SONY WORLD PHOTOGRAPHY AWARDS 2013

WORLD PHOTOGRAPHY ORGANISATION
World Photography Awards Limited
9 Manchester Square
London W1U 3PL
United Kingdom

Company Registration Number: 5704470
www.worldphoto.org

WPO CONTACTS
Scott Gray, Managing Director
scott@worldphoto.org

Astrid Merget, Creative Director
astrid@worldphoto.org

Ania Wadsworth, Student Focus Manager
ania@worldphoto.org

Cecily Breese, Event Director
cecily@worldphoto.org

Melanie Philippe, Marketing Manager
melanie@worldphoto.org

Giulia Messina, Project Manager
giulia@worldphoto.org

Kaley Sweeney, Communications Manager
kaley@worldphoto.org

Jill Cotton, PR Manager
jill@worldphoto.org

DESIGN
Isabel Solé López-Pinto
isabel@alan-bates.com

EDITOR
Katie Sanderson, Freelance Editor

PRINTER
Gruppo Editoriale Zanardi, Padova, Italy

ISBN 978-0-9572010-2-6

Legal deposit: April 2013

Front cover: Klaus Thymann, Denmark, 1st Place, Fashion & Beauty, Professional Competition

Back cover: William Eggleston. *Untitled*. 1695-1968 (fr. *Los Alamos*)
© Eggleston Artistic Trust. Courtesy of Gagosian Gallery.

Sony World Photography Awards

WPO
World Photography Organisation

SONY WORLD PHOTOGRAPHY AWARDS 2013

“I find this reflective storytelling of human life intriguing, and that it can be done so emphatically through photography is a testament to the medium’s diversity.”

WPO INTRODUCTION

Once again, this year's book shows a selection of extraordinary images from some remarkable photographers. I am taken aback by the commitment shown by these photographers in detailing their stories from all corners of the world, lending each series a depth that goes beyond the single image. The diversity with which these photographers have chosen to document their subject challenges our approach, prompts a narrative, stimulates thought and invites judgment.

Conventionally it is easier to understand classic reportage photo essays; by definition they are in themselves the story. Yet this would not do justice to the interpretations shown here. Valerio Bispuri's images of prison life in Latin America, for example, clearly depict the story he has chosen to tell, but his images impart a certain normalcy to incarceration. He has elegantly made a "heaven of hell" and the consistency of the images, despite being taken in many locations across the continent, give you an unexpected sense of familiarity and the uniformity of confinement.

Where the narrative becomes more challenging and suggestive is in works such as Vanessa Colareta's winning Still Life images. Traditionally, this style rarely offers a greater substance, yet here, unpredictably, Colareta considers the immense subjects of familial break-up and urban migration as reflected through food and flowers. Vanessa demonstrates true commitment to a narrative, foregoing more obvious channels, whilst maintaining an aesthetic quality. This series politely dictates a certain amount of thought from the viewer.

From Jens Juul's haunting portraits through to Roman Pyatkovka's reflections on Russian restructuring, each series is crying out to be silently observed with a degree of thought. None more so than Andrea Gjestvang's arresting images, which have so simply and concisely captured the strength of feeling and incomprehensible emotion lying deep within each subject. The grief for Norway's victims has never been so transparent to me than in viewing Gjestvang's images.

I find this reflective storytelling of human life intriguing, and that it can be done so emphatically through photography is a testament to the medium's diversity.

Thanks must go to the photographers for their outstanding efforts: I have thoroughly enjoyed looking through the works submitted. Thank you also to Sony for working with us to create such a platform for photographers to express themselves and for supporting the culture of image making itself.

SCOTT GRAY

FOUNDER & MANAGING DIRECTOR
WORLD PHOTOGRAPHY ORGANISATION

"I firmly believe everybody has a story to tell, and at Sony we are committed to developing cameras that facilitate the sharing of that story with the world through the medium of images."

SONY INTRODUCTION

Working for Sony has afforded me many opportunities to travel and see parts of the world that I would not otherwise have experienced. From each of these journeys I have seen, tasted and heard things that shape my memories of those different cities and countries and I feel honoured to have done this. However, there are still so many places that I would like to visit and spend time in but, logistically, this is impossible. It is then a wonderful thing that I am able to look through the entries to the Sony World Photography Awards and be offered ultra-vivid glimpses into locations that I have never visited and gain perspectives on places that I have been and could not have imagined.

I am always amazed at the photographer's skill to capture the moment and create art to share with the world. It is therefore doubly pleasing to see the entries into the Sony World Photography Awards continue to increase with over 122,000 submissions this year spanning 170 different countries, making this a truly global competition. However, it is the continual increasing quality of the entries, which gives me the most pleasure to see. I applaud all of the judges for making the tough decisions that no doubt faced them in choosing the winners this year.

I firmly believe everybody has a story to tell, and at Sony we are committed to developing cameras that facilitate the sharing of that story with the world through the medium of images. We will continue to produce cameras for every kind of photographer and, with the blessing of light, enable them to realise their visions, believing in the power of imaging.

I very much hope that you enjoy the journey that this book will take you on and that it will inspire you to get your camera out and start shooting. I would like to congratulate all of the shortlisted and winning photographers for producing work that stimulates the emotions in a wonderful way and I hope they all take pride in seeing their work on display at Somerset house in London and published in this book.

YOSHIYUKI NOGAMI

SENIOR GENERAL MANAGER, MARKETING DIVISION,
DIGITAL IMAGING BUSINESS GROUP SONY CORPORATION

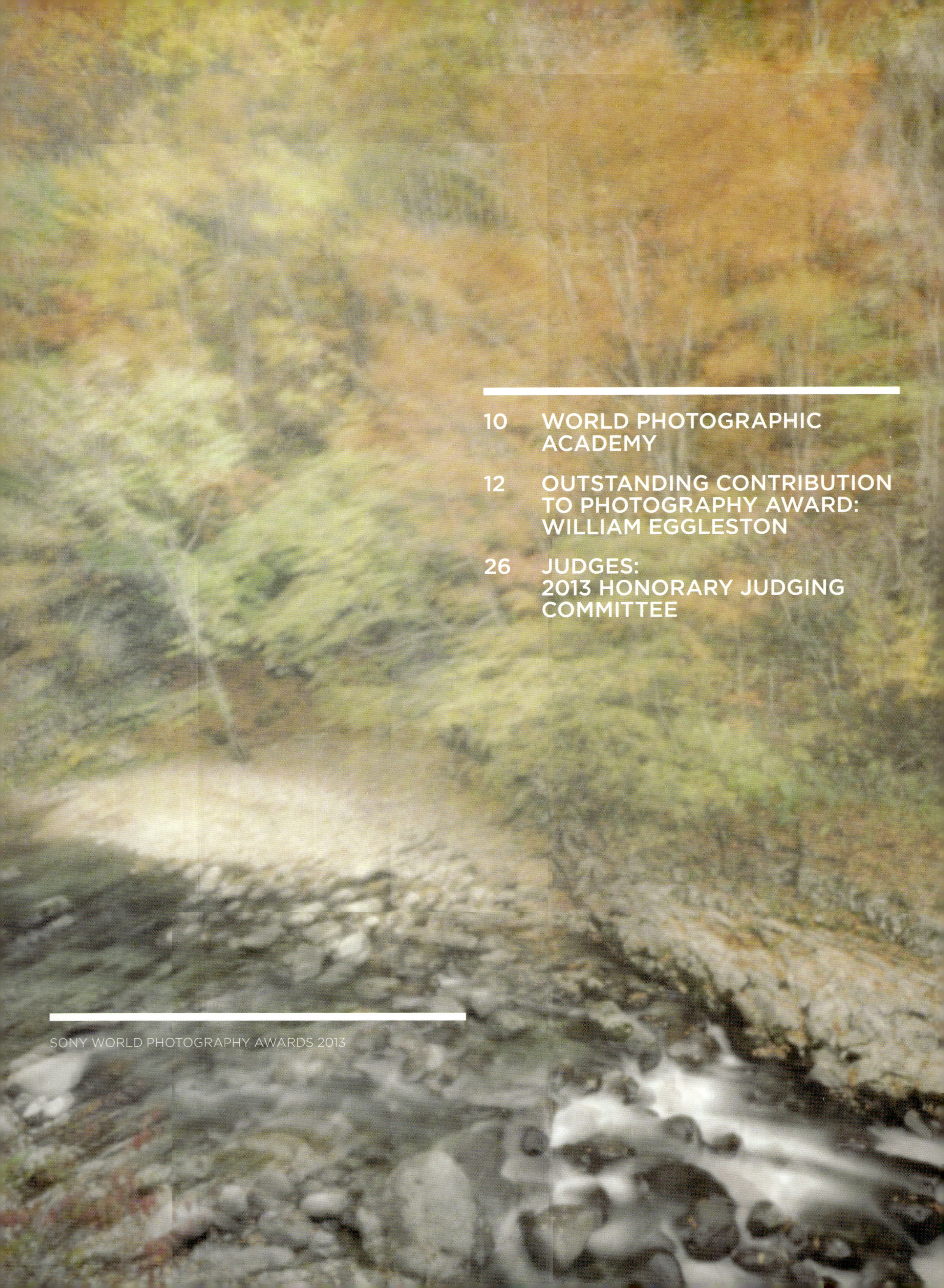

CONTENTS

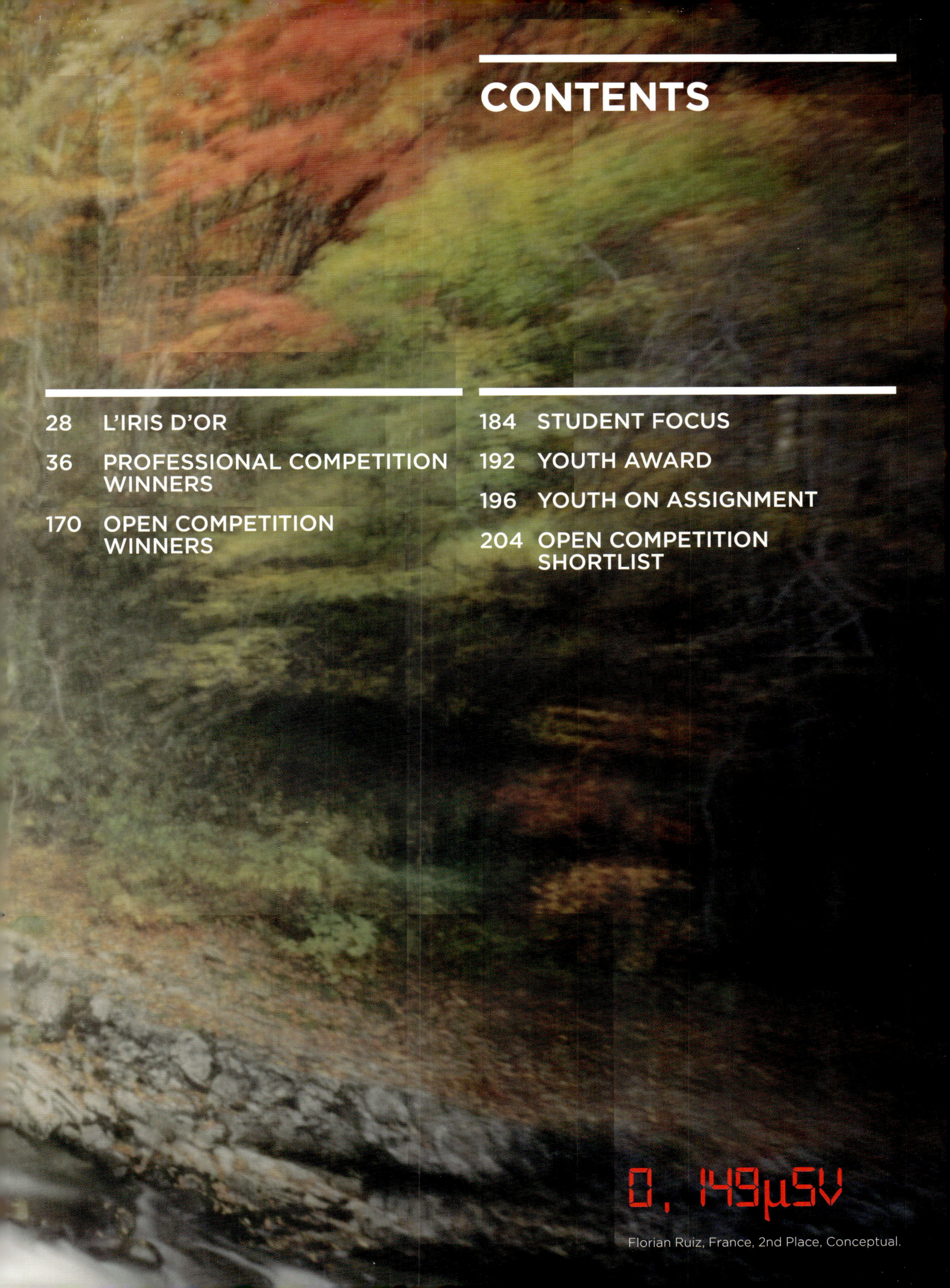

Florian Ruiz, France, 2nd Place, Conceptual.

WORLD PHOTOGRAPHIC ACADEMY

AZERBAIJAN

Rena Effendi, Photographer

AUSTRALIA

Delly Carr, Sports Photographer

Brian Rope, President of the Australian Photographic Society

BELGIUM

Carl De Keyzer, Magnum Photographer and Co-founder/ Co-director of XYZ Photography

Roger Szmulewicz, Founder of Fifty One Fine Art Photography Gallery

BRAZIL

Eder Chiodetto, Curator of Photography at the Museum of Modern Art of São Paulo - MAM-SP

CANADA

Stephen Bulger, President of AIPAD and Owner of Stephen Bulger Gallery

Maryann Camilleri, Director of Magenta Foundation

CHINA

Yao Lu, Associate Professor at School of Design, The Central Academy of Fine Arts

Heung Shing Liu, Author and Pulitzer Prize Winning Photographer

CZECH REPUBLIC

Daniela Mrazkova, Chair of Executive Board of Czech Photo

DENMARK

Casper Dalhoff, Press Photographer

FINLAND

Esko Männikkö, Photo Artist

FRANCE

Arnaud Adida, Founder Acte 2 Agence & Acte 2 Gallery, Paris

Alain Genestar, Director of Polka Magazine and Gallery

Eric Larrouil, General Manager of Agence VU

Guy Le Querrec, Magnum Photographer

Sarah Moon, Photographer

Marc Riboud, Photographer / Winner of 2009 Lifetime Achievement Award

Gilles Taquet, President of SNAPIG and Co-President of Photononstop

Esther Woerdehoff, Director of Galerie Esther Woerdehoff

William Klein, Photographer

GERMANY

Ruth Eichhorn, Director of Photography for GEO Magazine

Dr. Caprice Horn, Director of Galerie Caprice Horn

Jurgen Schadeberg, Photographer

Monica Suder, International Coach & Consultant to the Photographic Community

Friederike von Rauch, Photographer

GREECE

Stratos Kalafatis, Photographer

HONG KONG

Norman Lau, Honorary President of Federation of Asian Photographic Art

William So, Photographer

HUNGARY

Peter Korniss, Documentary Photographer

INDIA

Pablo Bartholomew, Photographer and Educator

Sudhir Saxena, Chairman of Photolovers India

IRAN

Reza Deghati, Photographer, Humanitarian & Founder of AÏNA

ITALY

Roberto Koch, Director, Contrasto Photo Agency & Publishing House / Founder of Forma Gallery

Grazia Neri, Founder and former President of Grazia Neri PhotoAgency

Federico Poggi, President of the Venice International Photo Contest

JAPAN

Michiko Kasahara, Chief Curator, Tokyo Metropolitan Museum of Photography

Shizuka Yokomizo, Artist

MEXICO

Pedro Meyer, Pedro Meyer Foundation, Photographer

Trisha Ziff, Curator, Journalist and Filmmaker (British, based in Mexico)

NETHERLANDS

Anton Corbijn, Photographer

Claudia Hinterseer, Managing Director and Founding Member, NOOR

Martin Rogge, Director of The Flatland Gallery, Utrecht

Inez van Lamsweerde and Vinoodh Matadin, Fashion and Fine Art Photographers

NEW ZEALAND

Chris Parker, President of the New Zealand Institute of Professional Photography

Leon Rose, President of the Advertising and Illustrative Photographers Association

POLAND

Tomasz Gutkowski, Director of Photomonth, Krakow / President of the Foundation for Visual Arts

Tomasz Tomaszewski, Press Photographer

PORTUGAL

José Luís Neto, Photo Artist

RUSSIA

Olga Sviblova, Director of the Moscow House of Photography

SINGAPORE

David P C Tay, President of The Photographic Society of Singapore

SLOVAKIA

Martin Kollar, Documentary Photographer

Professor Vaclav Macek, President of The Central European House of Photography

SOUTH AFRICA

Jodi Bieber, Photographer

Pieter de Ras, Photographer and President of Professional Photographers of Southern Africa

Dennis da Silva, Partner, Photographic Printing Company

SOUTH KOREA

Bohnchang Koo, Photographer

SPAIN

Juana de Aizpuru, Director of Galeria Juana de Aizpuru and Creator of ARCO Art Fair

Daniel Beltra, Photographer

Claude Bussac, Director of PhotoEspaña

Cristina Garcia Rodero, Magnum Photographer

SWEDEN

Anders Petersen, Photographer

SWITZERLAND

Stefan Wittwer, President of SAB/ASBI, Co-Owner of Prisma, Switzerland

TAIWAN

Chien-Chi Chang, Magnum Photographer

THAILAND

Thavorn Ko-Udomvit, Founder of Ardel Gallery

Joakim Leroy, President of Aperture Asia

UK

Monica Allende, Picture Editor, Sunday Times Magazine

Carol Allen-Storey, Photographer

Tom Ang, Photographer and Author of Digital Photography Books

Simon Bainbridge, Editor, British Journal of Photography

Simon Baker, Curator of Photography and International Art, Tate

Michael Benson, Director Candlestar and Co-founder Prix Pictet

Adrian Boot, Photographer

Hamish Brown, Photographer

Zelda Cheatle, Portfolio Manager and Curator

John Chillingworth, Photojournalist

Edmund Clark , Photographer

Jez Coulson, Reportage Artist

Kevin Cummins, Photographer

Lucy Davies, Picture Editor and Photography Critic, Telegraph

Damien Demolder, Editor of Amateur Photographer

Adrian Evans, Director, Panos Pictures

Stuart Franklin, Photographer

Julia Fullerton-Batten, Photographer

Philippe Garner, International Head, Photographs and 20th Century Decorative Art & Design, Christie's

Mark George, Photography Agent

David Graham, Photographer

Dominique Green, International Film & Photography Consultant

John Harrison, Chairman of Northern Ireland Press Photographers Association

Francis Hodgson, Photo Critic, Co-founder of Prix Pictet

Dafydd Jones, Social Photographer

Jon Jones, Director of Photography, Sunday Times Magazine

Idris Khan, Artist

Chloe Limpkin, Picture Editor of Harpers Bazar

Terri Manduca, Photographers Agent

Gered Mankowitz, Photographer

Kingsley Marten, Managing Director of The Association of Photographers

Dylan Martinez, Senior Photographer, UK & Ireland, Reuters

Caroline Metcalf, Director of Photography, Conde Nast Traveller

Johanna Neurath, Design Director of Thames & Hudson

John Offenbach, Photographer Specialising in Advertising

Terry O'Neill, Photographer

Tim Paton, Director, Balcony Jump

Steve Pyke, Photographer

Dr. Michael Pritchard, President of The Royal Photographic Society

Yasmina Reggad, Independent Curator and Founder of Photo-Festivals.

James Reid, Photography Director, Wallpaper*

Edward Robinson, Photographer and Owner of OneRedEye Consultancy

Andrew Sanigar, Commissioning Editor, Thames & Hudson

Mark Sealy, Director of Autograph (The Association of Black Photography)

Francesca Sears, Director of Panos Profile, Panos Pictures

Fiona Shields, Picture Editor, The Guardian

Paul Smith, Photographer

Alan Sparrow, Chairman of the Picture Editors Guild and Executive Picture Editor of Metro UK

Sue Steward, Photography Critic for The Evening Standard

Tom Stoddart, Photojournalist

Aidan Sullivan, Vice President Photo Assignments, Getty Images

Roger Tooth, Head of Photography at The Guardian, The Observer and Guardian.co.uk

Sarah Toplis, Freelance Digital Producer

Amelia Troubridge, Photographer

Michael Trow, Picture Editor, British Vogue Magazine

Tim Walker, Photographer

Hannah Watson, Managing Editor, Trolley Books

Jonathan Worth, Photographer and Author of the Open Photography classes #phonar and #picbod

Elizabeth Zeschin, Photographer

UKRAINE

Boris Mikhailov, Photo Artist

USA

Janette Beckman, Photographer

Elisabeth Biondi, Independent Curator

Alvin Booth, Photographer

Nick Brandt, Photographer

Julie Castellano, Director of Edwynn Houk Gallery

Catherine Chermayeff, Director of Special Projects, Magnum Photos

Stephen Cohen, Gallerist and Founder of Photo L.A., Photo MIAMI, ART LA and other Art Fairs in New York, San Francisco & Santa Fe

Bruce Davidson, Magnum Photographer

Michelle Dunn Marsh, Design and Publishing Consultant

Elliott Erwitt, Magnum Photographer

Sasha Erwitt, Senior Associate Photo Editor, Vanity Fair

Macduff Everton, Photographer

Hossein Farmani, Founder of Lucie Awards Foundation

Jim Fiscus, Advertising and Editorial Photographer

Nan Goldin, Photographer

Lynn Goldsmith, Photographer

Guy Hepner, Contemporary Art Dealer

W.M. Hunt, Photographic Consultant

Sonia Katchian, Social Photographer

Geoff Katz, Founder of Creative Photographers Inc.

Gary Kemper, Director, North America European Press Photo Agency

Elliott Landy, Photographer

Neil Leifer, Sports Photographer

Rebecca Lewis, Vice-President and Senior Agent with Art + Commerce Agency

Susie Linfield, Critic, Writer and Director of the Cultural Reporting and Criticism Program, NYU

Mary-Ellen Mark, Photographer

Stephen Mayes, Managing Director of VII Photo Agency

Susan Meiselas, Photographer

Cristina Mittermeier, President Earth in Focus, Inc. and Fellow of the ILCP

Kathy Moran, Senior Editor, Natural History, National Geographic Magazine

Virginia Morrison, Executive Director, Society for Photographic Education

RJ Muna, Photographer

Nigel Parry, Photographer

Daniel Power, Founder of powerHouse Books and powerHouse Arena

Jack Reznicki, President of the Professional Photographers of America

Gary Shenk, Chief Executive Officer of Corbis

Rose Shoshana, Founder and Owner of ROSEGALLERY

Mike Smith, President of the National Press Photographers Foundation

Phil Stern, War and Celebrity Photographer / Winner of 2008 SWPA Lifetime Achievement Award

Scott Thode, Freelance Curator and Photo Editor

Jonathan Torgovnik, Photographer

Dr. Deborah Willis, Chair and Professor of Photography and Imaging at Tisch School of the Arts (NYU)

L'IRIS D'OR WINNERS

Vanessa Winship (UK) 2008

David Zimmerman (USA) 2009

Tommaso Ausilli (Italy) 2010

Alejandro Chaskielberg (Argentina) 2011

Mitch Dobrowner (USA) 2012

Andrea Gjestvang (Norway) 2013

MEMBERS IN MEMORIAM

Jean Desaunois, President of The Fédération Nationale des Agences de Presse Photos et Informations

Martine Franck, Magnum Photographer

Prabuddha Dasgupta, Photographer

Gigi Giannuzzi, Founder and Managing Director, Trolley Books

Bob Willoughby, Photographer

WILLIAM EGGLESTON

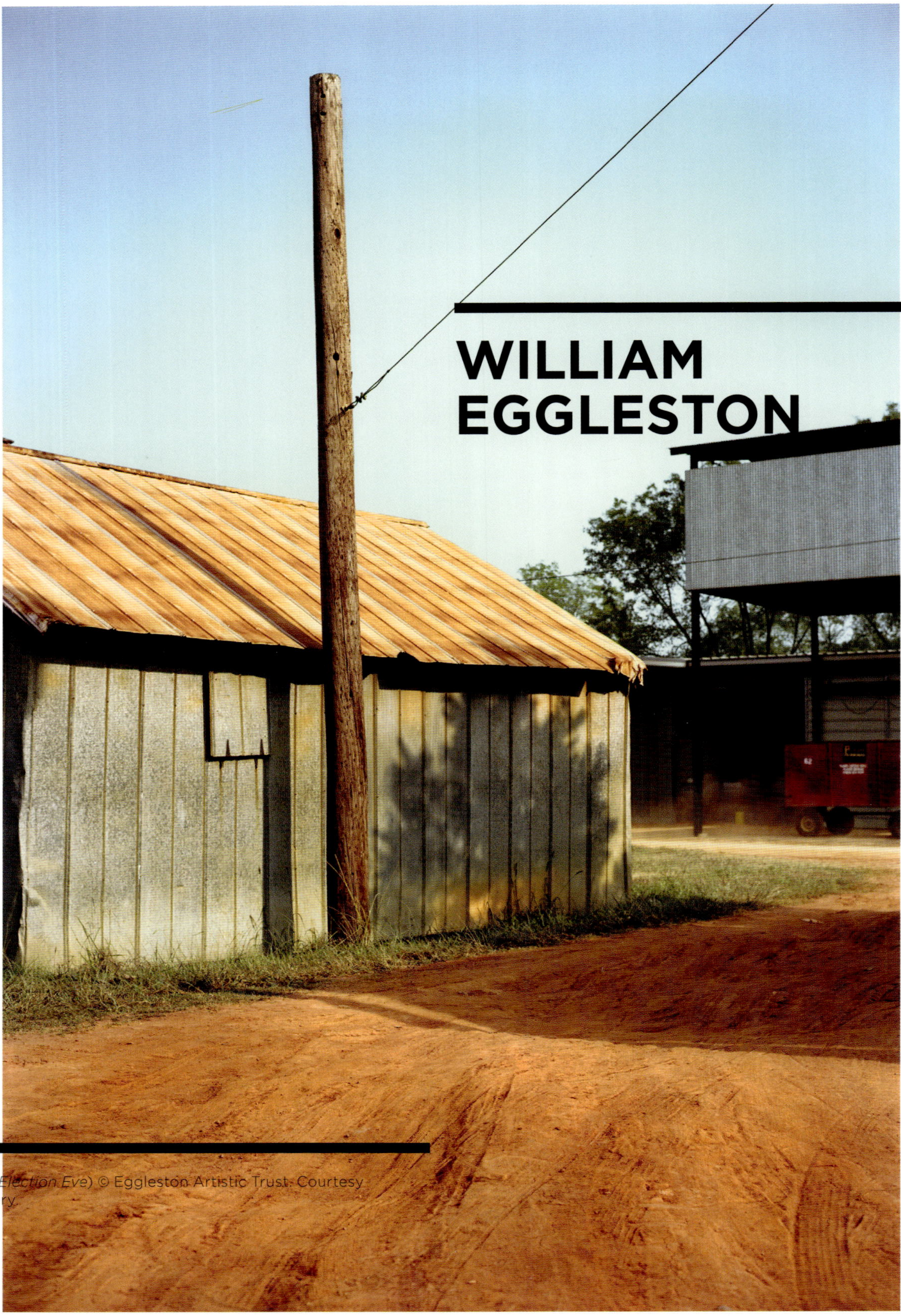

Untitled. 1976 (fr. *Election Eve*) © Eggleston Artistic Trust. Courtesy of Gagosian Gallery.

OUTSTANDING CONTRIBUTION TO PHOTOGRAPHY AWARD

Until William Eggleston, photography's tradition had been formed in monochrome. Although black and white is not innately natural, photographers had applied conventional concepts of composition to this graphic economy so that pictures could ultimately mean something.

In contrast, William Eggleston has avoided ascribing meaning in his work:

"The trouble is – whatever it is about pictures, photographs – it's just about impossible to follow up with words ... Art, or what we call that, you can love it and appreciate it, but you can't really talk about it. Doesn't make any sense."

Eggleston emerged out of a certain formality. He once said that the images in his seminal 1976 exhibition at the Museum of Modern Art (MOMA) and accompanying monograph, William Eggleston's Guide, were "based compositionally on the Confederate flag." While frustrating any possible rational analysis of his work, this statement is accurate. Many of his early works contain diagonal lines of composition emanating from a central object, the most literal example being the Red Ceiling. This image is in fact at the crossroads of colour and subject: a blatant 'use' of colour in painterly form against a centrally framed light bulb. In other images the simplicity of Eggleston's subjects can belie his use of colour, 'as though the blue and the sky were one thing.' (John Szarkowski, Guide). A critical tension of form exceeds subject in his work.

Degas took a similar stance: 'People call me the painter of dancing girls, it has never occurred to them that my chief interest in dancers lies in rendering movement and painting pretty clothes.' The danger, of course, in distinguishing between the two is simply that one begins to identify the work more on the content than on the rest of the conversation, especially the part in the non-word language of colour. And this perhaps gets to the core of Eggleston's aversion to ascribing meaning to his work: it draws the attention squarely onto the object.

'I am afraid that there are more people than I can imagine who can go no further than appreciating a picture that is a rectangle with an object in the middle of it, which they can identify. They don't care what is around the object as long as nothing interferes with the object itself, right in the centre. Even after the lessons of Winogrand and Friedlander, they don't get it.' William Eggleston, The Democratic Forest

Eggleston made this statement more than ten years after the publication of the Guide. What was true in his early work is no less true at this point for him: formality and order overlay form with similar consideration, only a different structure is now being imposed by his camera. Simplicity has progressed. A very large part of his archive contains unseen work that fits into this progression.

When Eggleston's landmark show opened at MOMA in 1976 his work was characterised by critics as rough 'snapshots' that were 'perfectly banal, perfectly boring... erratic and ramshackle.' In the years since, what has transpired is that almost every contemporary artist has found a new way of looking at the world through Eggleston's work. The next generation continues to be drawn to his work, as it is a new language, a new perspective that is still being discovered.

WILLIAM EGGLESTON III
Los Angeles, March 2013

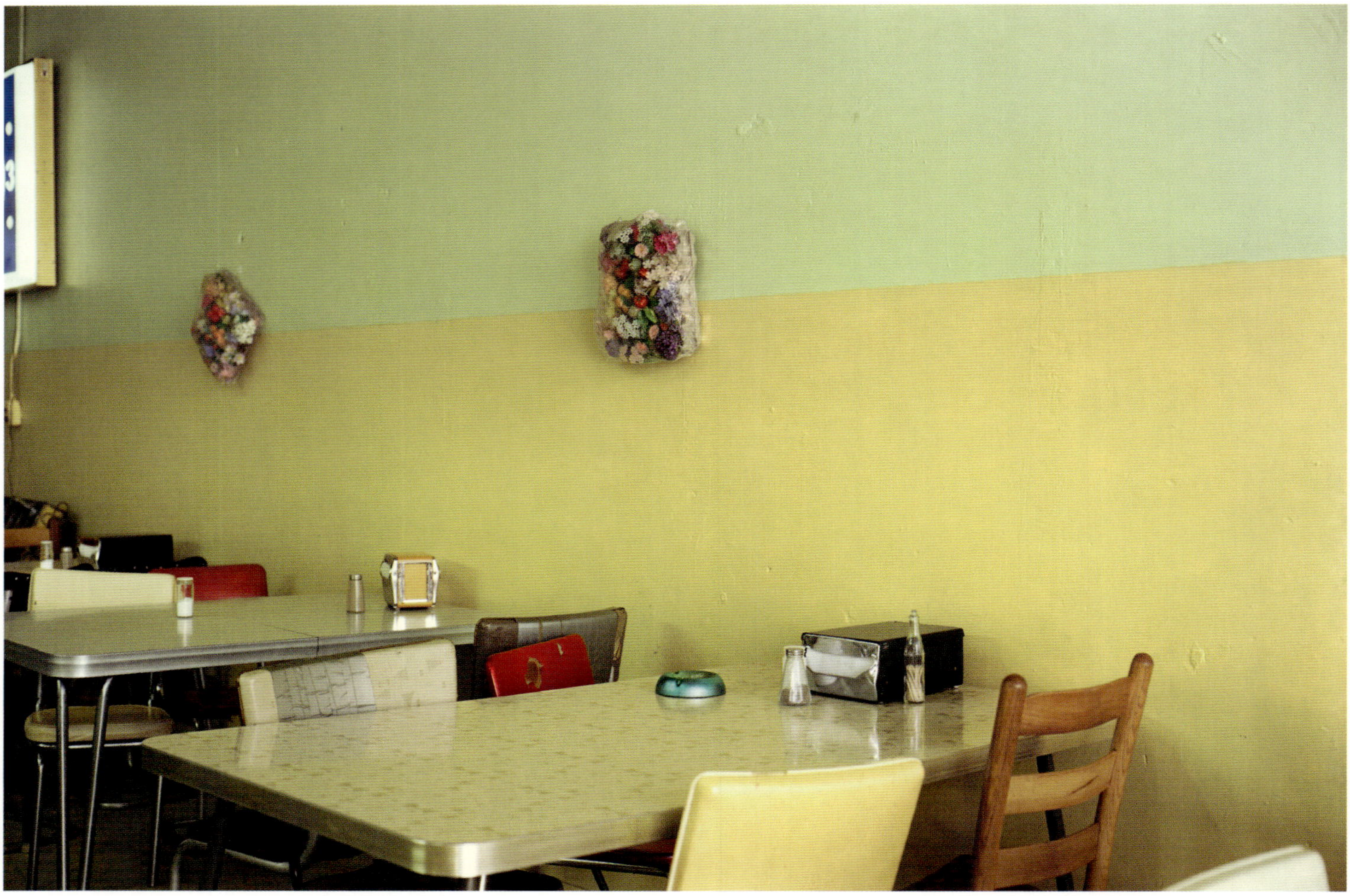

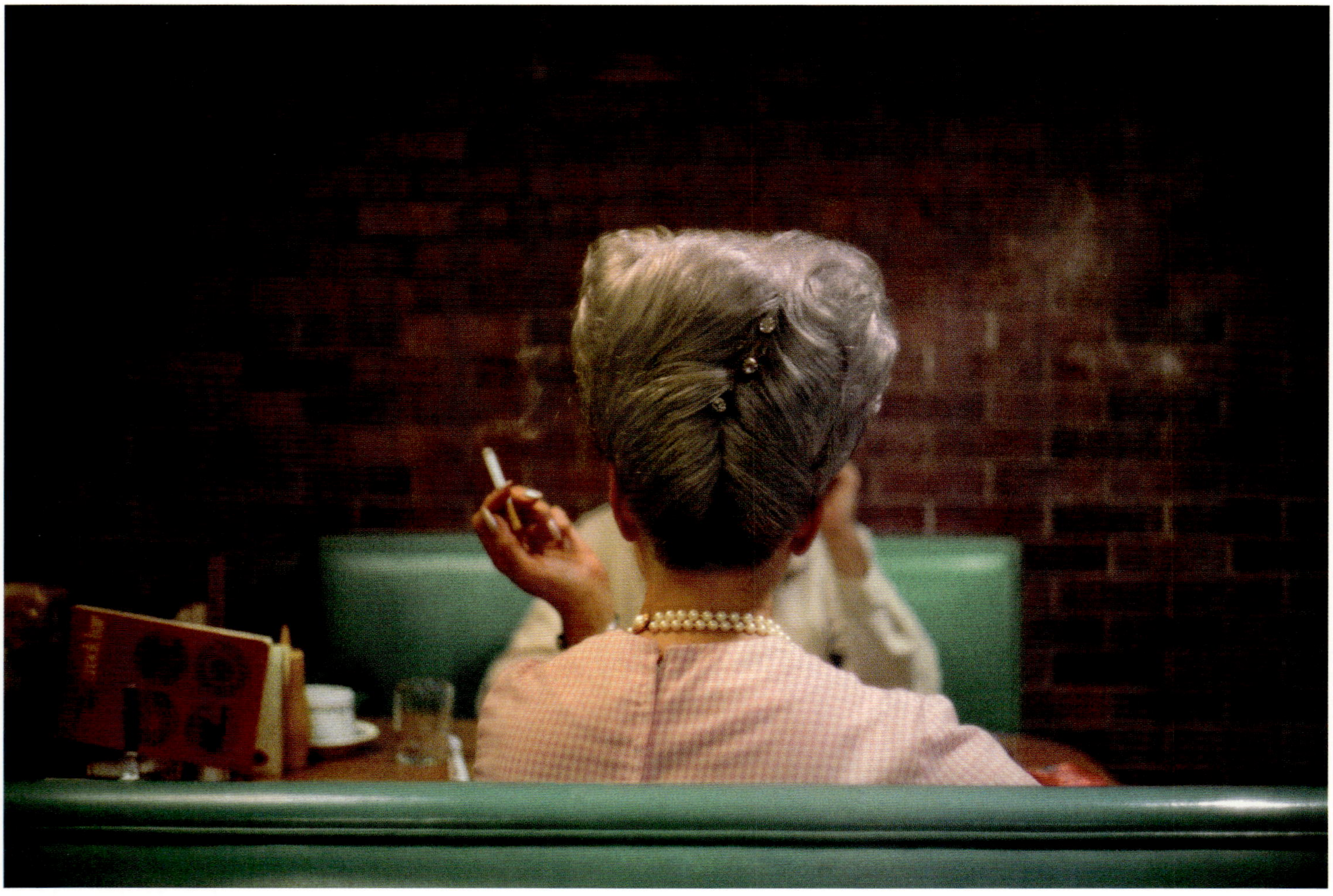

Top image: *Untitled*. 1976 (fr. *Election Eve*) © Eggleston Artistic Trust. Courtesy of Gagosian Gallery.
Bottom image: *Untitled*. 1695-1968 (fr. *Los Alamos*) © Eggleston Artistic Trust. Courtesy of Gagosian Gallery.

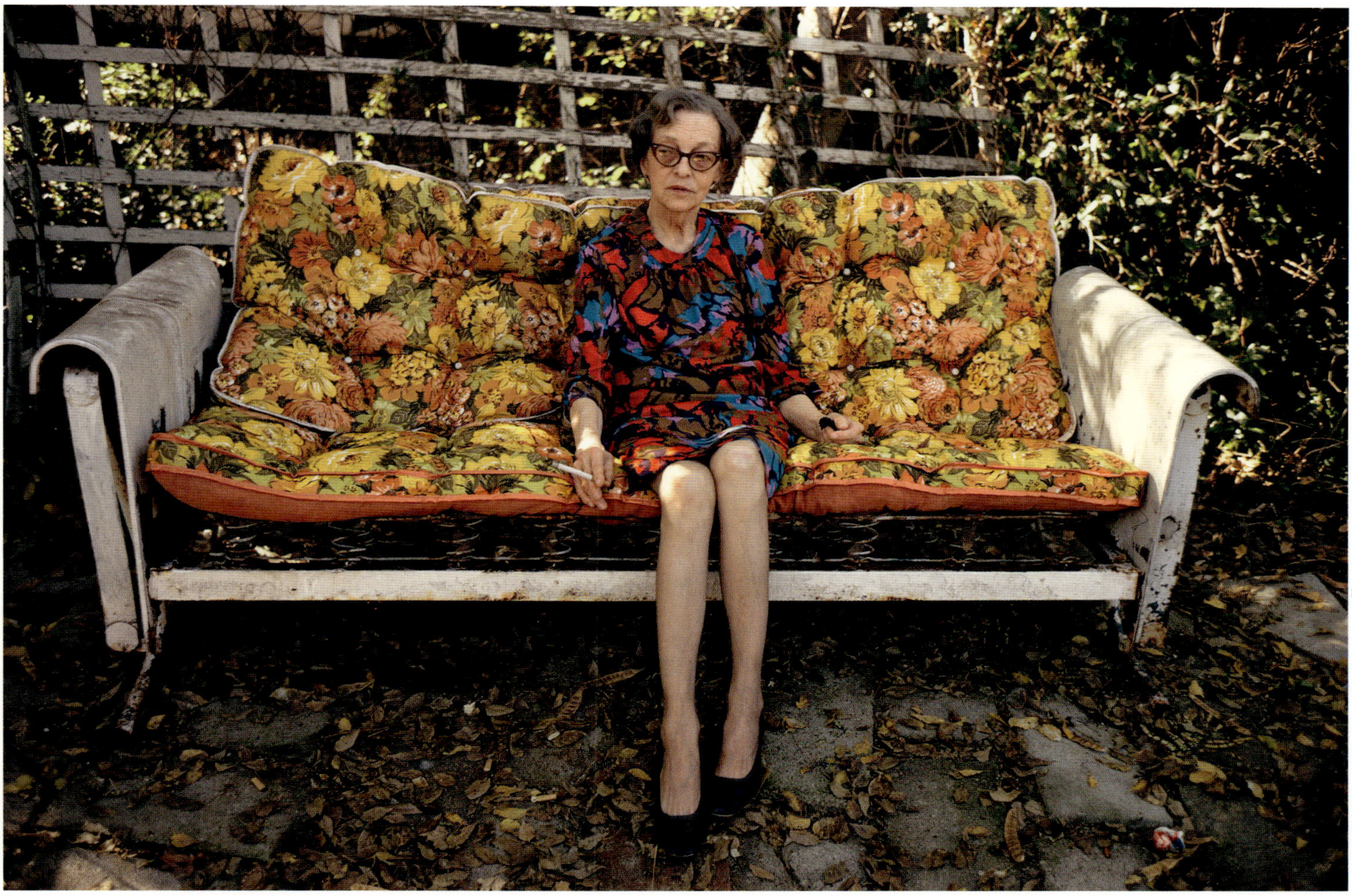

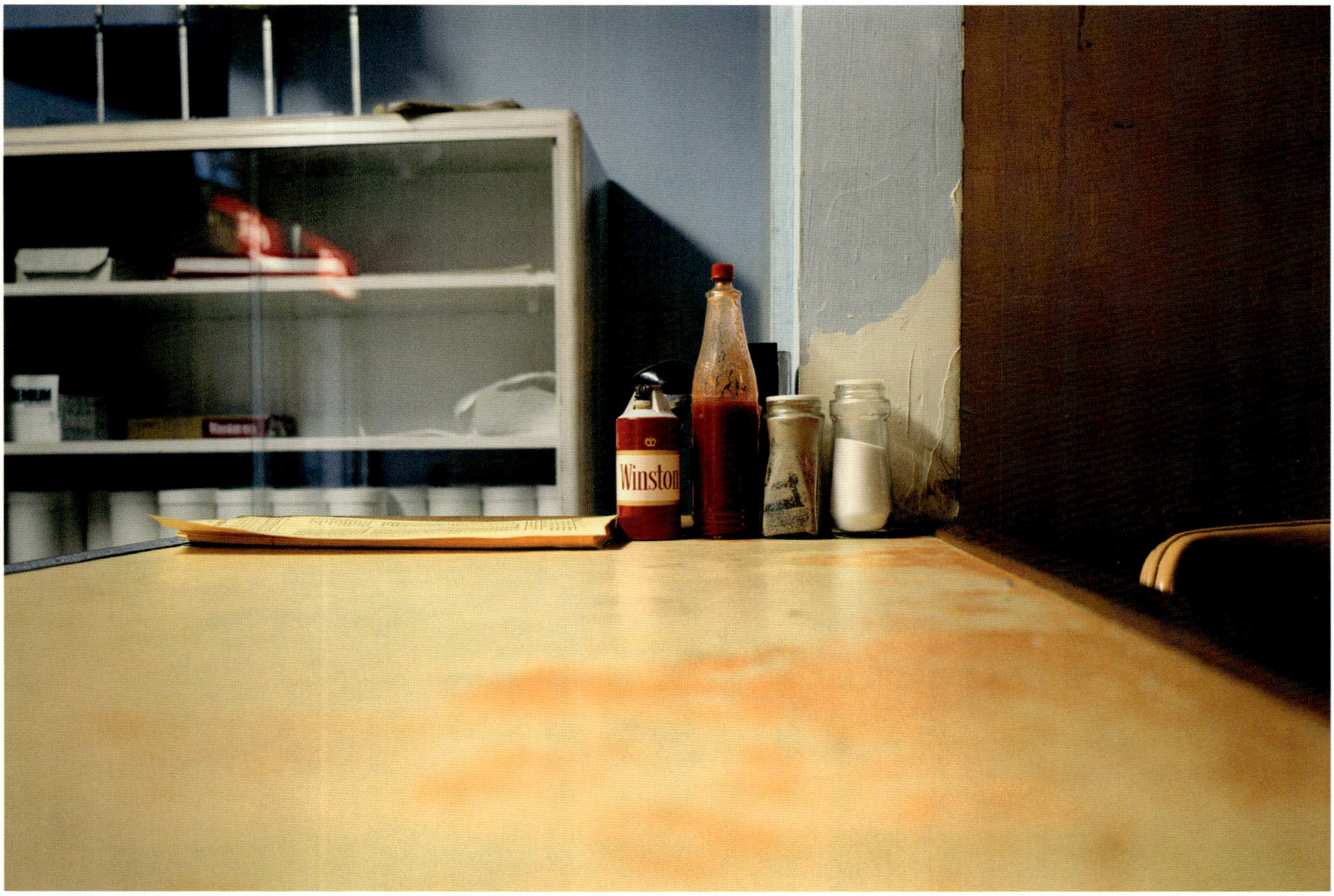

Top image: *Untitled.* 1970 (fr. *Guide*) © Eggleston Artistic Trust. Courtesy of Gagosian Gallery.
Bottom image: *Untitled.* 1980 (fr. *Lousianna Project*) © Eggleston Artistic Trust. Courtesy of Gagosian Gallery.

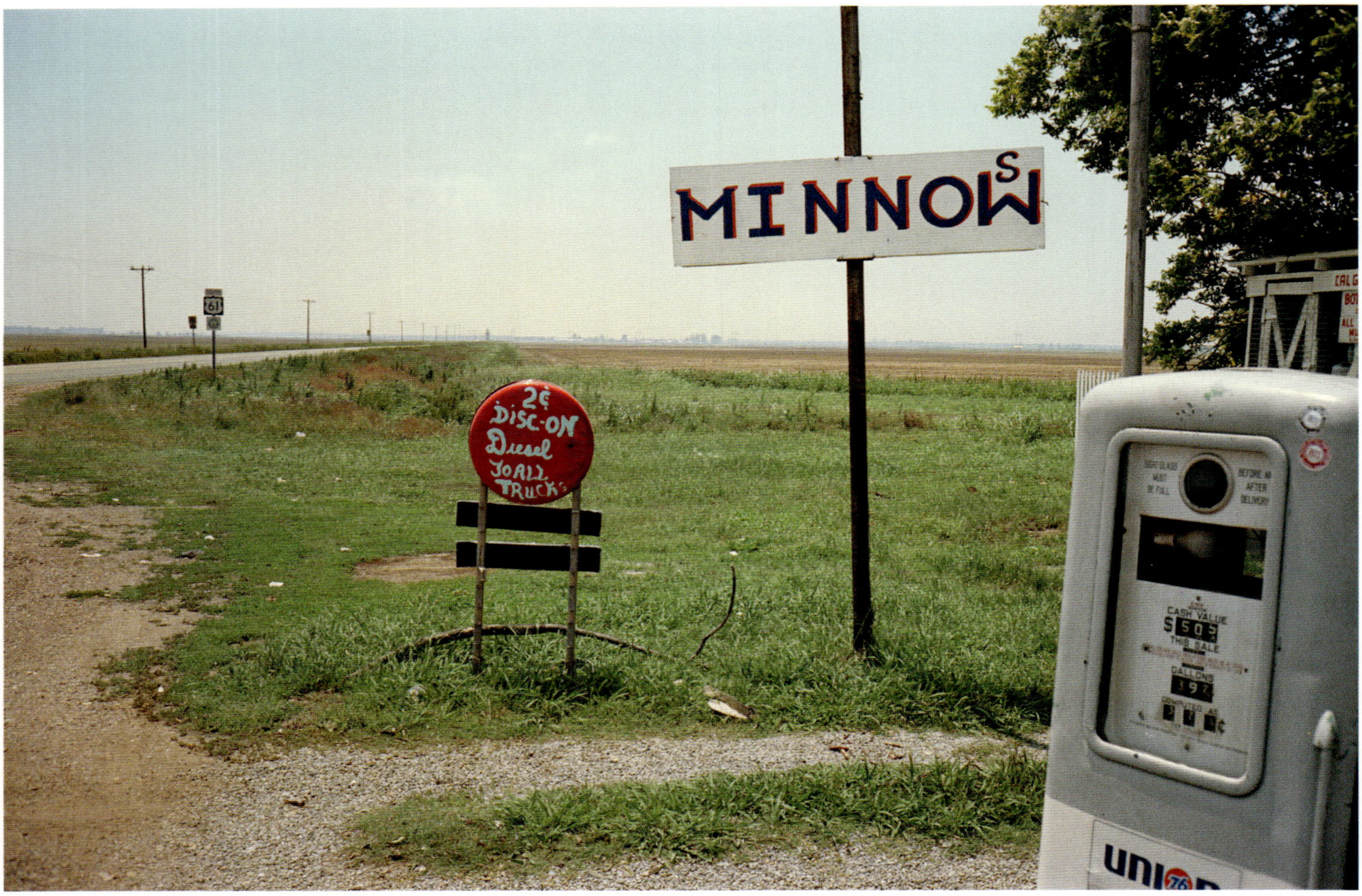

Untitled. 1971-1974 (fr. *Los Alamos*) © Eggleston Artistic Trust. Courtesy of Gagosian Gallery.

"Art, or what we call that, you can love it and appreciate it, but you can't really talk about it. Doesn't make any sense."
William Eggleston

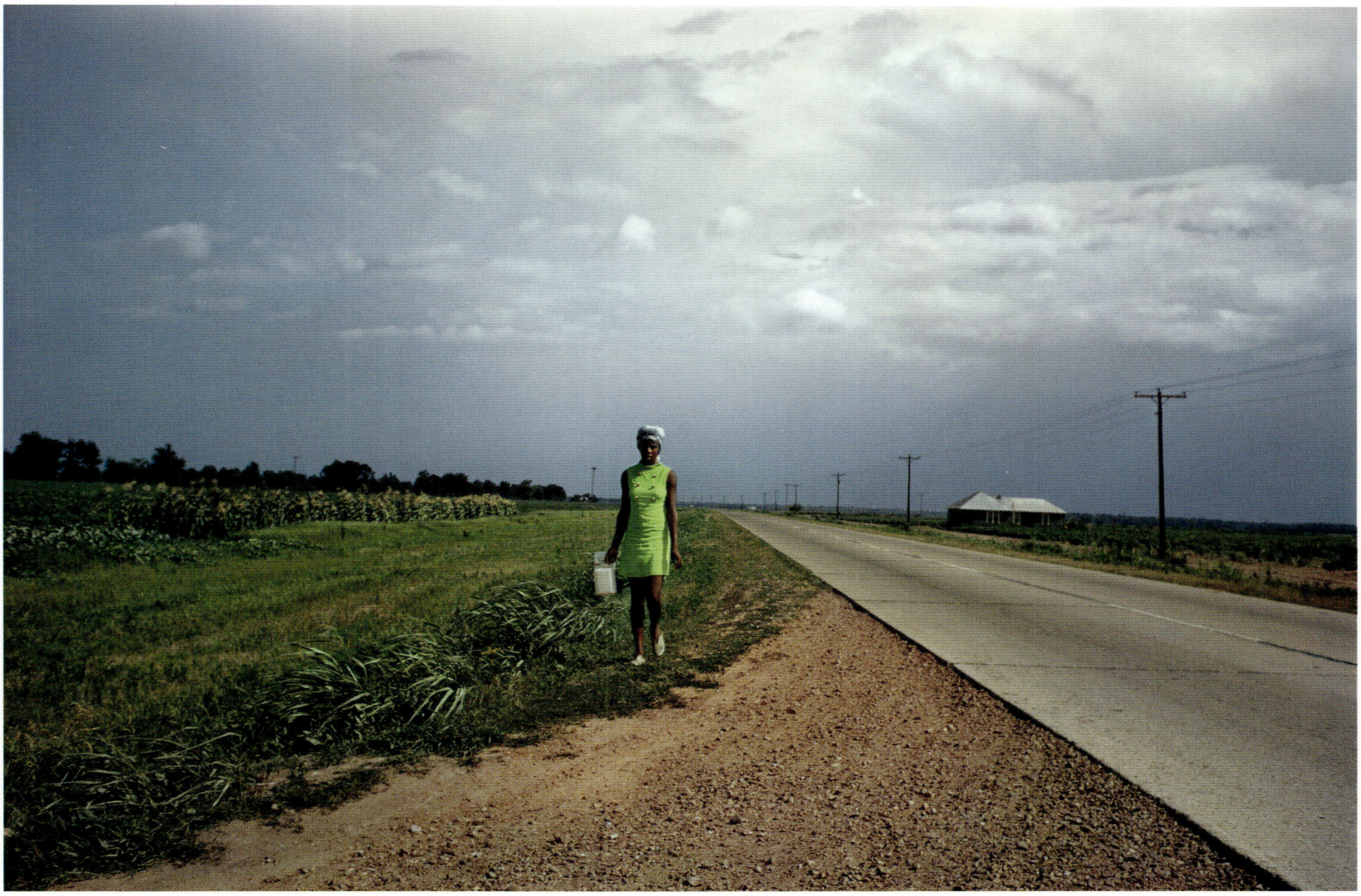

Untitled. 1970 (fr. *Guide*) © Eggleston Artistic Trust. Courtesy of Gagosian Gallery.

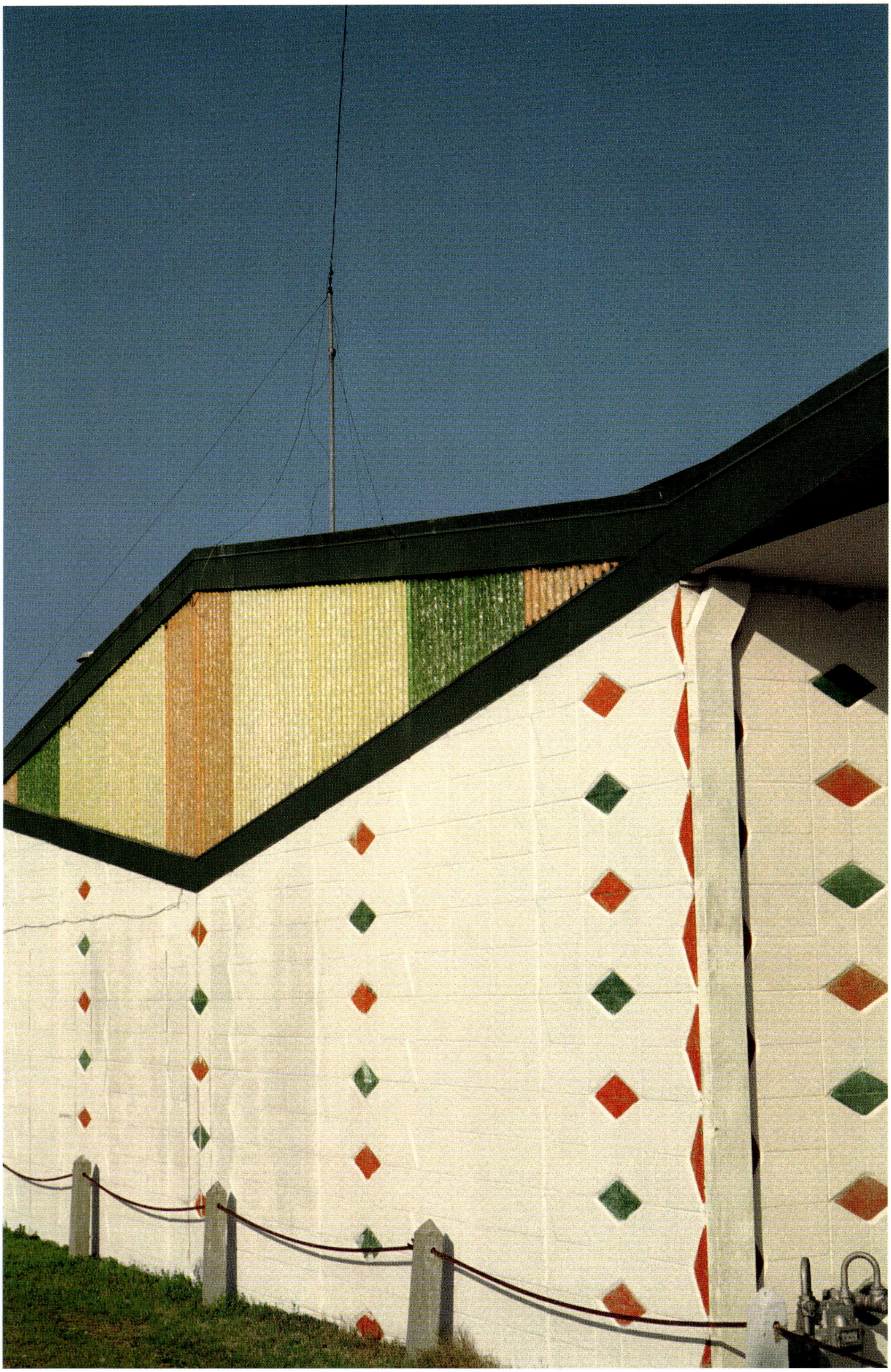

Untitled. 1971-1974 (fr. *Los Alamos*) © Eggleston Artistic Trust. Courtesy of Gagosian Gallery.

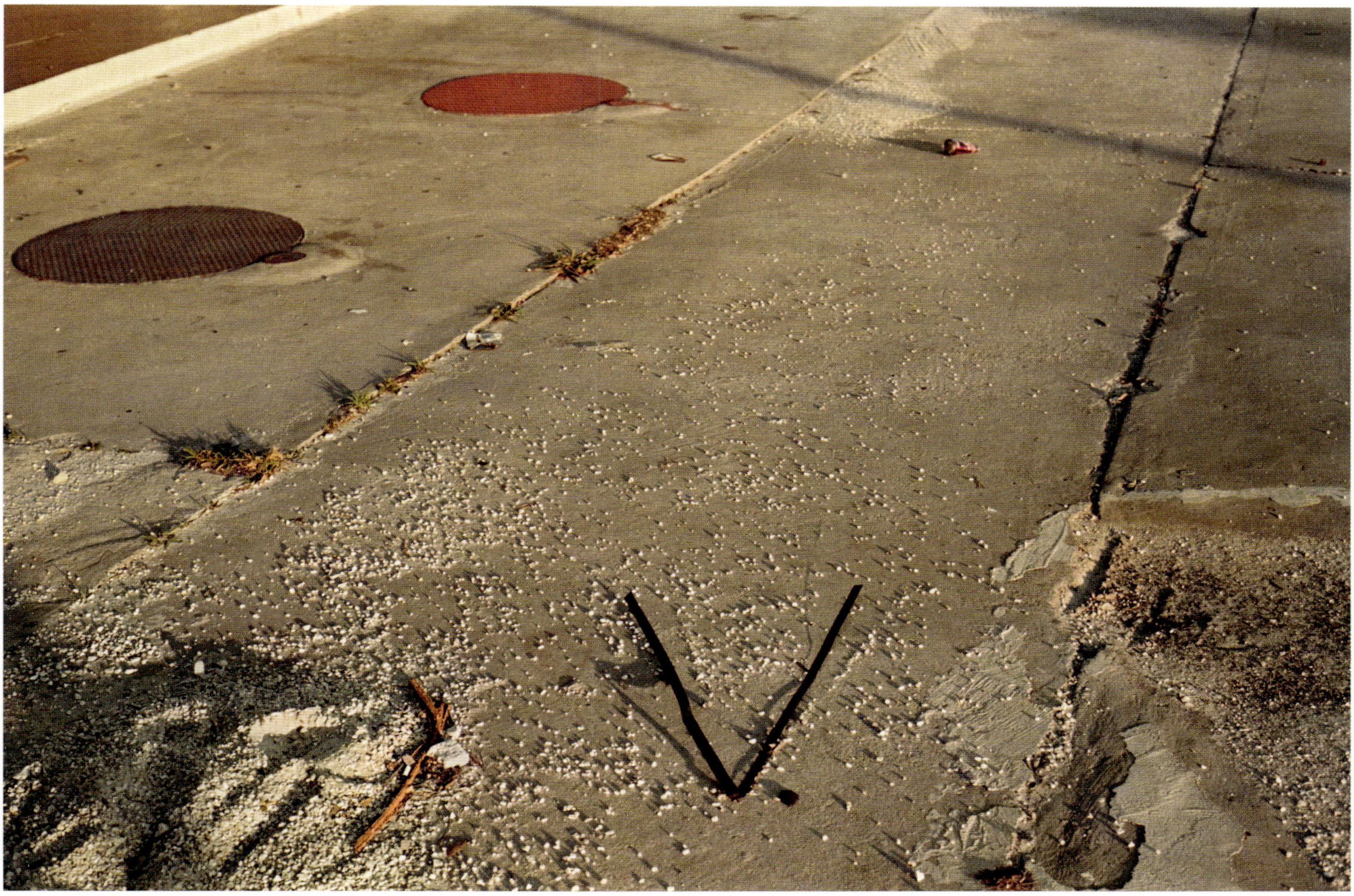

Untitled. 1971-1974 (fr. *Los Alamos*) © Eggleston Artistic Trust. Courtesy of Gagosian Gallery.

This perhaps gets to the core of Eggleston's aversion to ascribing meaning to his work: it draws the attention squarely onto the object.

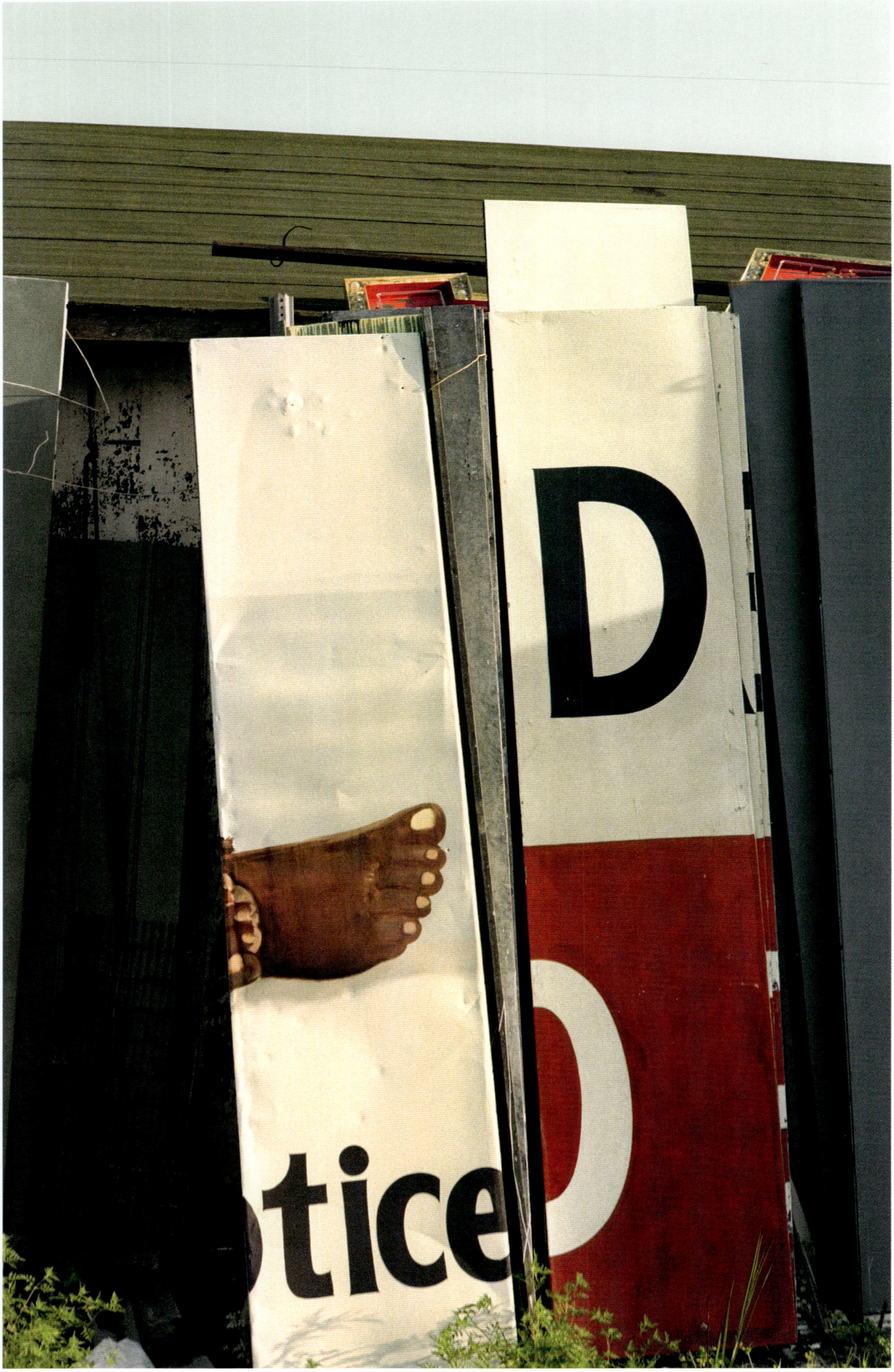

Untitled. 1971-1974 (fr. *Los Alamos*) © Eggleston Artistic Trust. Courtesy of Gagosian Gallery.

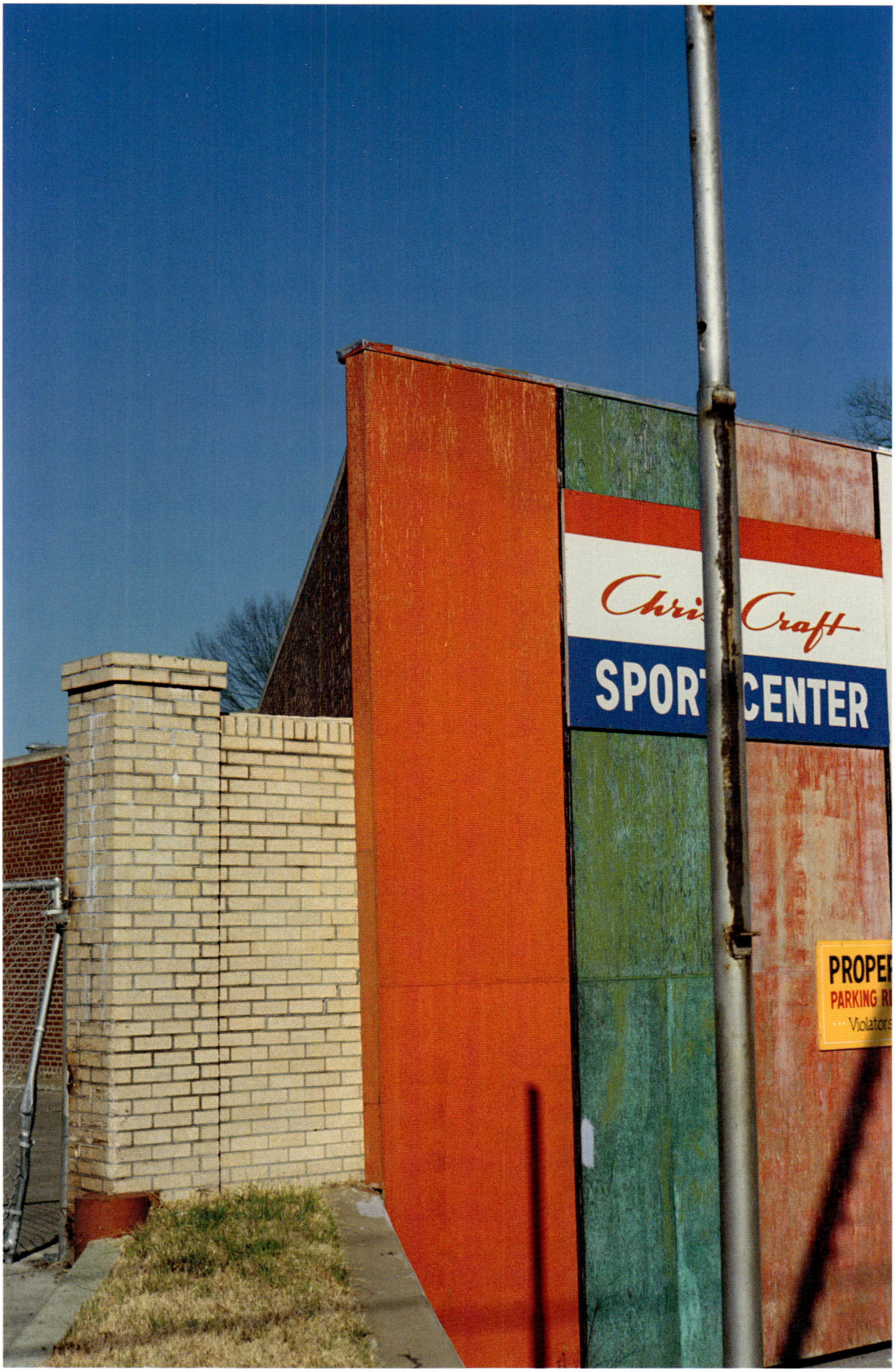

Untitled. 1971-1974 (fr. *Los Alamos*) © Eggleston Artistic Trust. Courtesy of Gagosian Gallery.

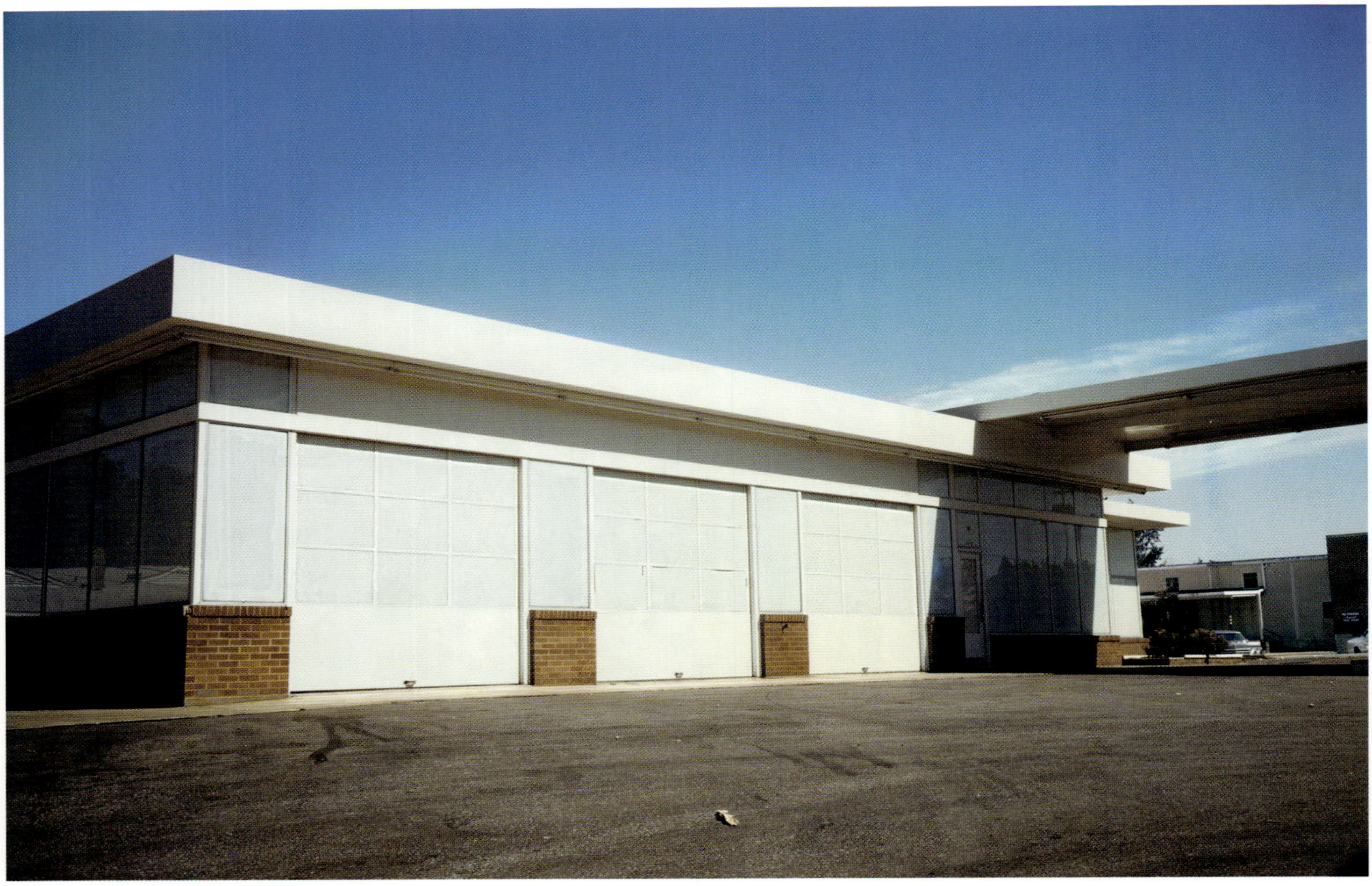

Untitled. 1971 (fr. *Chromes*) © Eggleston Artistic Trust. Courtesy of Gagosian Gallery.

"When you see a picture he's taken, you're stepping into some kind of jagged world that seems like Eggleston World."
Ed Ruscha

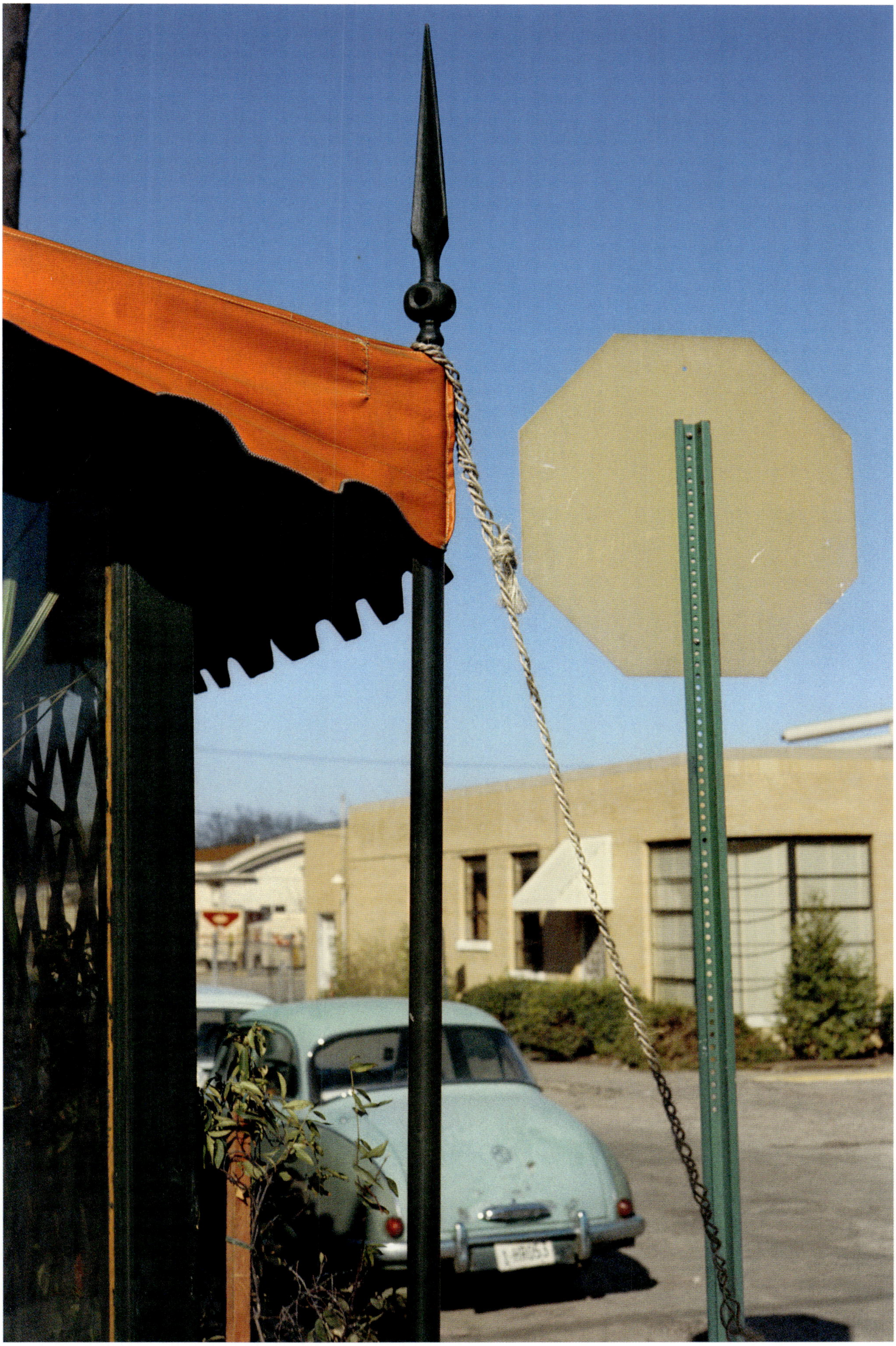

Untitled. 1971-1974 (fr. *Los Alamos*) © Eggleston Artistic Trust. Courtesy of Gagosian Gallery.
Next page image: *Untitled*. 1982-1985 (fr. *Democratic Forest*) © Eggleston Artistic Trust. Courtesy of Gagosian Gallery.

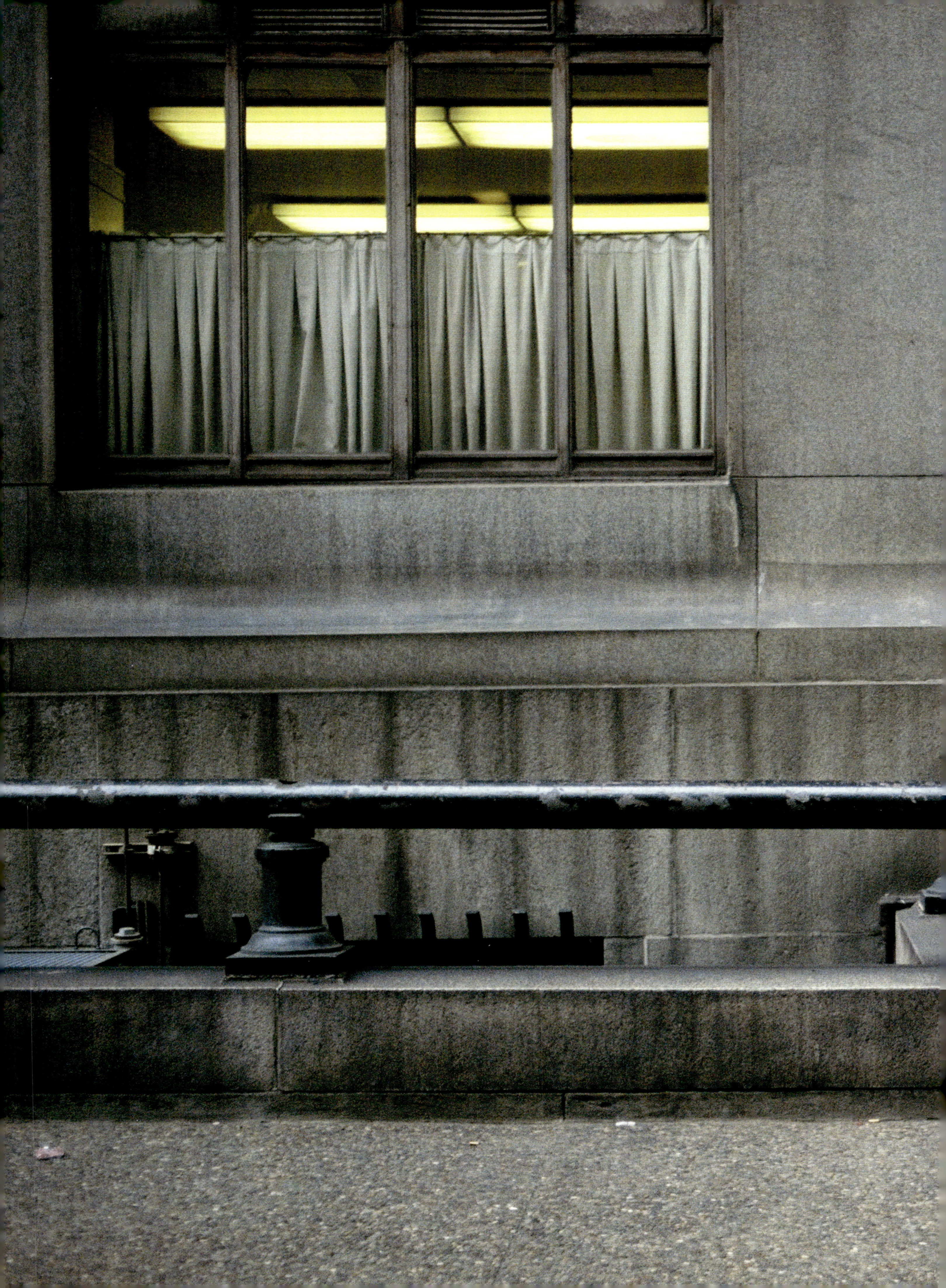

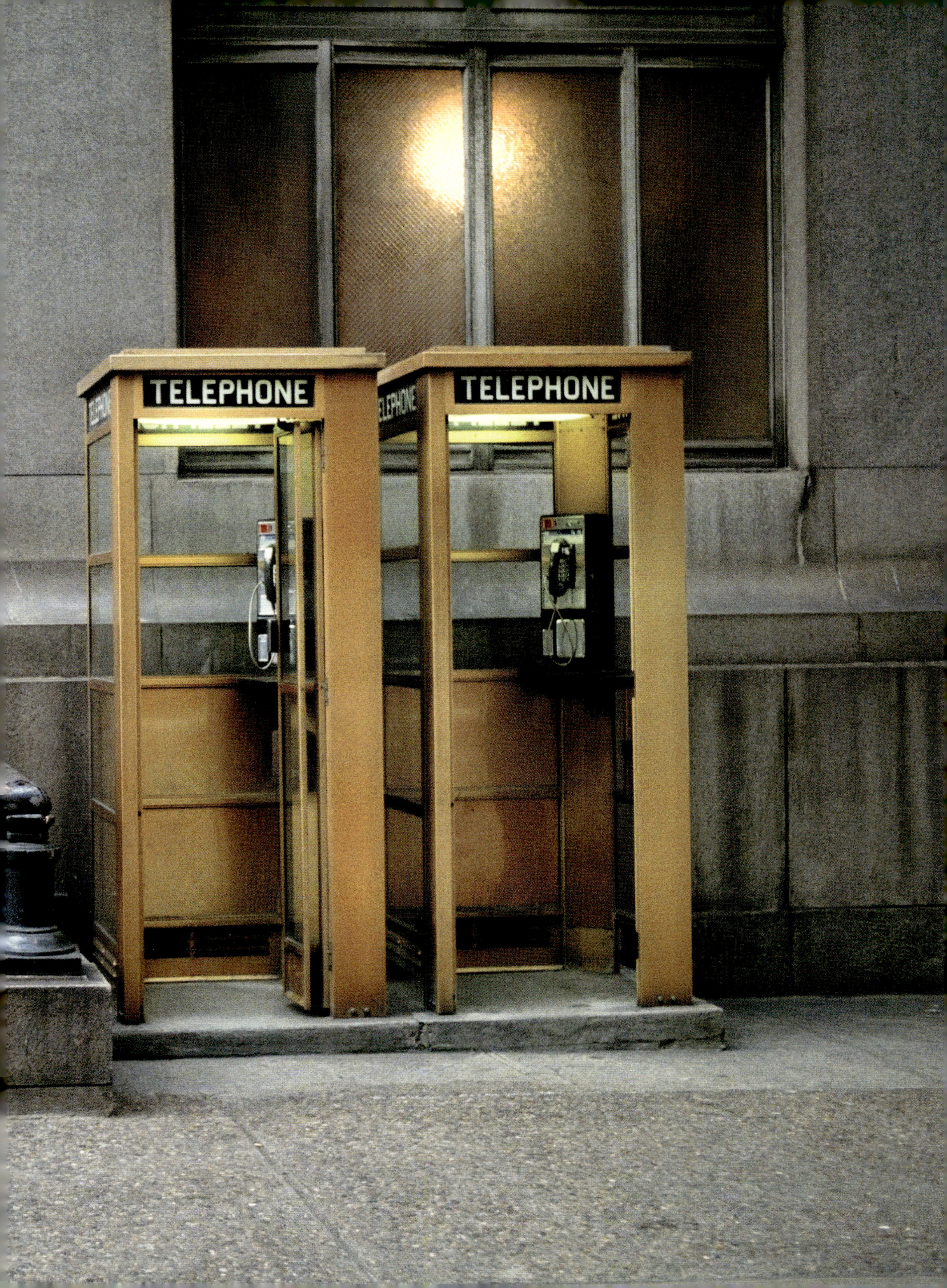
TELEPHONE
TELEPHONE

2013 HONORARY JUDGING COMMITTEE

A new Honorary Jury is chosen each year to form a diverse group of distinguished industry experts. These members are faced with the challenging task of sorting through thousands of images and finding those deserving of award commendations. Each of these individual experts, approached this task with a great sense of responsibility and professionalism.

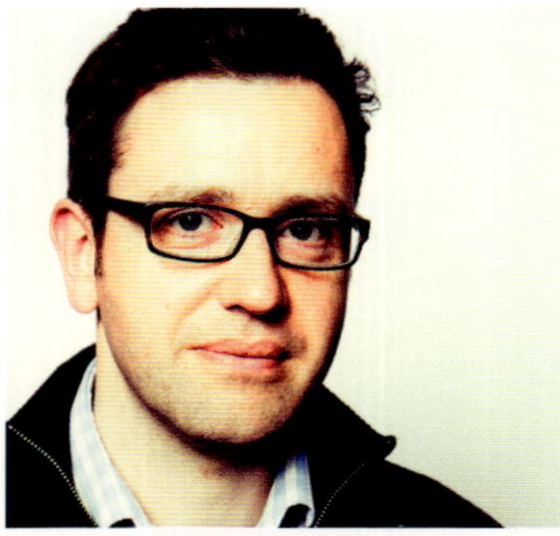

ANDREW SANIGAR

COMMISSIONING EDITOR,
THAMES & HUDSON (UK)

As a commissioning editor at Thames & Hudson, Andrew has selected a number of high profile and internationally successful photography publications, including Magnum Magnum (2007), Magnum Contact Sheets (2011), Coming into Fashion (2012), Eve Arnold's People (2009), and Mary McCartney From Where I Stand (2010). Alongside his activity in photography publishing, Andrew also commissions books on advertising, most notably Hegarty on Advertising (2011) and Goodvertising (2012), as well as a number of titles in areas such as design, illustration and popular culture.

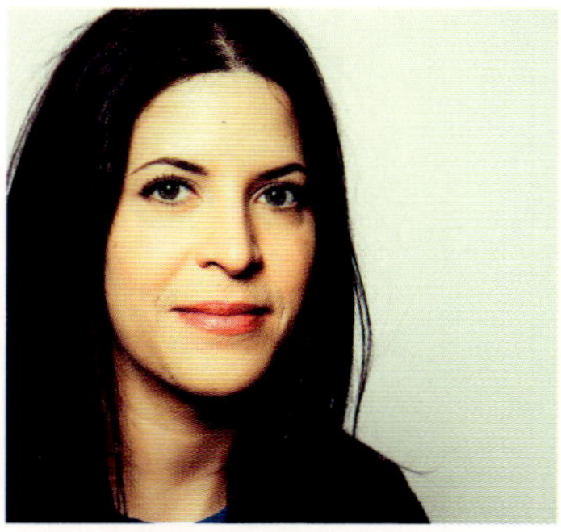

BRANDEI ESTES

ASSOCIATE DIRECTOR,
GALERIE NELSON FREEMAN
(FRANCE)

Brandei has served as manager and director for a variety of London galleries over the past ten years. After graduating with Honours from University College London in History of Art and Italian, she began her career as the gallery manager of David Gill Galleries, followed by four years at Michael Hoppen Gallery, where her passion and expertise in photography developed. This led to her post as director of Brancolini Grimaldi, a London gallery specialising in contemporary photography and video. In February 2013 Brandei took up a position at Galerie Nelson Freeman in Paris.

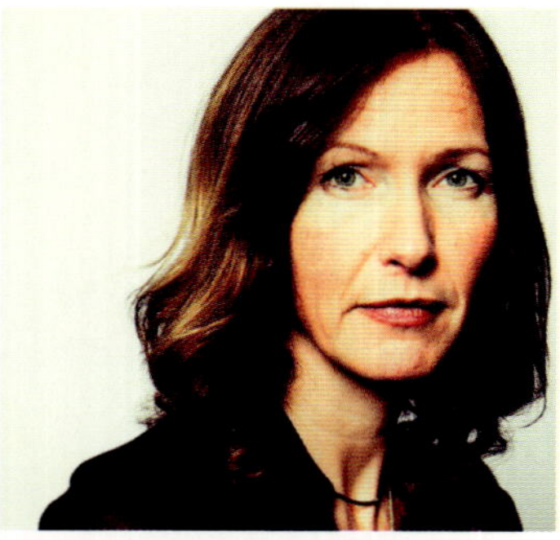

FIONA SHIELDS

PICTURE EDITOR,
THE GUARDIAN (UK)

Originally trained as a print journalist, Fiona moved into photojournalism in the early days of digital photography and has worked on a range of national newspaper titles from The Daily Mail to The Observer. She joined The Guardian in 1994 and became the paper's picture editor in 2009. Recently Fiona has taken on responsibility for the representation of current affairs on The Guardian's website, Guardian Unlimited, with involvement in web galleries, slideshows and the development of a news picture blog.

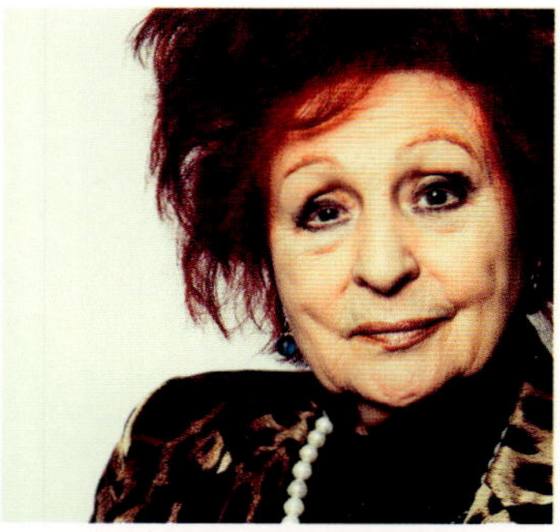

JUANA DE AIZPURU

GALLERY DIRECTOR,
GALERIA JUANA DE AIZPURU
(SPAIN)

Juana opened her gallery in Seville in 1970. The space is dedicated to the promotion of new tendencies, and Juana has consistently worked to exhibit both Spanish and international work. In 1982 she opened her gallery in Madrid. Her commitment has won her numerous awards, among them the Medallion for the Arts from the Cultural Ministry of Egypt, Gold Medallion for the Arts from the King of Spain, and Chevalier dans l'Ordre des Arts et des Lettres. In 1978 Juana conceived the idea of creating an international art fair, a concept that was realised in 1982 with the first edition of ARCO.

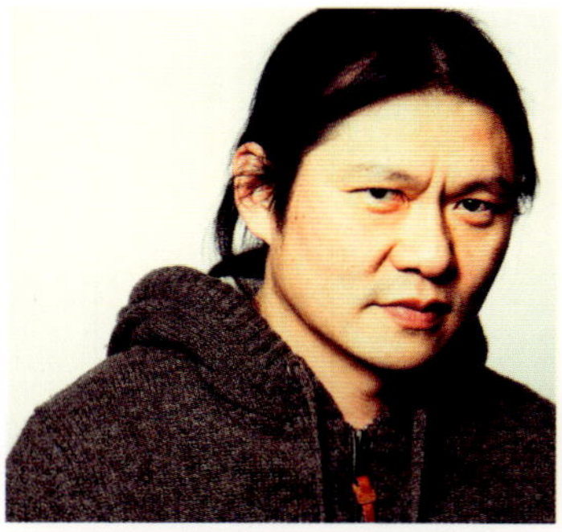

CHIEN-CHI CHANG

MAGNUM PHOTOGRAPHER
(TAIWAN)

Chien-Chi Chang often explores themes of alienation and connection through long-term documentary projects such as The Chain (1993-1999) and Double Happiness (2003-2009). The ties of family and of culture are also the theme of an ambitious project – China Town (1992 to present). For 21 years Chang has documented the bifurcated lives of Chinese immigrants in New York's Chinatown, along with those of their wives and families back home in Fujian. Chang joined Magnum in 1995 and became a full member in 2001.

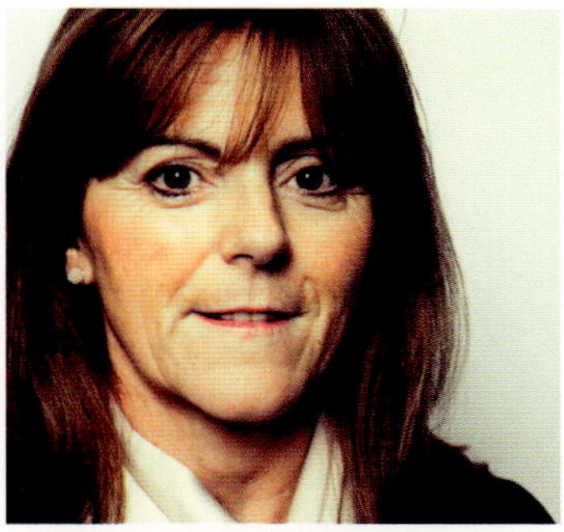

CAROLINE METCALFE

CONDÉ NAST TRAVELLER, DIRECTOR OF PHOTOGRAPHY (UK)

Caroline is responsible for commissioning and overseeing the photographic content of Condé Nast Traveller (non-fashion stories). Her career began in newspaper magazines, working at The Observer, The Independent and the Financial Times. Caroline has worked on advertising campaigns for Leo Burnett, Ogilvy and JWT and projects for design groups Pentagram and Vince Frost. She is a member of the World Press Photo Masterclass and YPA committees, nominating individuals for participation in their mentoring programmes. Her other judging roles have included TPOTY, HIPA, AOP and Azerbaijan Through the Lens.

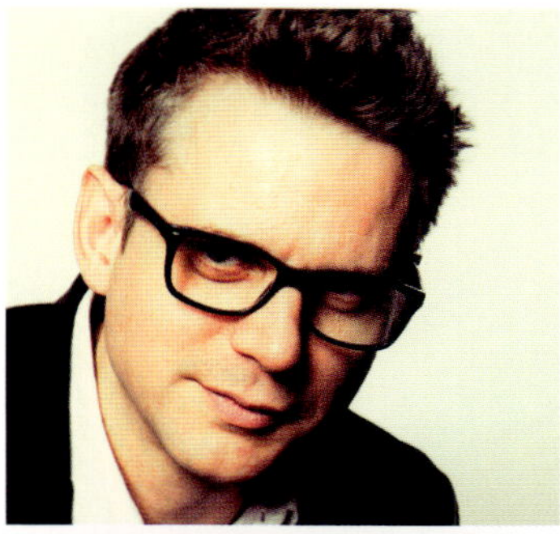

TIM PATON

MANAGING DIRECTOR, BALCONY JUMP (UK)

Tim began his career in the industry as a photographer, working his way up from local newspapers to shooting for the music magazine NME. By 1995 he realised that many of his contemporaries struggled with the business side of photography, so he created Balcony Jump, a photo agency. The company began by specialising in music photography, but has developed over the years, bridging into various areas and media. It is now a highly regarded agency for photography, fashion, illustration and advertising. Tim also lectures at Bournemouth University, assisting students with the benefits of commercial practice.

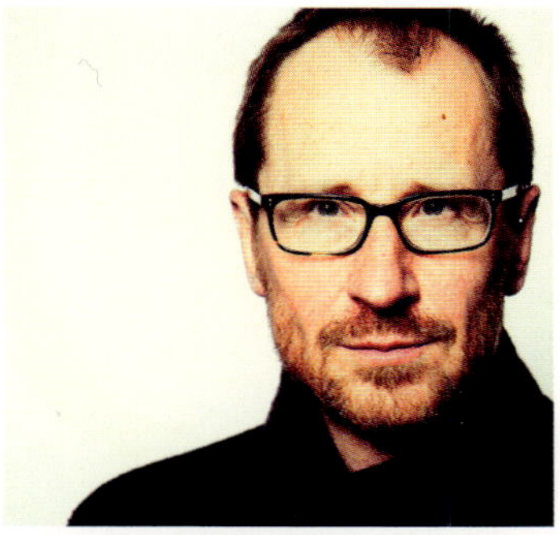

EDMUND CLARK

PHOTOGRAPHER (UK)

Edmund is best known for his award-winning work on the representation of control and incarceration through the monographs Guantanamo: If the Light Goes Out (2010) and Still Life Killing Time (2007). After studying History at the University of Sussex and the University of Paris, he worked in international research in London and Brussels before gaining a postgraduate photojournalism diploma at the London College of Communications. In 2011 he was awarded the Royal Photographic Society Hood Medal for outstanding photography for public service.

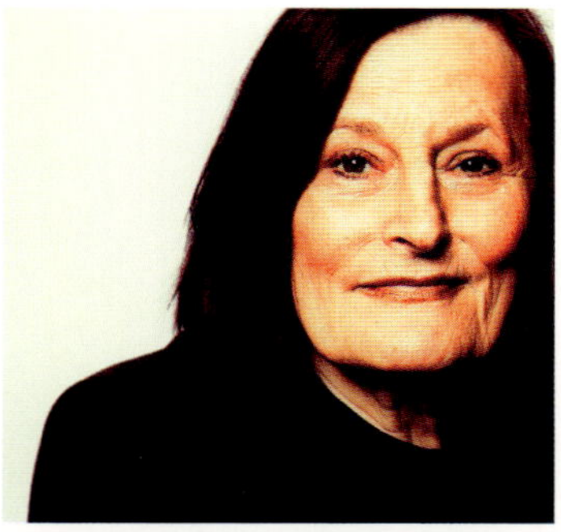

MONICA SUDER

PHOTOGRAPHY CONSULTANT AND COACH (GERMANY & USA)

Monica works with the international photographic community as a creative and career coach, consultant, lecturer, panellist and educator. She has been an award-winning photo editor, and has worked as a director of photography and consultant to publishers. She worked at Magnum Photos, Time-Life, and Rolling Stone, and has been assisting photographers for 15 years in developing websites, portfolios, books and personal projects in the US and in Europe. Monica has been a portfolio reviewer for many years in New York City and San Francisco, as well as in France and Germany.

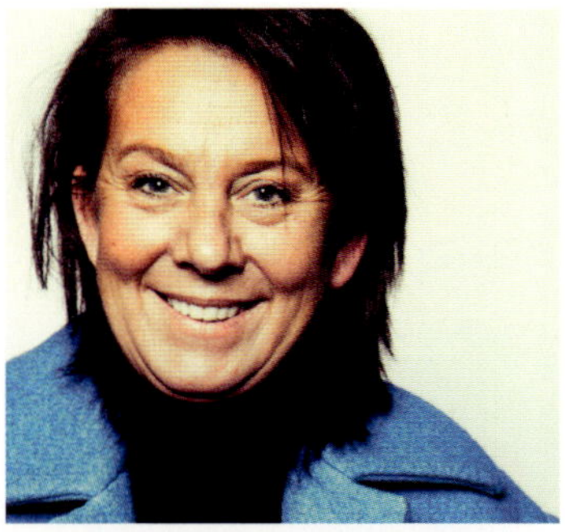

CATHERINE CHERMAYEFF

DIRECTOR OF SPECIAL PROJECTS, MAGNUM PHOTOS (USA)

In 1985 Catherine became the Director of Special Projects at Magnum Photos, the international photo agency. She developed, produced, sold and secured funding for exhibitions, editorial and corporate projects, along with publications. In 1991 she co-founded Umbra Editions, a publishing house that specialised in packaging visual books. In 2000 she wrote and edited Fashion Photography Now and in the same year founded i2i Photography, an international photographic agency currently representing 27 photographers. Catherine has now returned to Magnum, alongside lecturing and other current ventures.

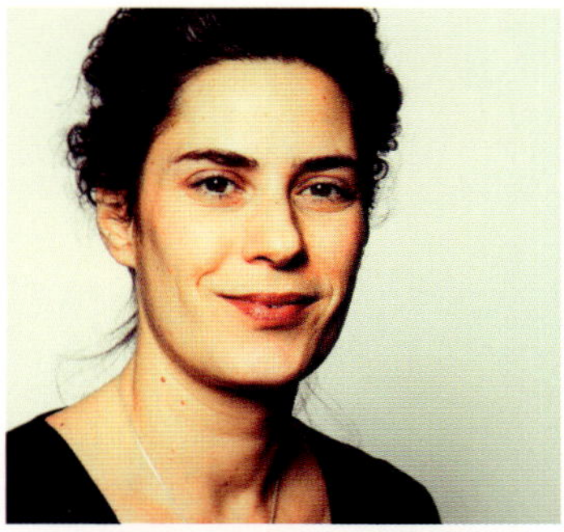

FRANCESCA SEARS

DIRECTOR, PANOS PROFILE AT PANOS PICTURES (UK)

Francesca started her professional career as a print journalist for Forbes magazine in New York, turning to photography in 2002, when she re-trained and graduated from Goldsmiths with an MA in Image and Communication. Before moving to Panos she worked at Magnum Photos as the Editorial Director in London, then as the agency's Global Editorial Director and manager of the London office. Francesca is currently Director of Profile at Panos Pictures in London. She is responsible for raising the company profile, for business development and for cultural projects.

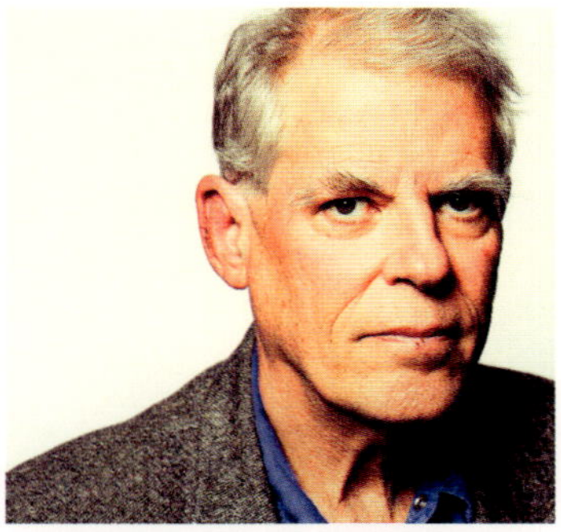

MACDUFF EVERTON

PHOTOGRAPHER (USA)

Macduff is a contributing editor at National Geographic Traveller, where he has photographed more than 20 stories. His many editorial clients also include Condé Nast Traveller, Life, NY Times Magazine and Smithsonian. His work is in the collections of many public and private institutions including the Bibliothèque Nationale in Paris, and the Museum of Modern Art in New York.

L'IRIS D'OR

ANDREA GJESTVANG
NORWAY

The Sony World Photography Awards is regarded as one of the most prestigious awards programmes in the photographic industry and each year members of this industry, across all genres of photography, are recognised and awarded.

Chosen by our esteemed Honorary Judging Committee, the L'Iris d'Or, our most distinguished award, is presented to one single photographer whose work represents the pinnacle of the entries received.

This photographer is chosen from within the first place winners of all the professional categories.

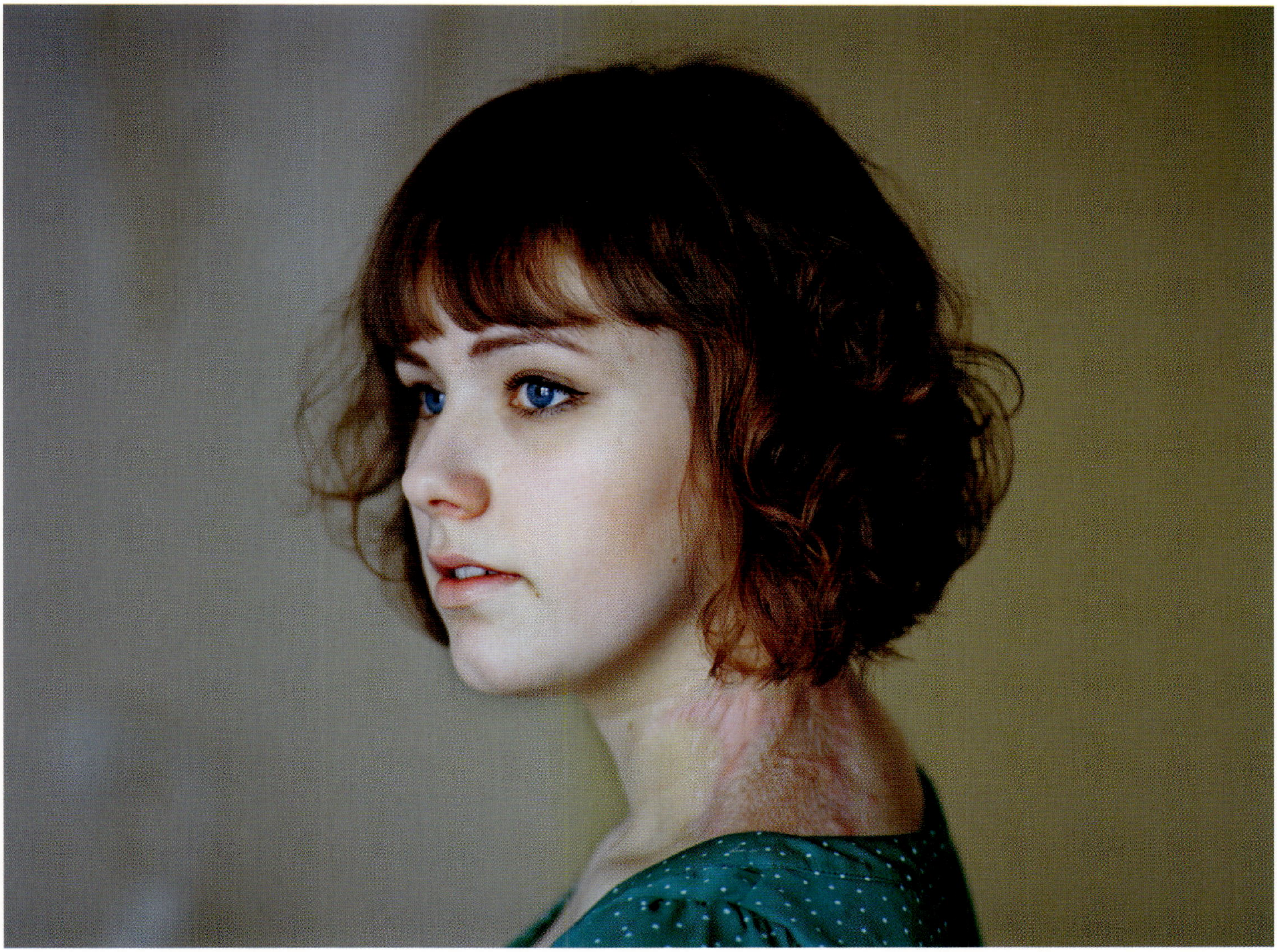

"I bear my scares with dignity, because I got them standing for something I believe in." Ylva Schwenke (15).

One Day in History. In Norway, the date of 22nd of July 2011 has forever etched itself into the collective and private memory. That day, a car bomb killed eight people and damaged the executive government quarter in Oslo. A few hours later, 69 young people were killed at a summer camp on the island of Utøya. The camp was organised by AUF, the youth division of the ruling Norwegian Labor Party.

Around 500 people survived the massacre, many of whom were badly wounded. More than half of the survivors were children and youths under the age of 18. They have now returned to their daily lives. They go to school, they hang out with friends and they fall in love. They go to bed every night and every morning they look at themselves in the mirror. However something has changed. The young survivors will live on with their scars — both visible and mental — many of which may never fully heal.

This is a series of portraits of children and youths who survived the massacre on the island of Utøya, outside Oslo, on 22 July 2011.

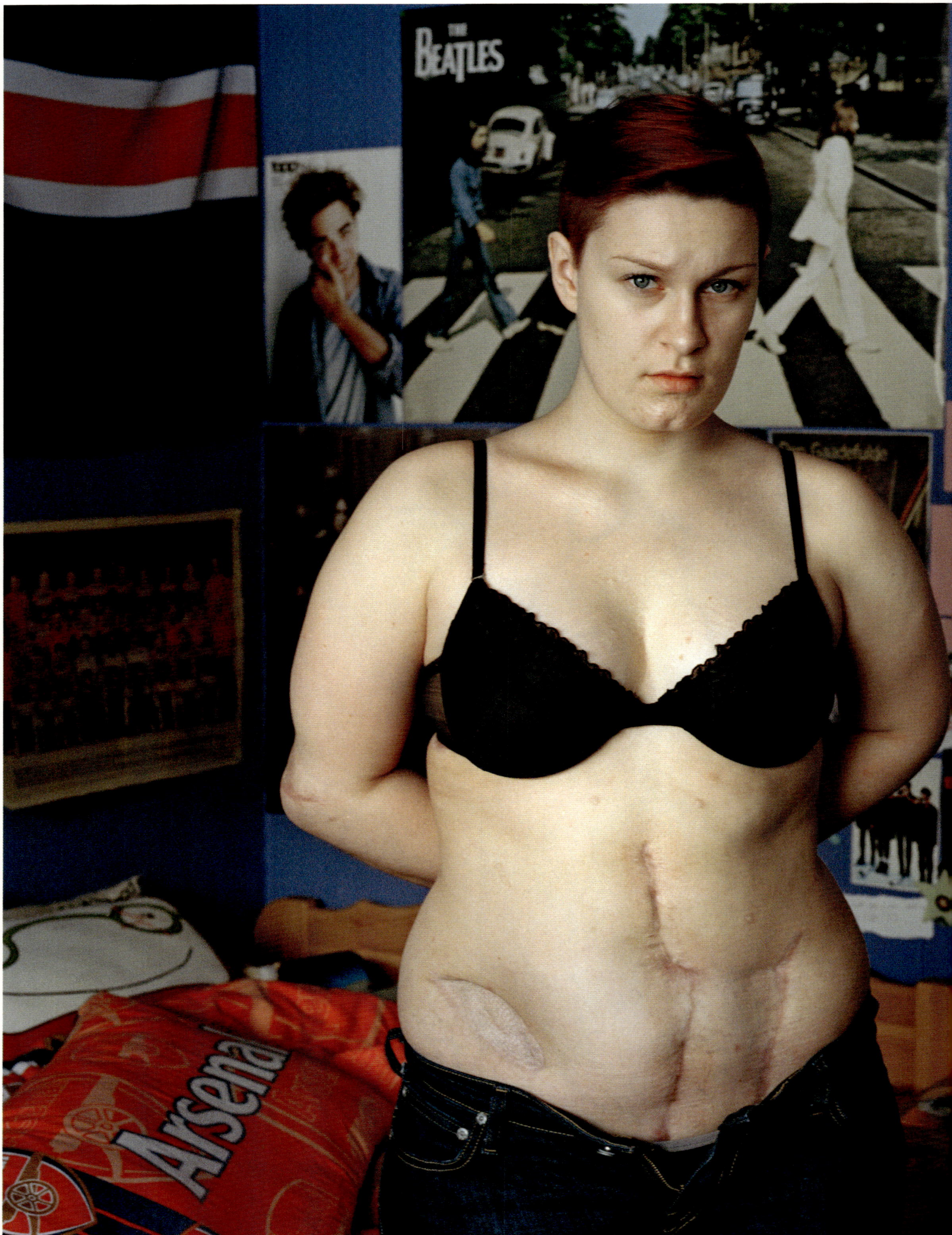
THE
BEATLES
Arsenal

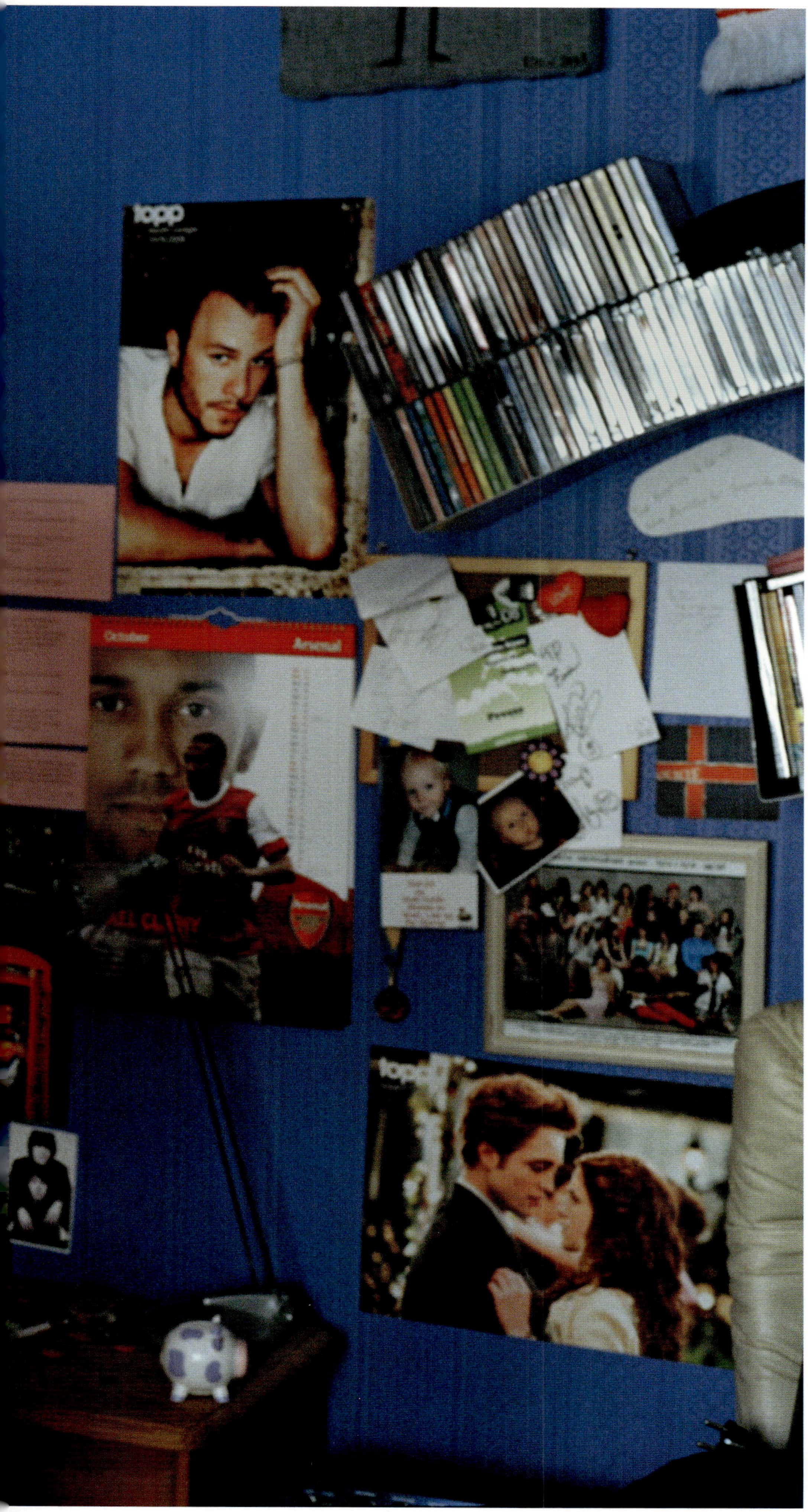

Eirin Kjaer (20) hid in a cave. She was shot in her stomach, arm, knee and armpit when trying to protect younger friends.

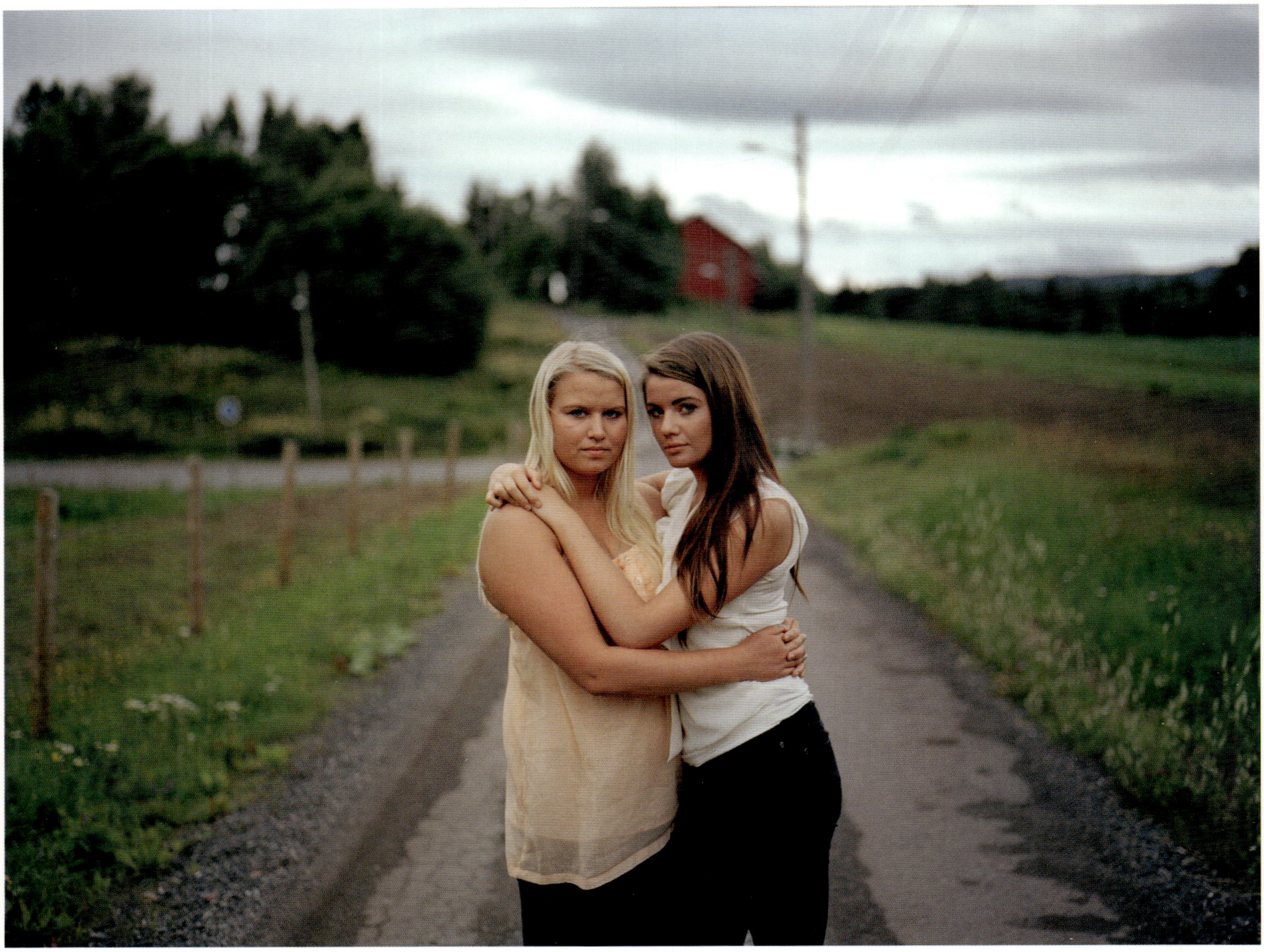

Best friends Victoria Froeyd (18) and Sofie Nilsen (17) hid together in the school building until the police rescued them.

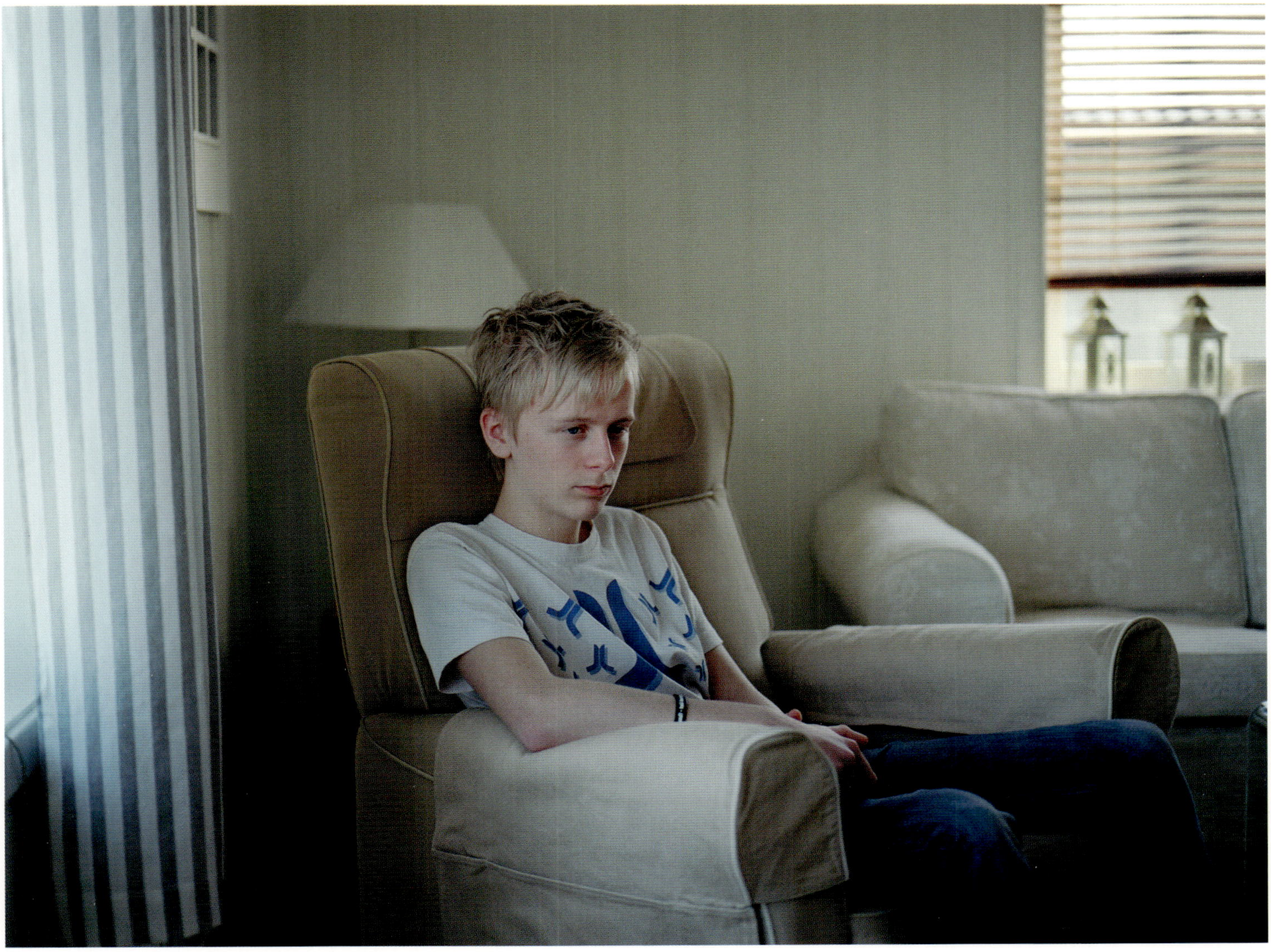

Alexander Sandberg (16) hid under a sofa in the school building, until the perpetrator was arrested.

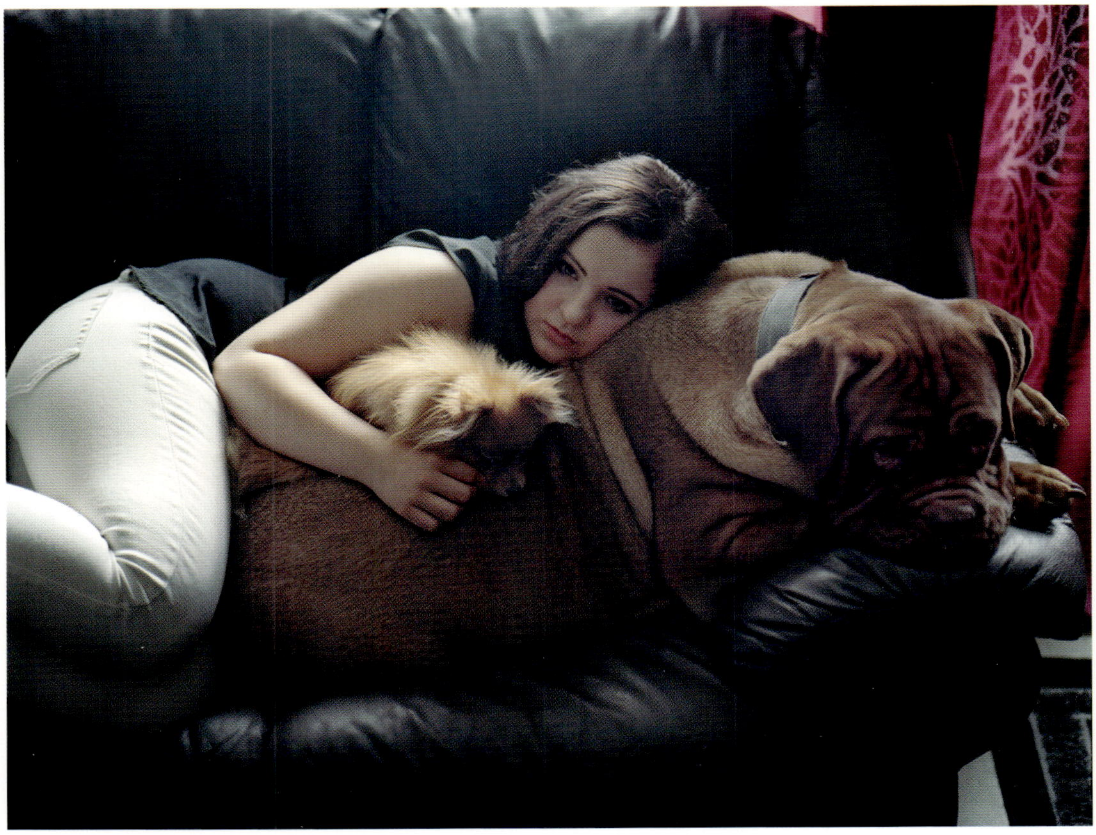

Iselin Rose Borch (15) suffered from nightmares. She got a little dog, which now sleeps on her stomach every night.

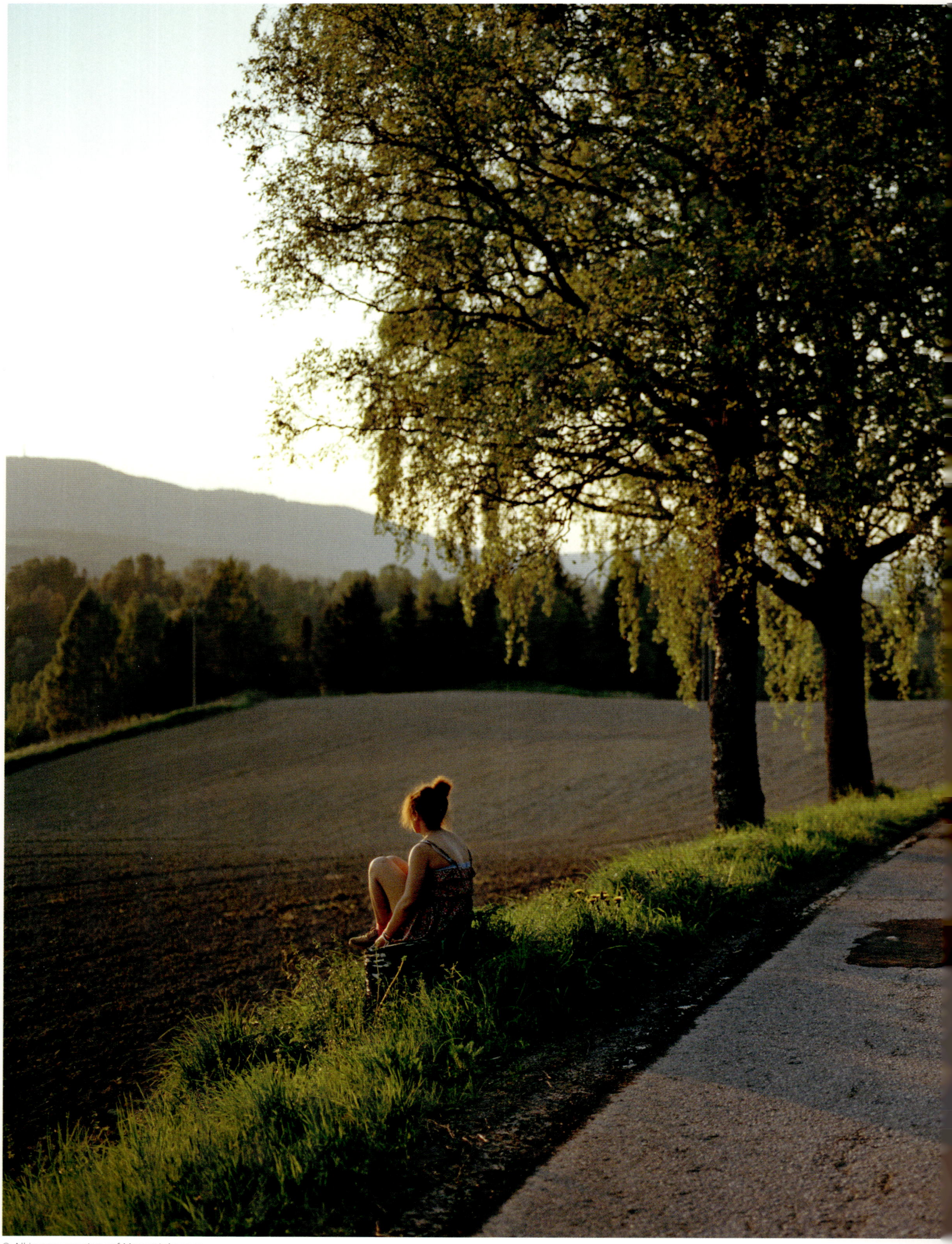

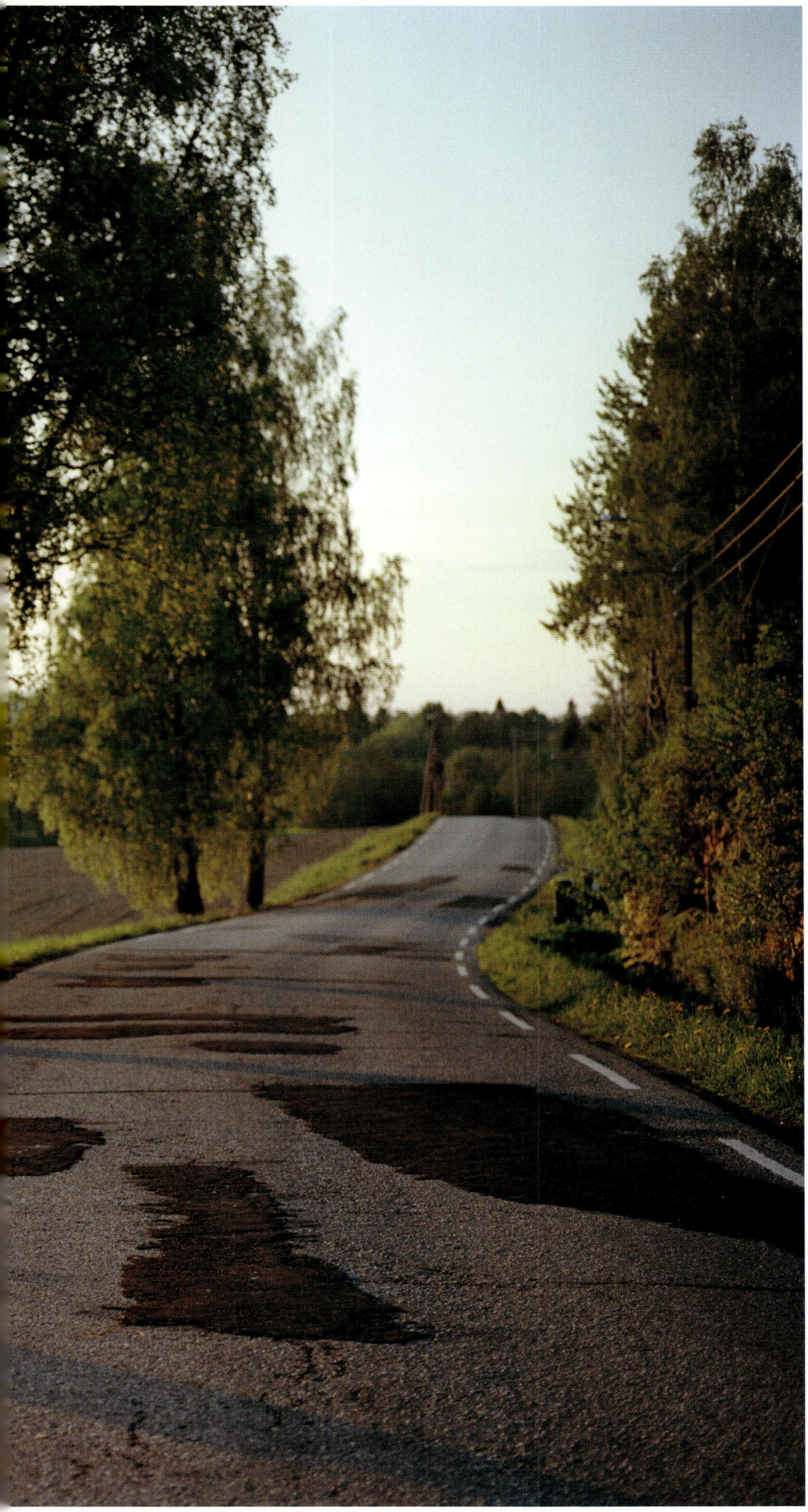

"I like to sit here, because I feel that my dead friends are in the nature that surrounds us."
Aina helgheim (19)

ARCHITECTURE
ARTS & CULTURE
CAMPAIGN
CONCEPTUAL
CONTEMPORARY ISSUES
CURRENT AFFAIRS
FASHION & BEAUTY
LANDSCAPE
LIFESTYLE
NATURE & WILDLIFE
PEOPLE
PORTRAITURE
SPORT
STILL LIFE
TRAVEL

PROFESSIONAL COMPETITION WINNERS

"Are we judges – or just judgmental?" This was uttered by one of my fellow jurors as we were led into a series of rooms on a snowy, rainy, cold day in London in late January. The job in front of us was daunting – actually slightly overwhelming. There were 15 categories, 12 judges, 3 days and thousands of photographs to look at. Our task was to carefully and thoughtfully look at them all, discuss them all, and come up with a short list and then in a single voice pick a single winner. Wow.

We were divided into four groups of three each and each group looked at three or four categories. It seemed unimaginable that we would find a common consensus – we did.

There were so many things to consider – we all find ourselves in a transitional moment in our visual culture – how do we understand the power of photography? Photographs impact all our lives, they do more than record the world, they give us a voice and a way to tell universal stories.

How do we, the jurors, look at literally thousands of photographic stories and find the most potent examples of how photographs tell these stories. So many photographs are made for so many reasons and so often the simplest are the most powerful.

After two days of looking and arguing, arm twisting and eliminating - all the jurors were reunited in one room with our 15 individual category winners. We were a diverse group – a photographic agency founder, gallery directors from France and Spain, a photographic book editor from the UK, a photo agency director, a newspaper picture editor, a magazine picture editor, an international consultant and three photographers coming from Taiwan, the UK and the USA. So truly a mixed bag.

My job was to wrangle this heady, smart, experienced and articulate group. Everyone had passionate opinions and made heartfelt arguments. We all found ourselves somewhat amazed at the level of work being discussed.

The shortlist was as diverse as we were – a whimsical extraordinarily clever sneaker campaign shot in Hong Kong, a gritty reportage of conflict in Syria, majestic black and white landscapes, a personal AIDS campaign shot with friends on an iphone, a quiet personal look at survivors of a Norwegian mass shooting. Every story had an advocate – a strong voice speaking for it. In the end, after much debate and discussion we were all completely united in our choice – which was such a satisfactory outcome.

I want to thank not only my fellow jurors but also the wonderfully supportive team that makes up the World Photography Organisation. And I want to congratulate not only the finalists represented in this book, but the entire shortlist of photographers – as well as the many photographers around the globe who submitted their work and made this such an engaging and lively debate.

CATHERINE CHERMAYEFF

DIRECTOR OF SPECIAL PROJECTS, MAGNUM PHOTOS (USA).
PRESIDING CHAIR OF 2013 HONORARY JUDGING COMMITTEE

FABRICE FOUILLET FRANCE

1ST PLACE
ARCHITECTURE

Corpus Christi. This series highlights the architectural aesthetic of these new places of worship, a genuine creative inspiration in modern religious architecture. Part of a movement originating in the 1920s, most of these churches were built in the 1950-60s. They reveal a new conception of the sacred, a representation of the divine imbued with modernity, a hymn to minimalism. I have sought to capture this break with centuries of architectural tradition, the reinforced concrete, plastic and the crystal.

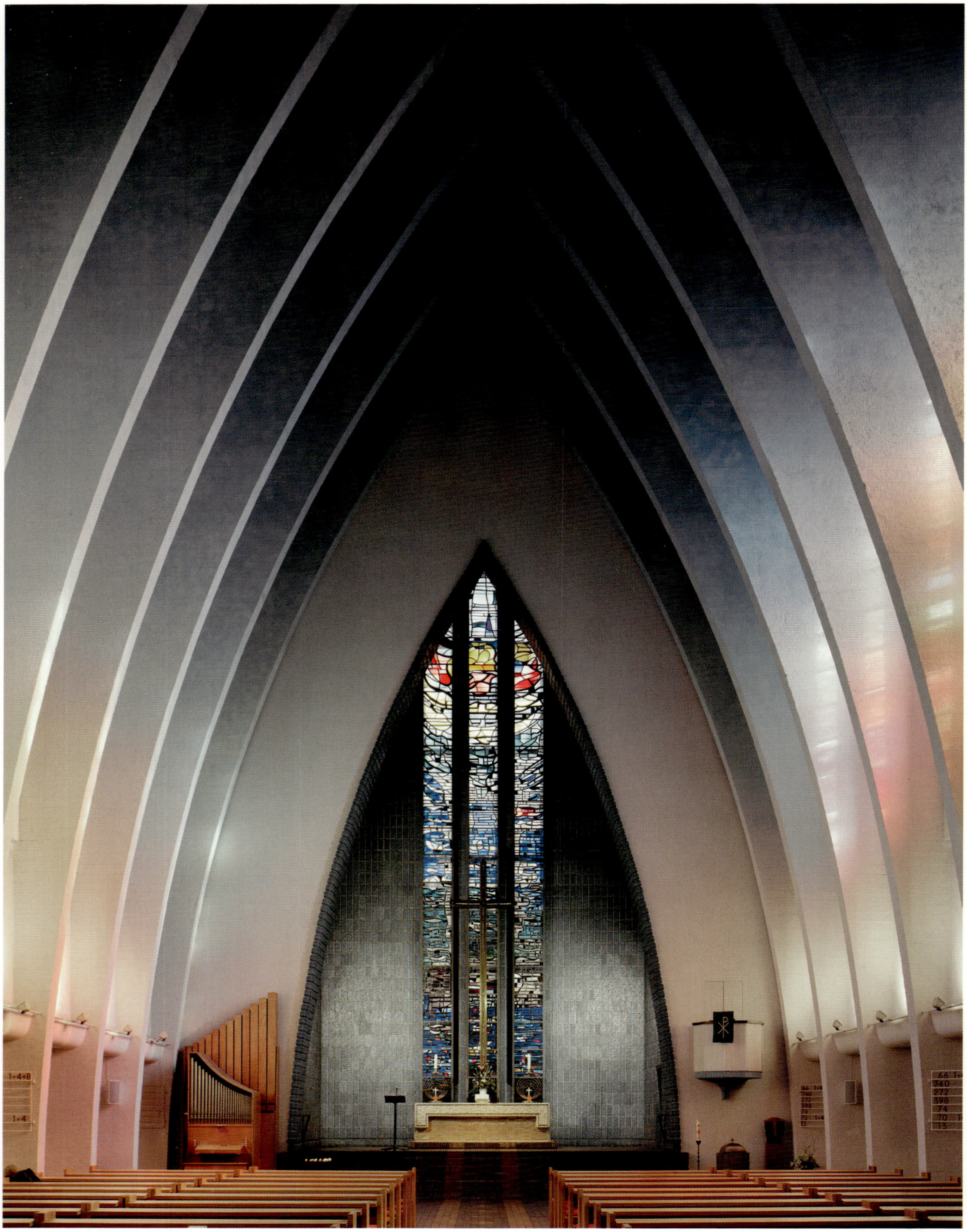

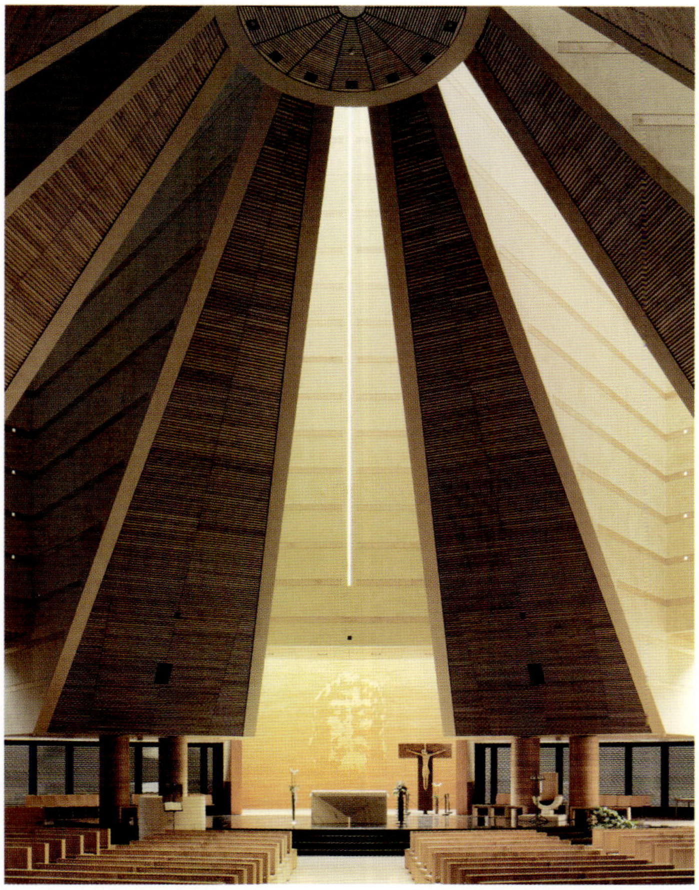
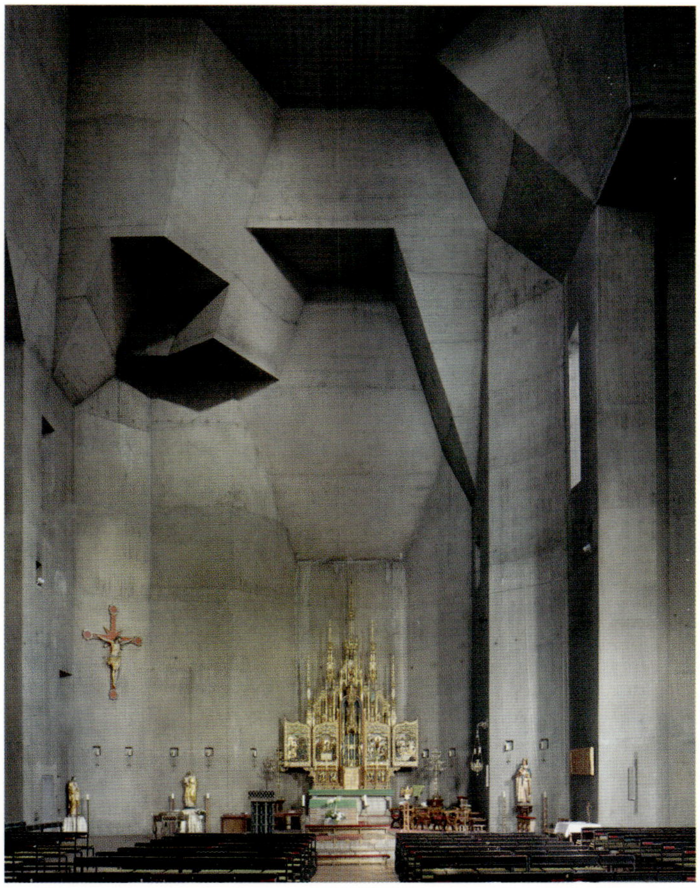
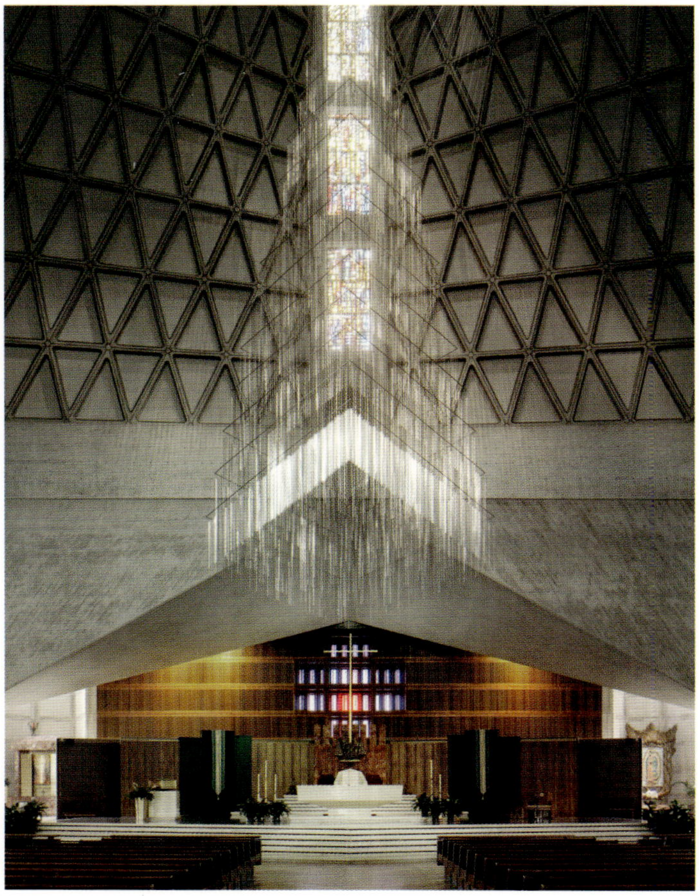
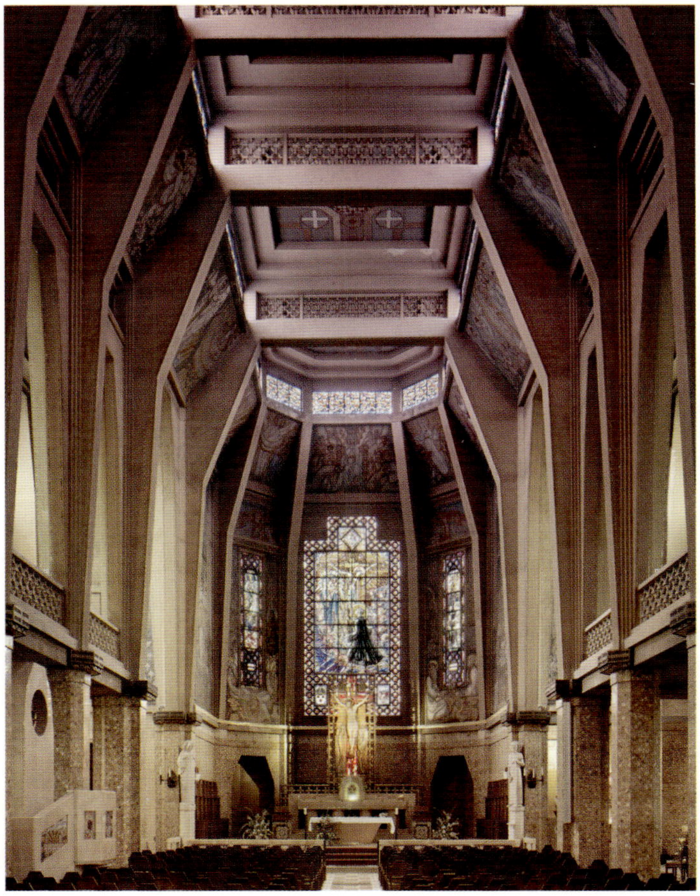

REINIS HOFMANIS LATVIA

2ND PLACE
ARCHITECTURE

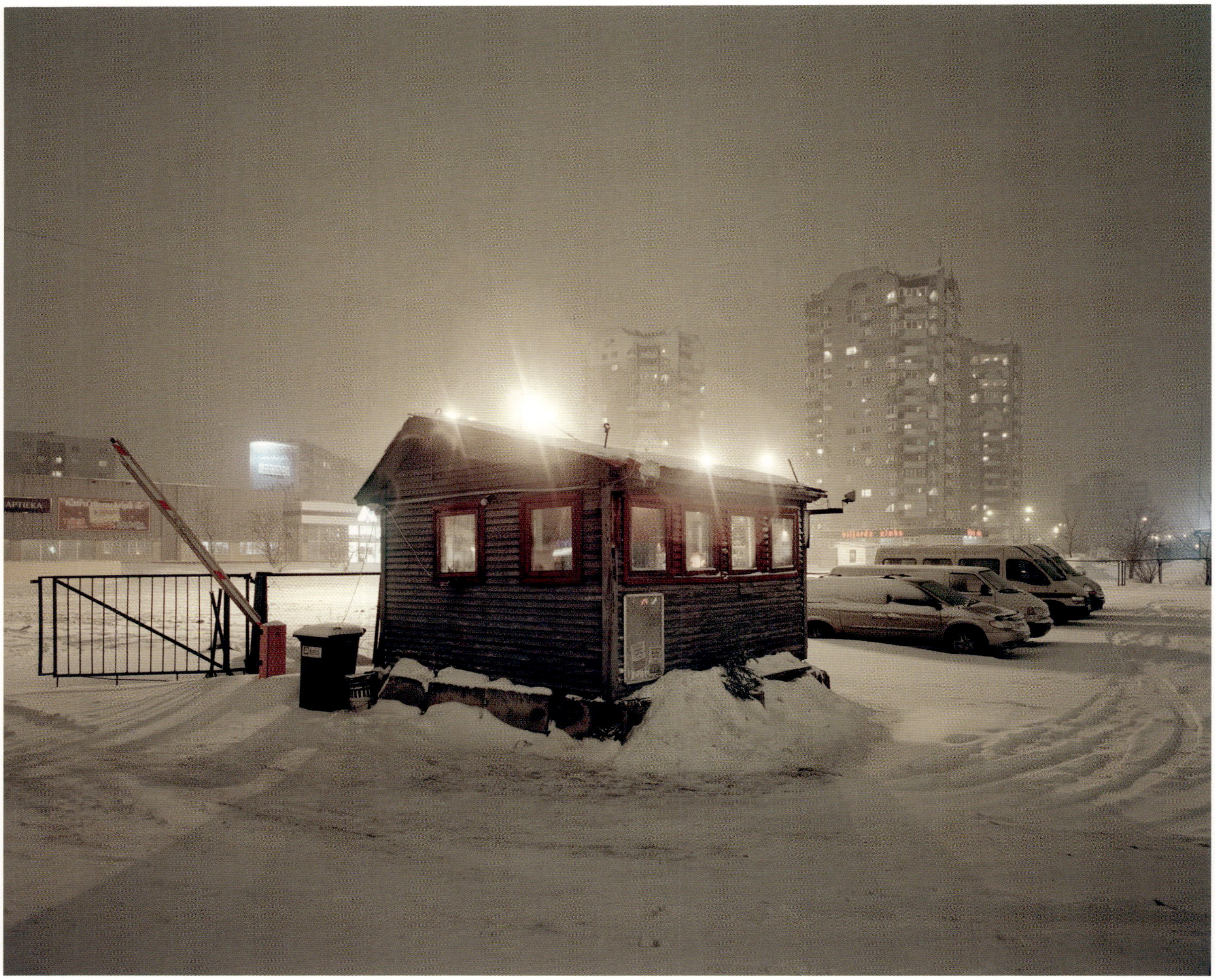

Territory. This series focuses on various aspects and boundaries in the urban landscape. There are boundaries between the public and the private space, and the specifics of vision and perception. Each image features a guard and his guardhouse. Guard booths are architecturally inexpressive and humble, although ubiquitous in the urban landscape. The images feature the moment at which the guard has spotted or is approaching the photographer. Photos are captured in twilight conditions, when the lighting is visible. Contemporary architecture is unthinkable without the light. Light plays an important role in highlighting and hiding.

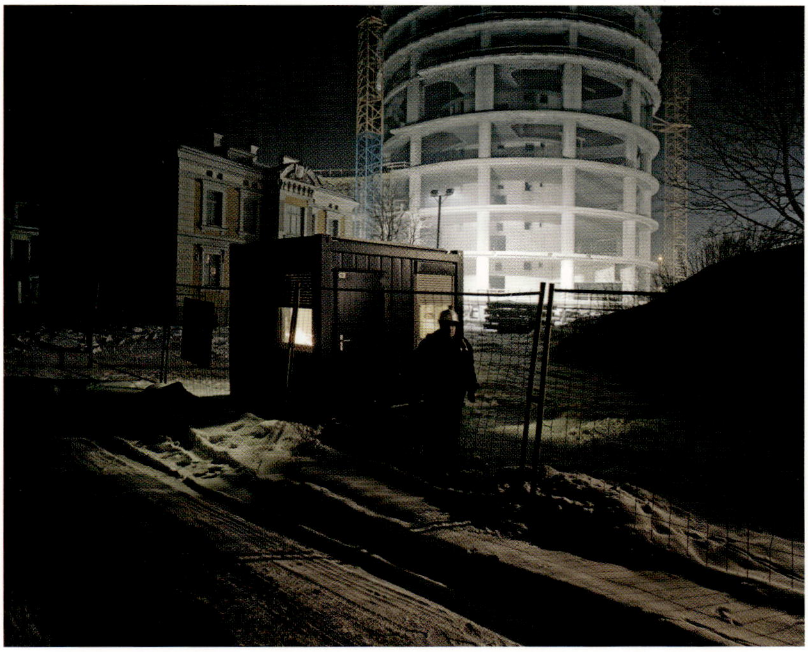

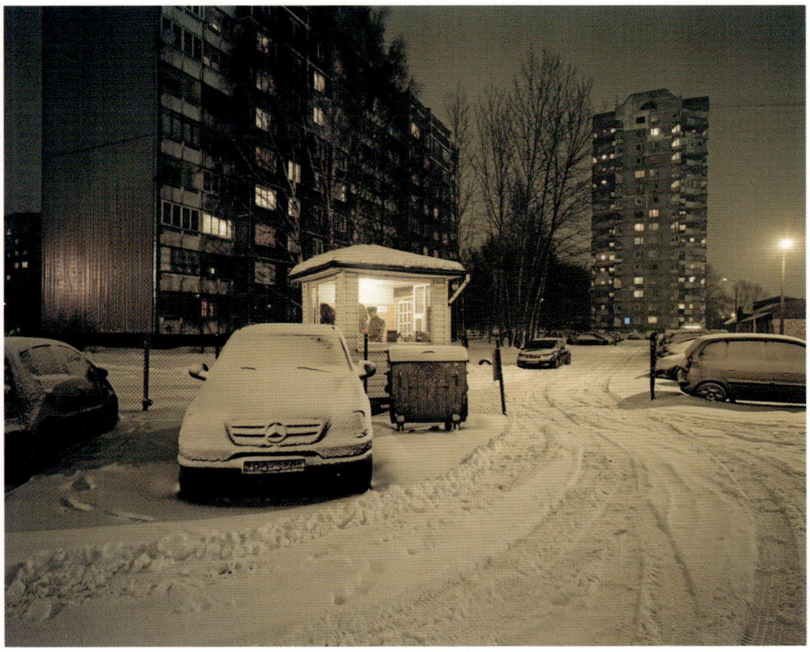

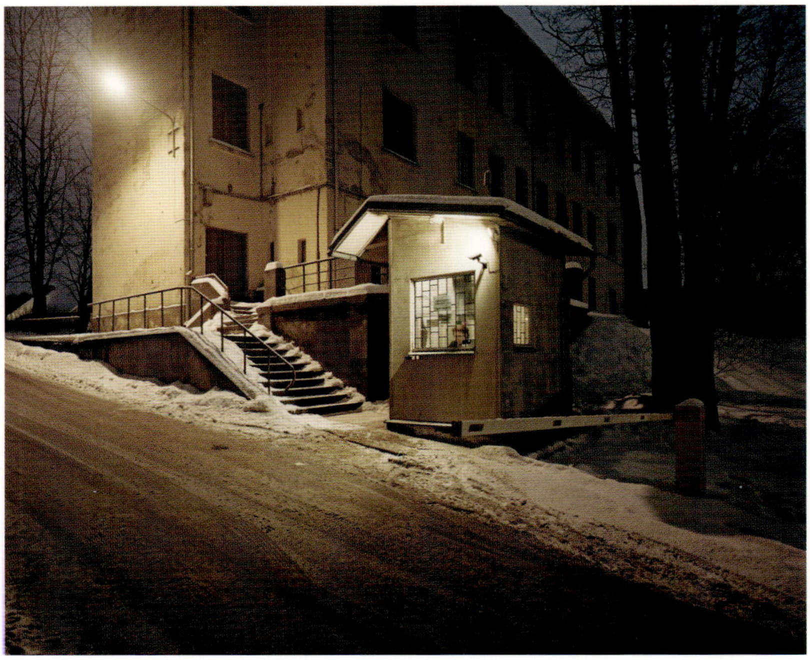

CHRISTOF PLUEMACHER GERMANY

3RD PLACE
ARCHITECTURE

Urban Darkness. These images are a reflection on the observation that energy is now being conserved at night in German urban spaces. Once lit-up monolithic urban structures now morph into ghostly colossi, an indicator of changing times. Light usually takes away the fears of the night - and was an indicator of wealth and prosperity in the western world. Dark cities and dark structures were once a hallmark of impoverished countries and the communist east. With that era behind us, the urban darkness has a new significance.

MYRIAM MELONI ITALY

1ST PLACE
ARTS & CULTURE

The Limousine. A luxury emblem, which used to transport politicians and rock stars in the '80s, is nowadays an icon of Argentinian popular culture. Brides in their white dresses, starlets, teenagers celebrating their birthdays and stag parties: they all share the same sensation of sitting for one night in a 1972 electric blue Ford Fairlane. 'The Limousine' explores an enclosed space in which many diverse things can happen. Ordinary people use the dark tinted windows to release their fantasies of transgression, under the curious eye of the passersby.

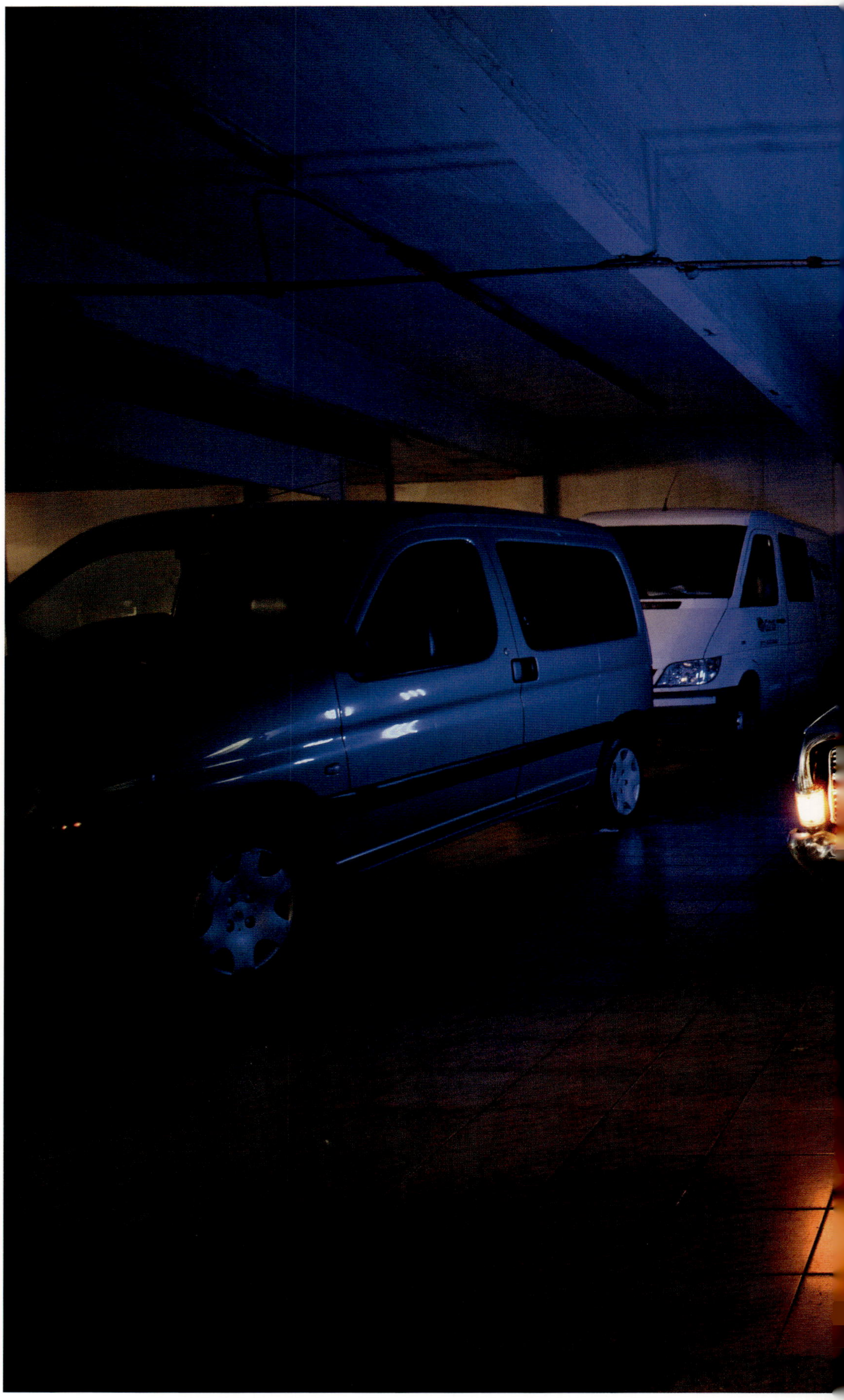

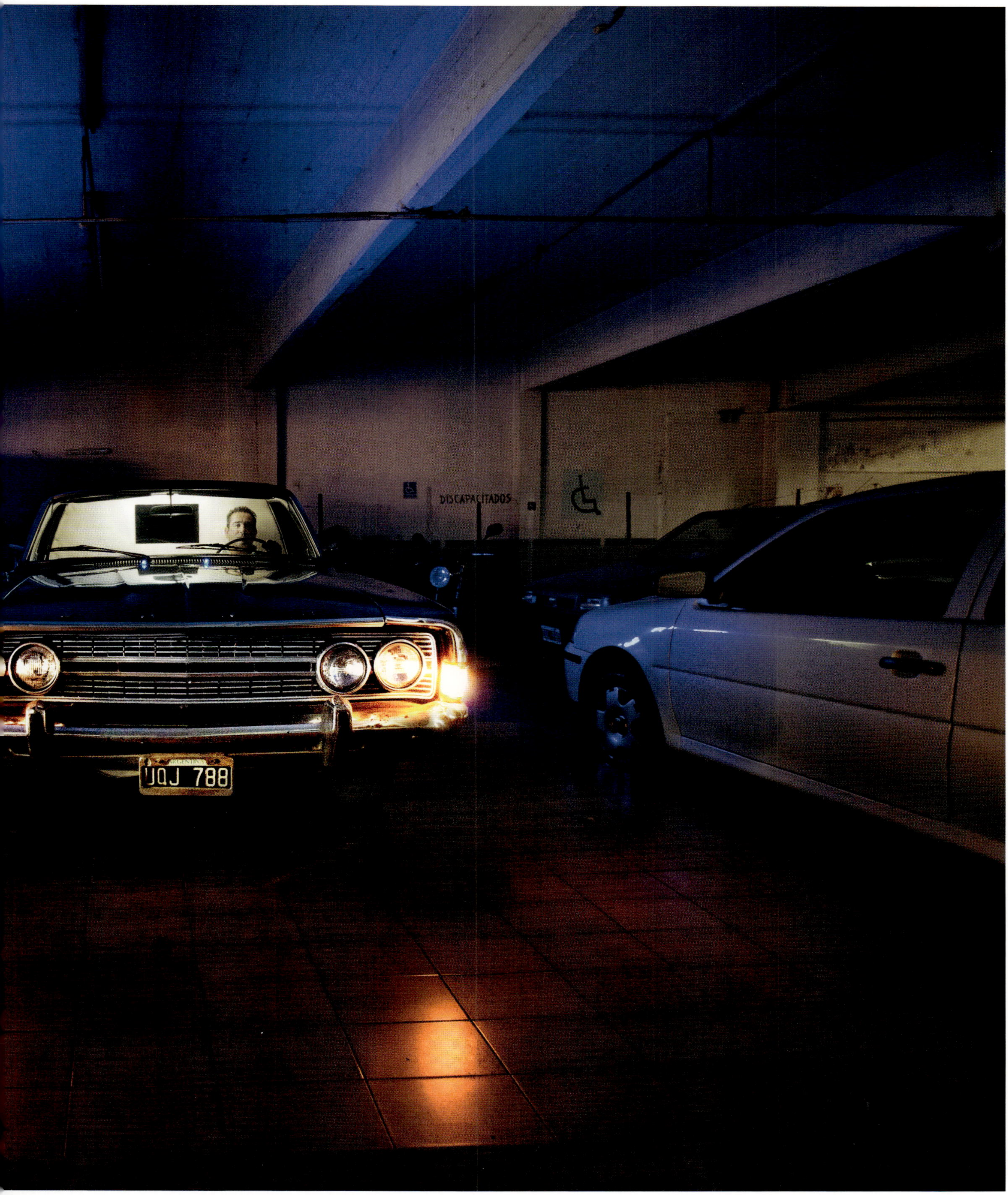
DISCAPACITADOS
JQJ 788

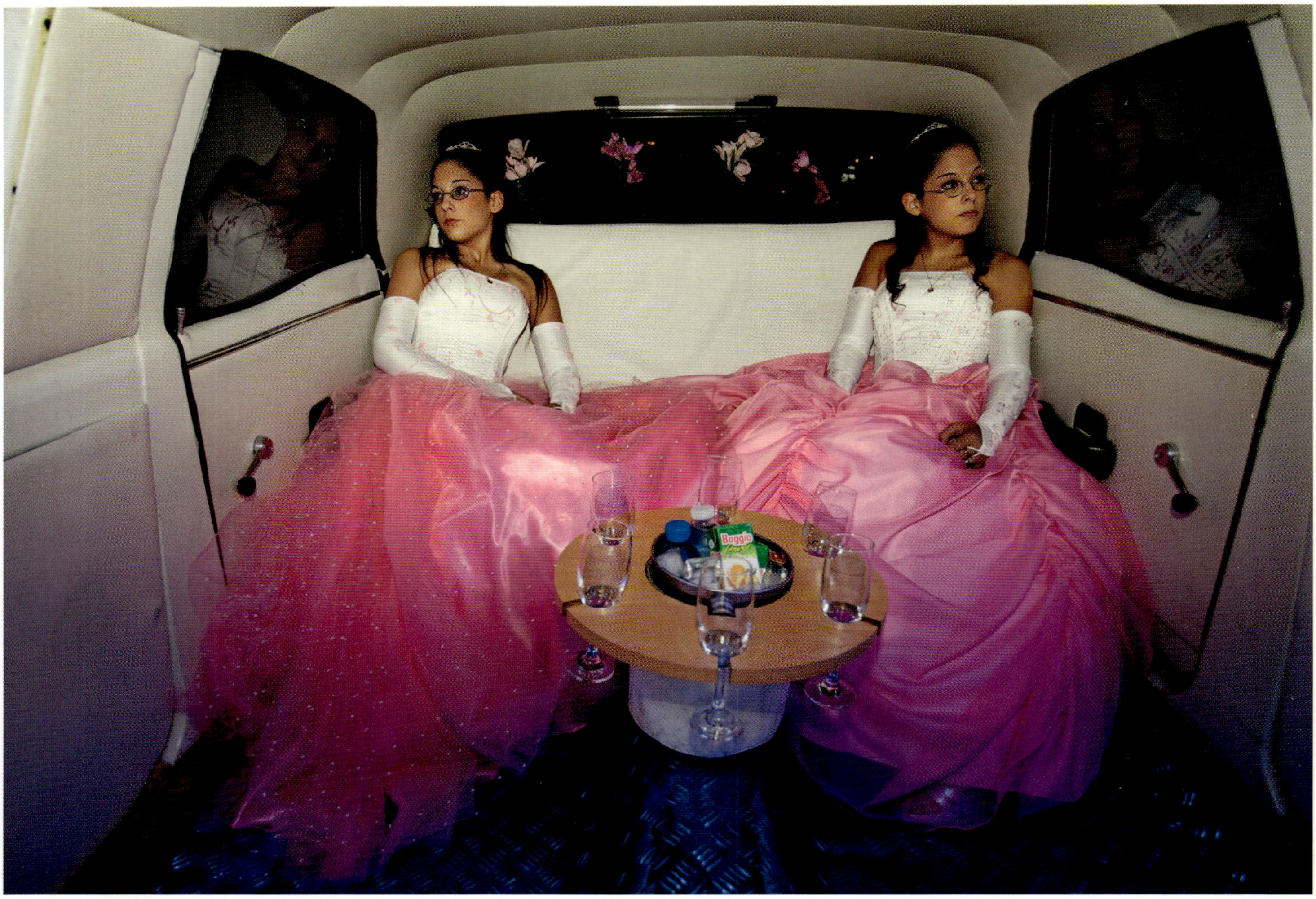
Baggio

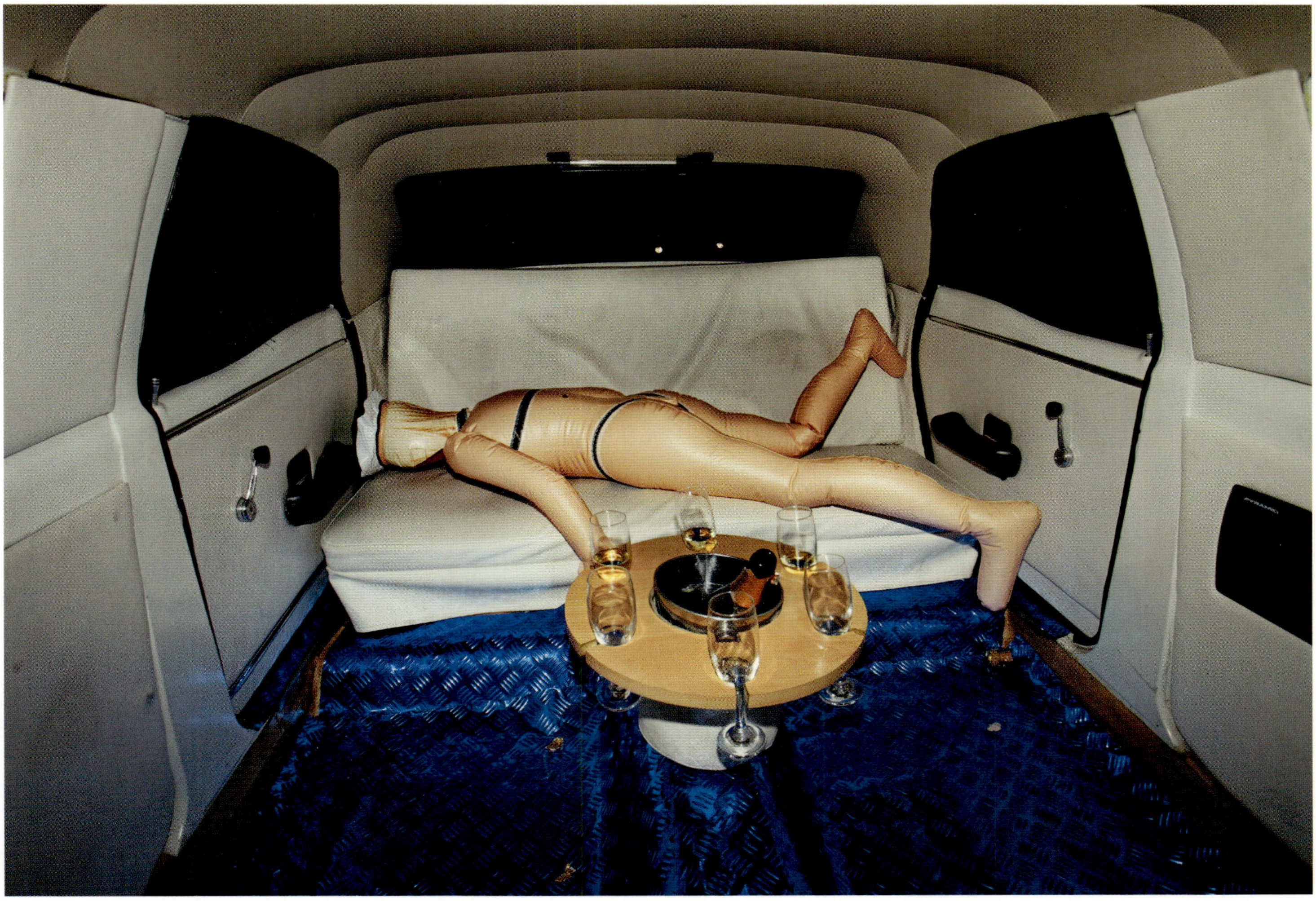

NICCOLÒ RASTRELLI & GIORGIO BARRERA ITALY

2ND PLACE
ARTS & CULTURE

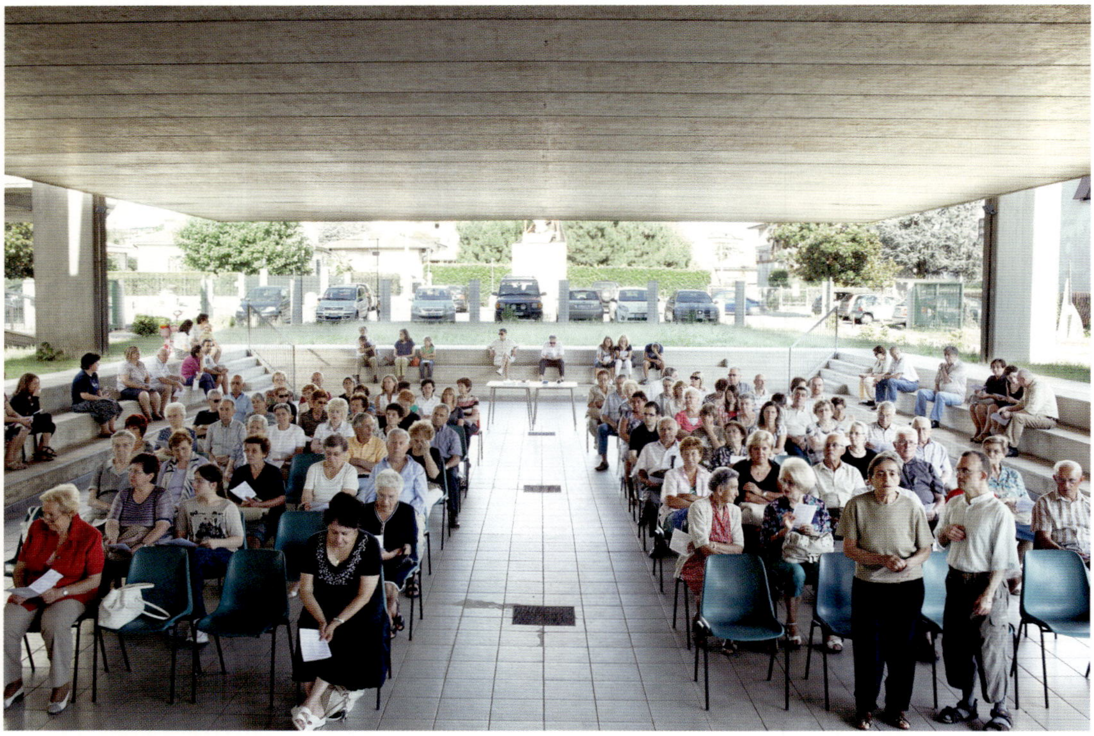

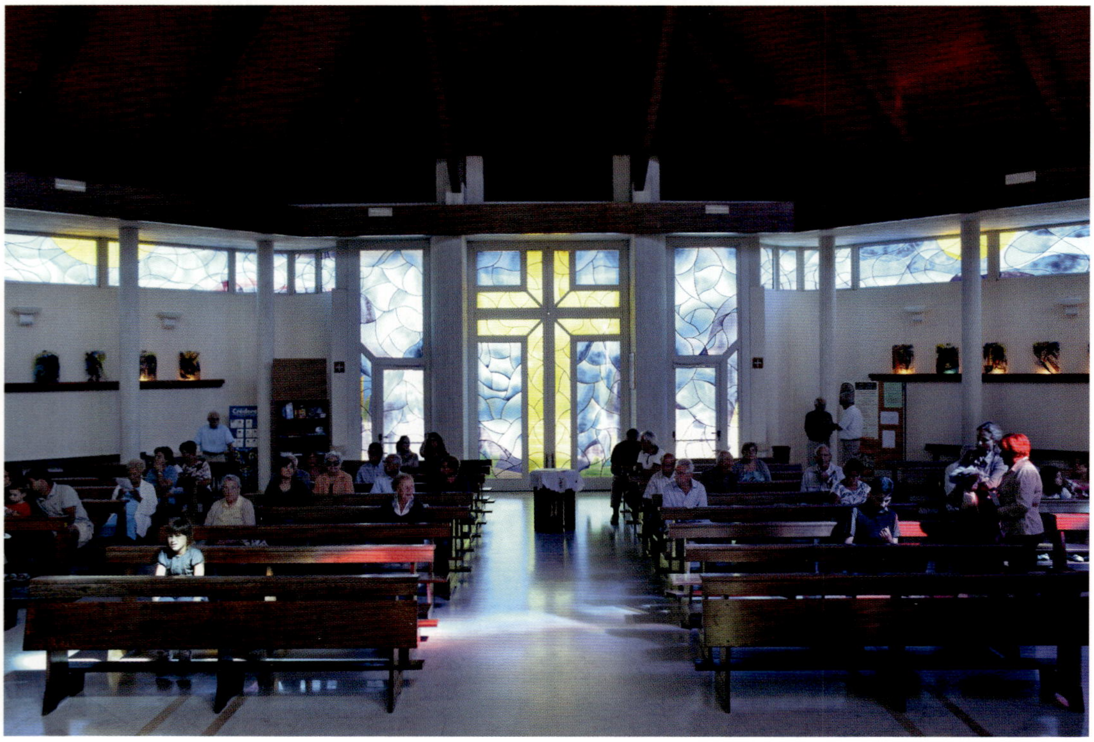

Andate in pace (go in peace). These images document the churches built after Vatican II (1962-65). The Church is not intended as a building but as a space made up of people of flesh and bone, of 'human material' or 'living stones'. The camera remains in front of the altar. Anyone who enters the church can see it but cannot see the photographers because the camera is operated by a remote control or time lapse. Post-Vatican II, the structure of the chancel was revolutionised; the priest now turns towards the churchgoer. The new vision of the priest is vital: we place the camera in front of the altar – as if it replaces the priest's gaze.

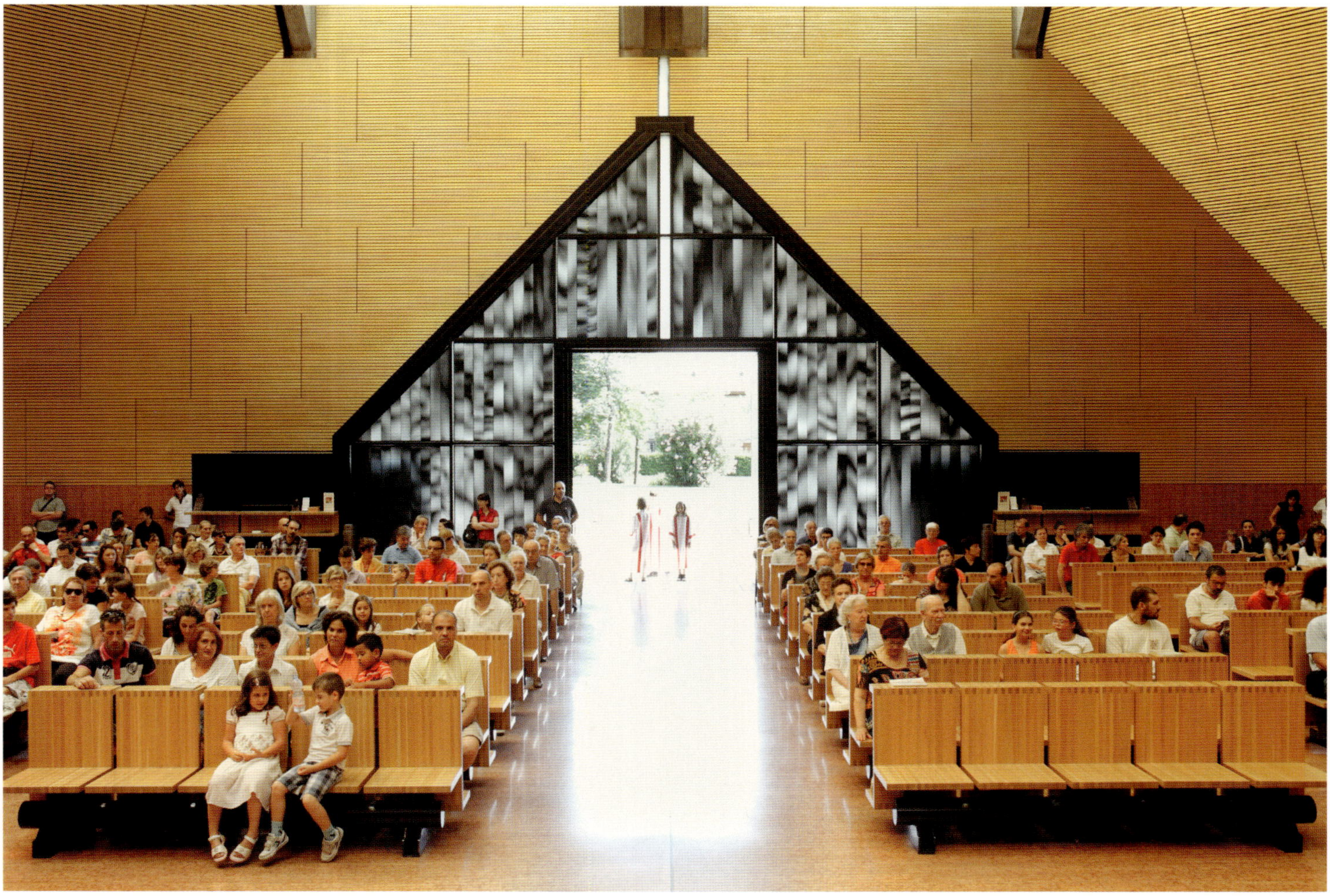

DANISH SIDDIQUI INDIA

3RD PLACE
ARTS & CULTURE

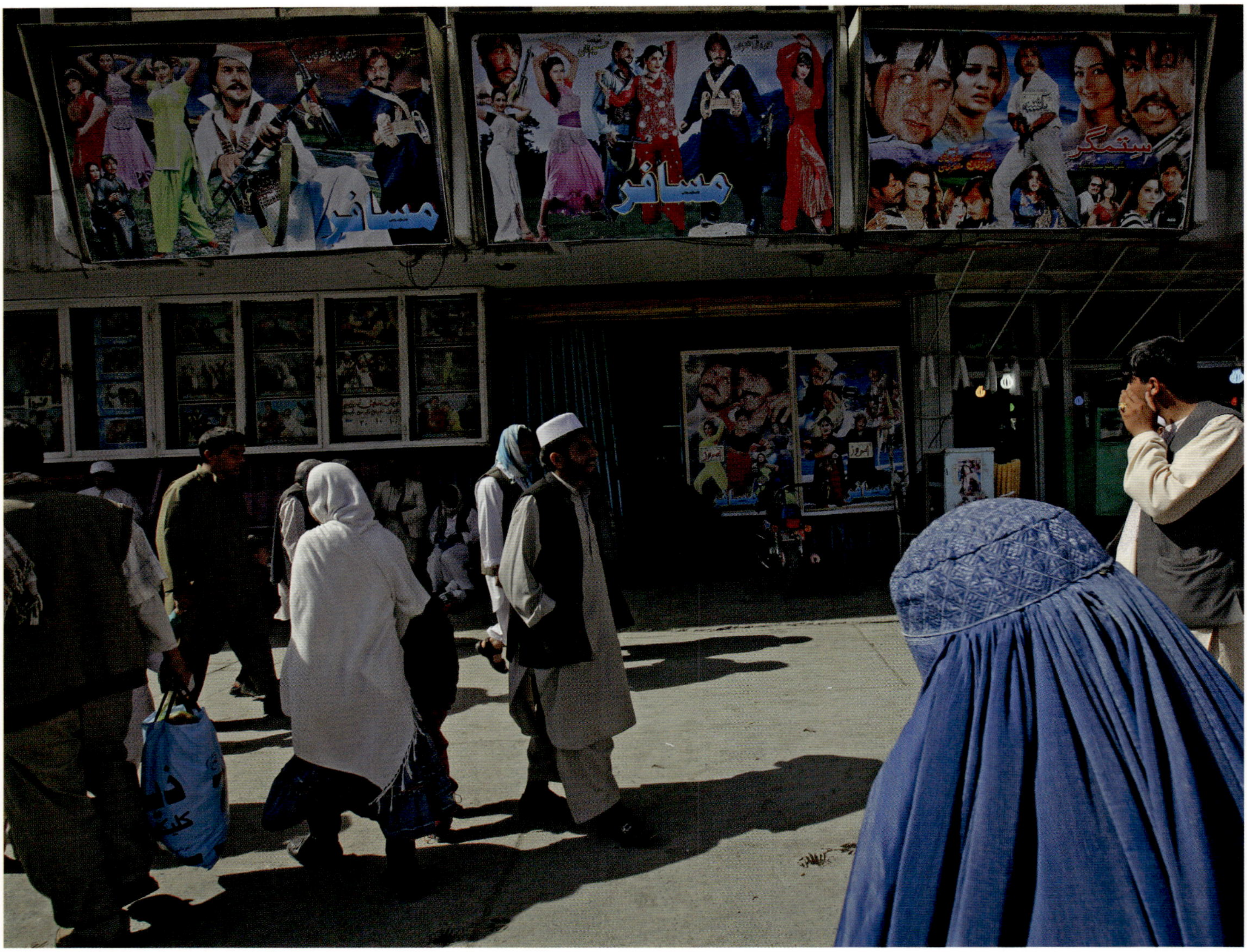

Inside Kabul's Screens. When the Taliban took over Kabul in 1996, cinemas were attacked and many films forbidden. Under the constant shadow of fear cinemas are slowly re-emerging. There are only half a dozen cinemas in the whole of Kabul. Now each has three films every day, the first one starting at 10a.m. Bollywood films from India, Pashto films from Pakistan and occasionally dubbed Hollywood films play on Kabul's screens, but the genre is always the same; Afghan movie fans love action films.

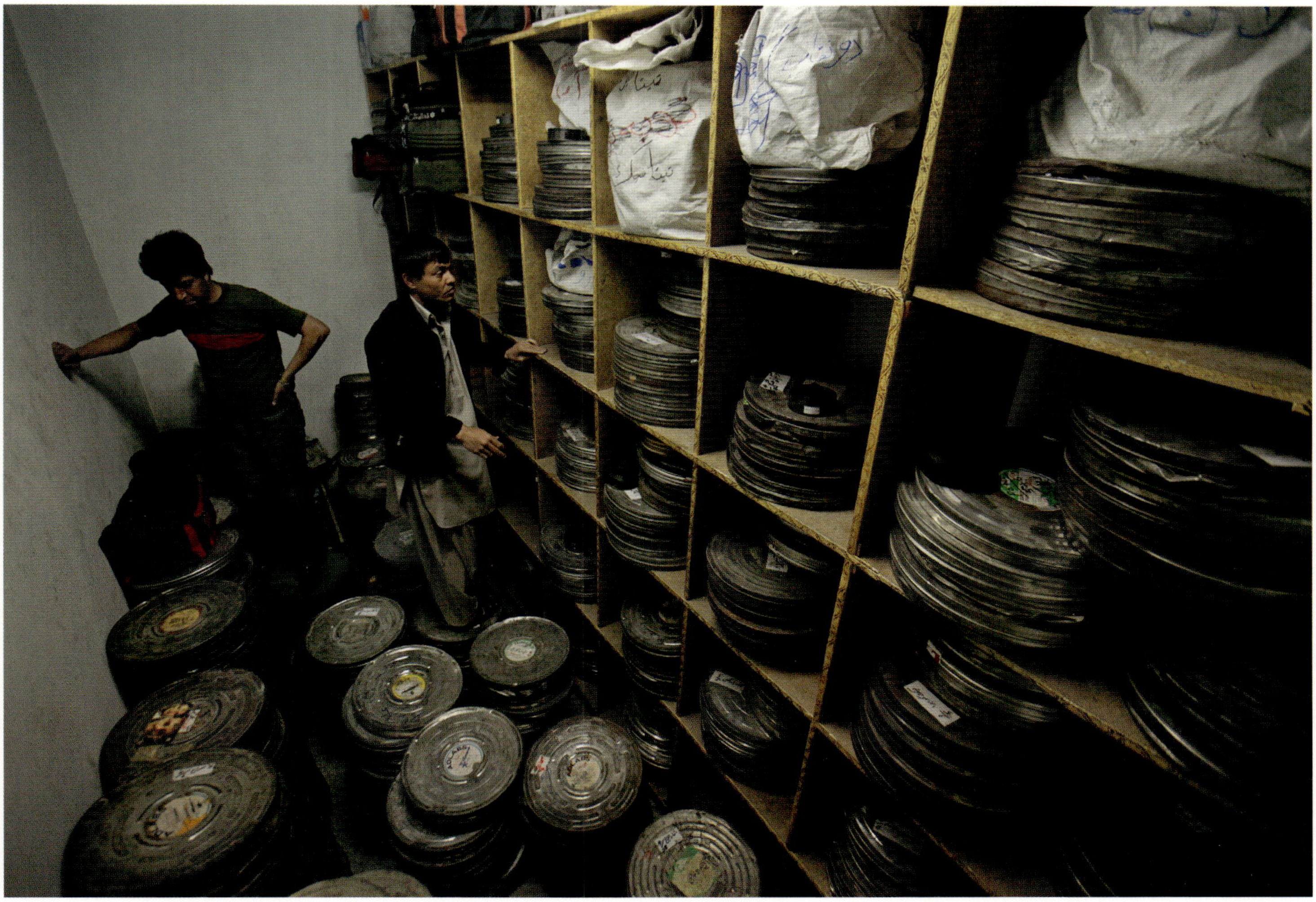

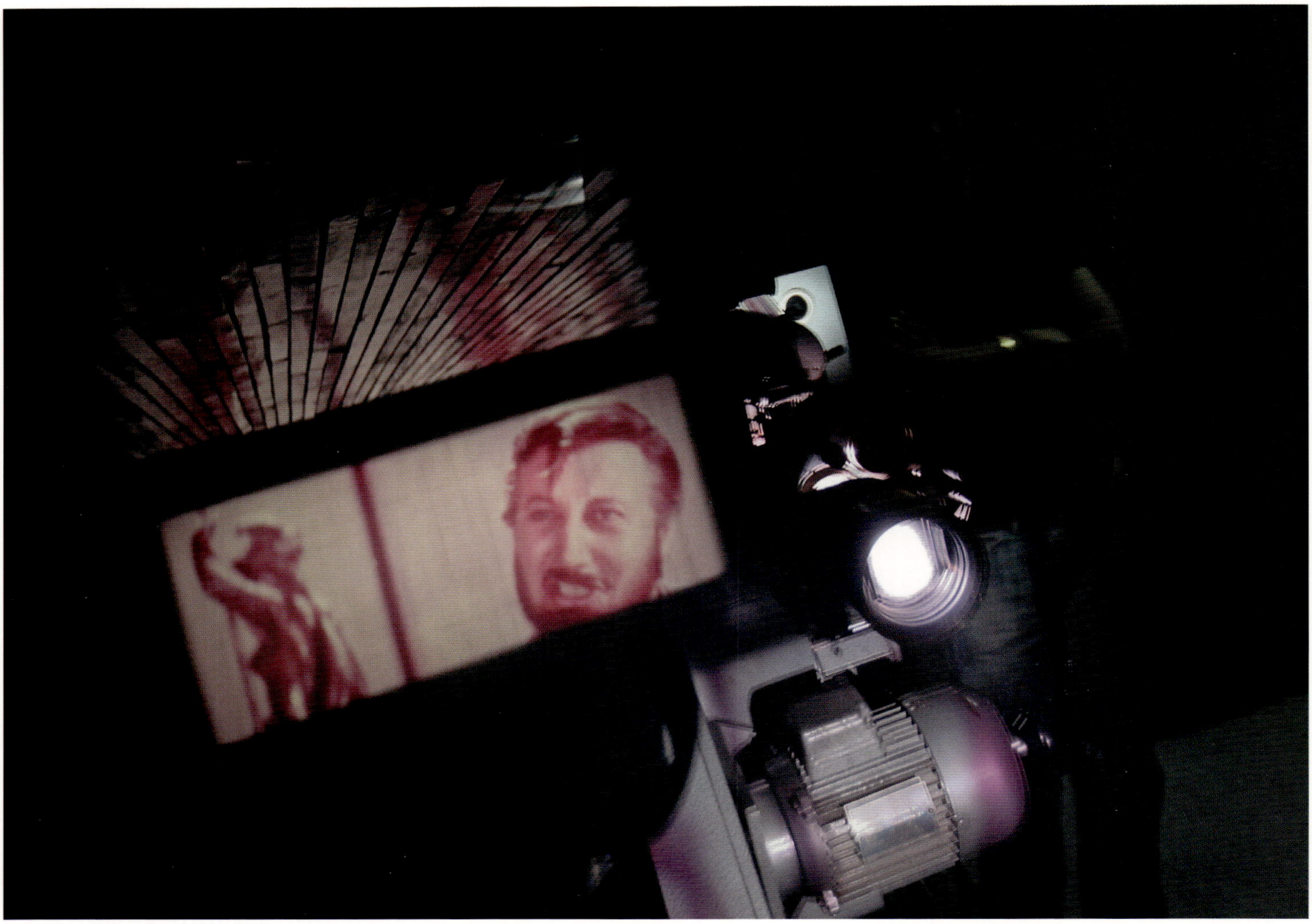

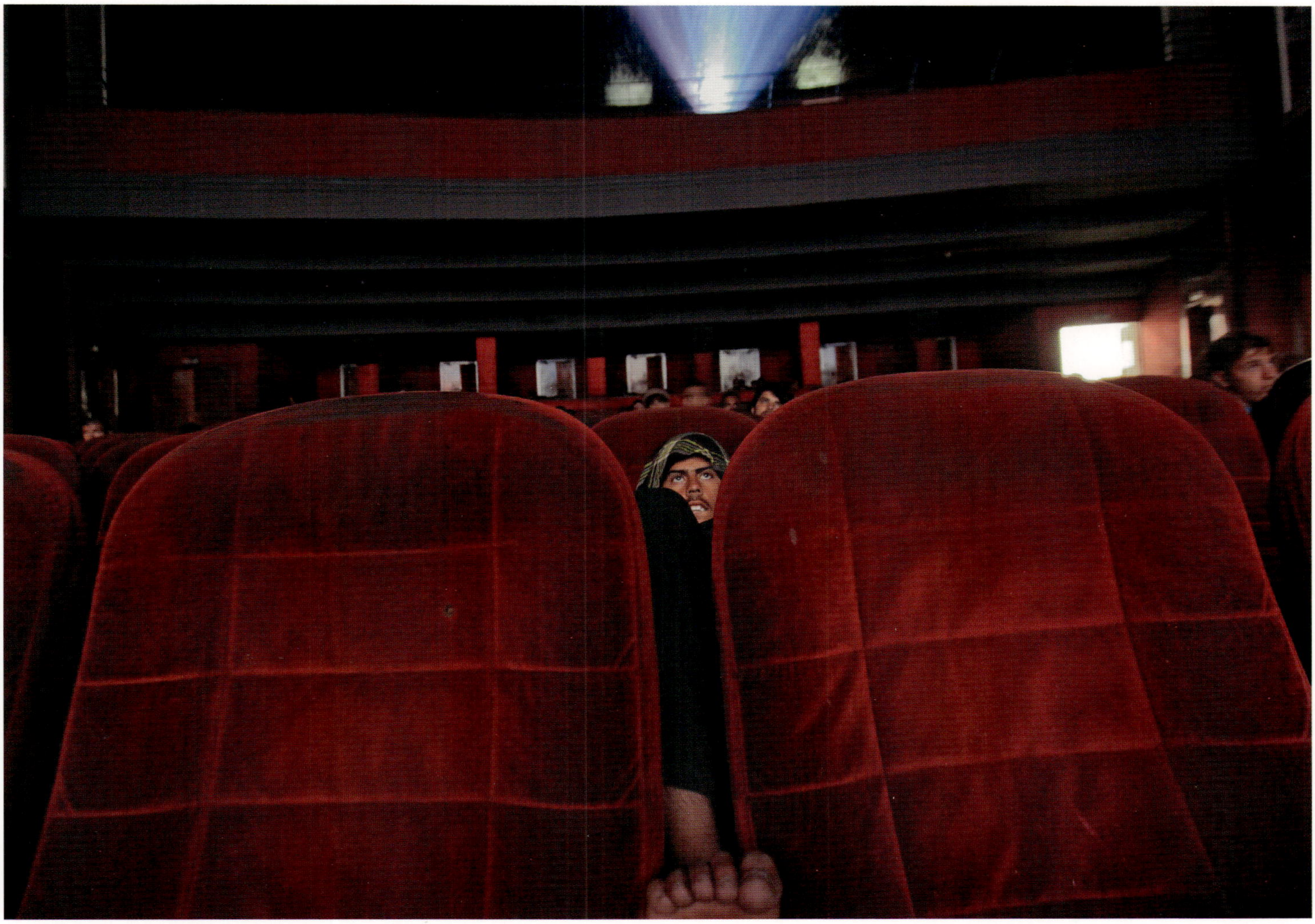

© All images courtesy of Thomson Reuters.

CHRISTIAN ÅSLUND SWEDEN

1ST PLACE
CAMPAIGN

Jim Rickey. Advertising campaign for the sneaker brand Jim Rickey. Project: Honkey Kong - a 2D platform game tribute. Shot on location in Hong Kong. Images were shot from skyscrapers toward the ground. A telephoto lens was used to make the image as flat as possible, so that they looked like a platform game.

Client: Jim Rickey / *Creative Director and Photographer:* Christian Åslund / *Production Manager:* Jan Andreen / *Unit Manager:* Loa Bie.

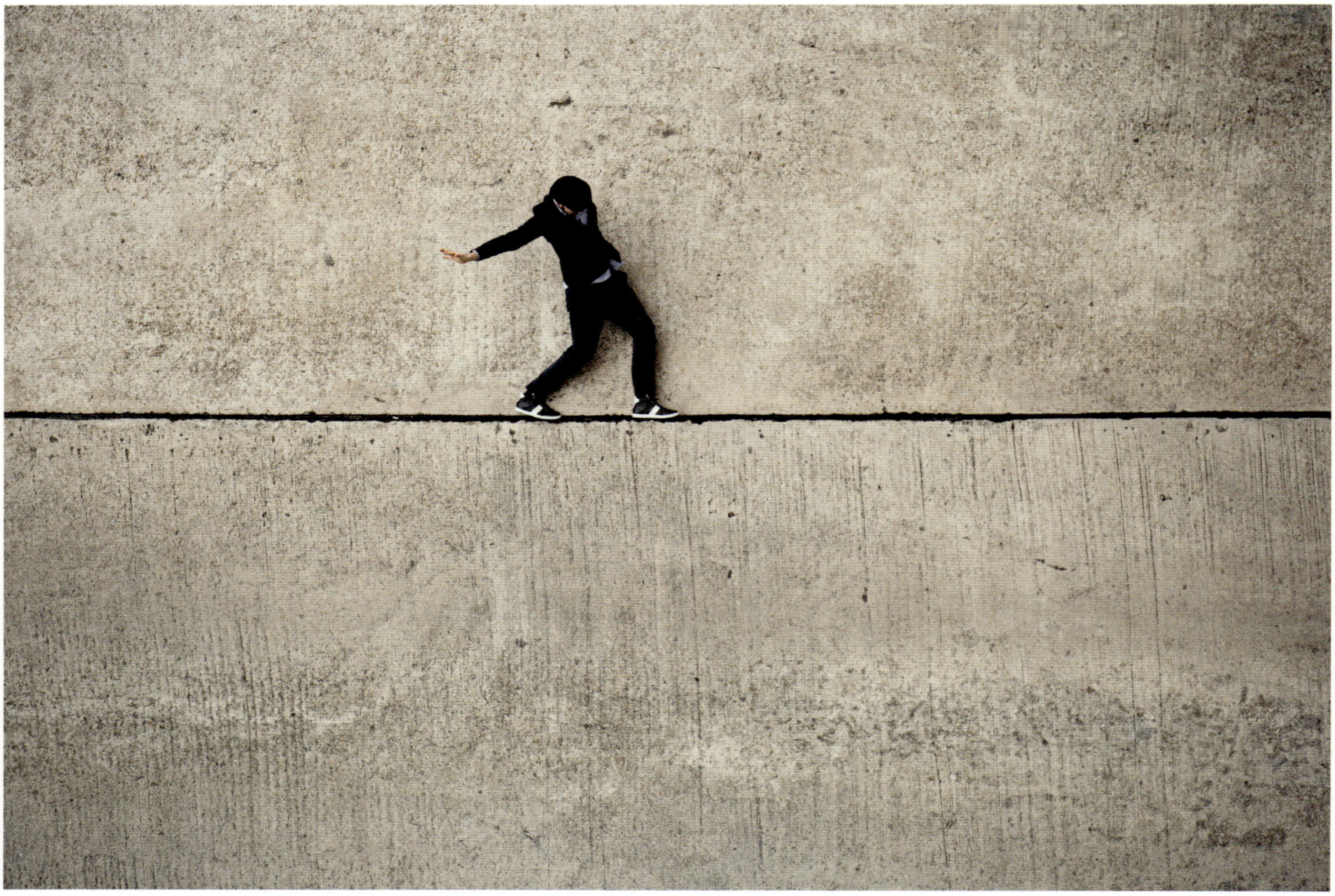

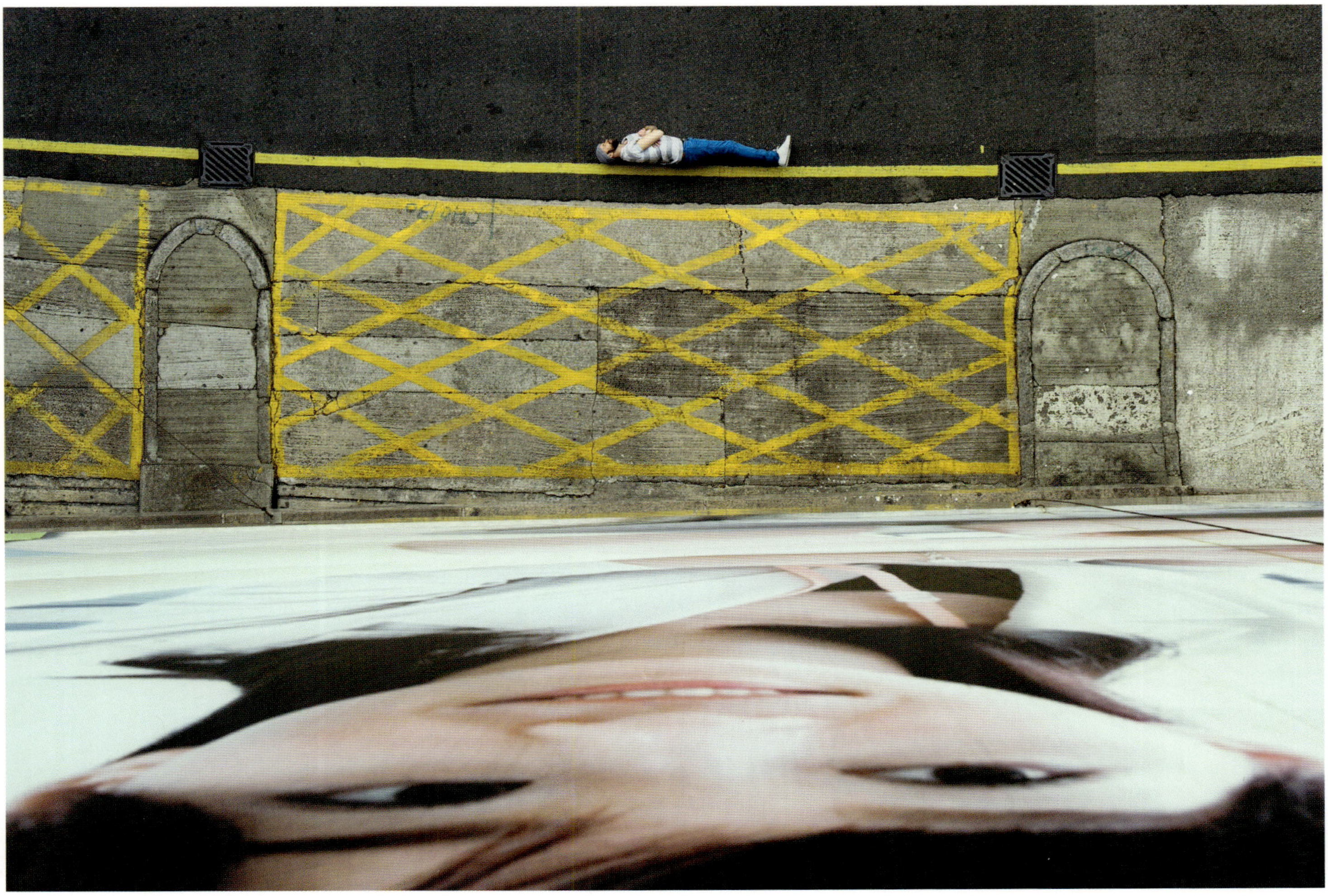

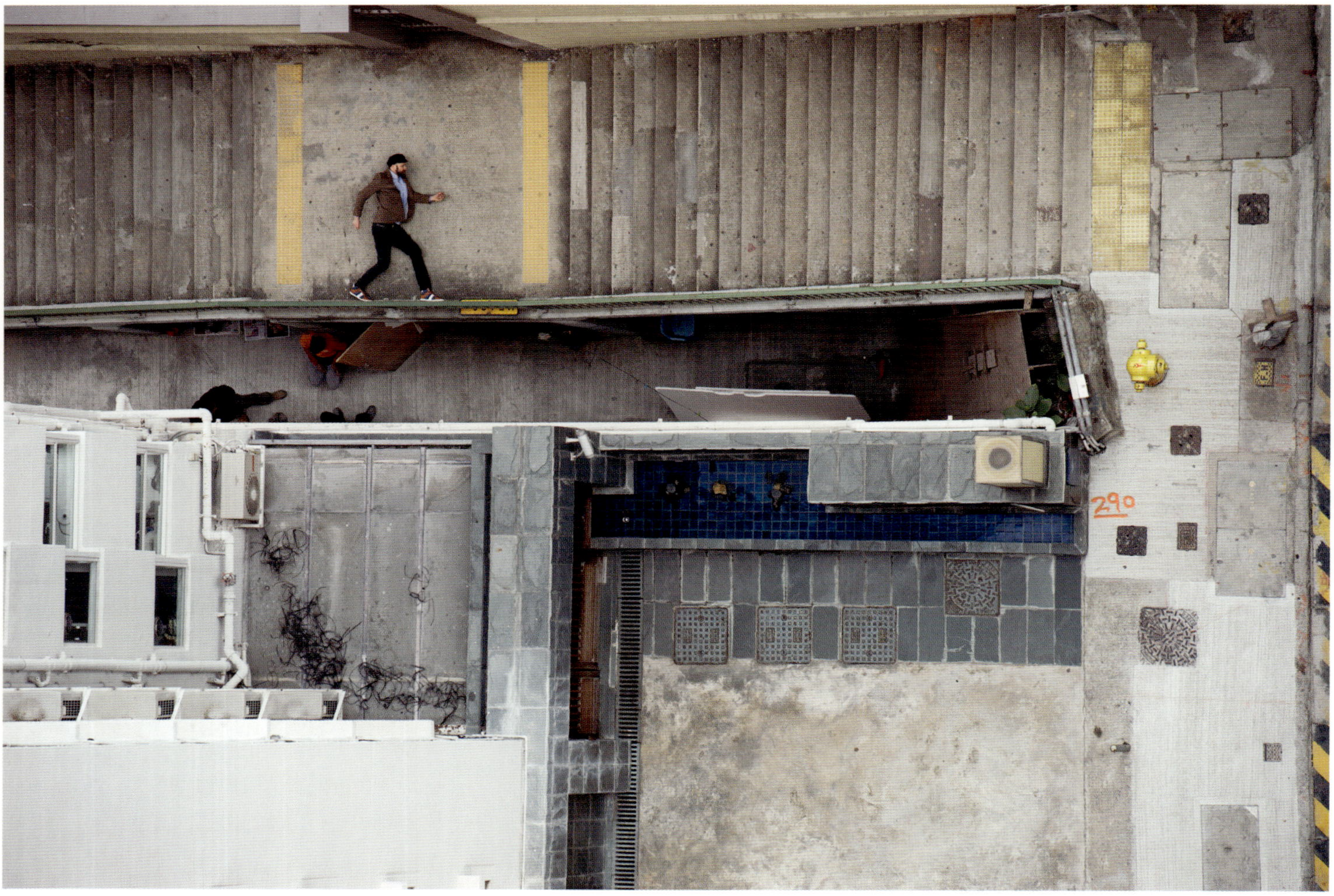
290

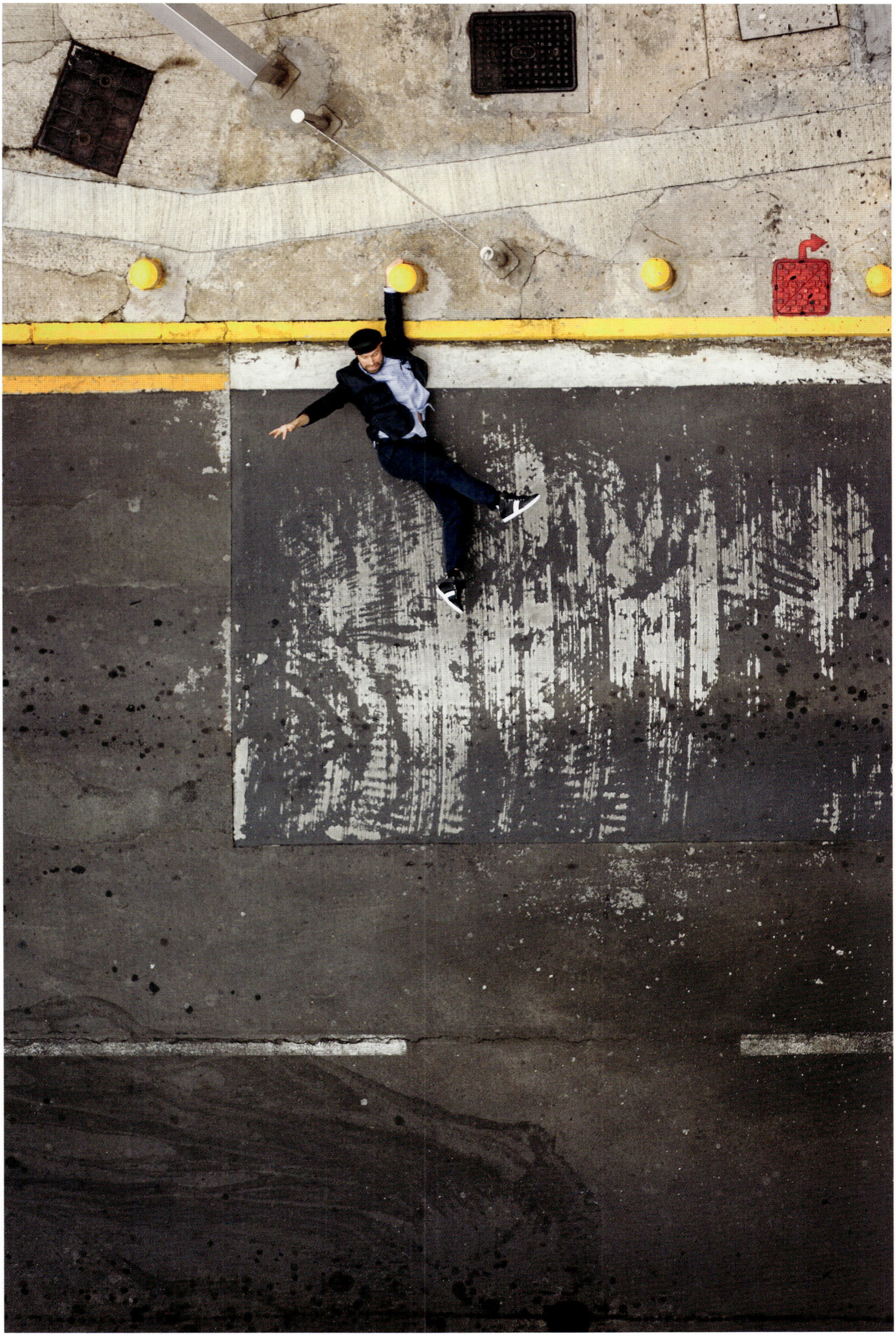

SCOUT TUFANKJIAN USA

2ND PLACE
CAMPAIGN

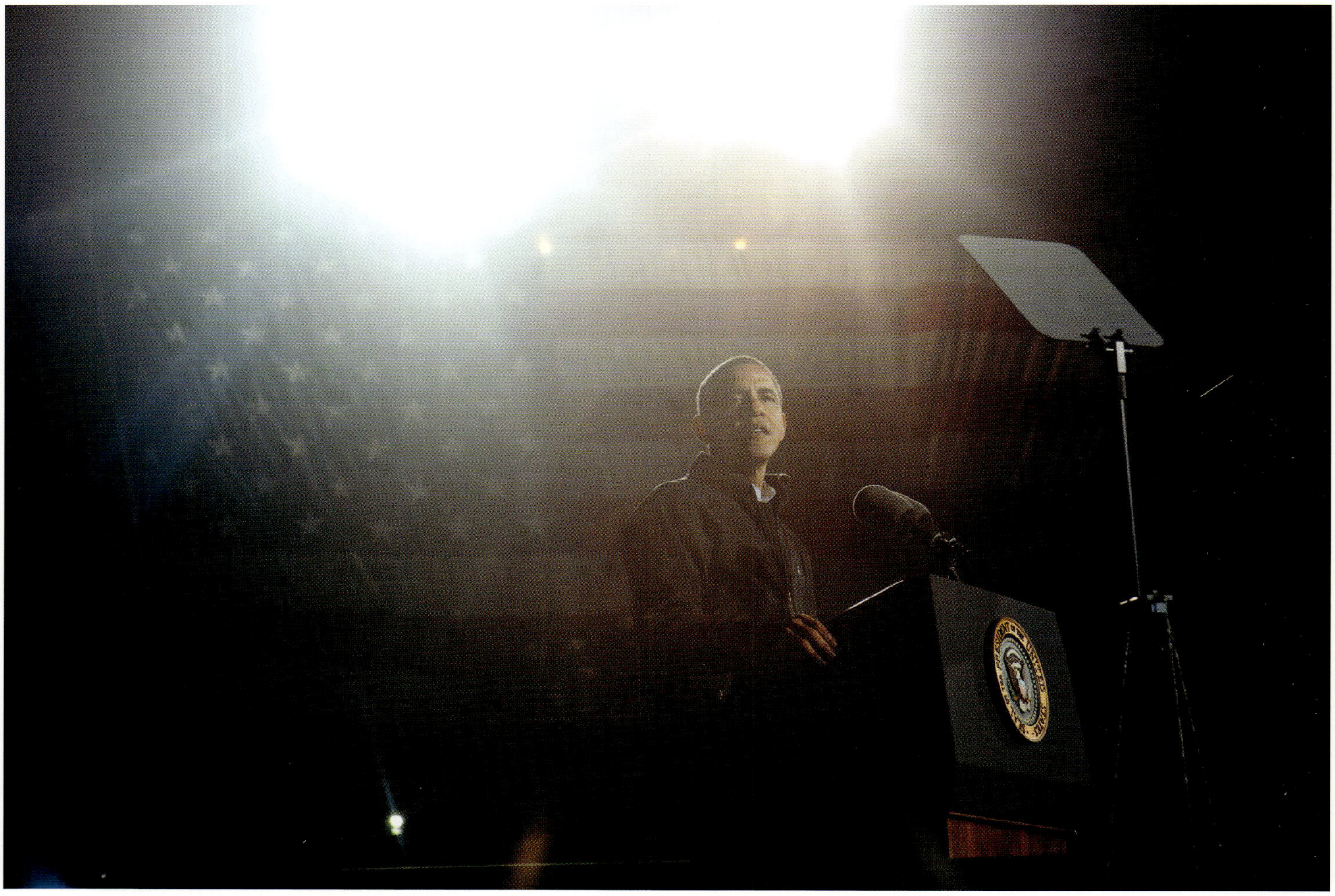

Four More Years: The 2012 Barack Obama Campaign. A selection of images taken during my tenure as a campaign photographer for President Barack Obama's 2012 re-election campaign. The images were taken throughout the last four months of Barack Obama's presidential campaign and were used by the campaign in television advertising, the web, social media, and print literature.

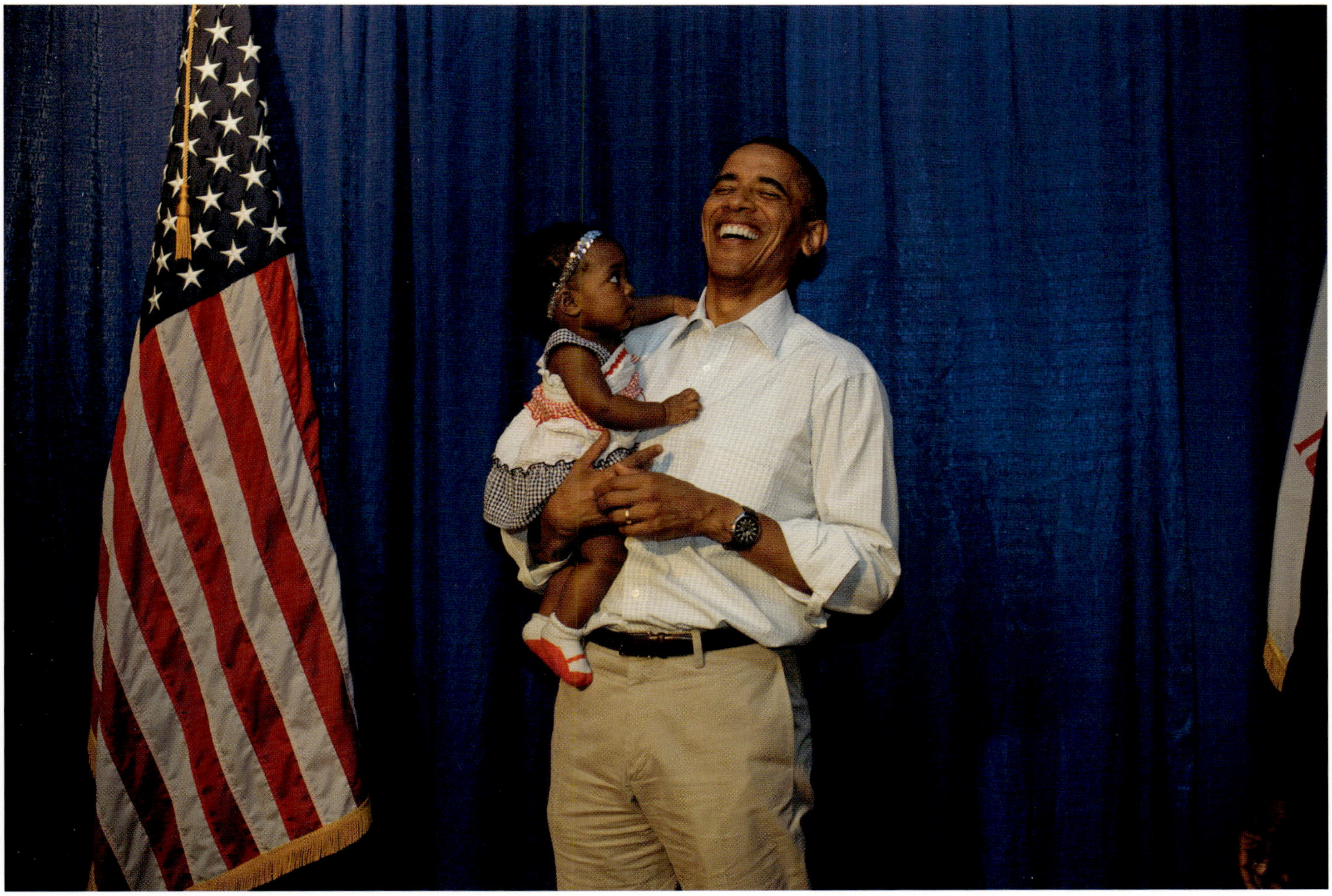

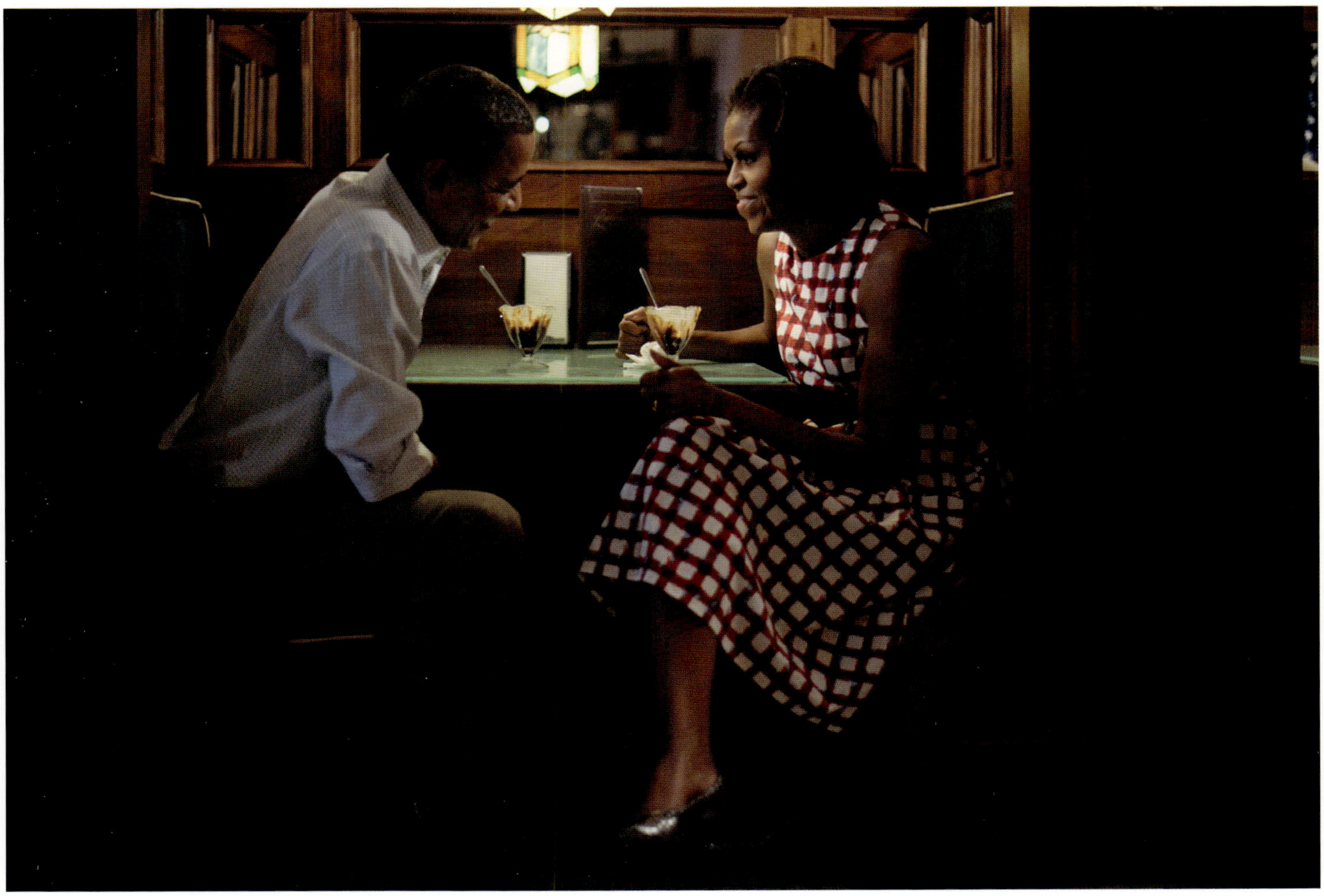

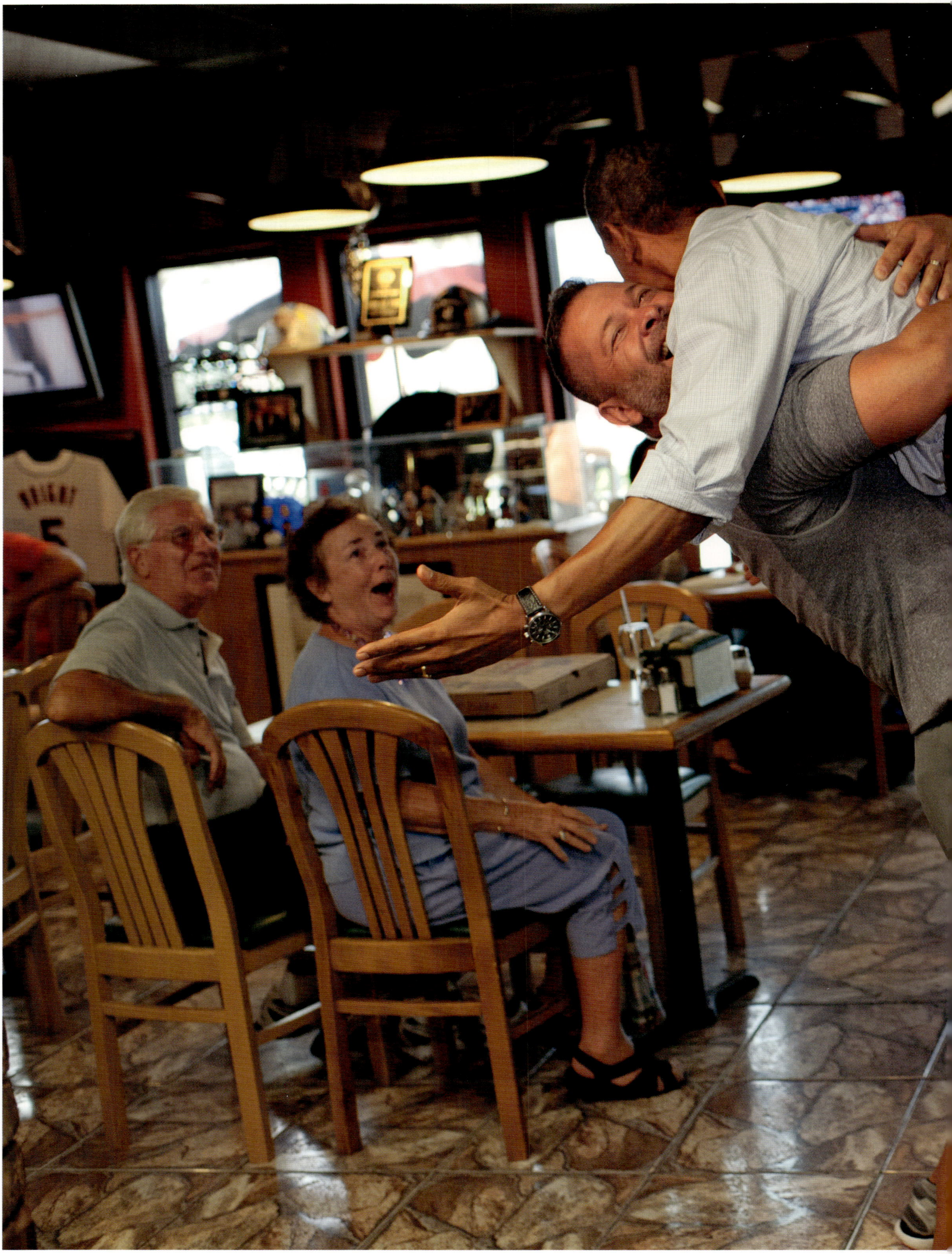

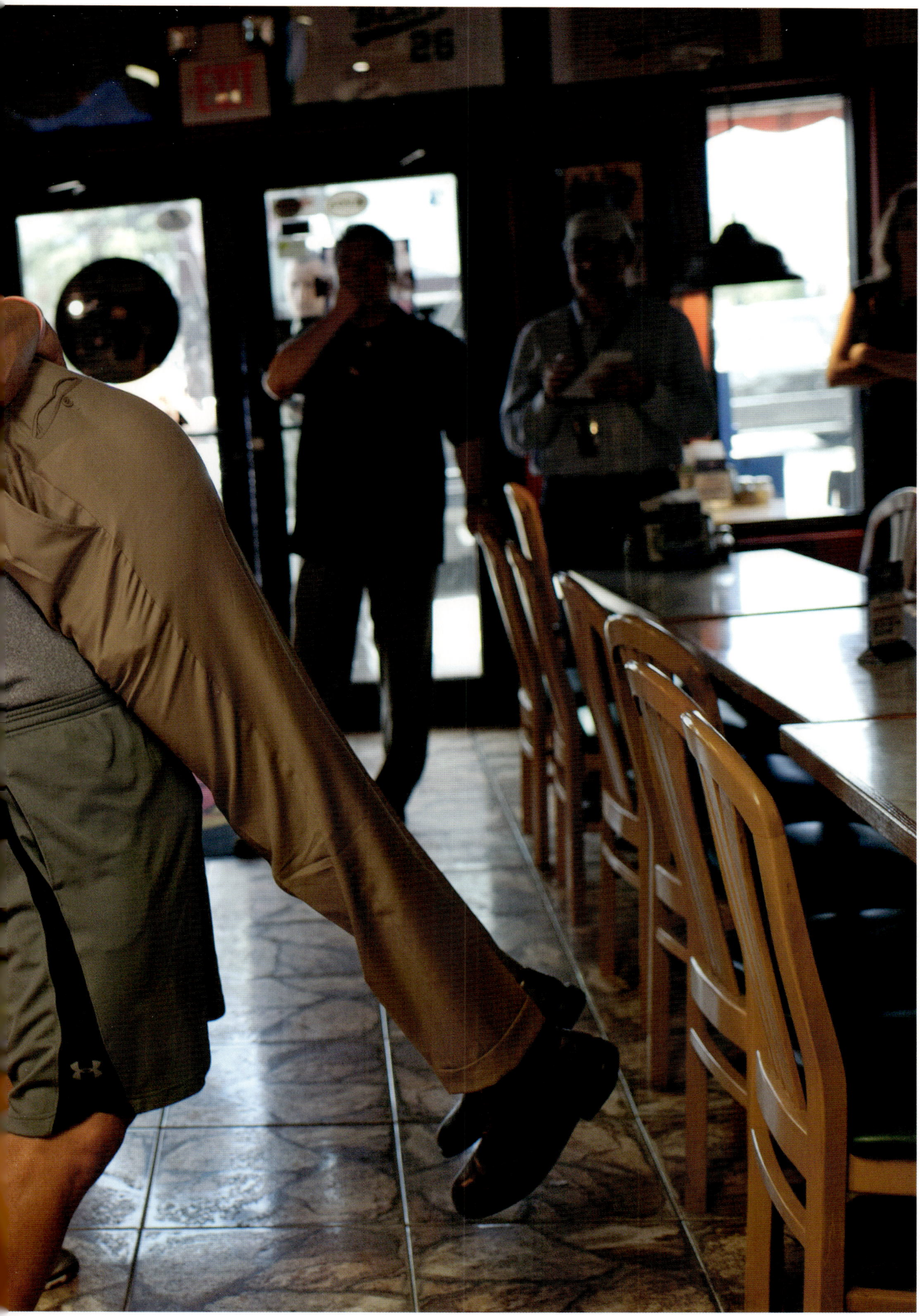
26

SPENCER MURPHY UNITED KINGDOM

3RD PLACE
CAMPAIGN

Surfer's Against Sewage - What If The Next Wave Never Comes. The Protect Our Waves (POW) campaign specifically promotes the protection of coastal regions, recognising the environmental, social, cultural and economic benefits of surfing resources. POW represents the surfing community to government, developers and other coastal stakeholders. The campaign aims to protect surf spots from unacceptable levels of environmental impact and degradation of surfing wave quality, and to advance recreational water users' right of access.

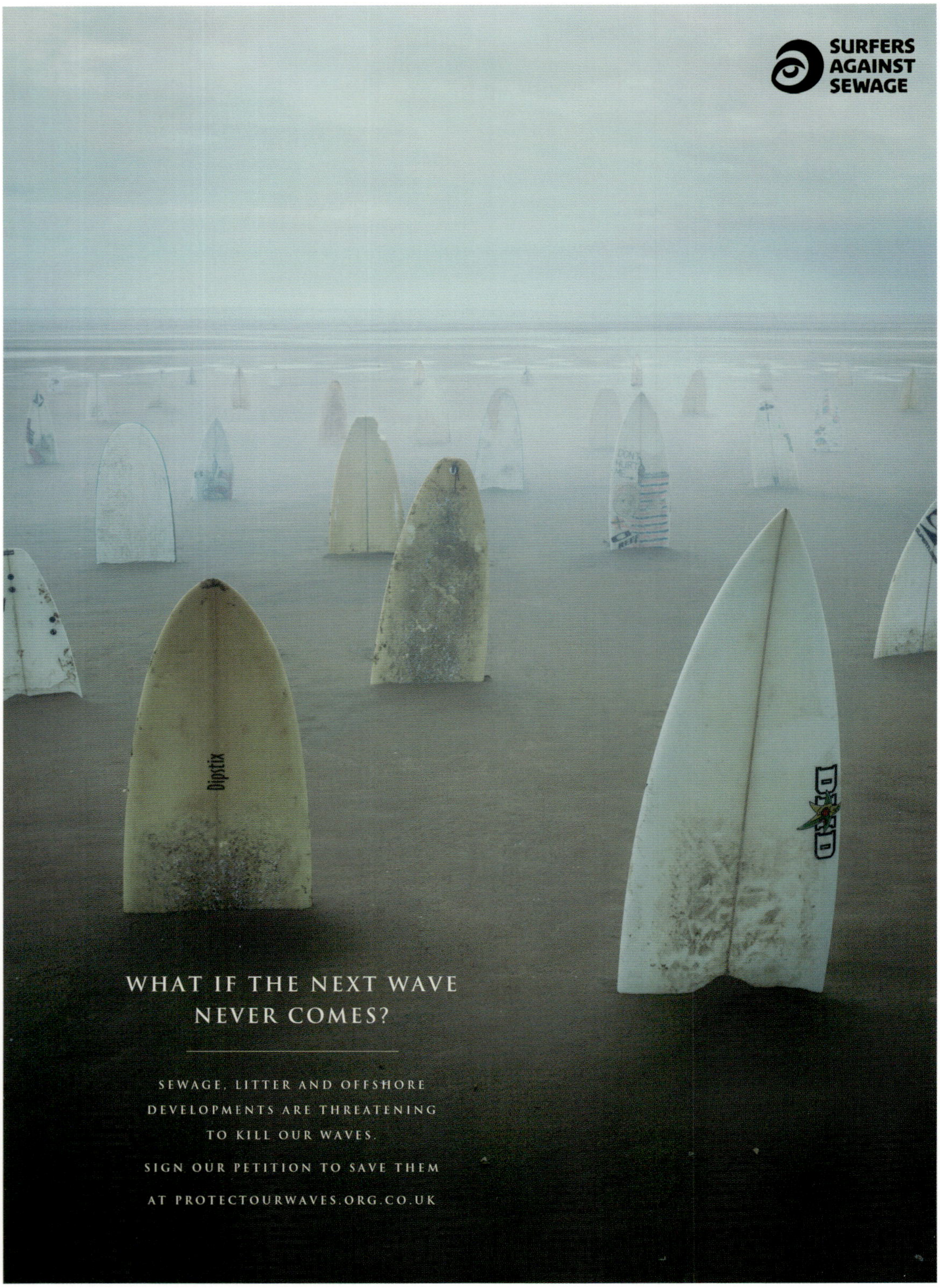

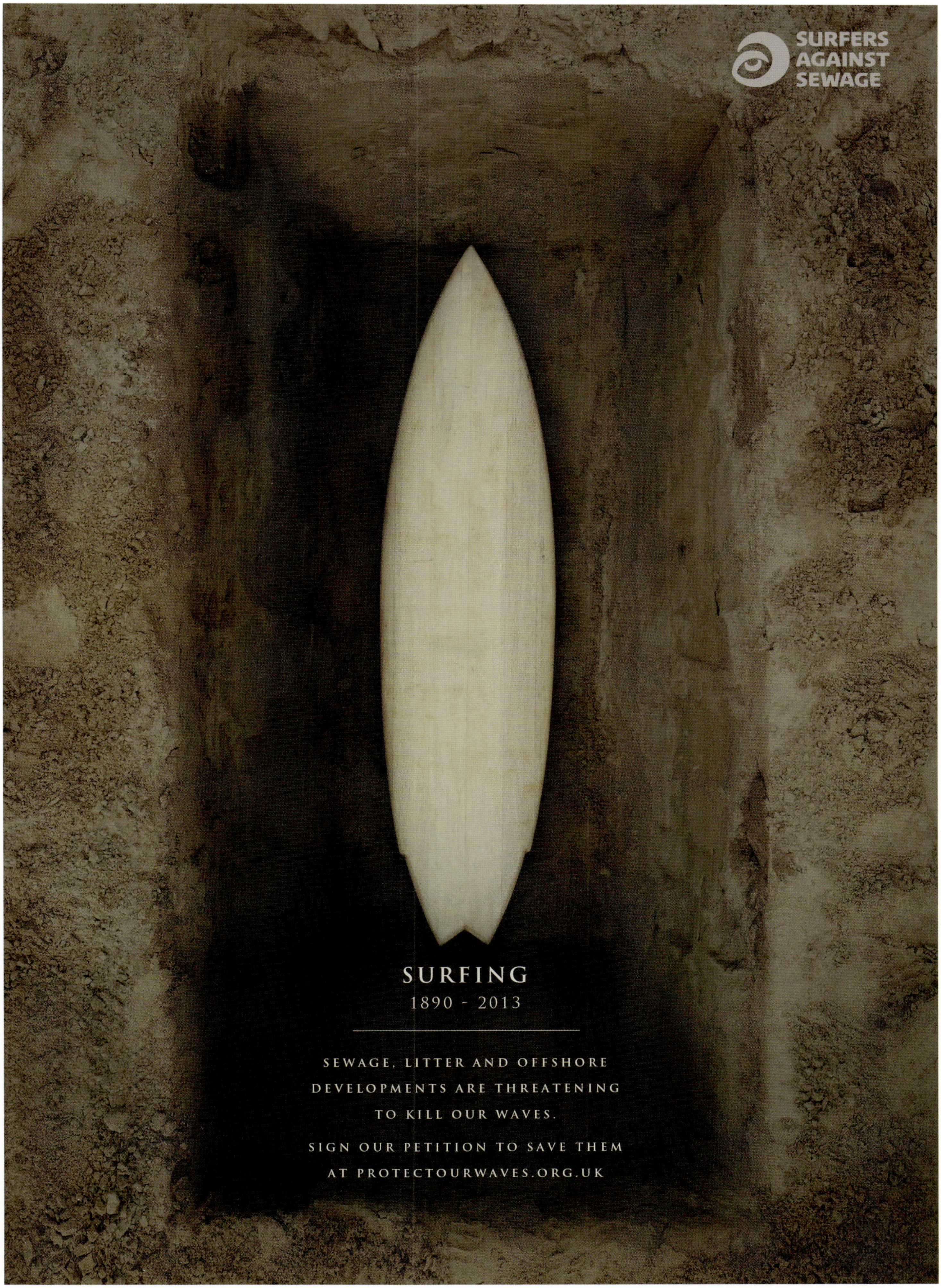
SURFERS
AGAINST
SEWAGE
SURFING
1890 - 2013
SEWAGE, LITTER AND OFFSHORE
DEVELOPMENTS ARE THREATENING
TO KILL OUR WAVES.
SIGN OUR PETITION TO SAVE THEM
AT PROTECTOURWAVES.ORG.UK

ROMAN PYATKOVKA UKRAINE

1ST PLACE
CONCEPTUAL

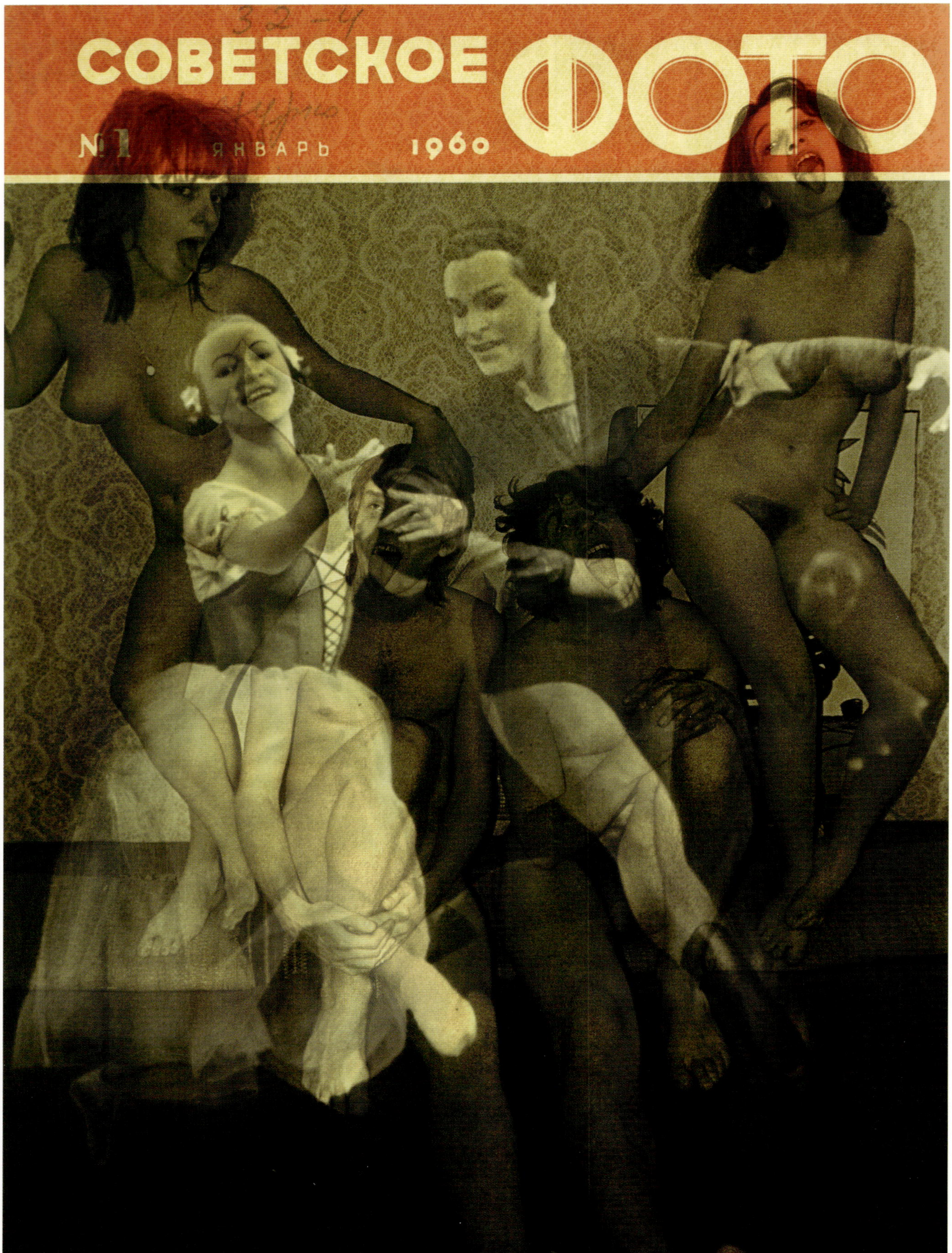

Soviet photo. 'Soviet photo' is a whole epoch, which has disappeared irrevocably. On the one hand it is an odious magazine, *Soviet Photo*, filled with communist propaganda. On the other, these were pictures of underground photographers of the time, pictures for which they risked imprisonment.

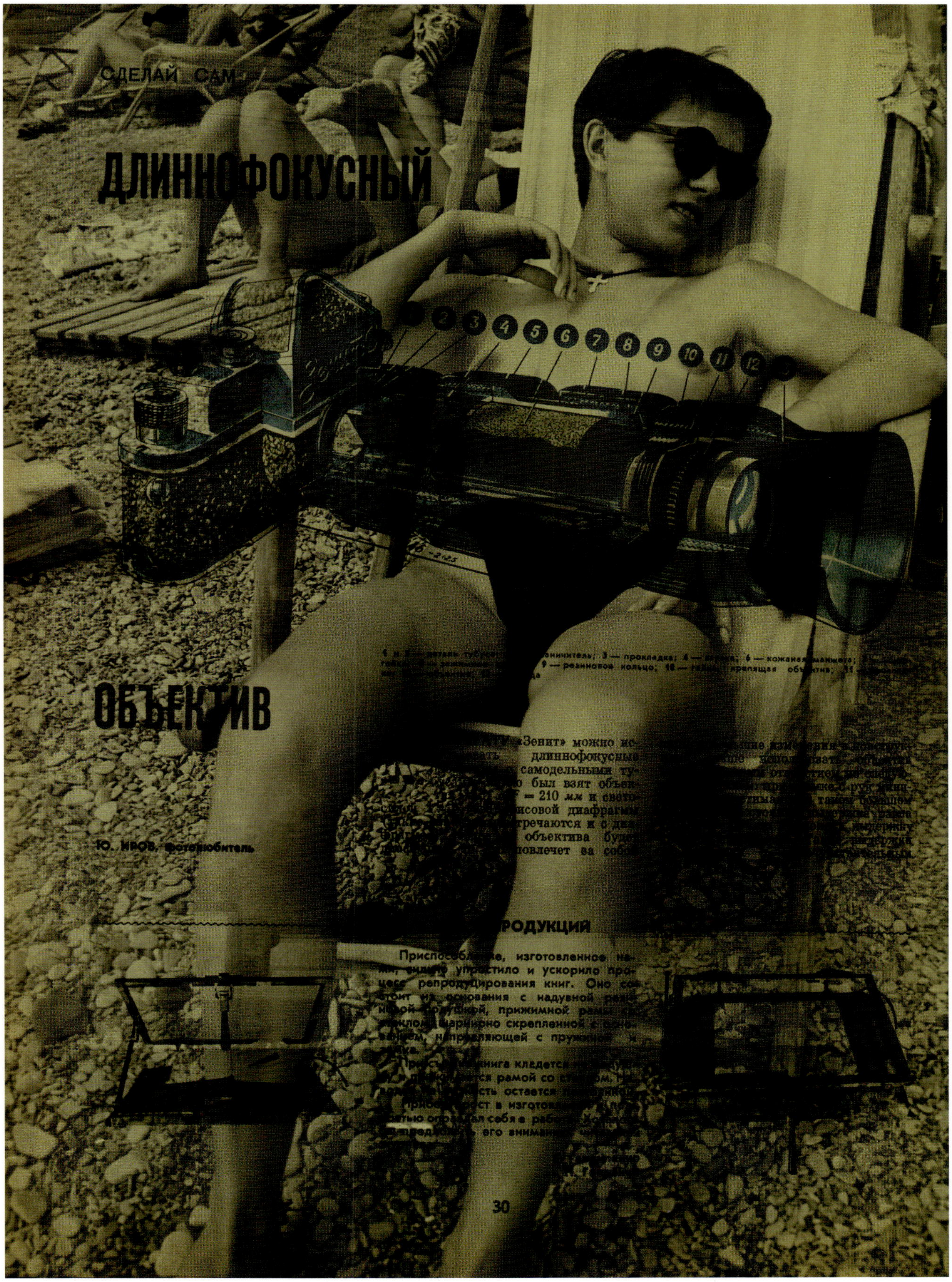

FLORIAN RUIZ FRANCE

2ND PLACE
CONCEPTUAL

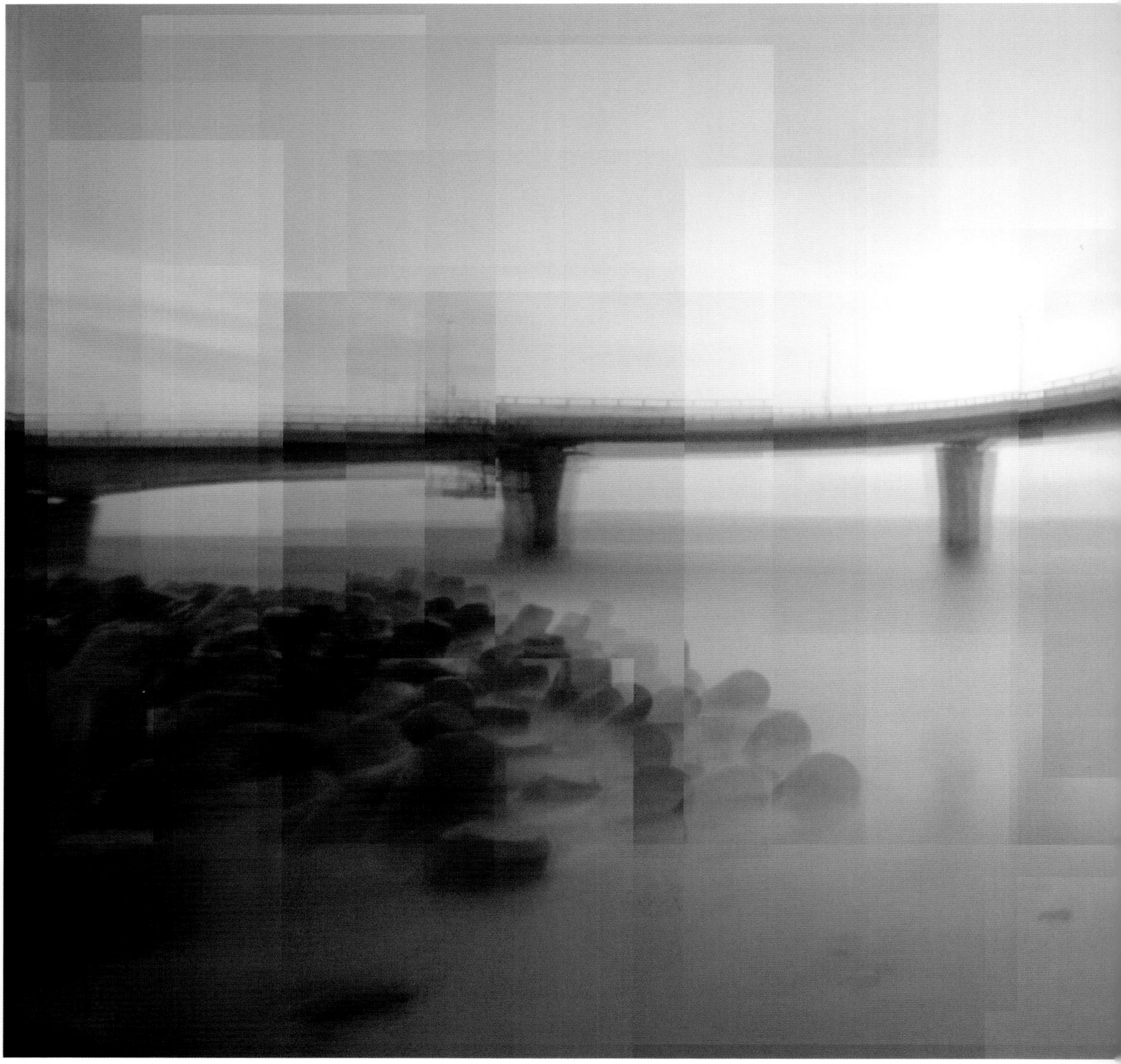

Fukushima, Invisible Pain. Within the natural environment and in the areas surrounding cities across Fukushima prefecture, I have captured the invisible pain of radiation. With an ear to the rhythm of the seasons as in traditional Japanese engravings, and inspired by their refined, uncluttered style, I hoped to capture the fleeting moments, the movements of climatic phenomena, and the ever-shifting perceptions of nature, where radiation accumulates the most. Each photo is an accumulation of visual fragments taken in the same location but from different angles, always accompanied by the radiation level to which my film was exposed.

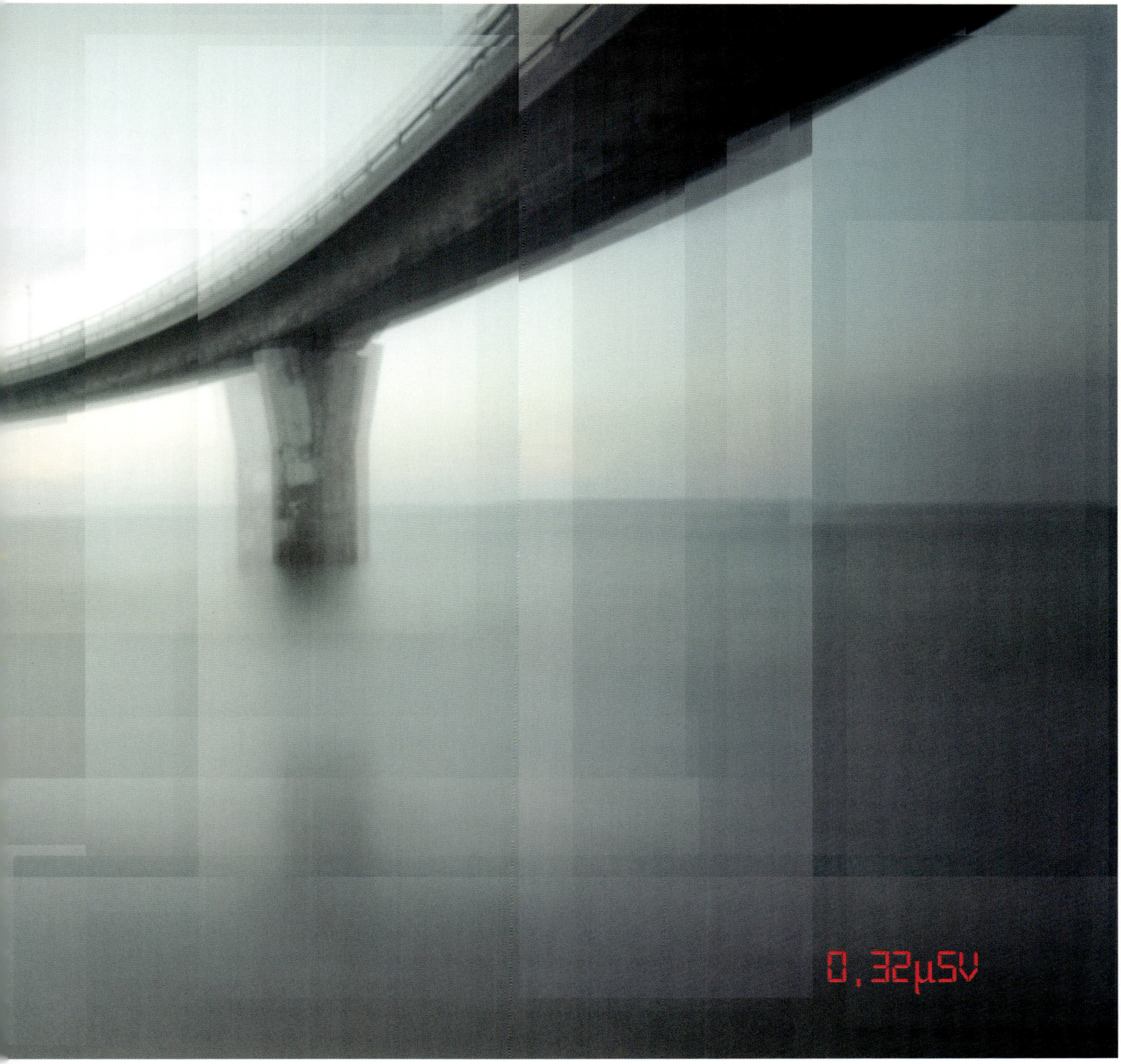
0,32μSv

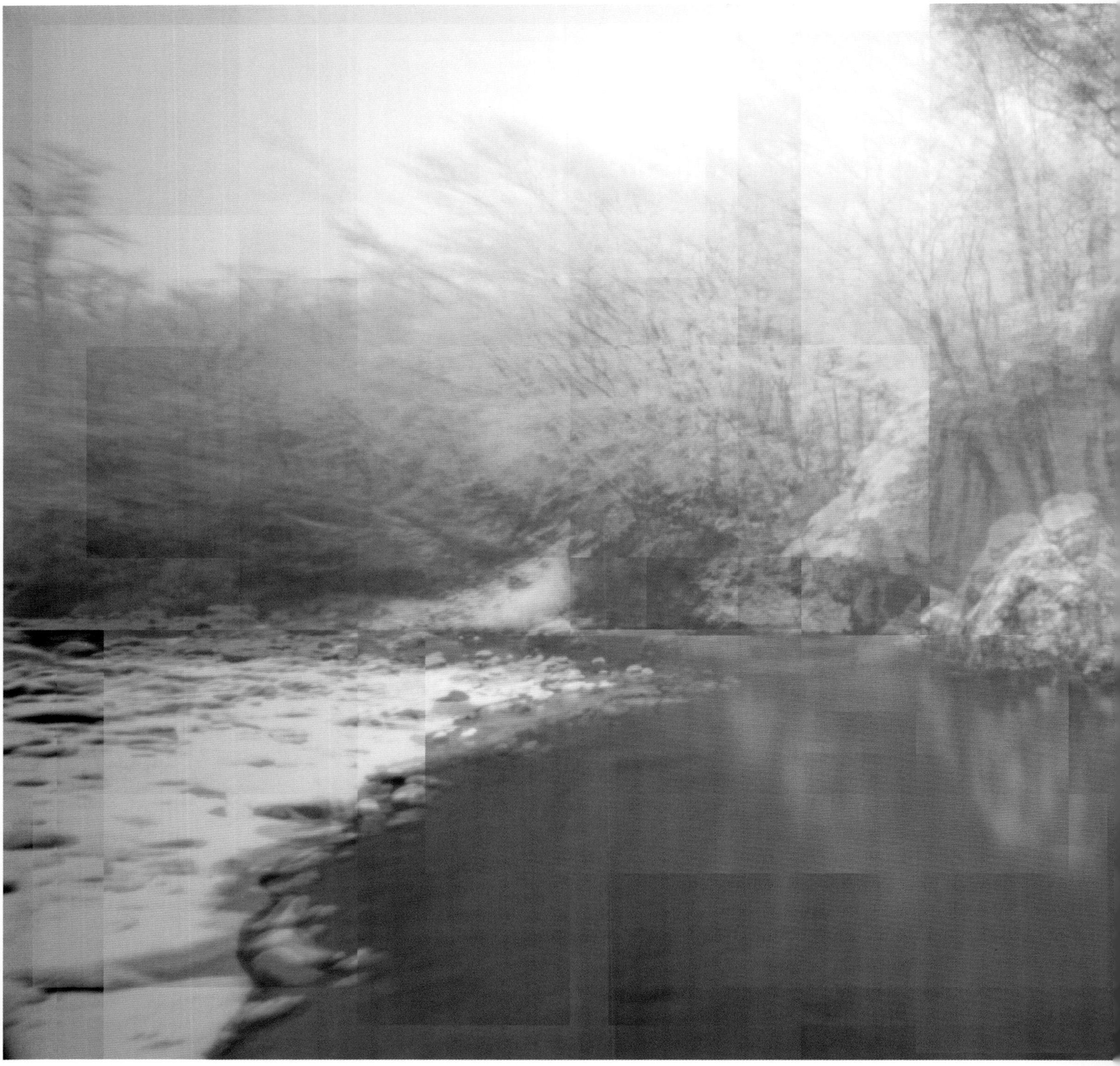

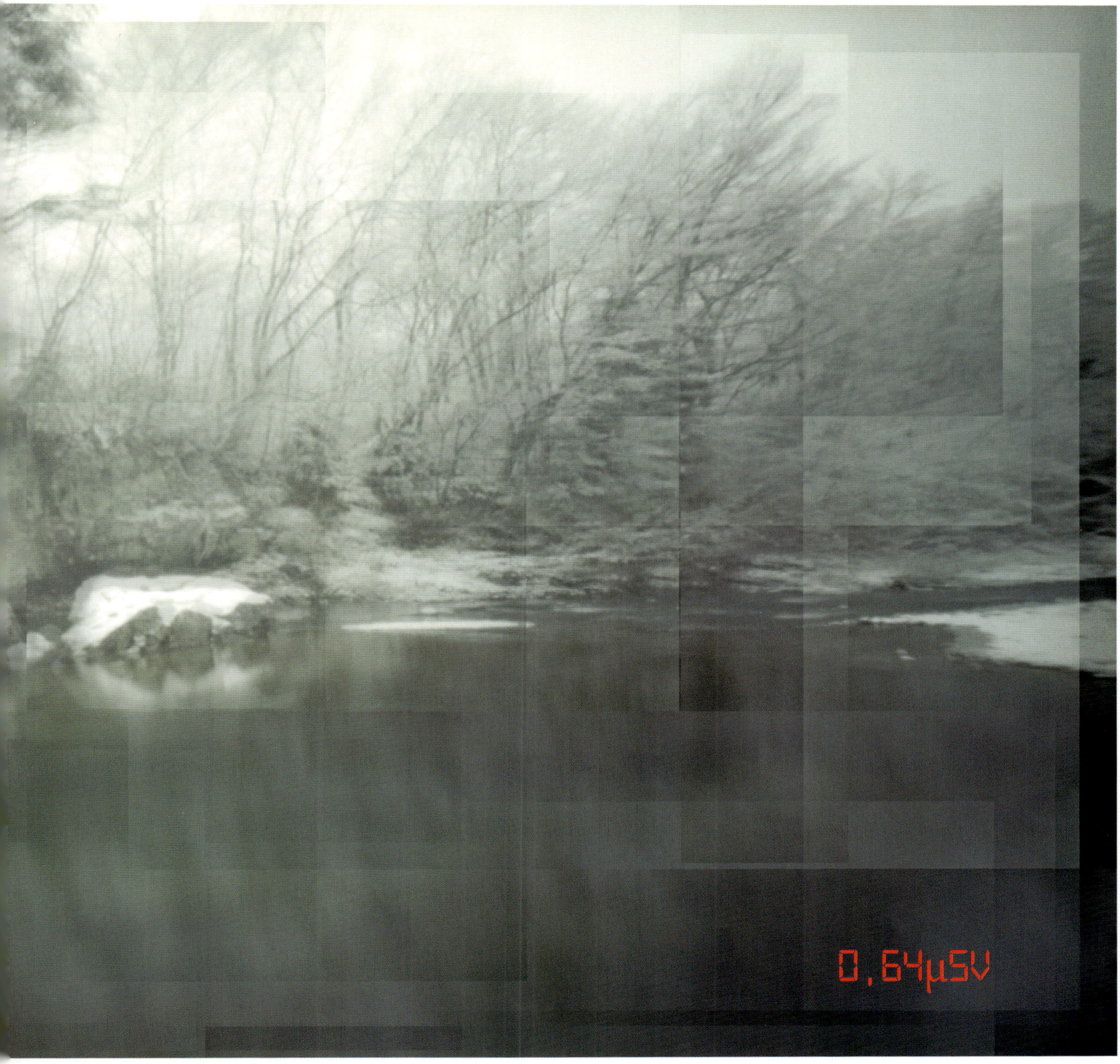
0,64µSV

EDURNE AGUINAGA SPAIN

3RD PLACE
CONCEPTUAL

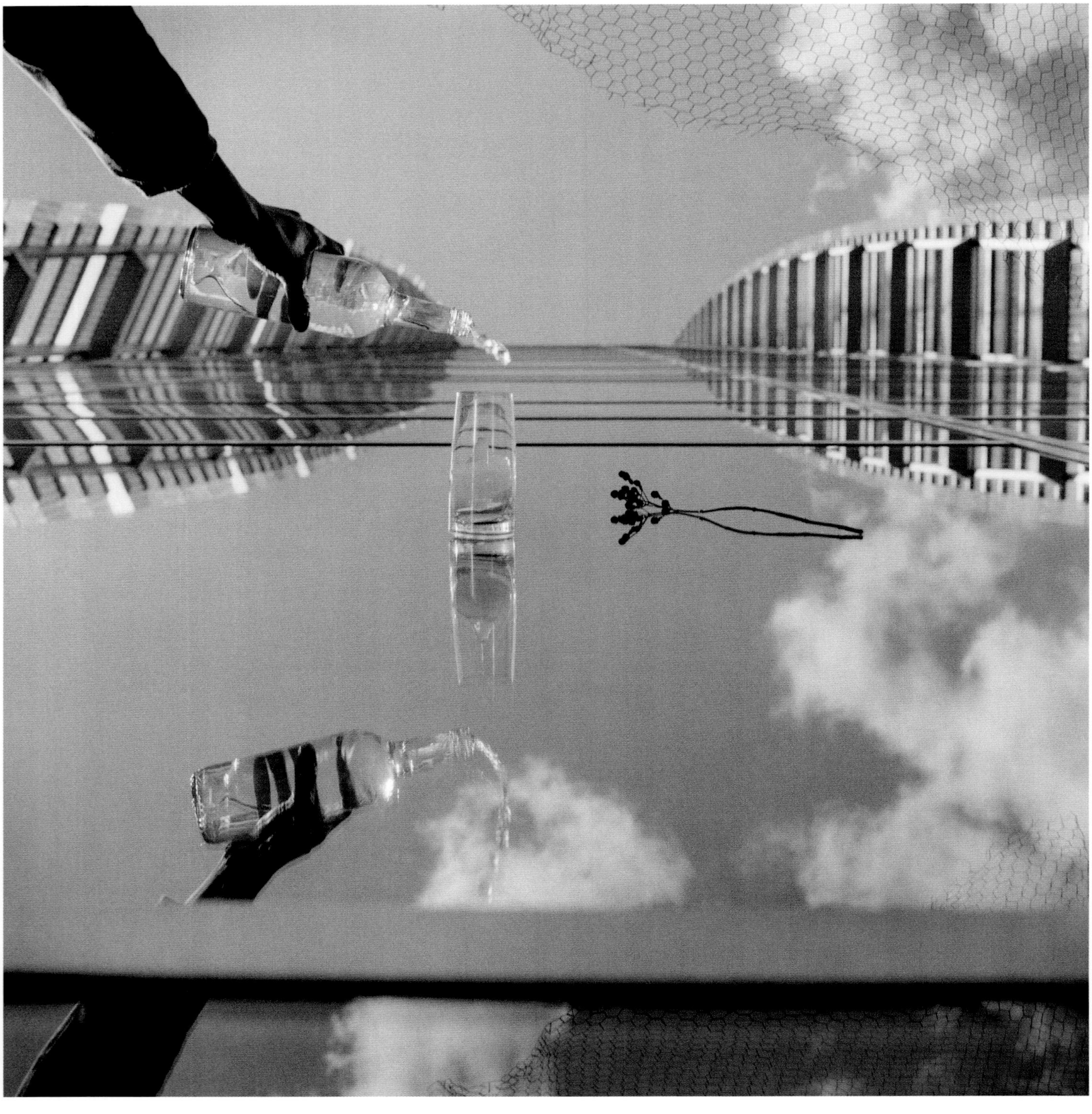

Lie Down. Lie Down is a series of surrealist pictures that create the feeling of being upright on a vertical surface. The objects on each image interact with the viewer's subjective associations and draw them into a distorted reality by creating installations influenced by natural light and reflections. The production was a technically and conceptually complex project that resulted from numerous analogue shots and the composing of different arrangements thus achieving a highly manipulated reality. It did not involve any combination printing or multiple exposure.

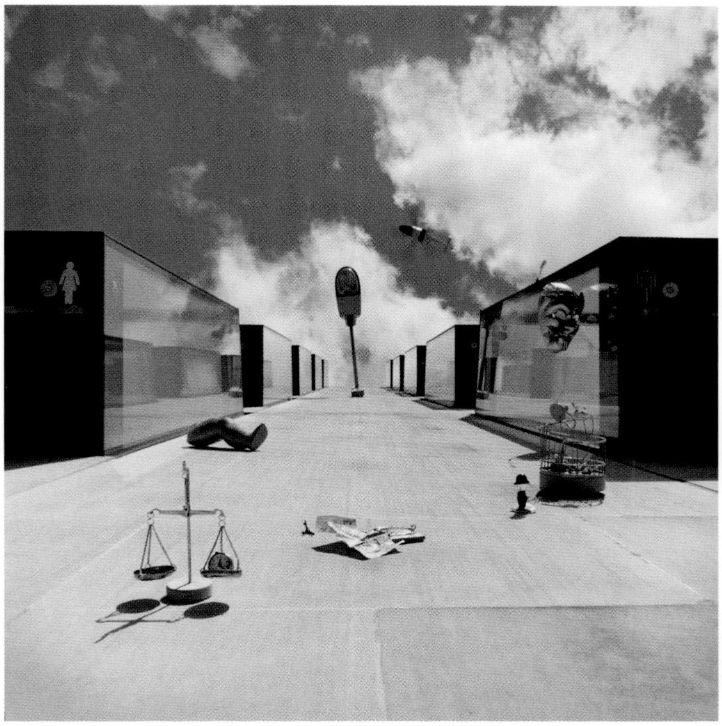

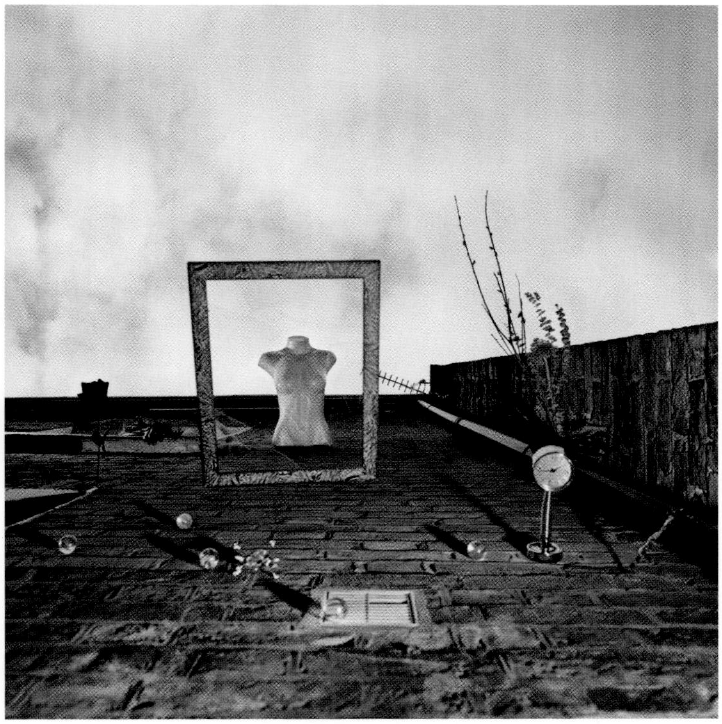

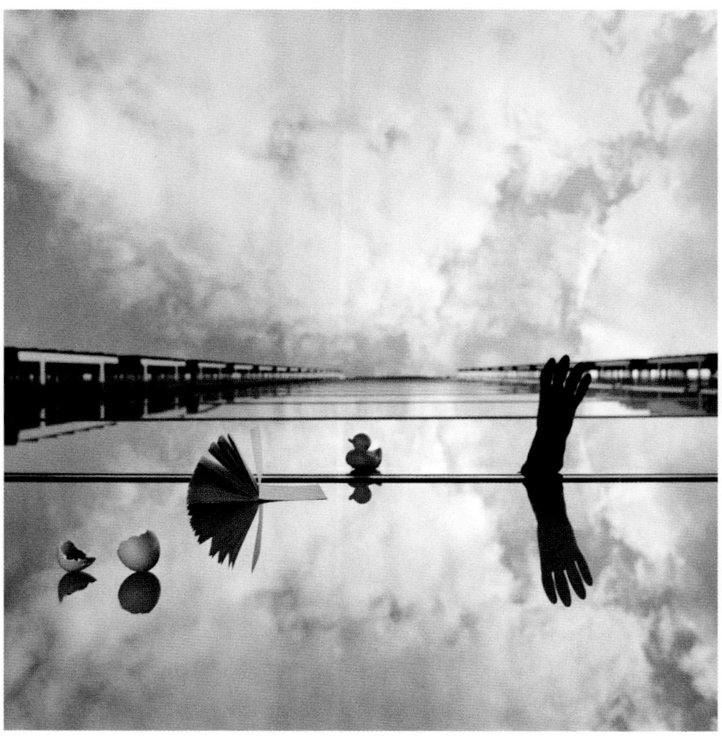

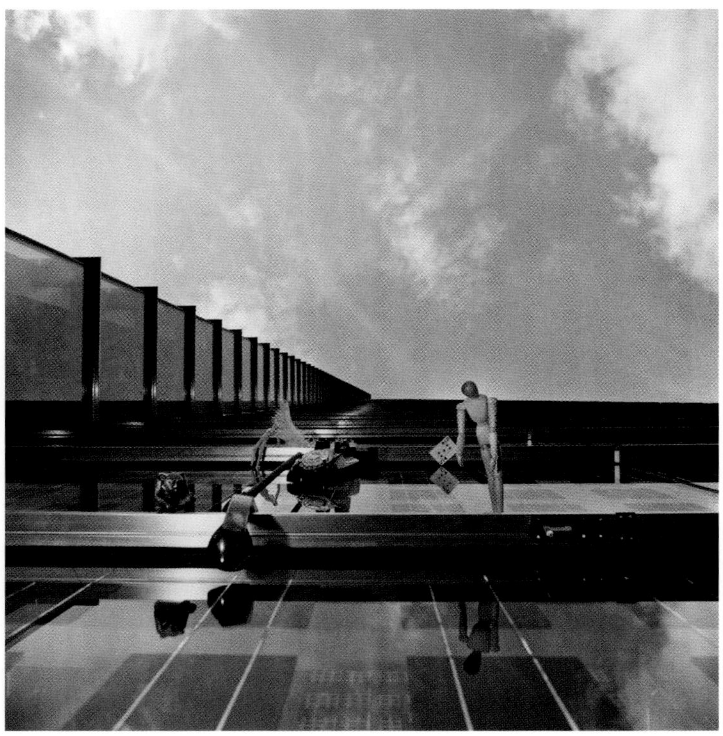

VALERIO BISPURI ITALY

1ST PLACE
CONTEMPORARY ISSUES

Encerrados. I spent 10 years travelling through South America's jails, a complex world in which violence and abuse are part of a convict's life. I saw how the convicts try to recreate a space similar to the one they had outside. They try to preserve their dignity. Some prisoners defiantly show their knives; whoever is unarmed becomes a kind of slave. The jails' rules are the same as those outside: authority comes with money and power. Some convicts considered me a distraction, others looked at me with envy, others again with contempt because they thought that I was there only to take pictures to sell of their confined lives.

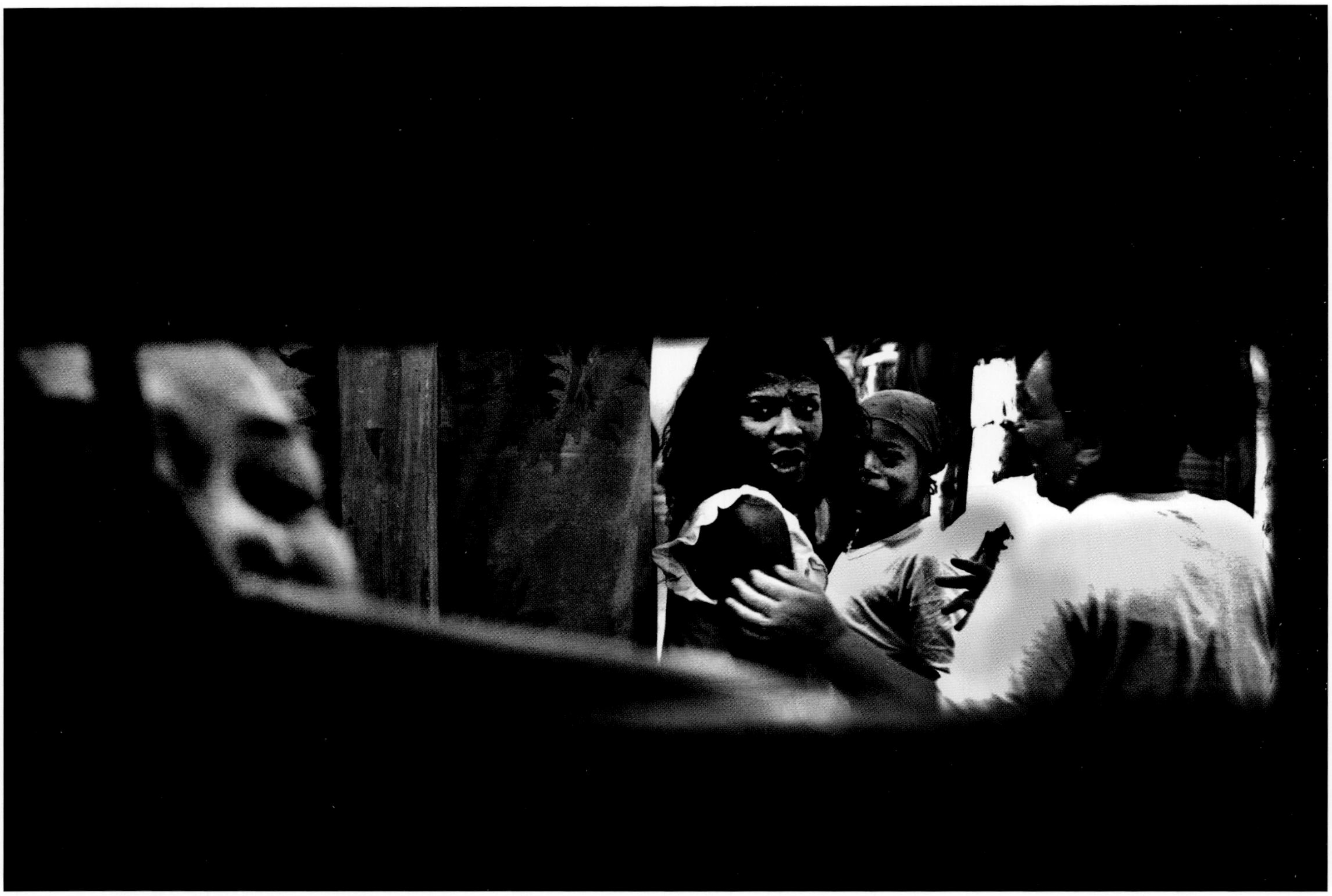

Above image: Women in a prison in Rio de Janeiro, Brazil.
Above right image: Prison for former Farc military soldiers, Bogota, Colombia.
Below right image: Over crowded conditions at Santiago de Chile prison; where 40 inmates should be housed, there are 150.

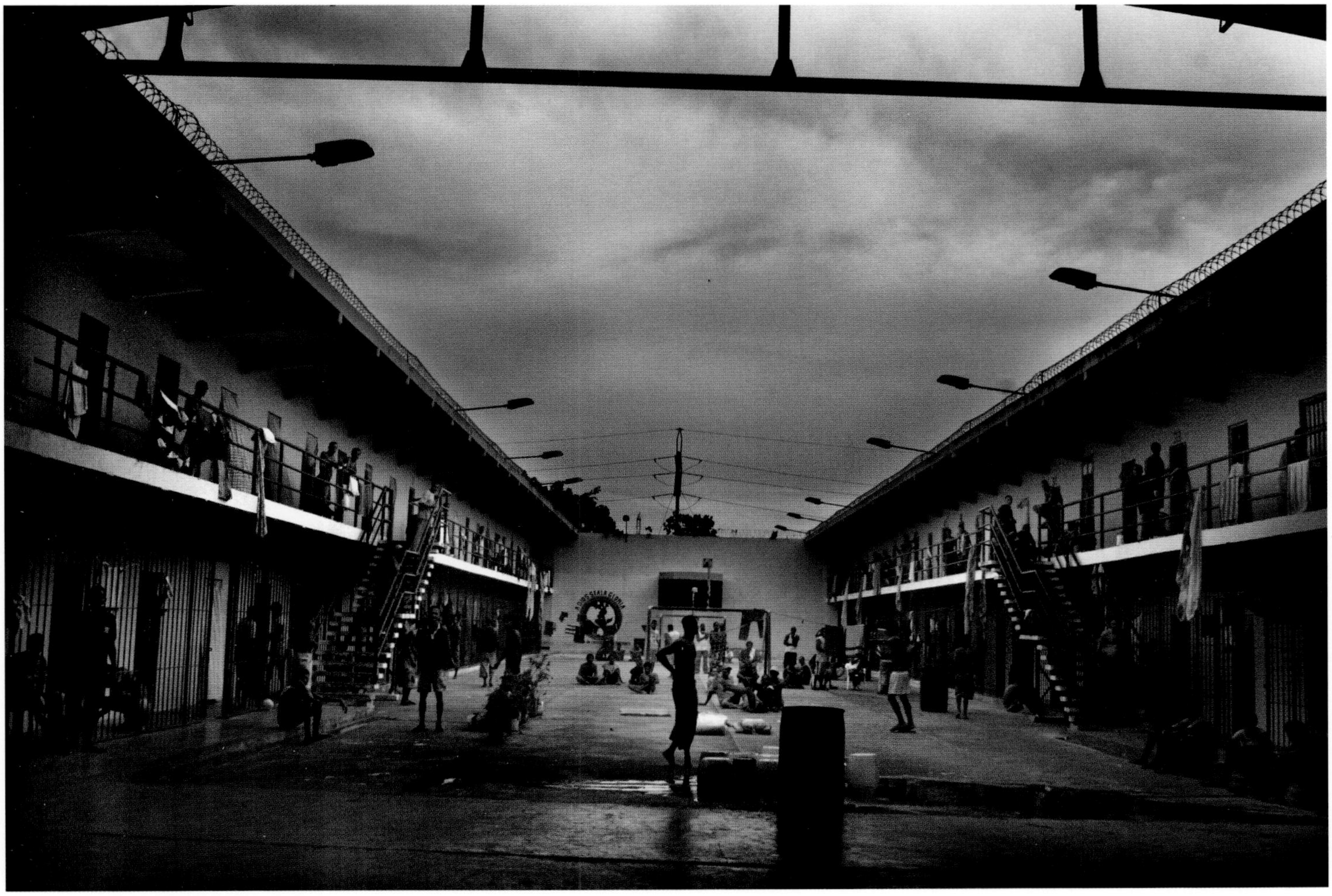

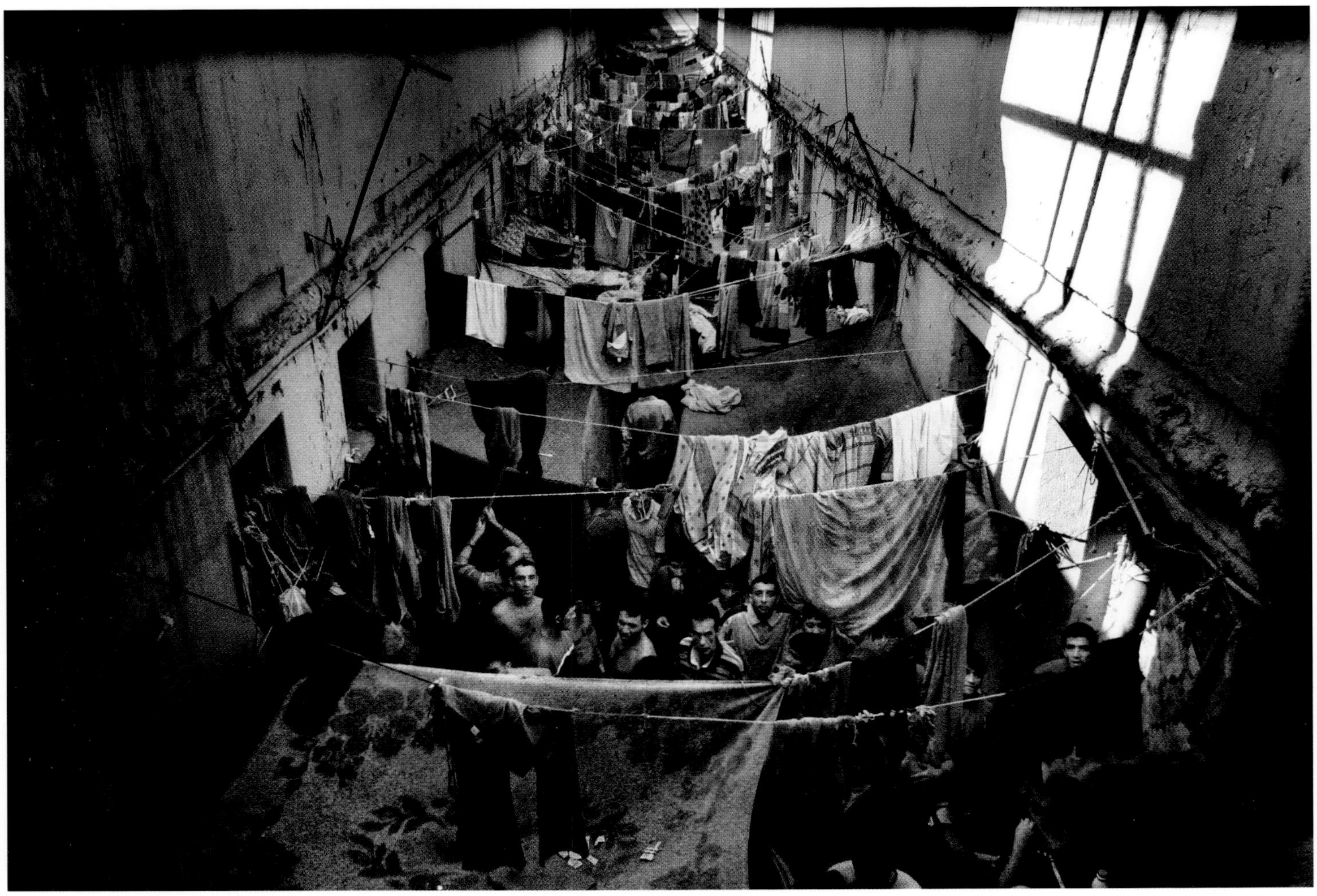

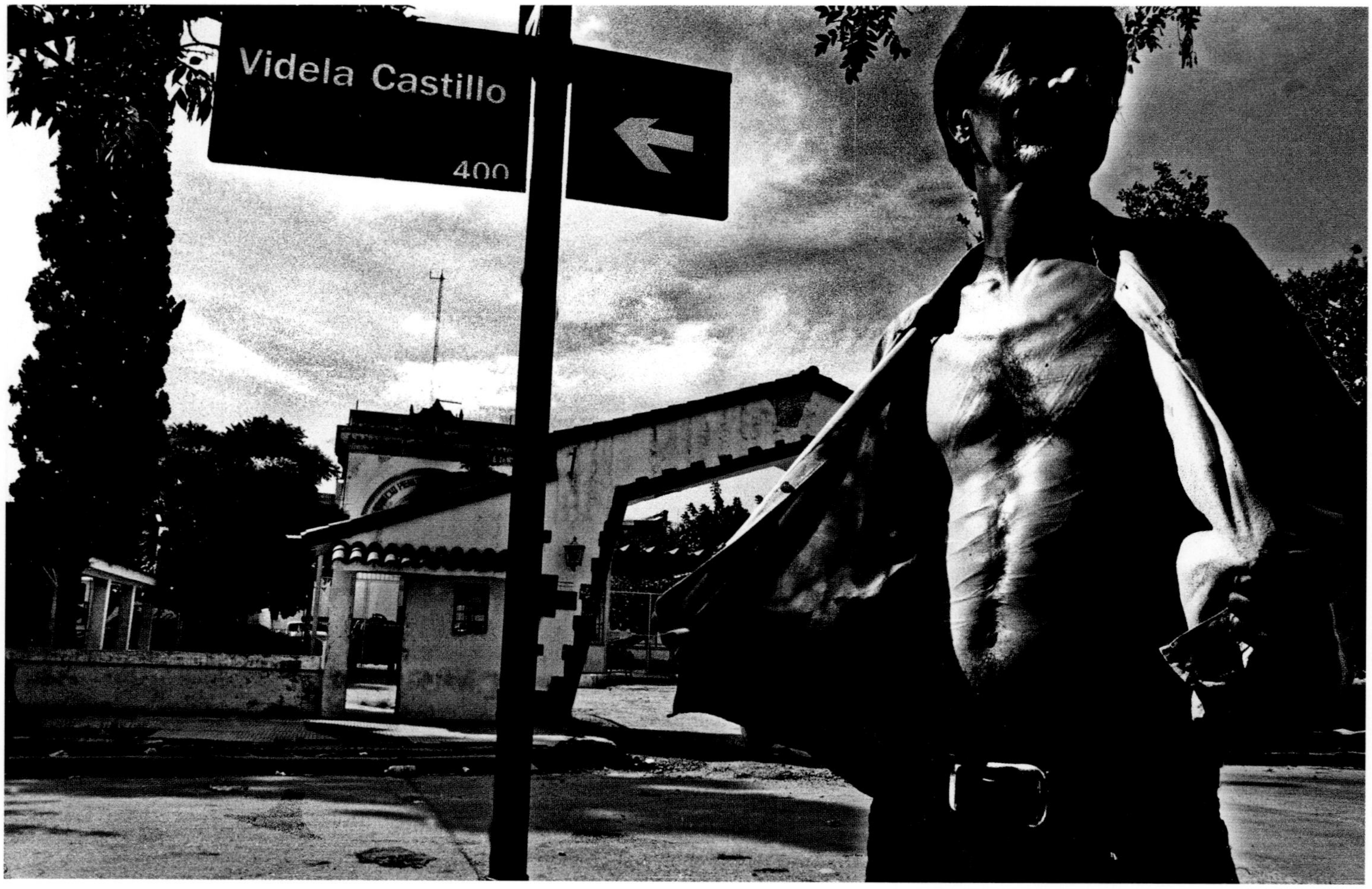

A man lifts his shirt to show the scars he sustained in prison, Cordoba, Argentina.

Prisoners in the bathroom at Santiago de Chile, Chile.

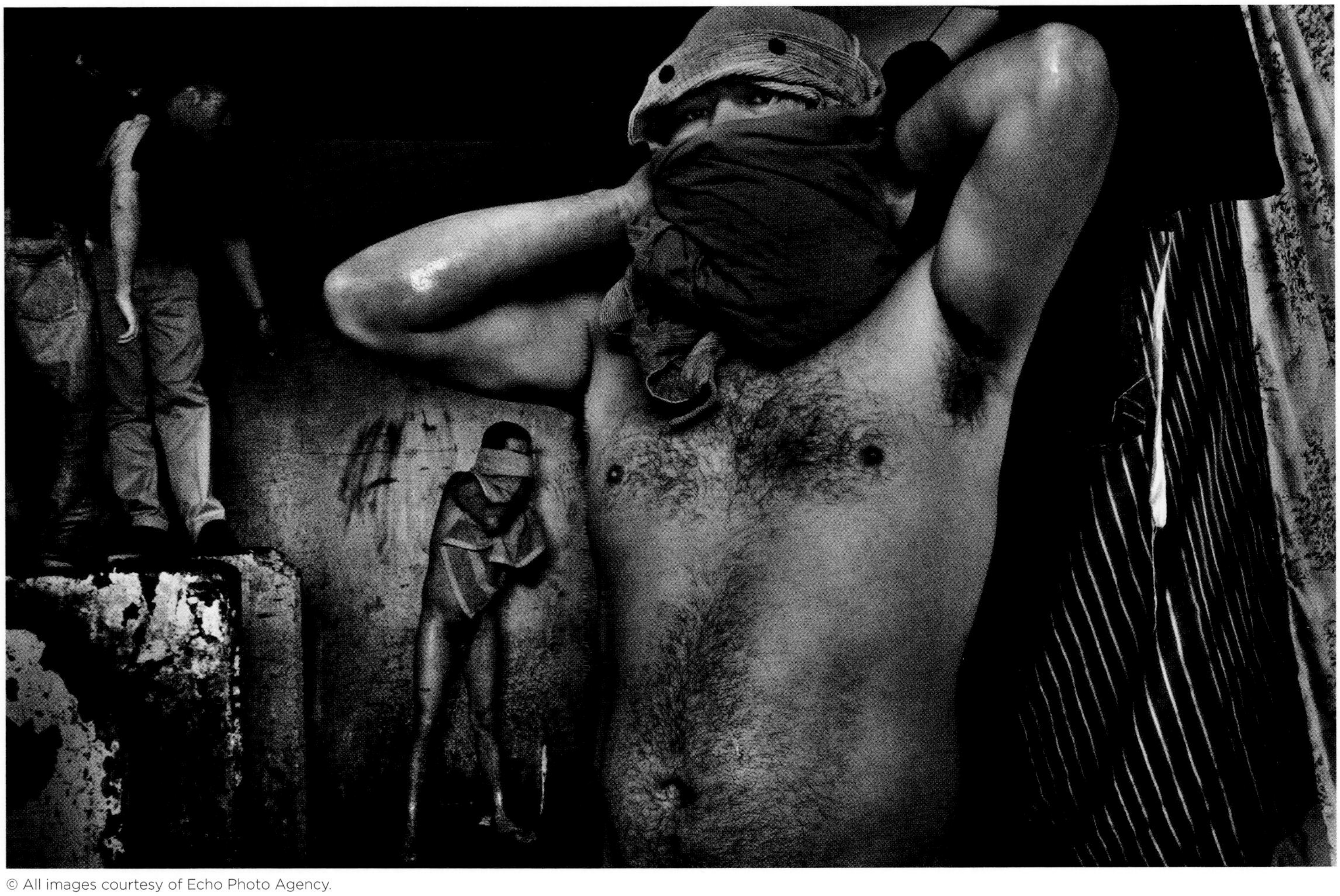

SAMUEL JAMES USA

2ND PLACE
CONTEMPORARY ISSUES

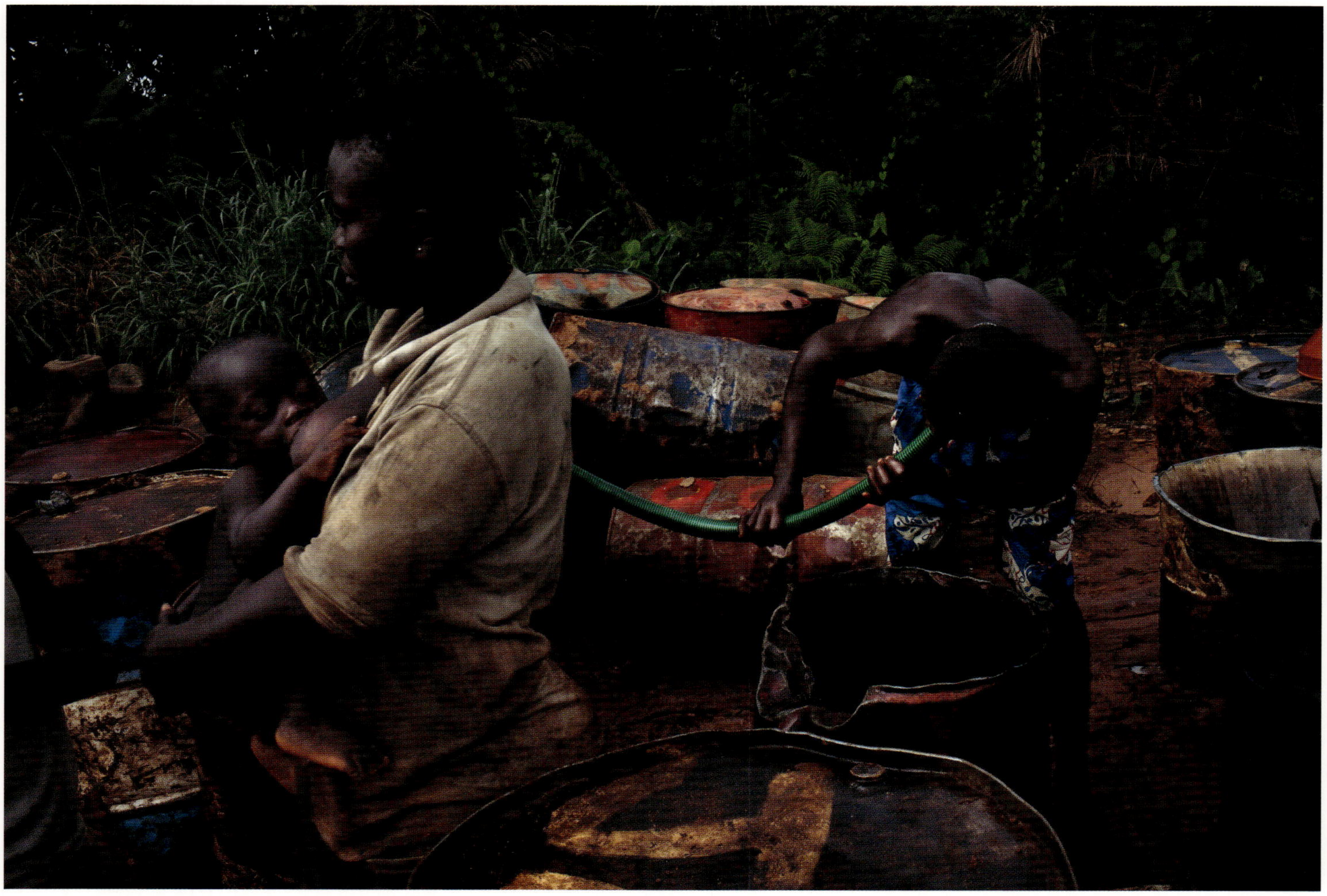

A woman takes a break from the rigorous labour of unloading diesel to nurse her small child. Behind her, a man siphons fuel from a large metal drum into a plastic jerrican.

The water of my land. Concealed deep within mangrove swamps and raffia forests, men work by flashlight, manually tossing stolen crude oil into burning pits to keep the refining process going. Little effort has been made to address the pollution, corruption, and political sponsorship of armed groups, which drive the underlying violence and endemic poverty in what is Africa's largest oil producing region and fifth largest supplier of crude to the United States. Decades of unchecked gas flaring and spillage from multi-national oil operations, sabotage of pipelines and bunkering has severely damaged vast swaths of one of the world's largest and most magnificent wetlands. Since 2008, I have been exploring the ruthless contradictions that define the post-colonial petro-state that is Nigeria. This work builds upon this passage, and stands as an inquiry into our collective relationship to the environment and each other.

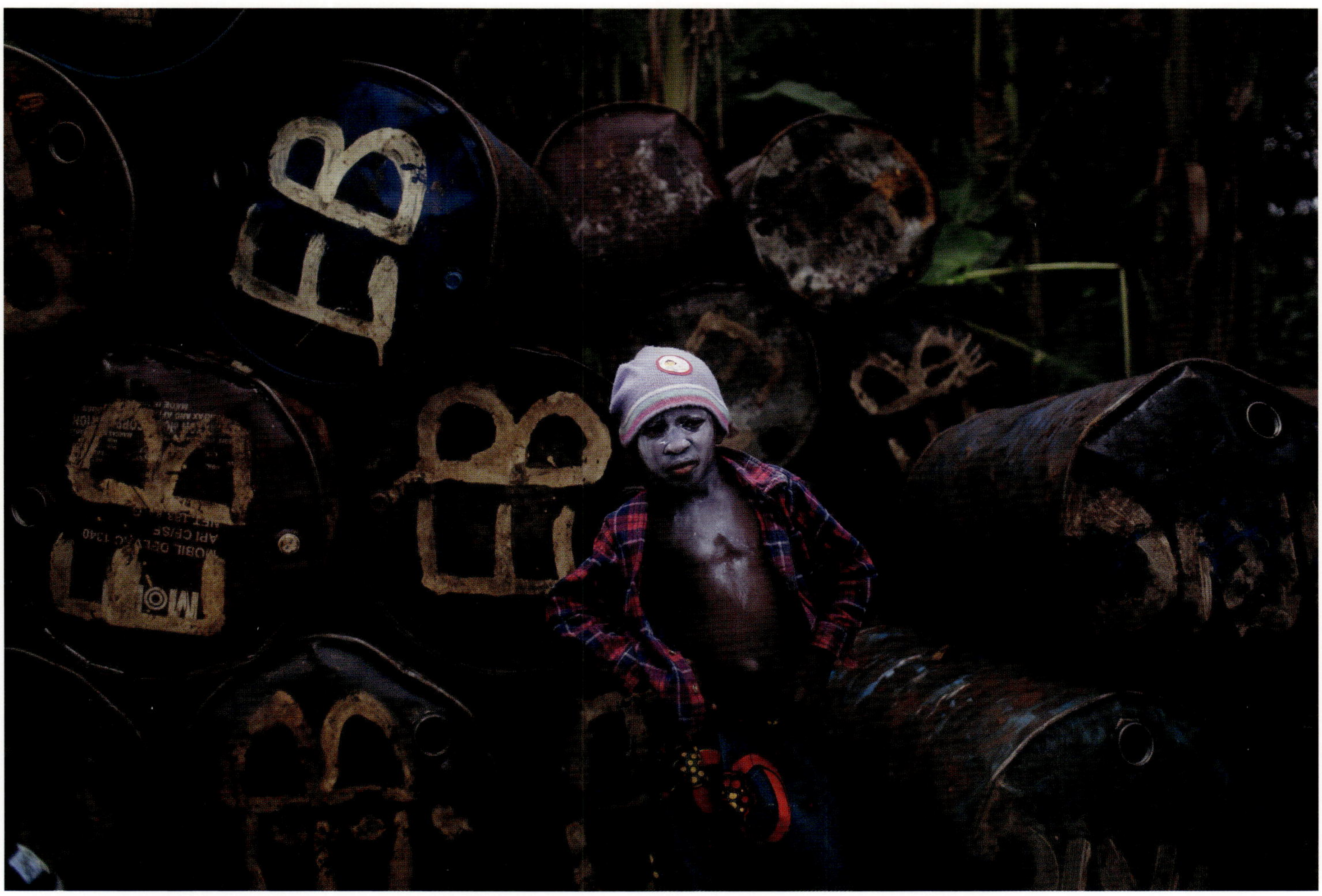

A child waits to unload drums of diesel at a jetty in the Niger Delta where illicitly refined fuel is sold on the black market to local filling stations. In many riverine communities throughout the delta, the entire local economy revolves around the illicit diesel trade, and young children often work at the unloading docks rather than going to school.

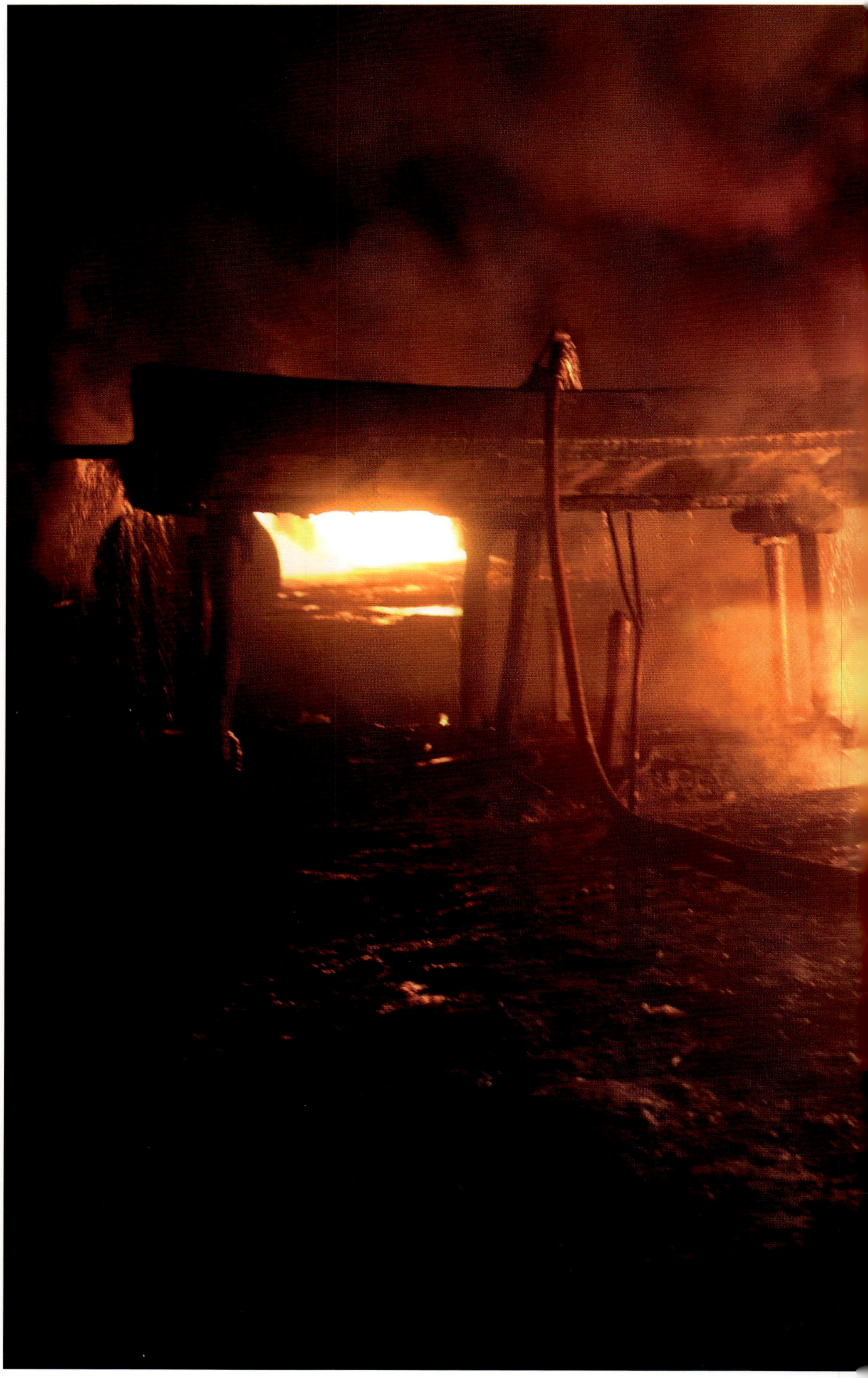

At an illicit refinery deep within the mangroves of the Niger Delta, a man works through the night in extremely dangerous conditions, cooking stolen crude oil into diesel, petrol and kerosene. Entire camps can easily, and often do, explode when the fumes produced during the refining process catch fire. The workers cook under the cover of the night to evade authorities tracking the smoke from their operations.

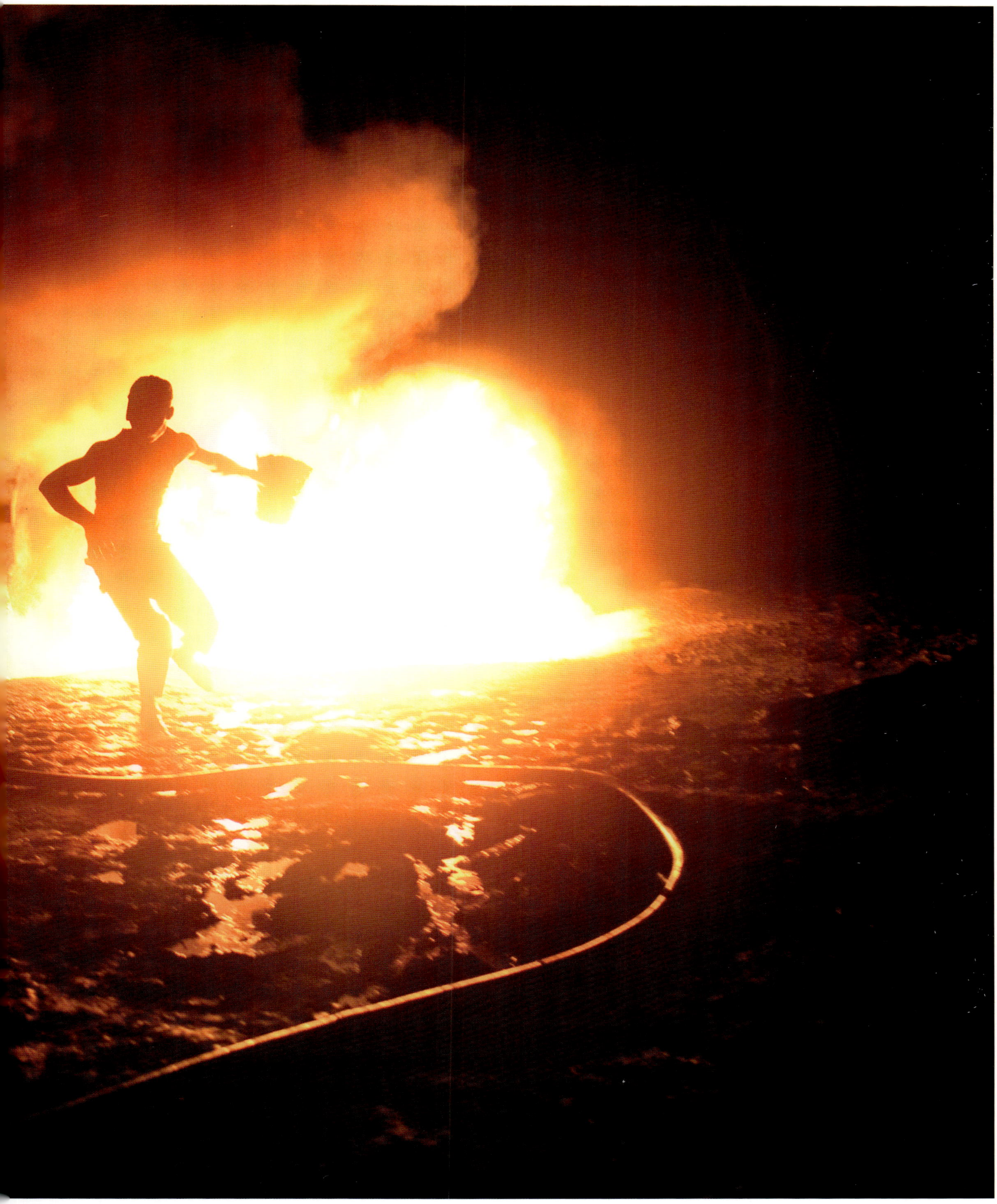

DAESUNG LEE REPUBLIC OF KOREA

3RD PLACE
CONTEMPORARY ISSUES

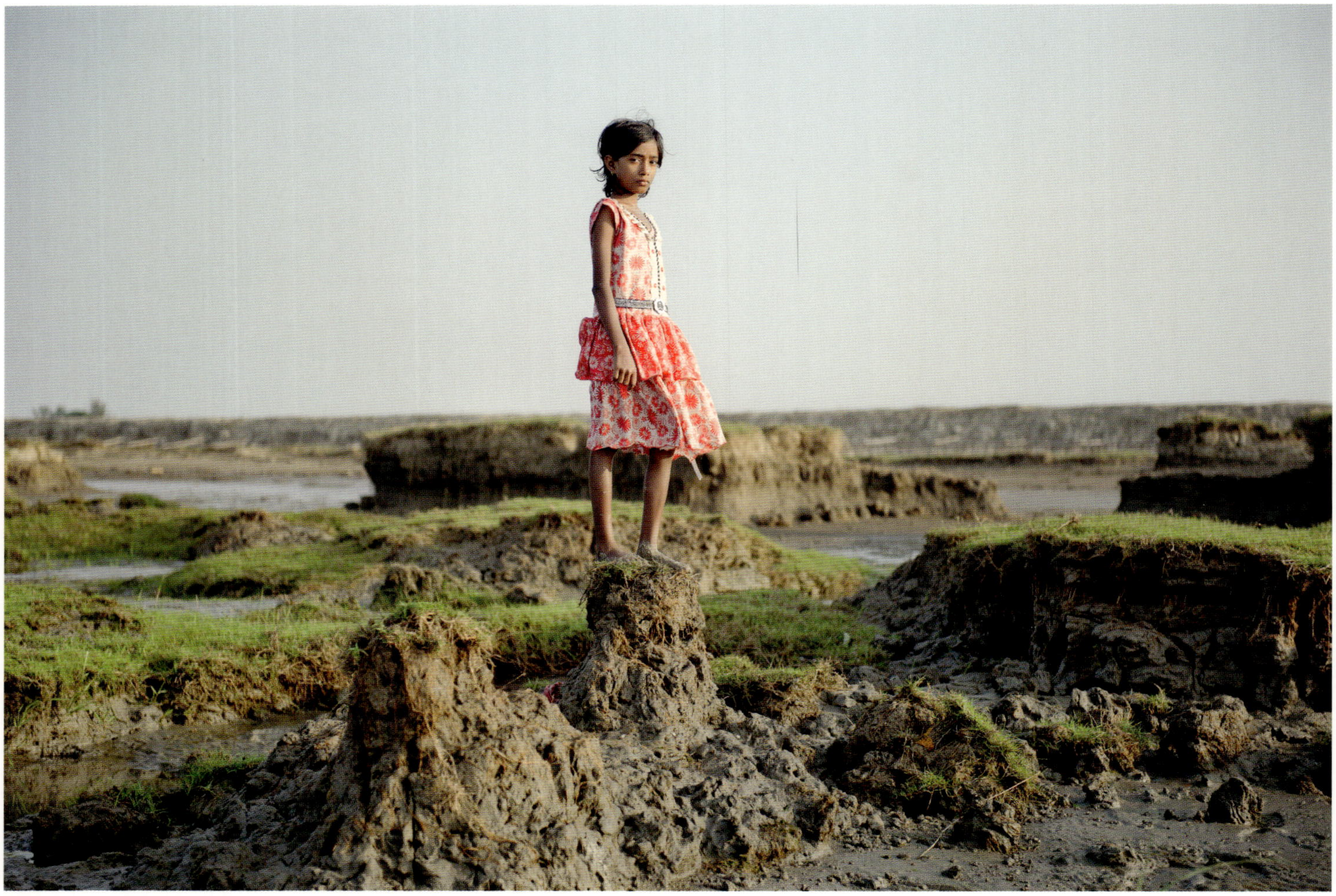

On the shore of a vanishing island. Ghoramara Island, West Bengal. A dramatic rise in sea level means that the shores of this island are being perpetually washed away. Since the 1980s more than half the territory has vanished, and two-thirds of the population have moved away. Many who remain are farmers and fishermen who depend on the island's resources for their livelihoods. According to a civil servant I met, in 20-25 years the Indian government could abolish the island, and have already formulated a plan to evacuate villagers to another island, Sagar. One day, this island on which they were born will exist only in their memories.

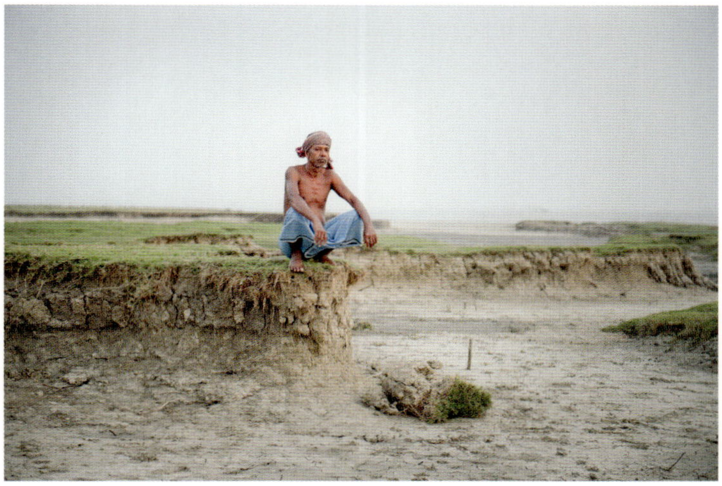

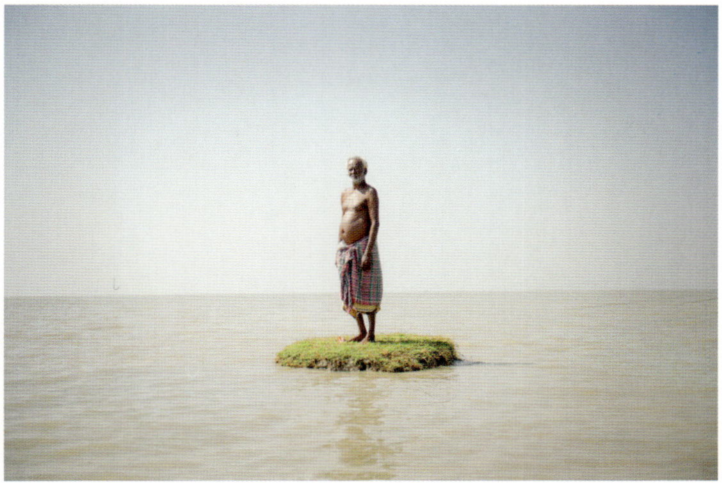

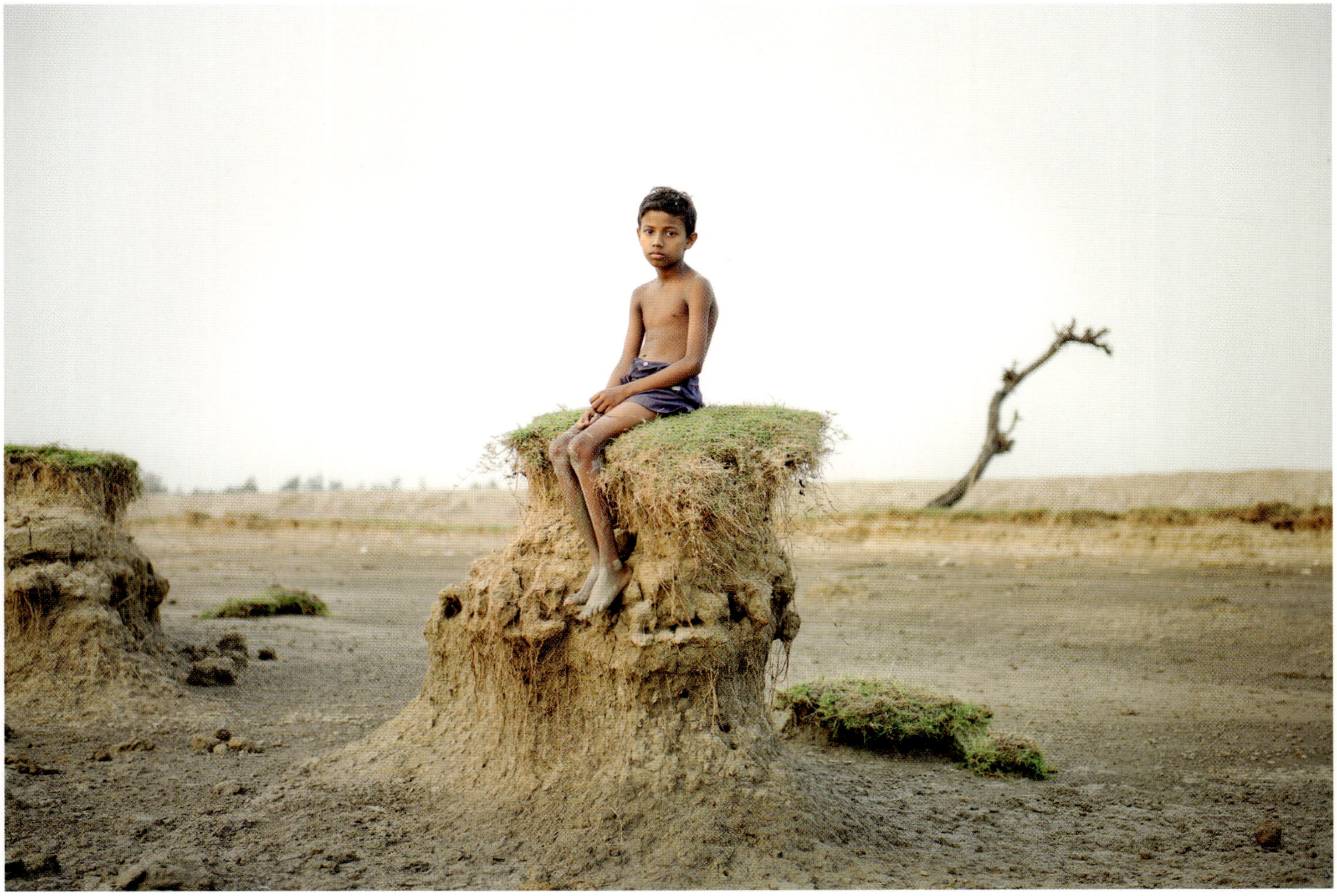

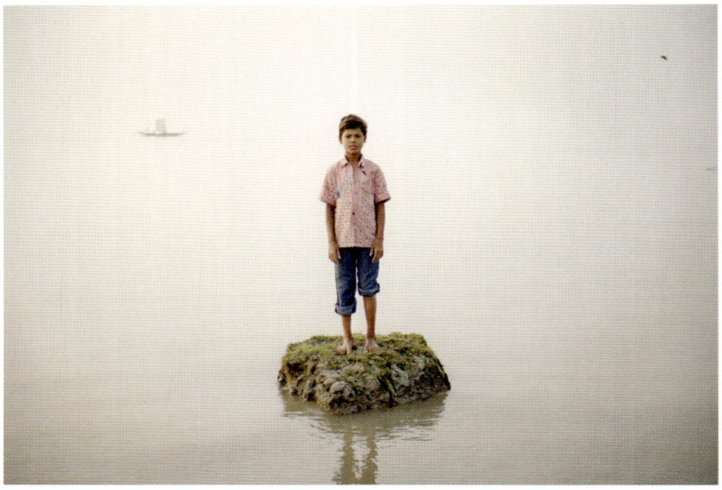

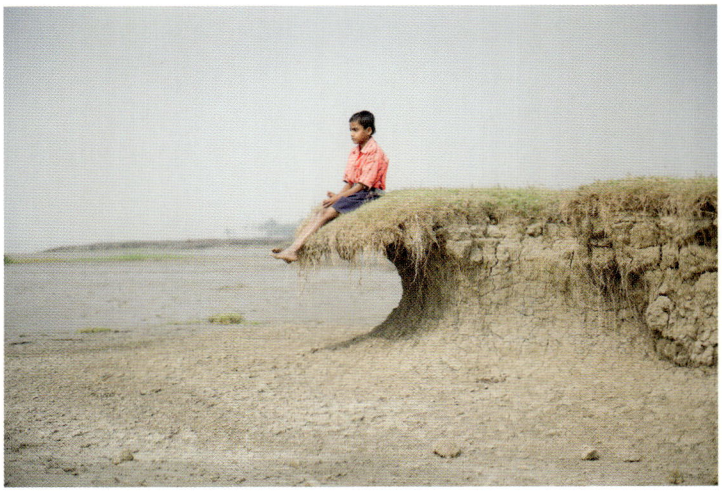

© All images courtesy of Sipa Press.

ILYA PITALEV RUSSIA

1ST PLACE
CURRENT AFFAIRS

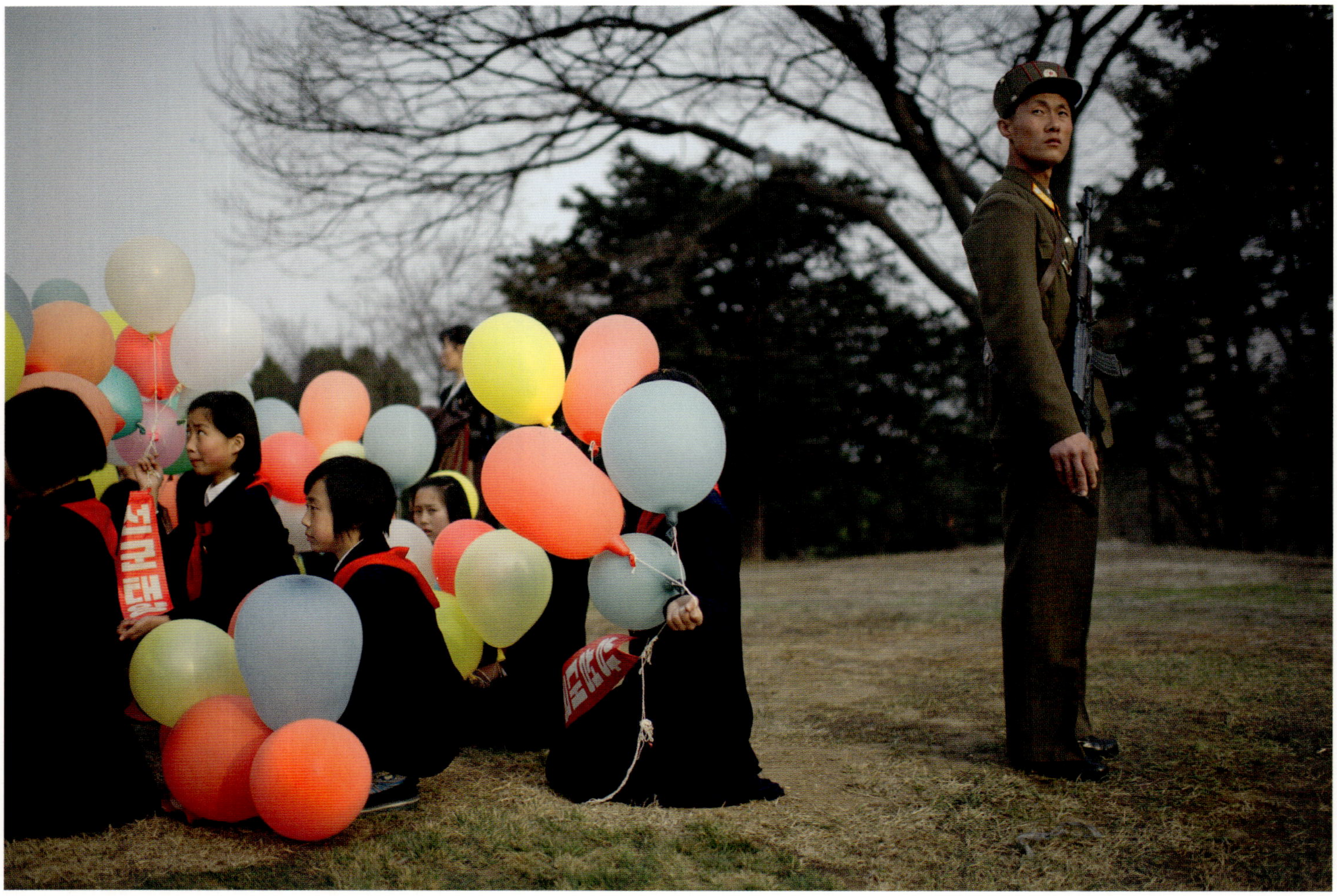

School students and soldier at an official ceremony of unveiling a monument to Kim Il Sung and Kim Jong Il.

Personality and society. Reality vs illusions. In 2012, the people of North Korea celebrated the centenary of the founder of their state, Kim Il Sung. Kim Jong Il, who had continued the policies of his father for many years, passed away in 2011. Because of the policies of Kim Jong Il, North Korea remained a closed country for many years. There has never been comprehensive, reliable information about developments in North Korea. Kim Jong Un, the grandson of Kim Il Sung, now rules the country. Will the new ruler break the nearly 100-year-long silence?

The military parade marking the centennial birthday of Kim Il Sung, the founder of North Korea.

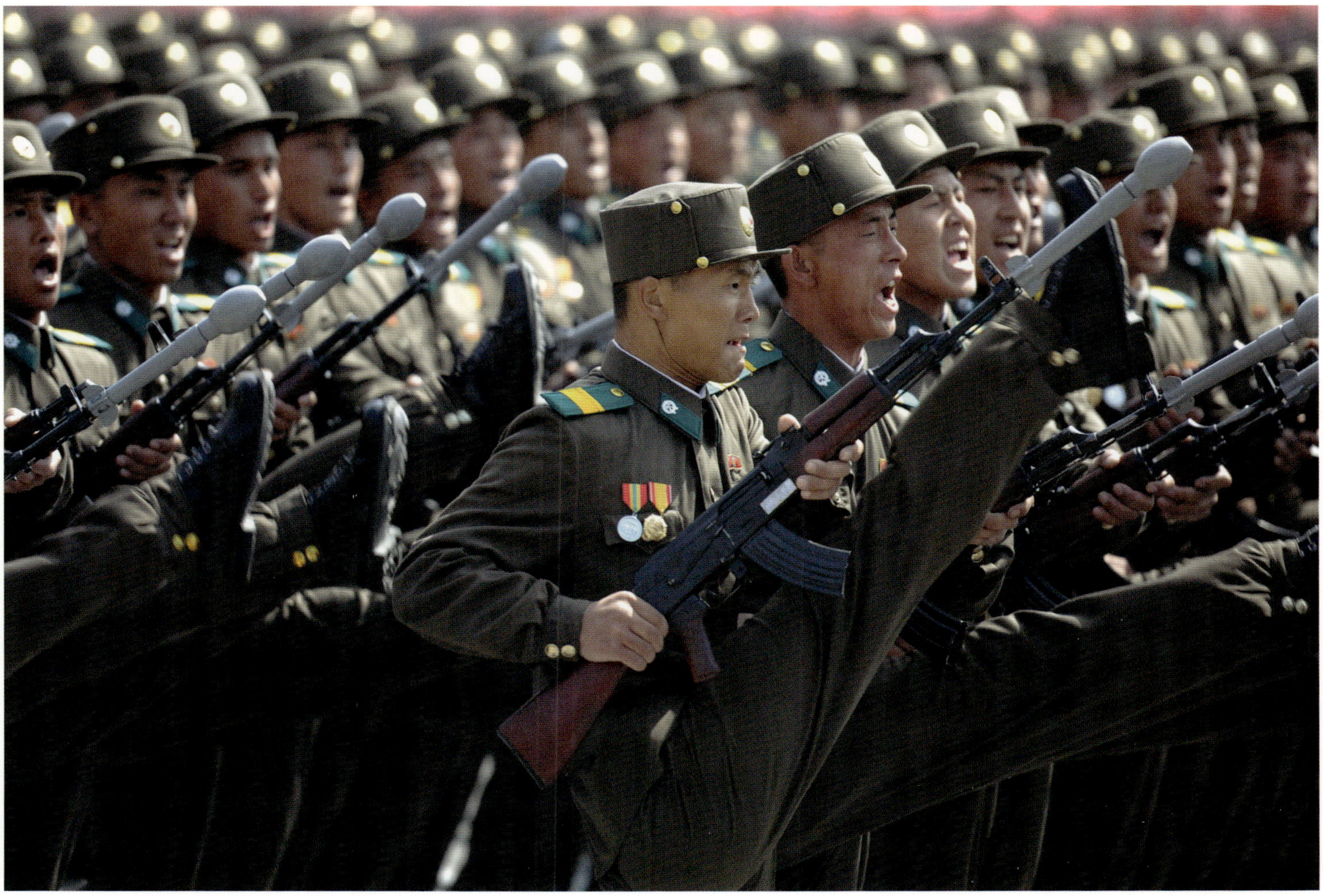

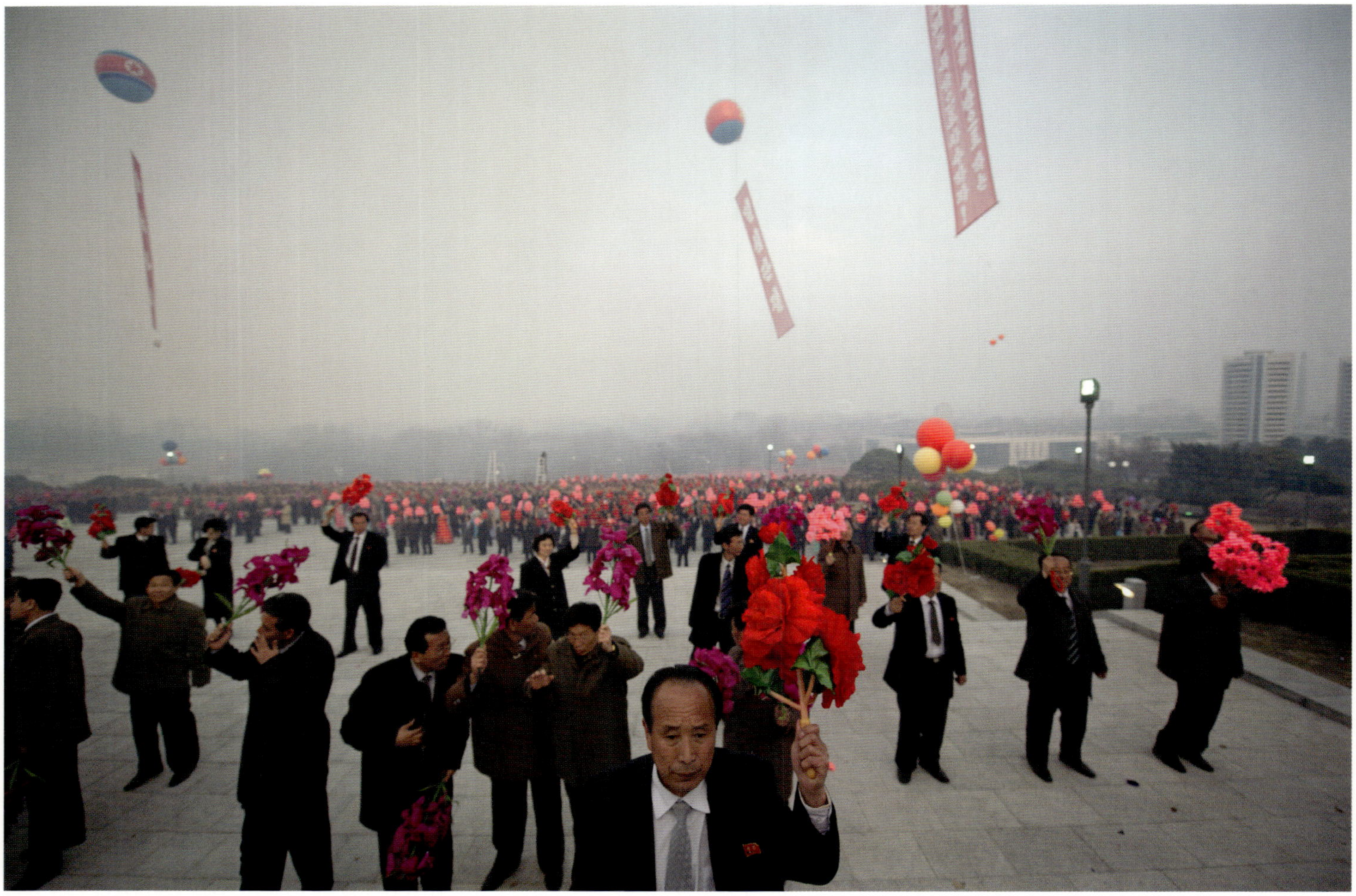

Above image: Pyongyang residents at official ceremony to unveil a monument to Kim Il Sung and Kim Jong Il. **Above right image:** North Korean Army soldiers and civilians on the stand of the Kim Il Sung Stadium. **Below right image:** Guests attending an official concert in honor of the centennial birthday of Kim Il Sung.

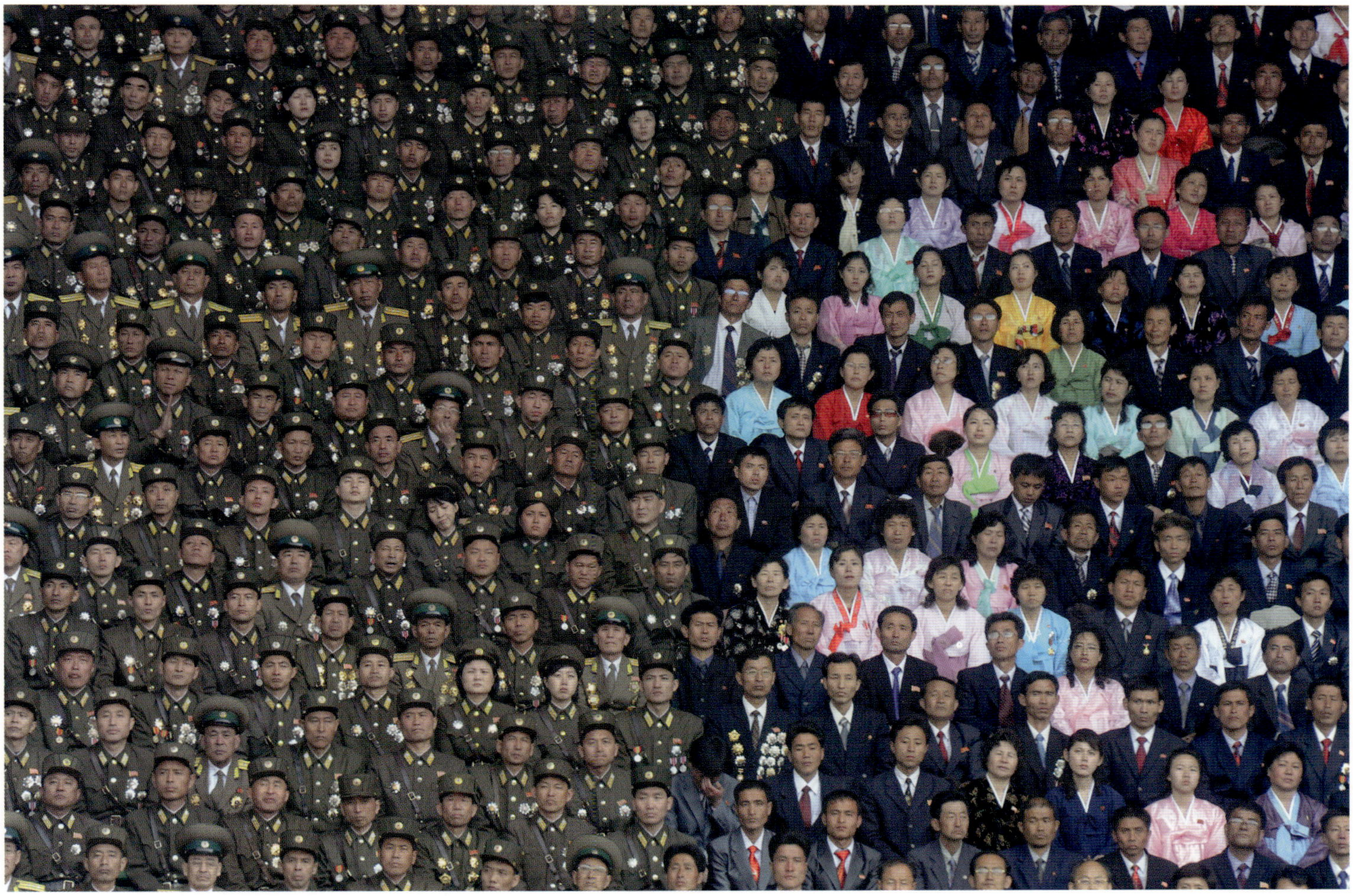

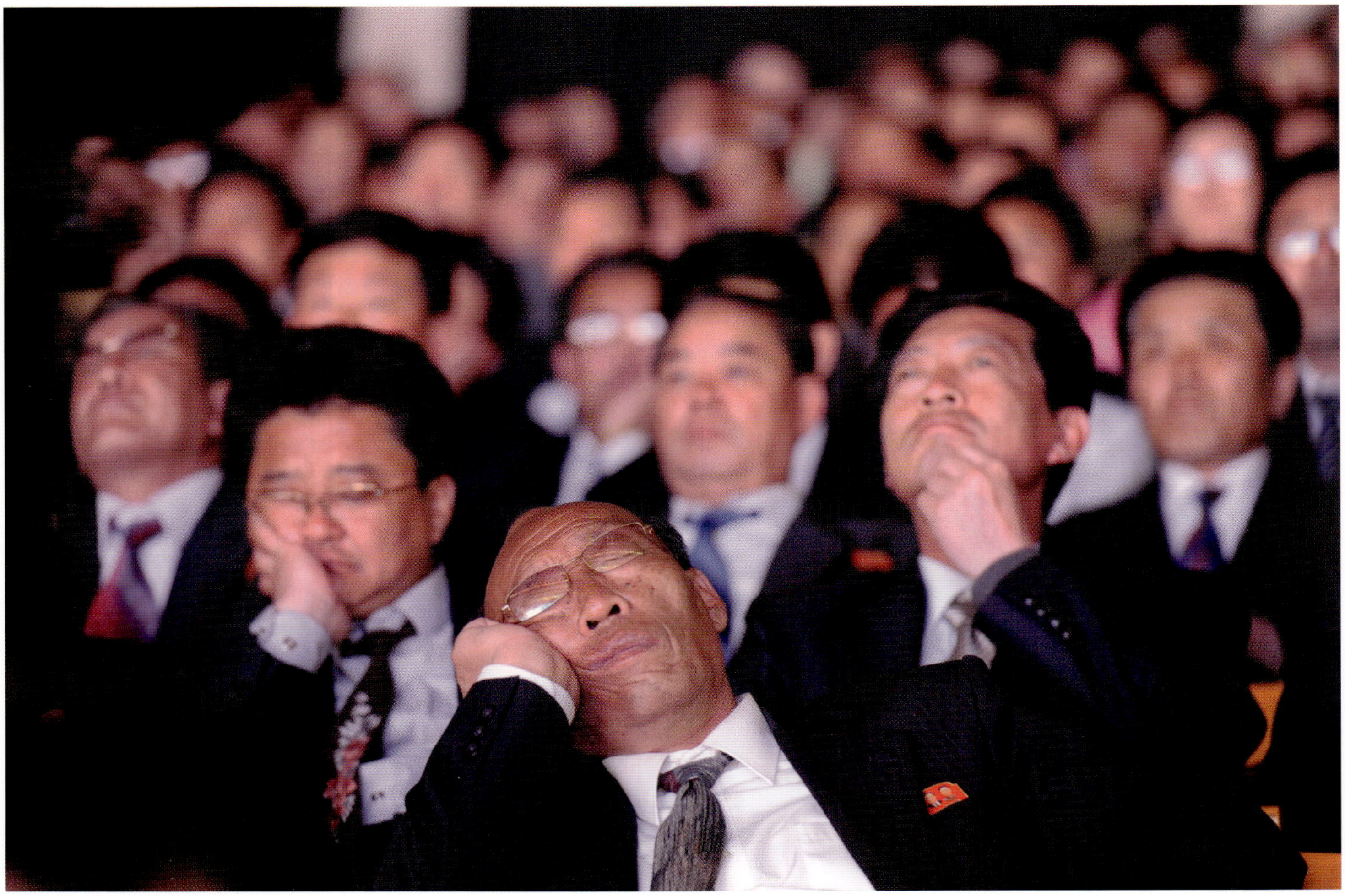

PAOLO PELLEGRIN ITALY

2ND PLACE
CURRENT AFFAIRS

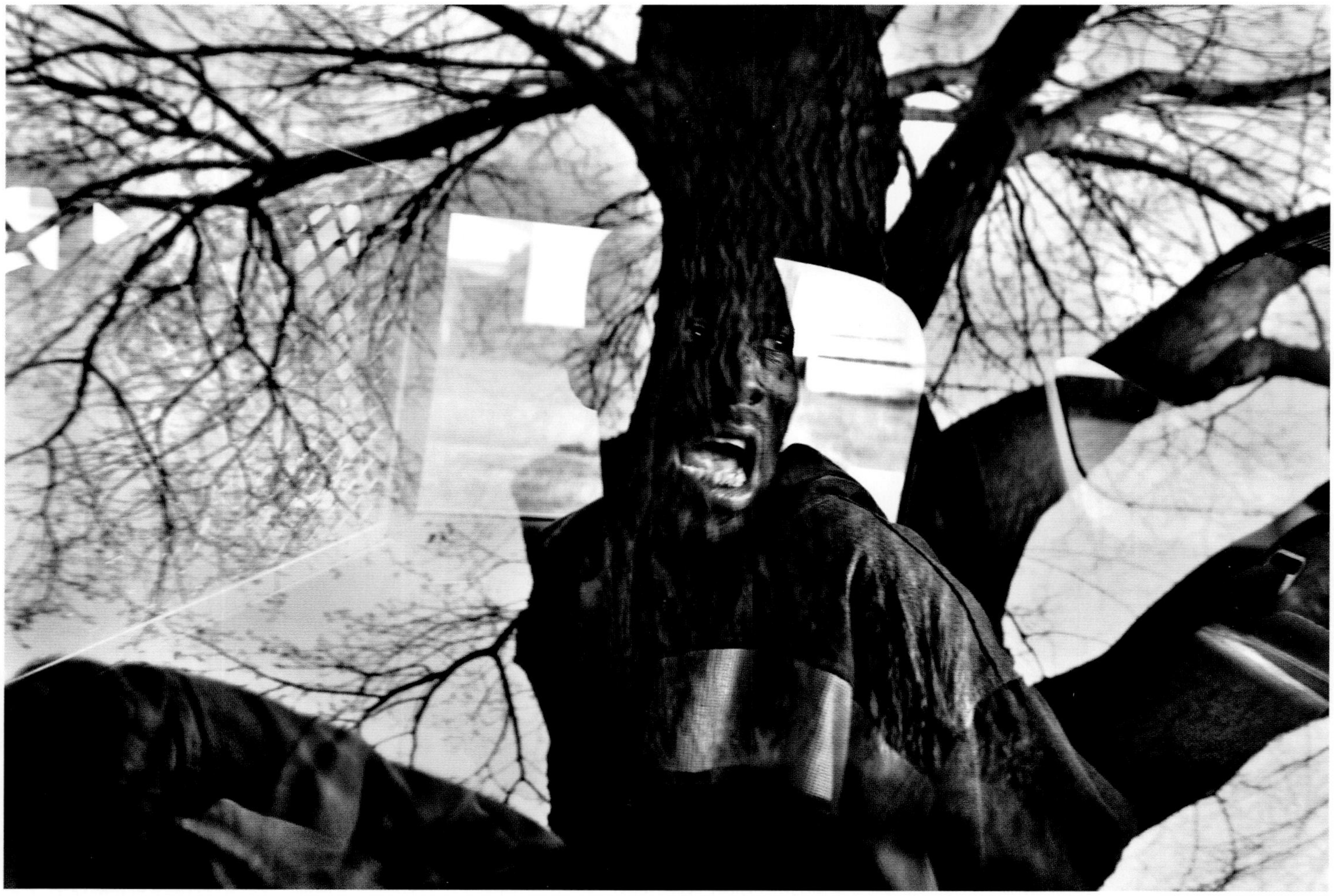

A man is arrested by the Rochester police after having assaulted his father with a samurai sword.

The Crescent. Rochester USA 2012. Rochester is part of the so-called 'Crescent', a moon-shaped area that runs across several Rochester neighbourhoods, where crime rates are significantly higher than the rest of the city. The Crescent is home to 27 percent of the city's residents and 80 percent of the city's homicides. The reasons behind the violence include the lagging upstate economy, a steady migration of residents to the suburbs and a growing number of abandoned houses prone to becoming drug dens. Rochester's school system also performs poorly. 'It's an area of great poverty and high consumption rate of drugs which fuels an incredibly high number of homicides,' said the Rochester police chief.

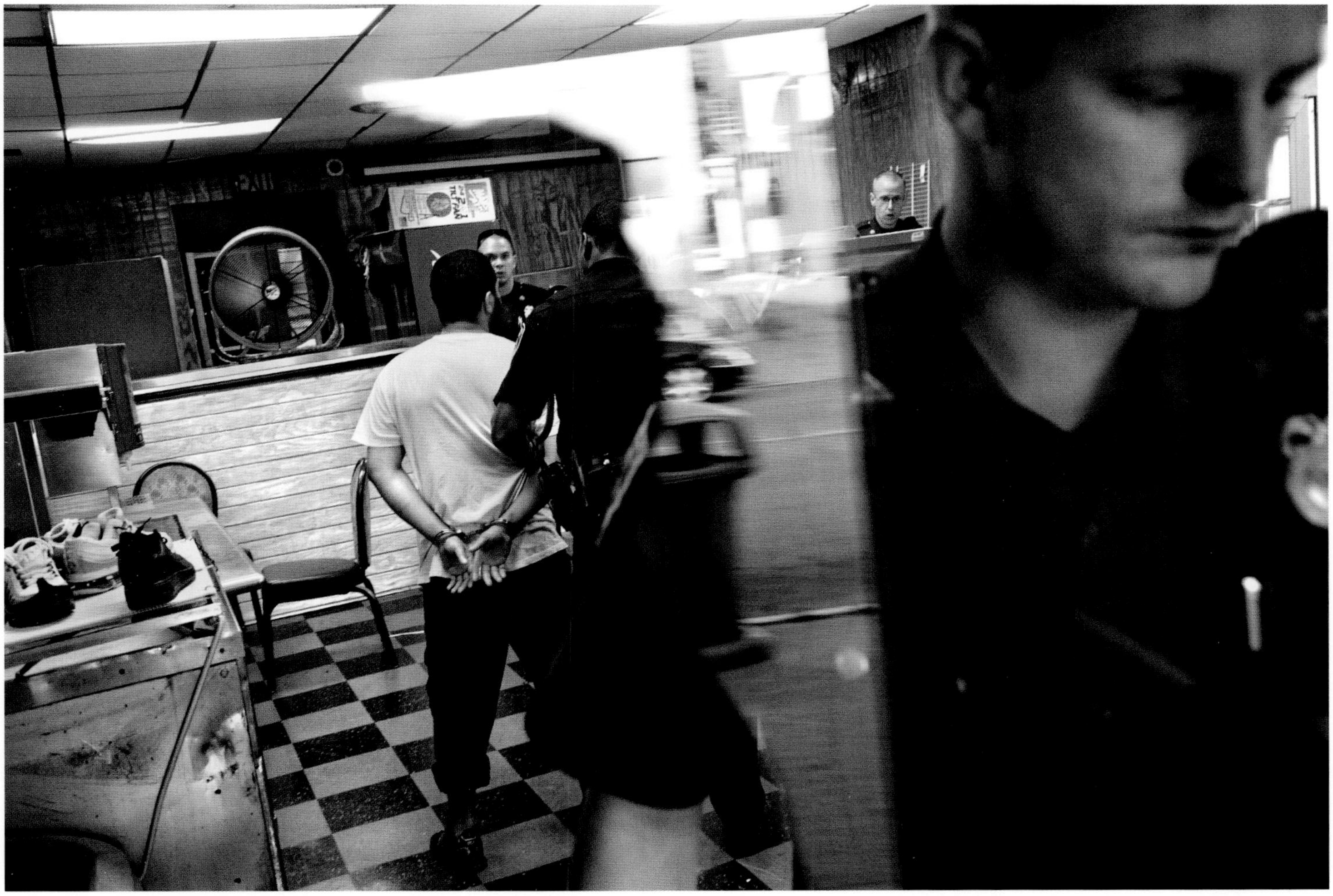

A Yemeni deli owner is questioned after allegedly threatening a customer with a shotgun in NE Rochester.

Bottom image: A man who was stabbed during a fight is treated by medics. He refused to give the name of the assailant to the police saying that he would take care of it himself. **Top right image:** A family in the Crescent area of Rochester. **Bottom right image:** The funeral of Max King, a 15 year old who was shot in the head and killed in NE Rochester at the end of August 2012. His was the 25th killing in Rochester in 2012.

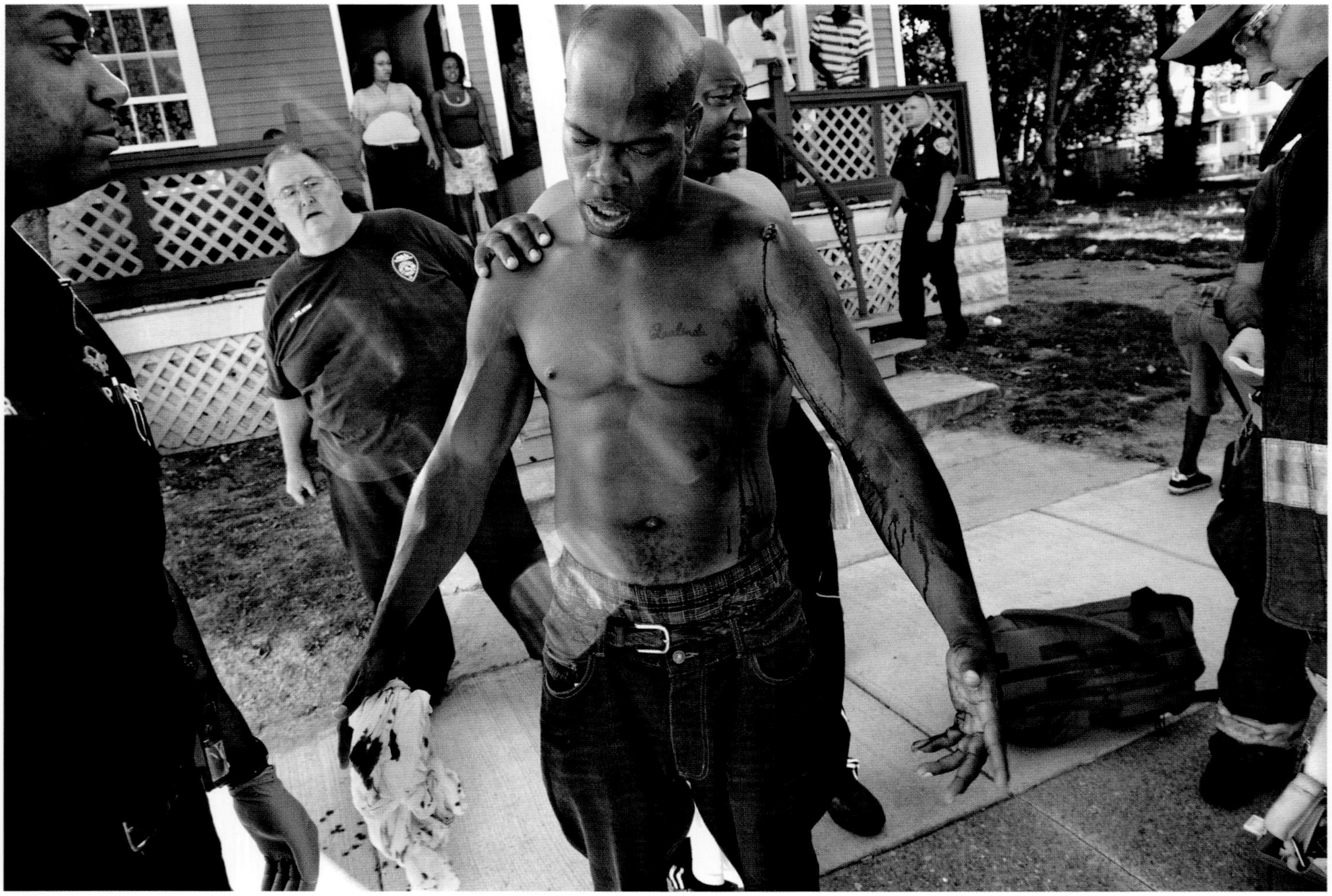

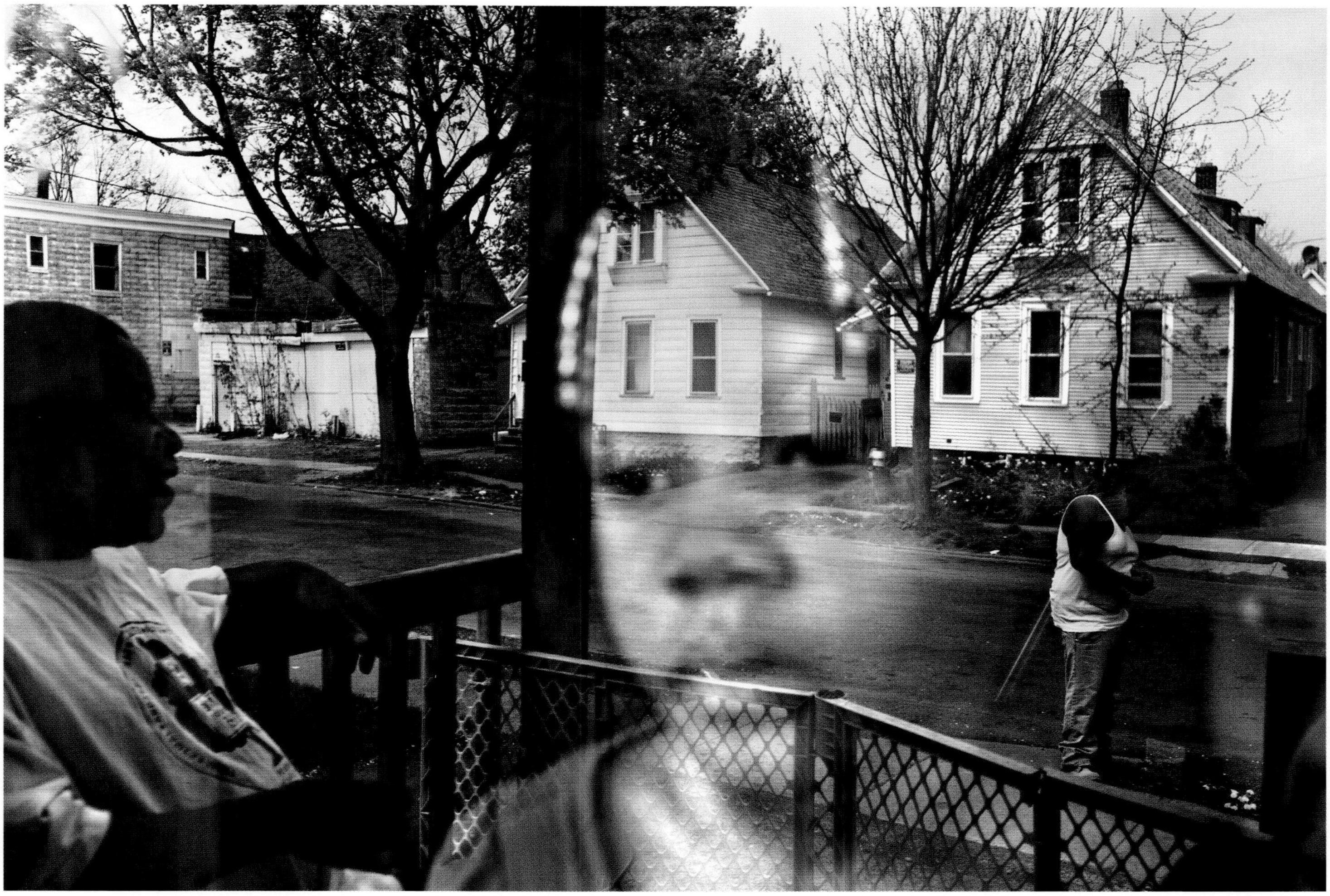

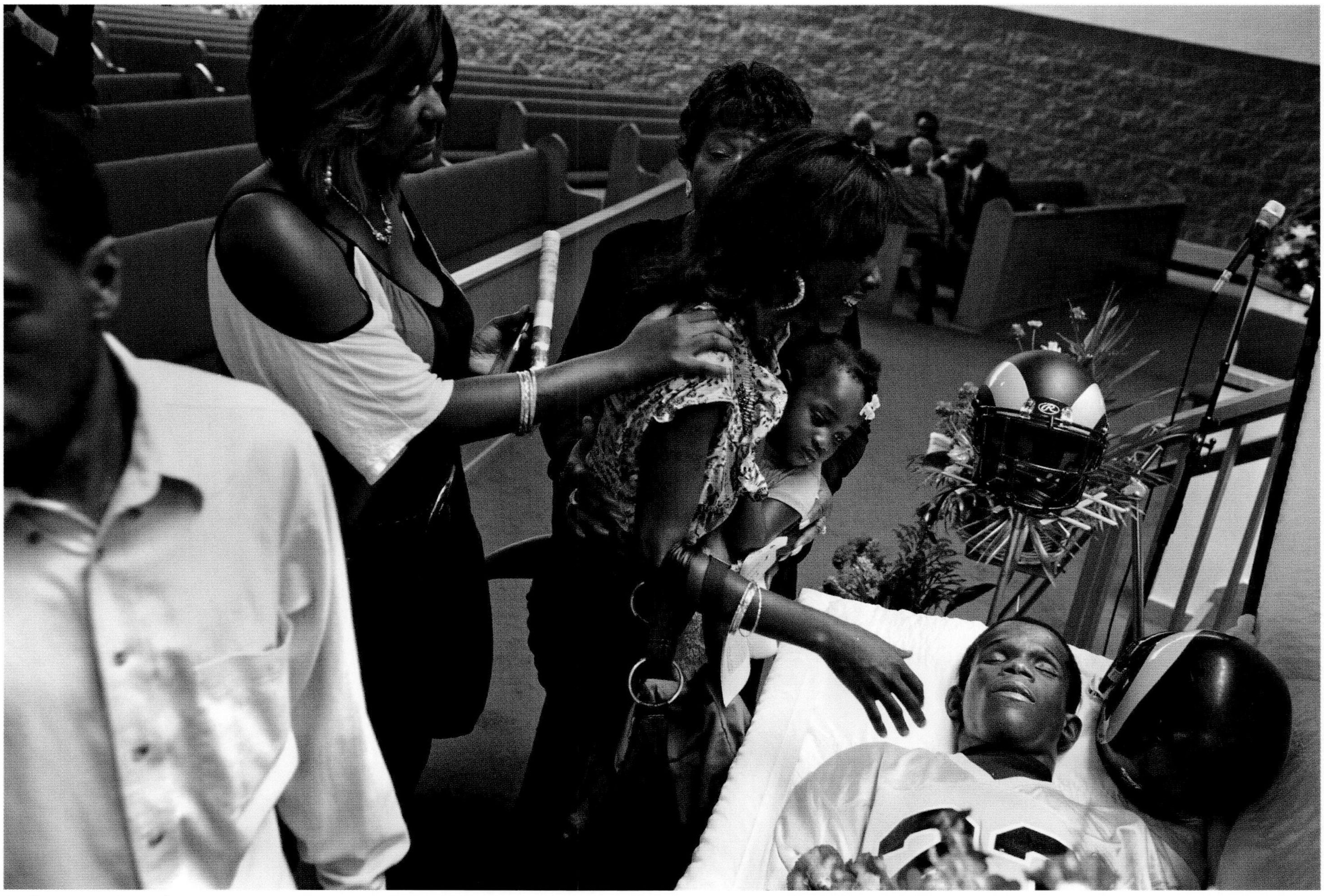

FABIO BUCCIARELLI ITALY

3RD PLACE
CURRENT AFFAIRS

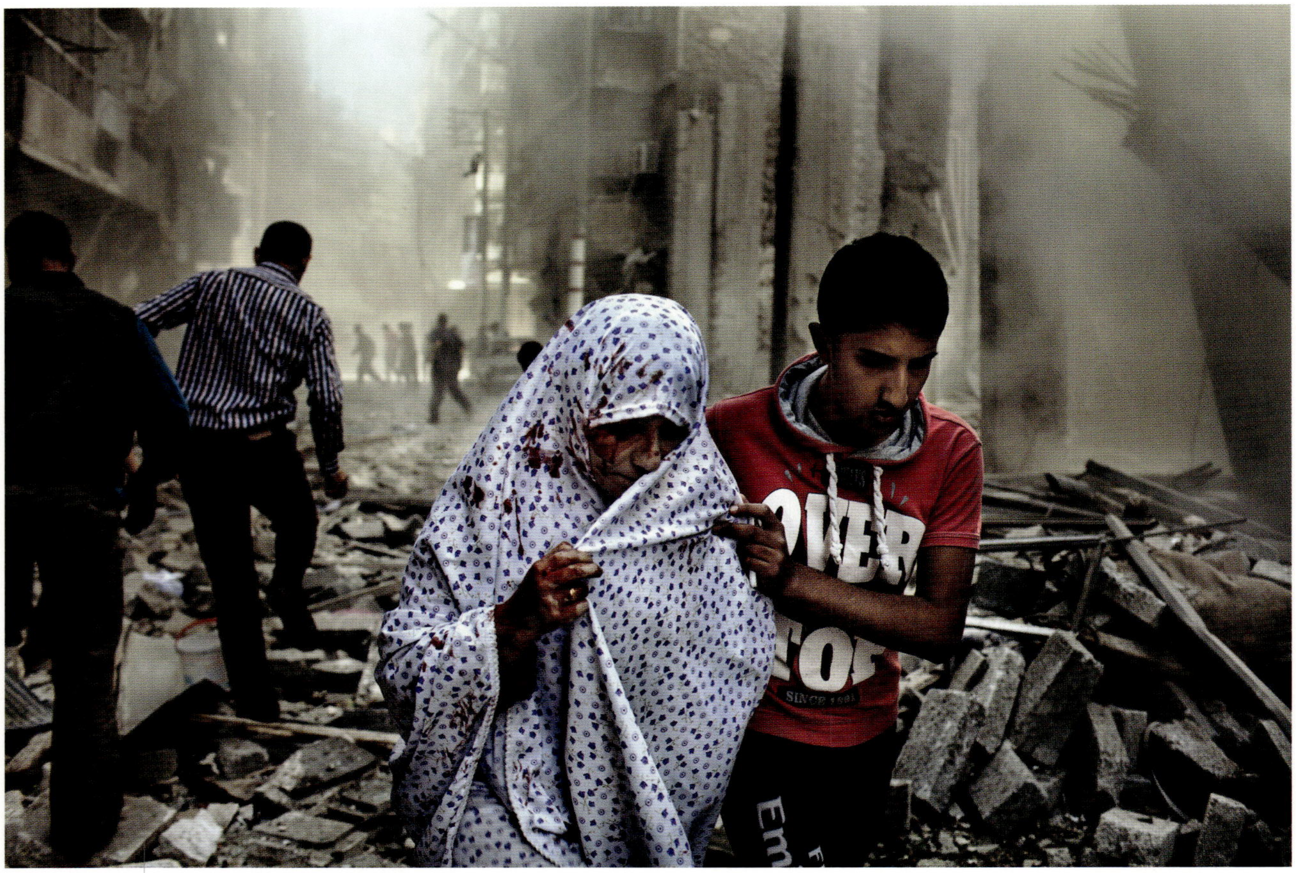

Above image: A Syrian woman is evacuated after being wounded in a shelling by President Bashar al-Assad forces, in the Shaar neighborhood of the northen city of Aleppo. The Syrian civil war begun on April 2011 and the battle for the control of Aleppo, the biggest Syrian city, started at the end of July 2012. The clashes between the Free Syrian Army and President Bashar al-Assad's forces cause hundreds of victims among the civilian population every month. **Above right image:** A woman embraces her child at the Dar al-Shifa Hospital in Aleppo. The child has been wounded by fragments of a mortar launched by President Bashar al-Assad forces. **Below right image:** Syrian men rescue a civilian who was trapped in the rubble of the Nur al-Shuhada mosque after it was shelled by forces loyal to Syrian President Bashar al-Assad, in the Shaar district of Aleppo.

Battle to death in Syria. During the summer of 2012, after more than a year of conflict, the Syrian civil war reaches Aleppo. The most populous city in Syria becomes a stronghold of the revolutionary forces. The battle for control of the city becomes a real massacre: every day the revolutionary fighters, armed only with Kalashnikovs, face the loyalist army and its tanks and aircraft. The media interest does not do justice to events in Syria: unlike Libya, Syria lacks oil, and the international community is just a spectator as a country fights alone against their President. The UN estimates the death toll at more than 60,000.

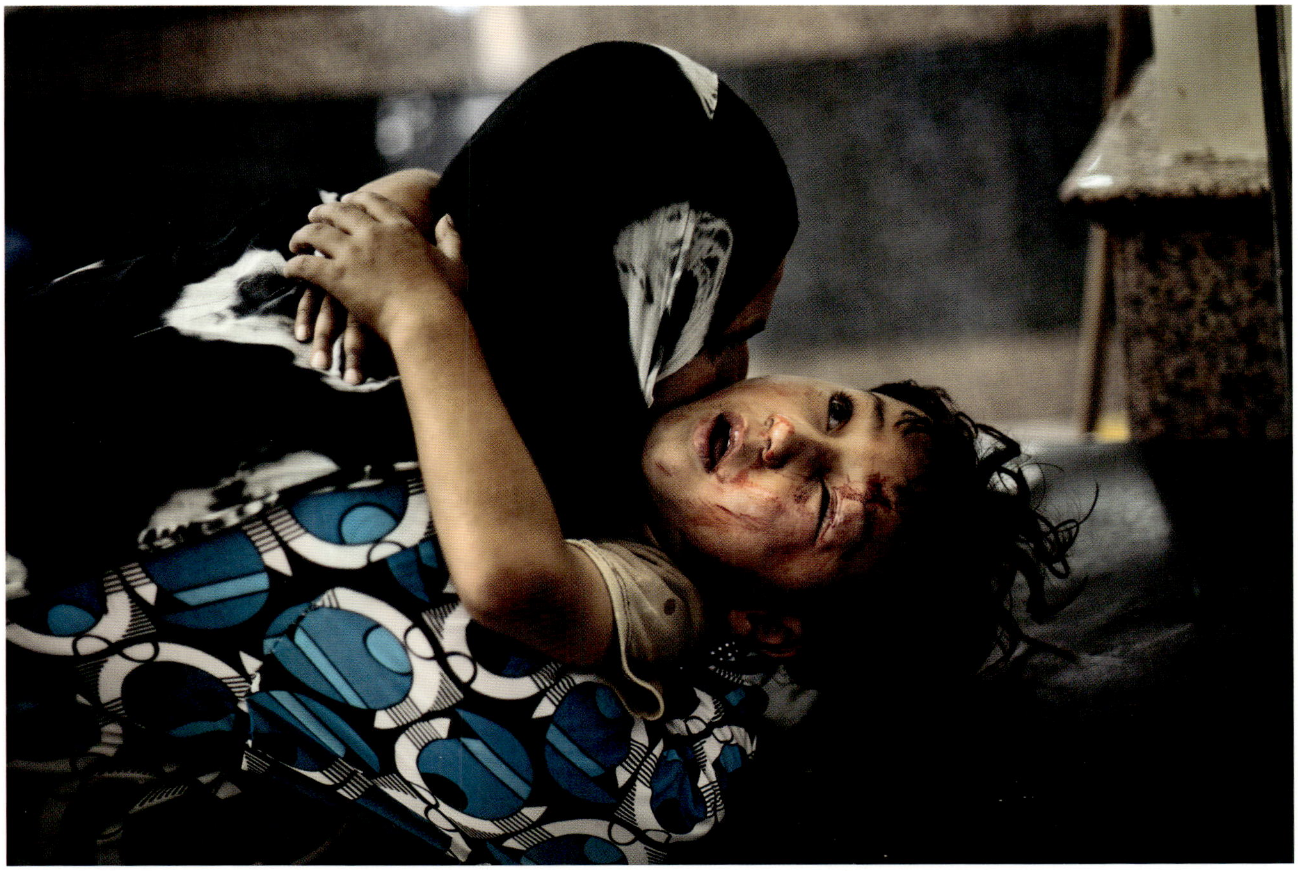

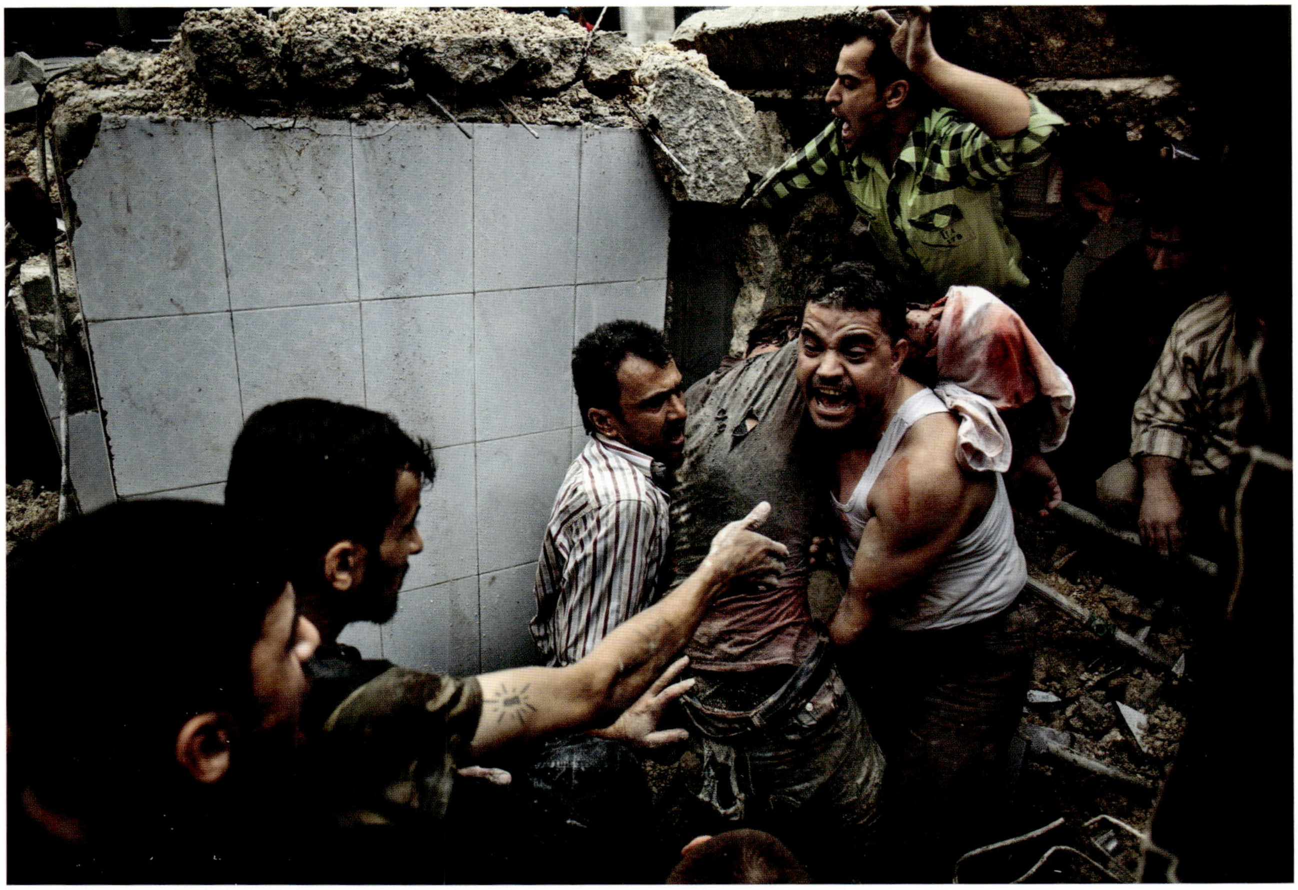

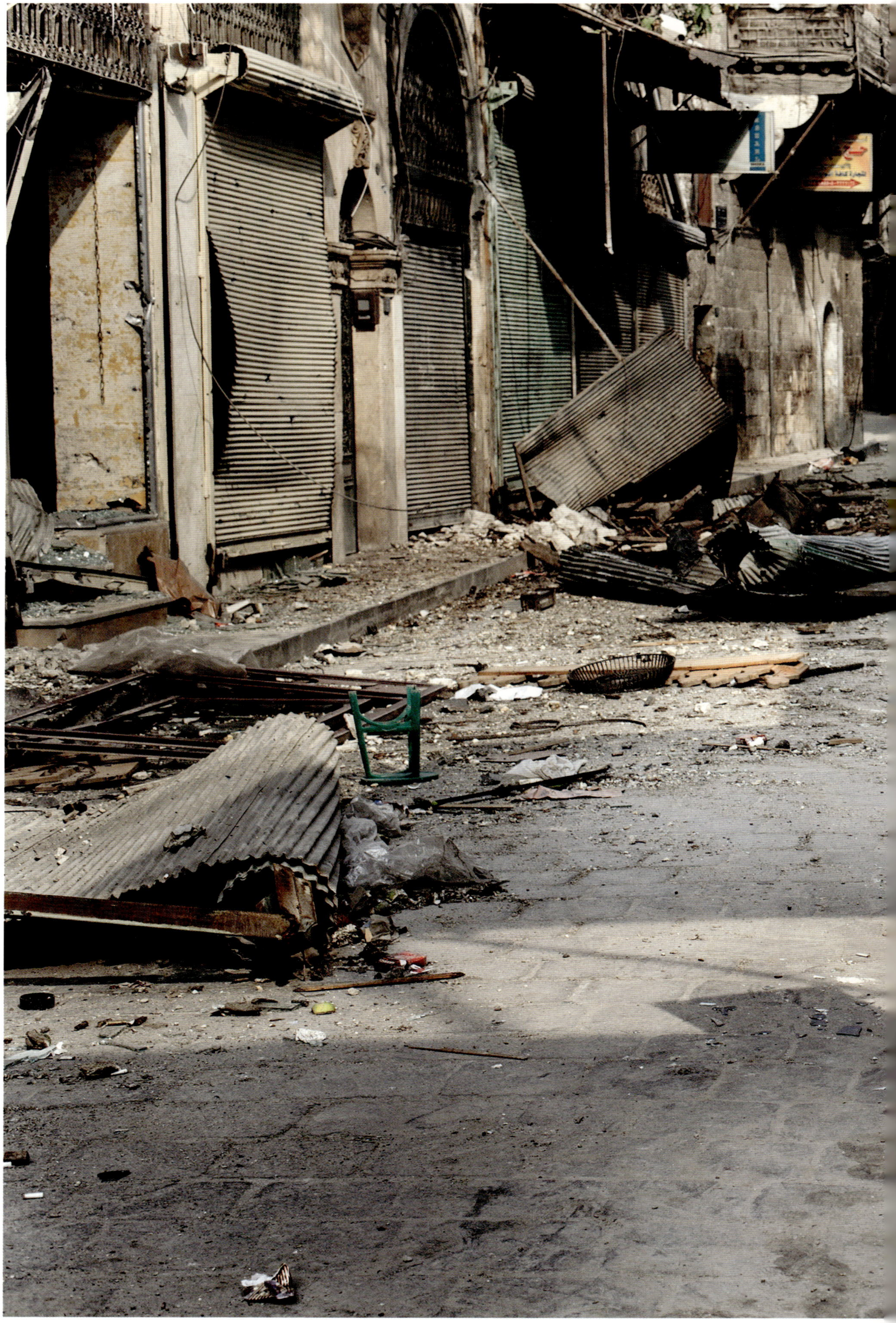

The reflection of a rebel fighter is seen on a mirror used to spot Syrian government forces' position in an Old City district of Aleppo during fighting on October 23rd, 2012.

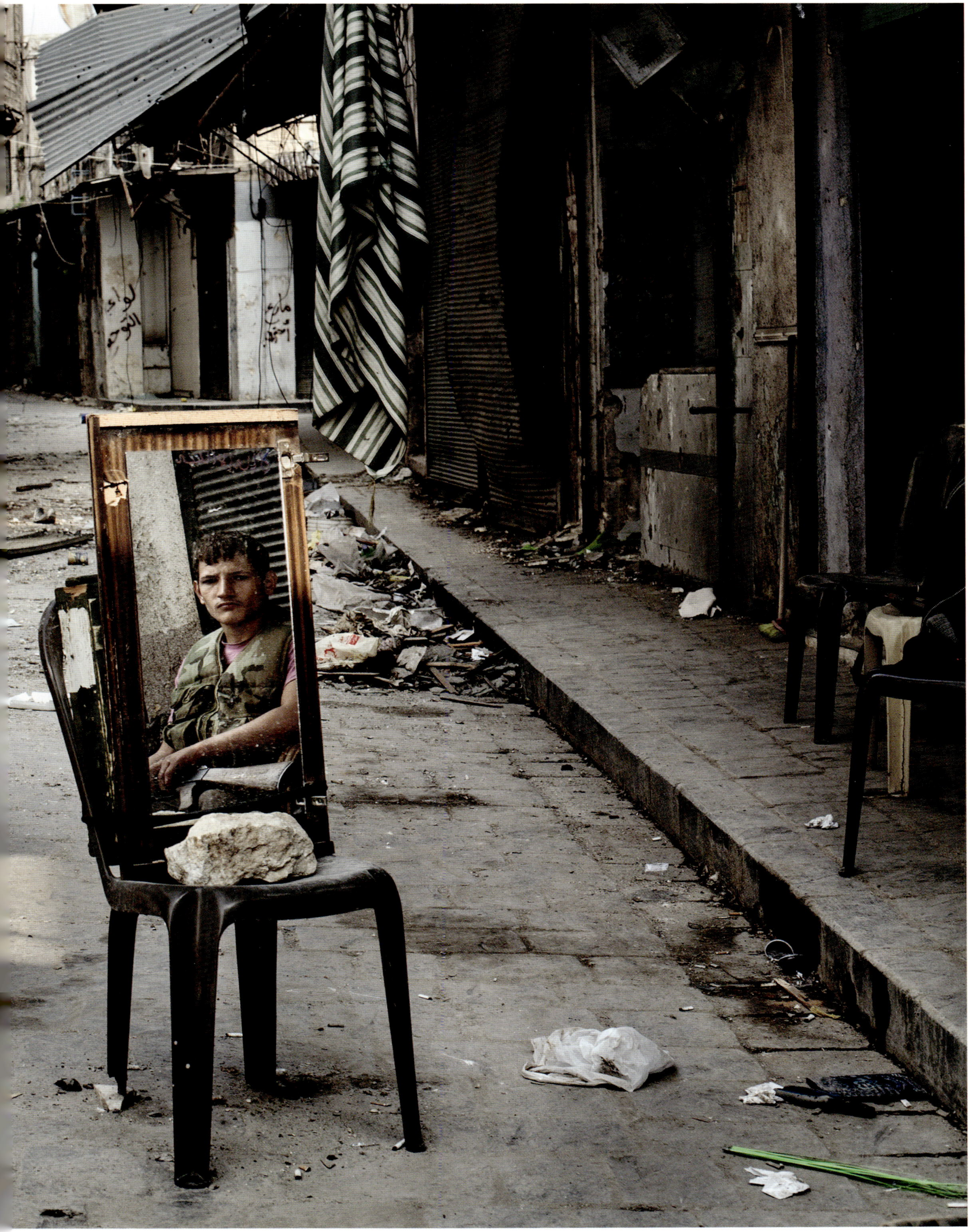

KLAUS THYMANN DENMARK

1ST PLACE
FASHION & BEAUTY

i-D Iceland. The story was photographed on the remote east coast of Iceland, on and around the glacier lake of Jokulsarlon. Under temperamental weather and light conditions Klaus Thymann let fashion and nature merge together in a bright and beautiful way.

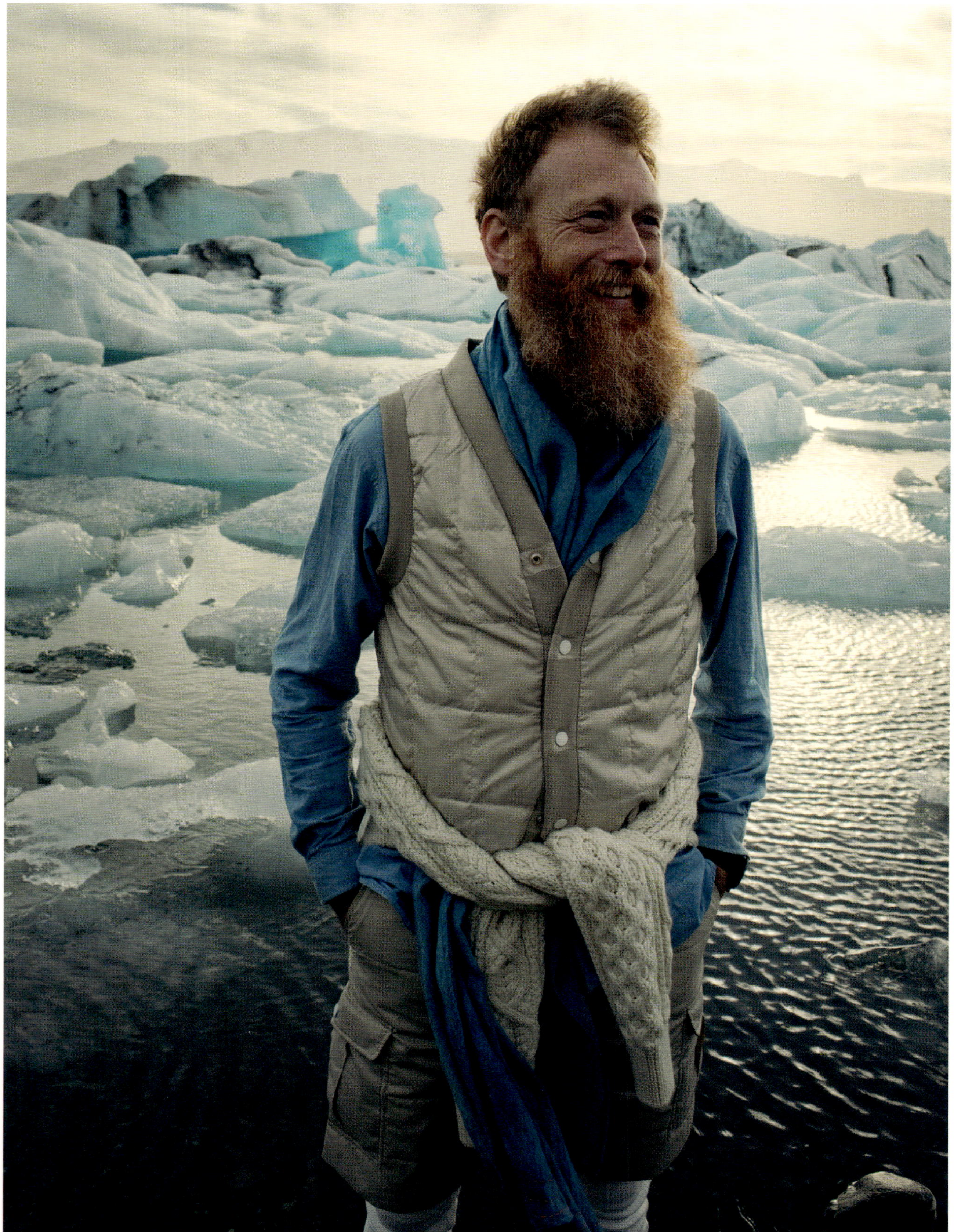

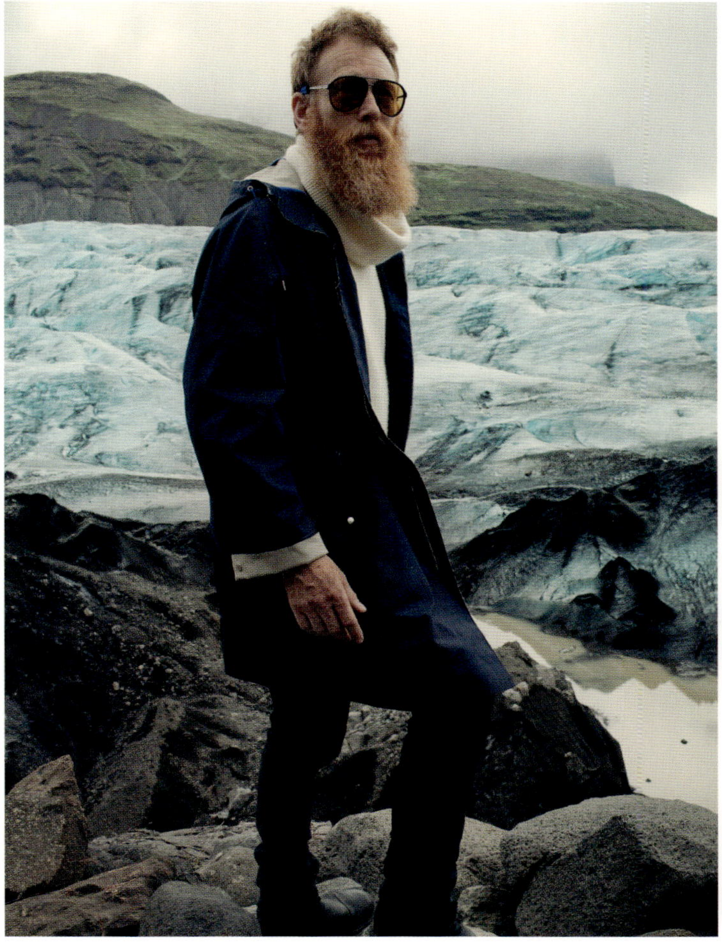

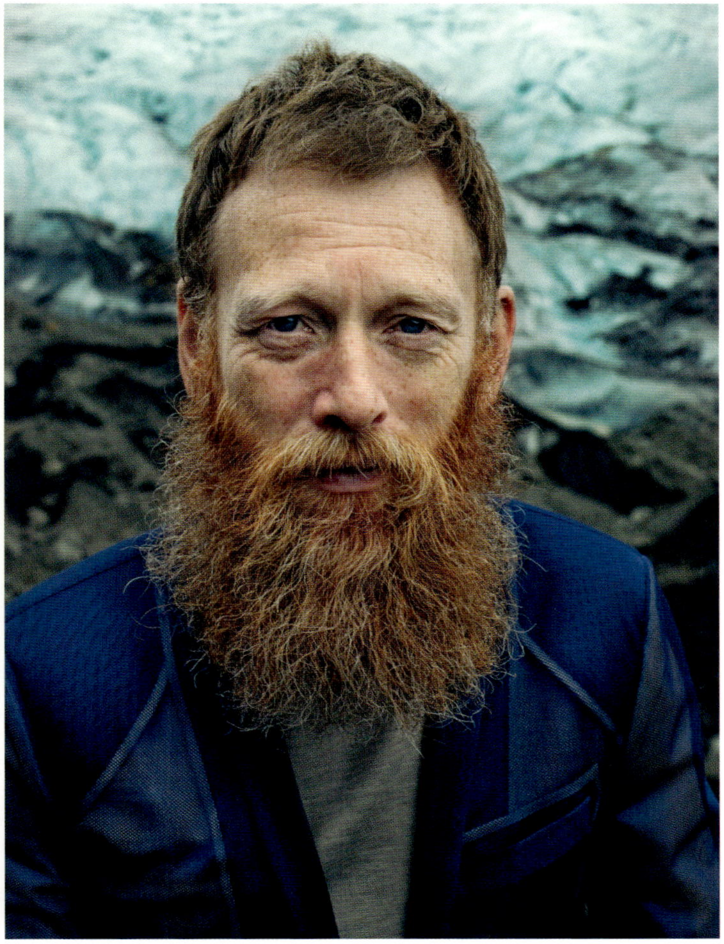

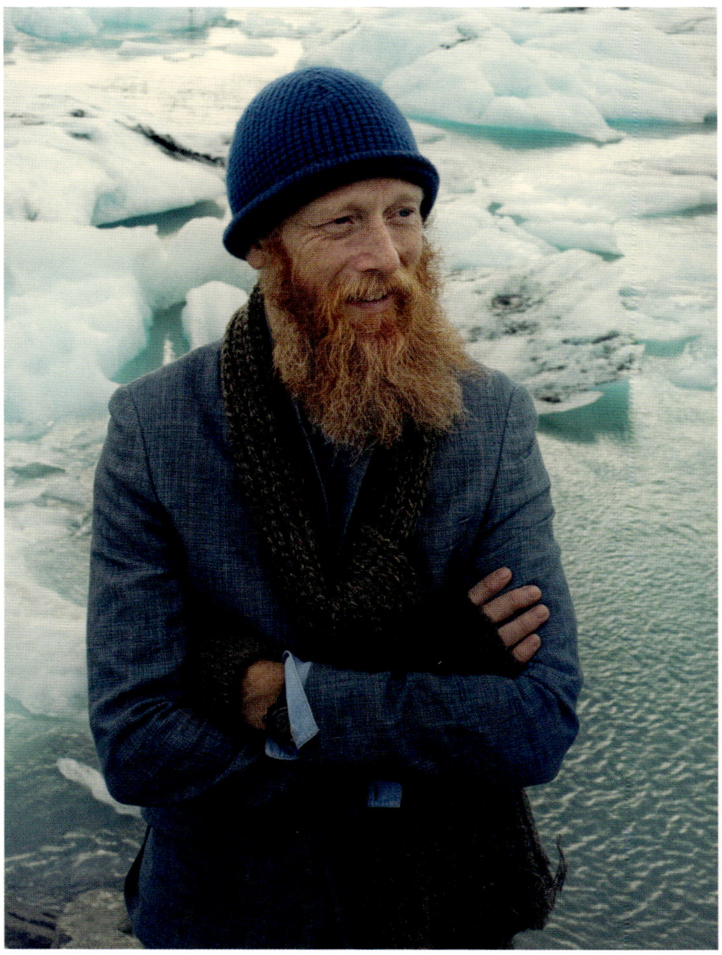

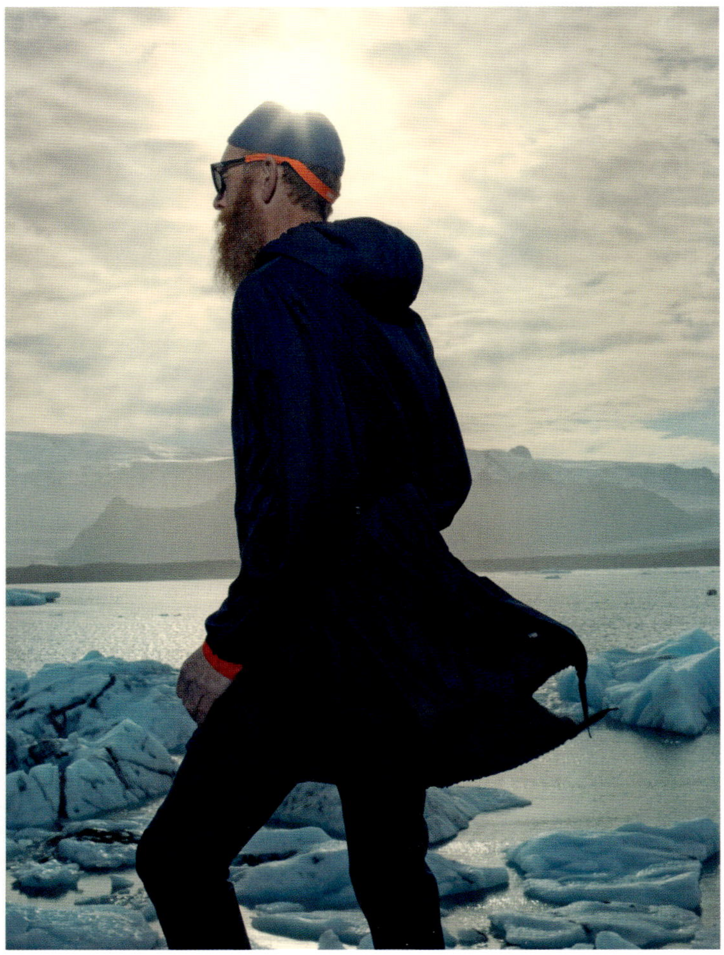

THIERRY BOUËT FRANCE

2ND PLACE
FASHION & BEAUTY

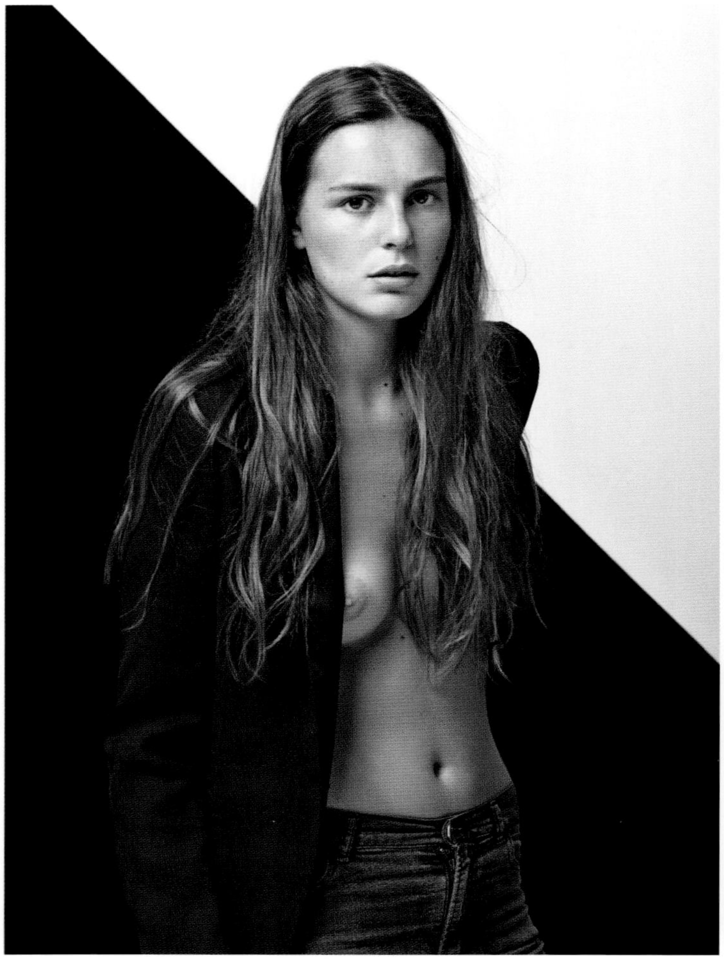

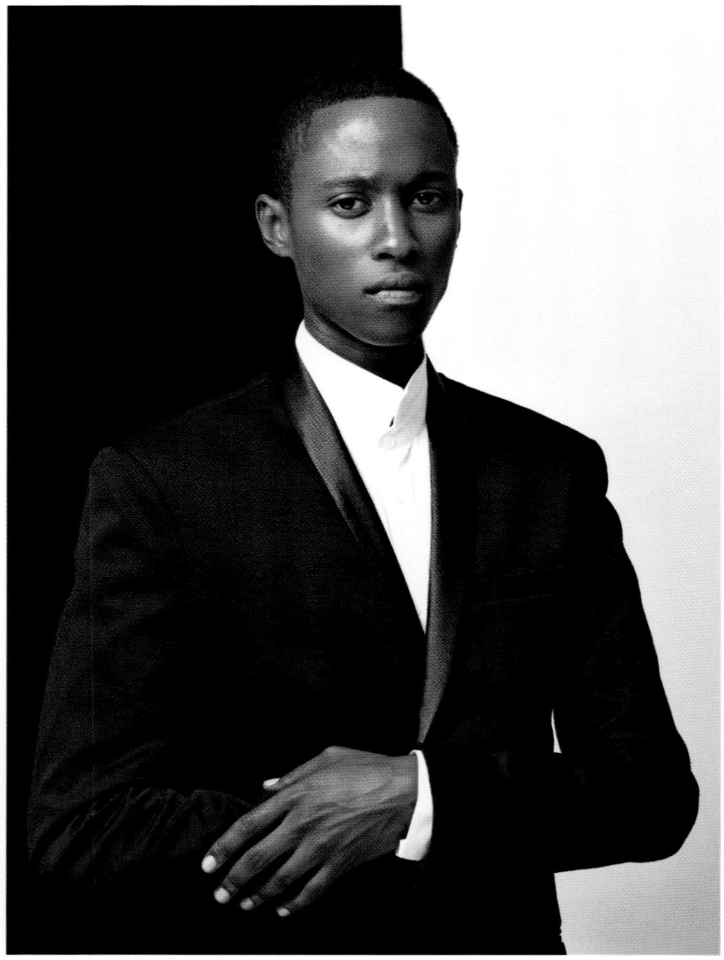

Parisian Twenties. Portraits of a generation in their twenties living in Paris. These privileged kids enjoy a carefree existence. These are studio portraits of people wearing the same jacket.

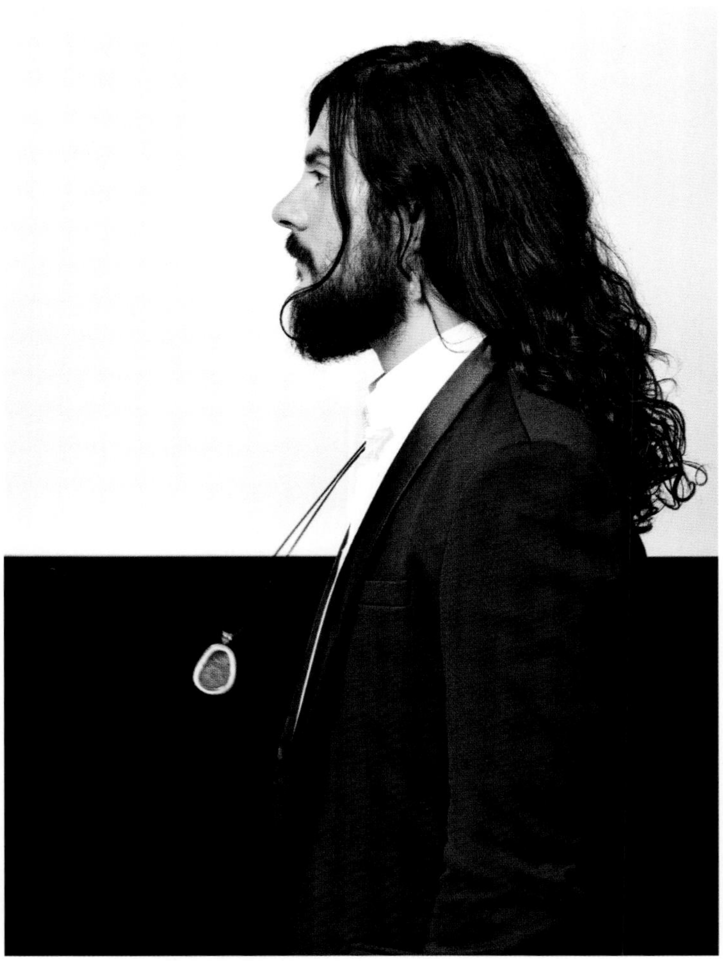

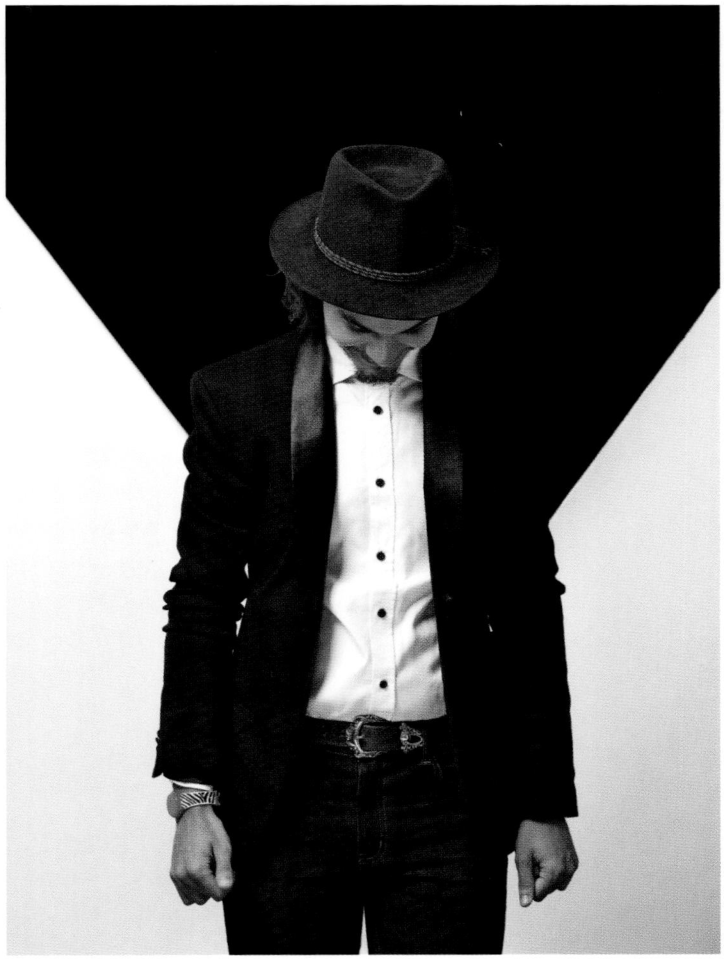

ALICE PAVESI FIORI ITALY

3RD PLACE
FASHION & BEAUTY

ATTESE - Expectations. Expectation is what inspired this work of fashion. The idea I began from is that every day, all of us are expecting different things in different ways to a greater or lesser extent. We are expecting the bus, a baby, the end of the day, a smile, promotion at work, our turn at the doctor's, the rain to stop falling, the love of our life. With these fashion photos I wanted to re-create stories of expectation which, even if suspended in time and space, belong to our daily lives.

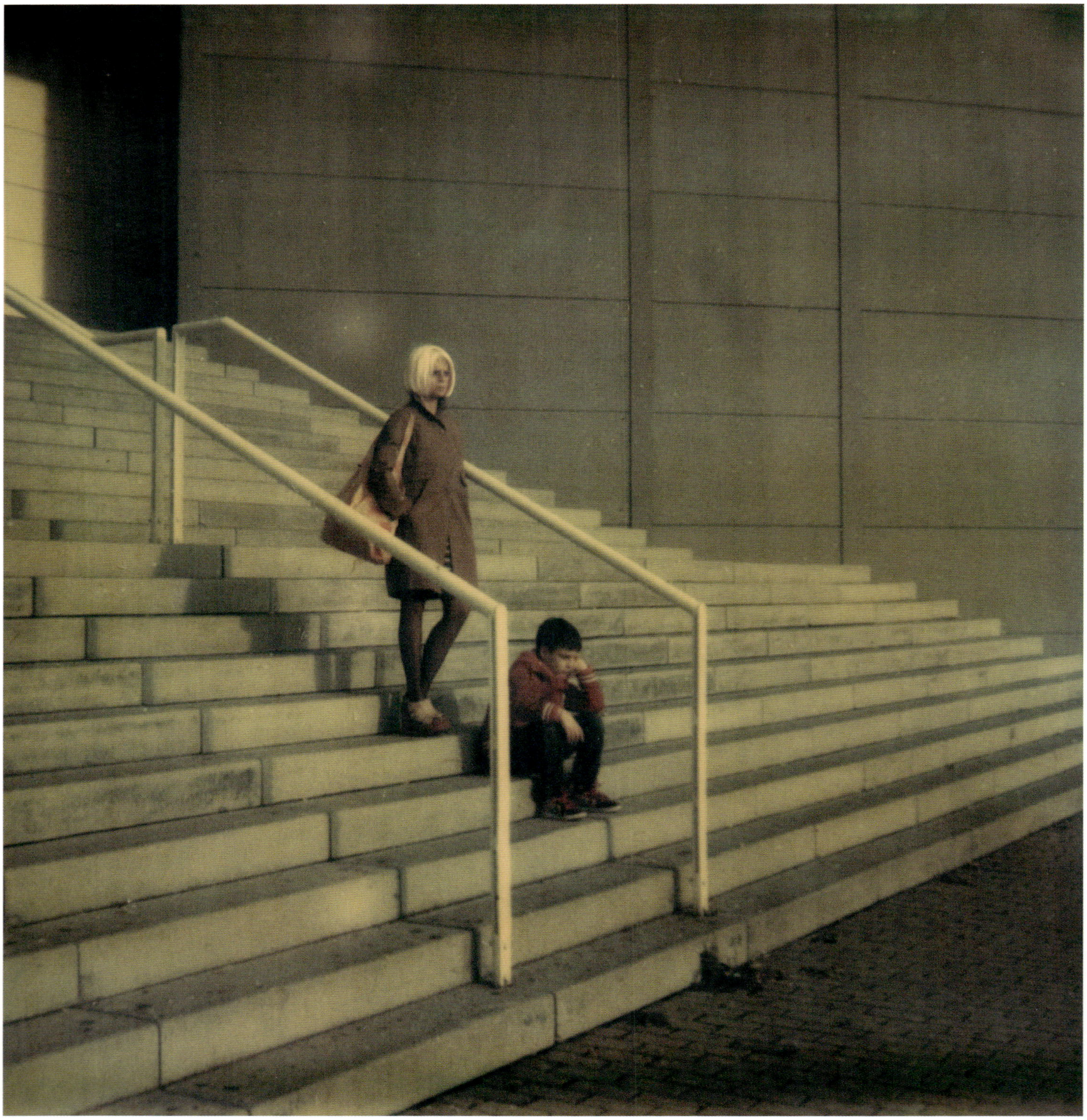

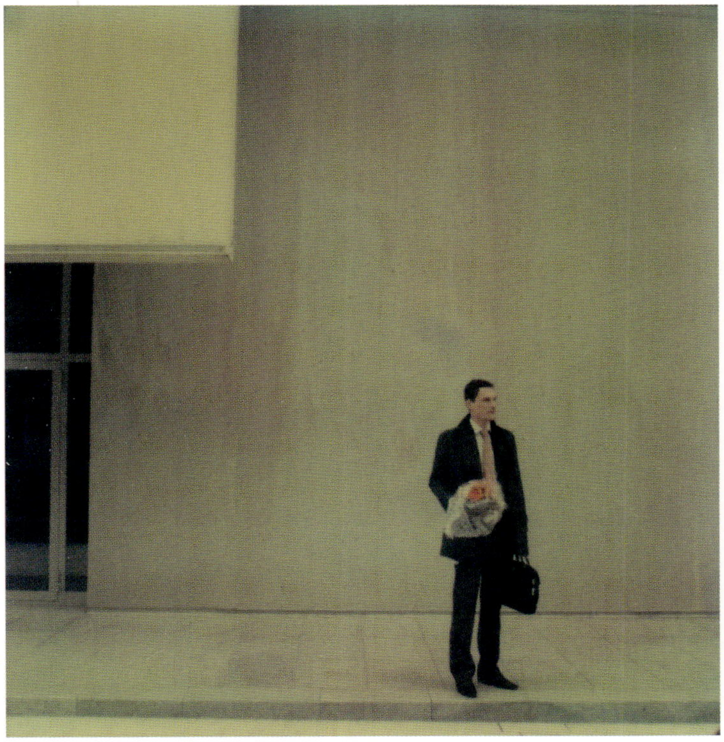

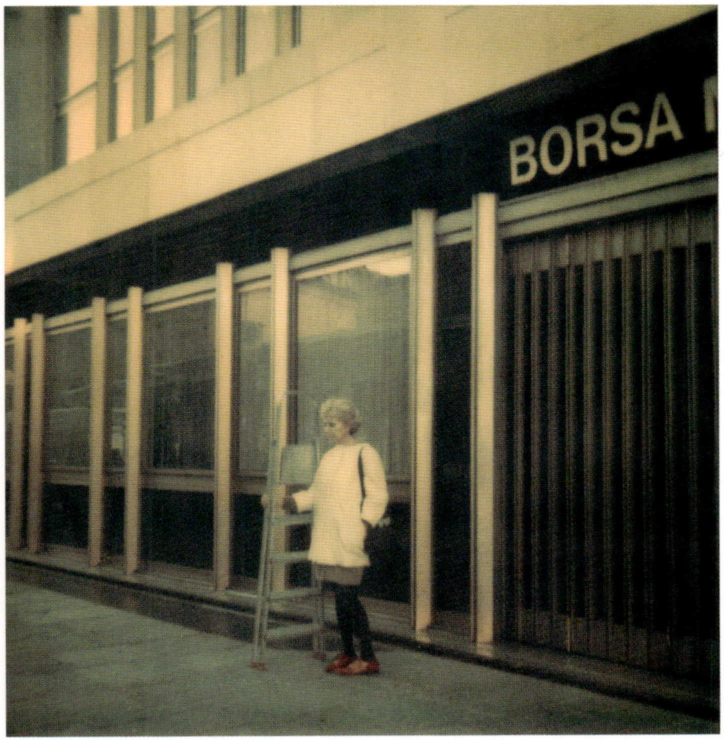
BORSA

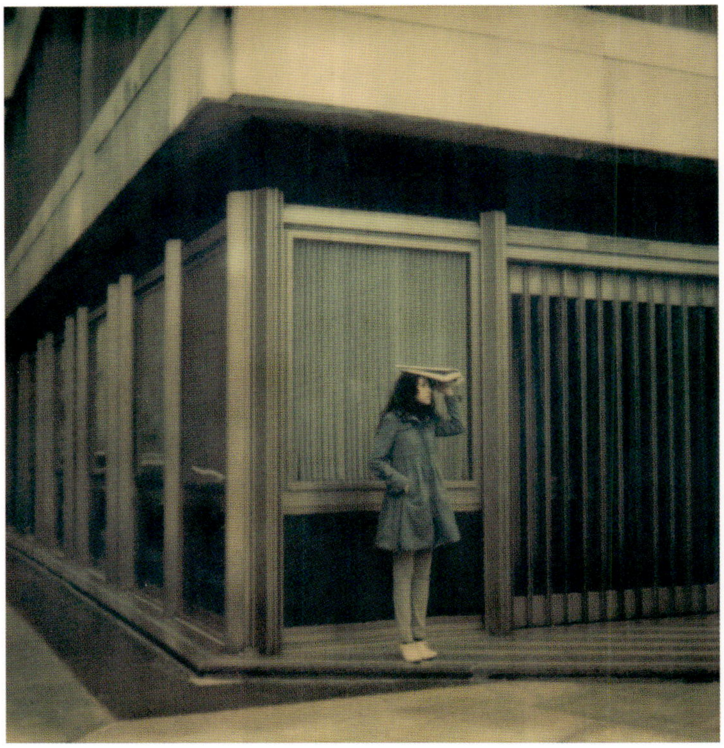

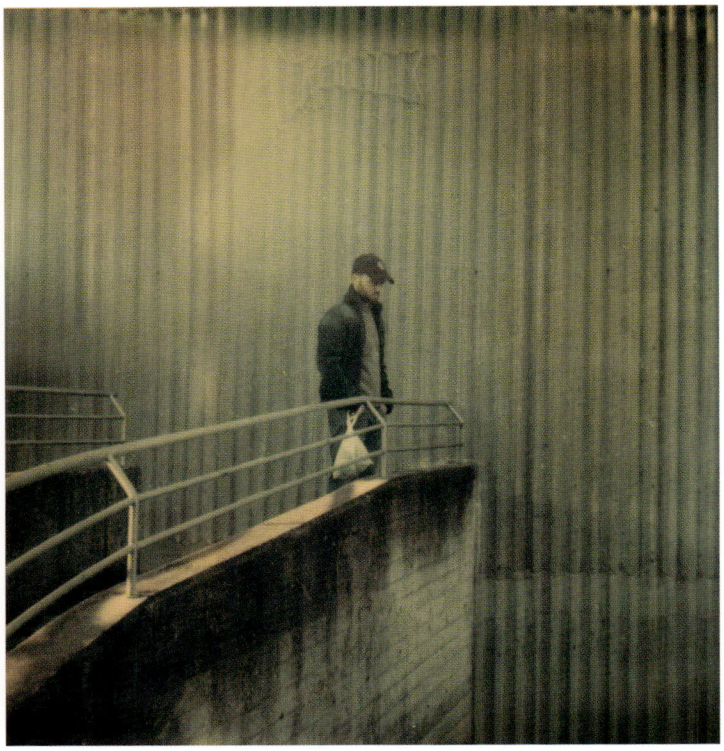

NENAD SALJIC CROATIA

1ST PLACE
LANDSCAPE

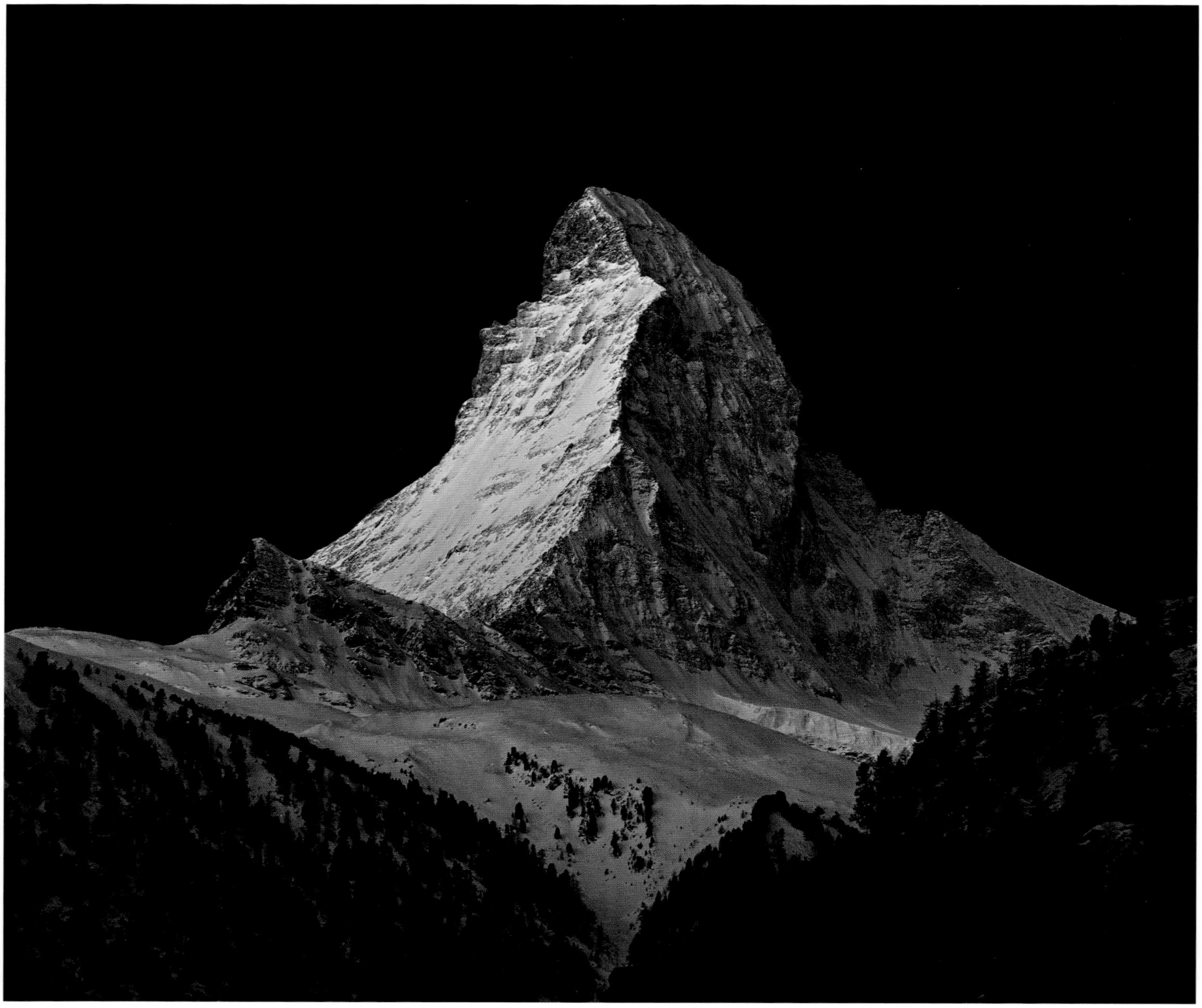

A Portrait of the Matterhorn. When I was young, I fantasised about climbing the Matterhorn, the last great Alpine peak to be conquered. Its first ascent in 1865 marked the end of the golden age of alpinism. Its North Face, among the 'Three Great Problems' in the Alps, was not climbed until 1931. I have been around Zermatt countless times, trying to capture the exquisiteness of this magical peak and its endless state of change; to compress the passing of time, the beauty of the wind and the clouds dancing around the mountain. This portfolio is a kind of memento to all climbers who dared to go there and for those who never returned.

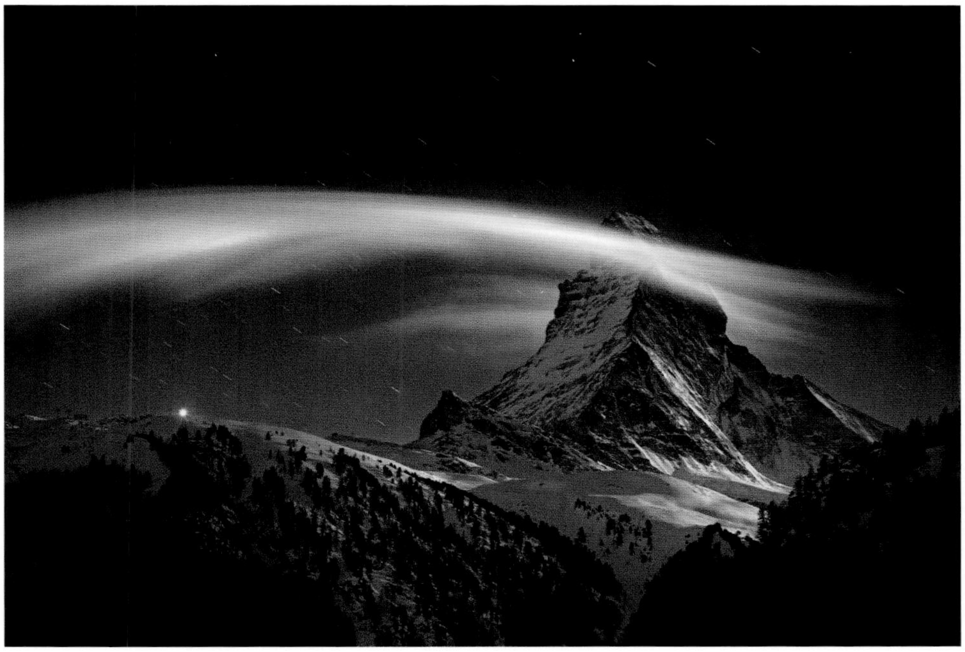

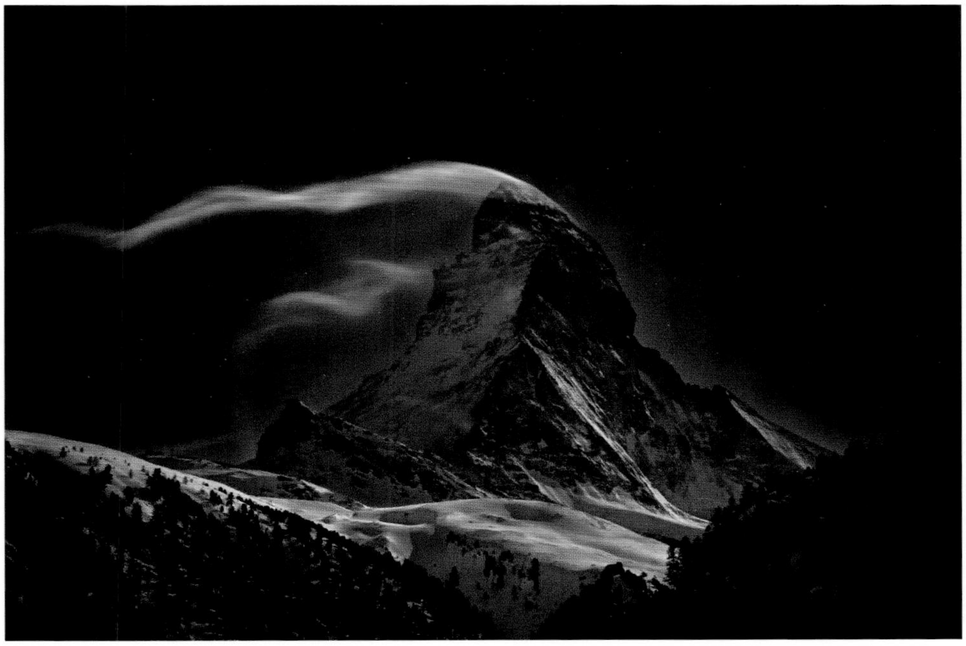

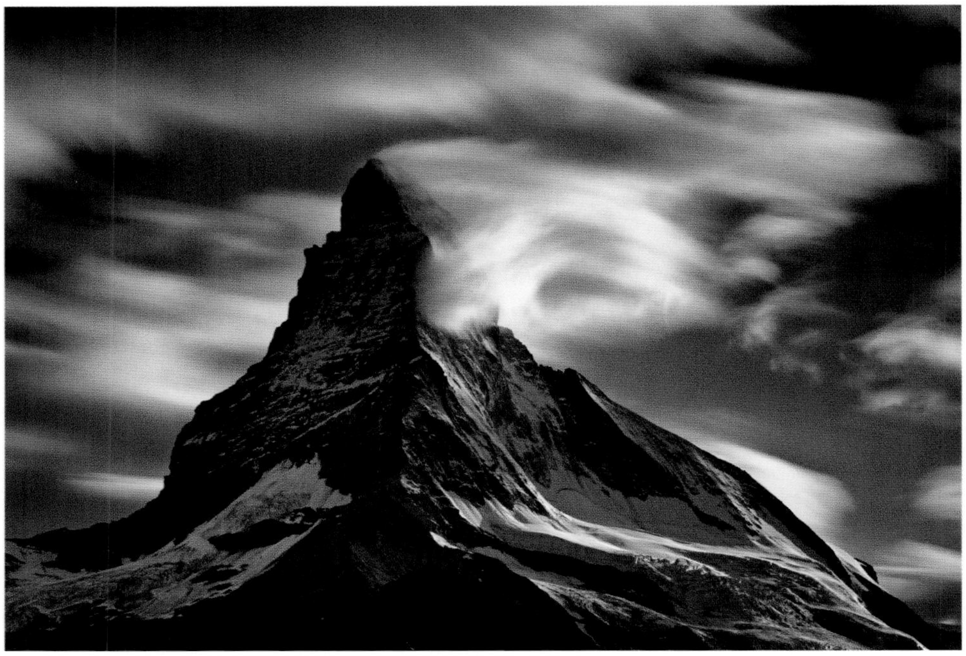

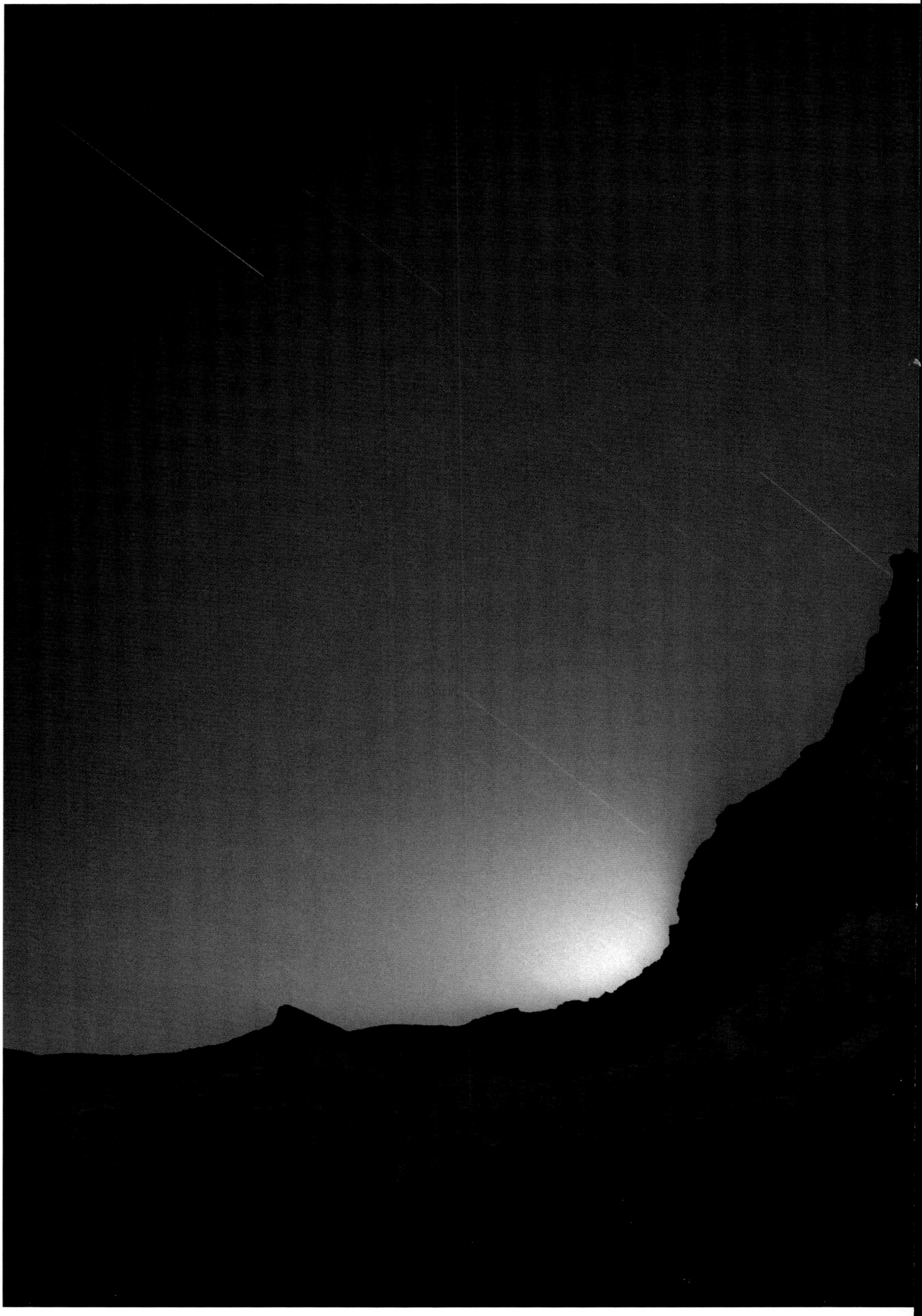

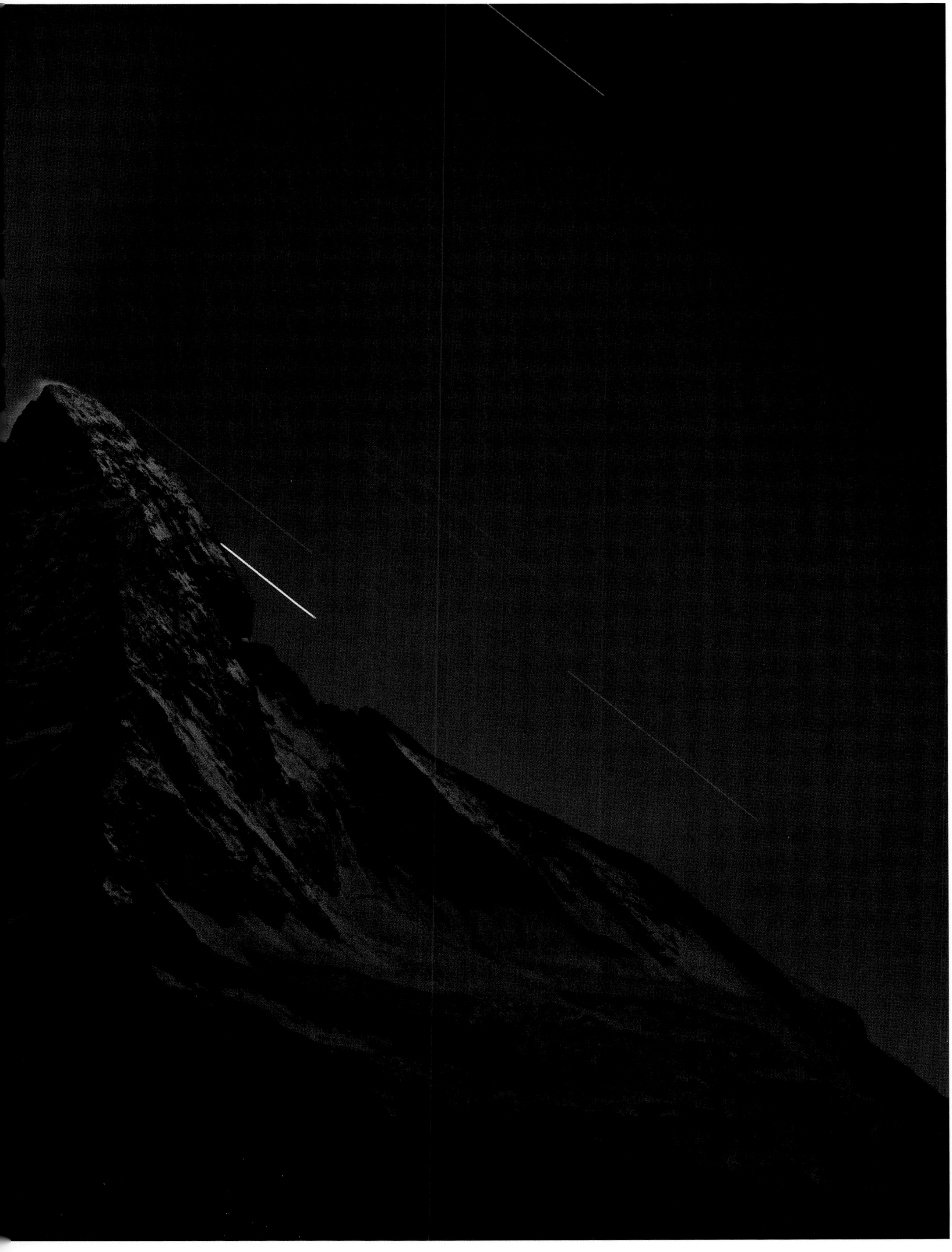

REGIS BOILEAU FRANCE

2ND PLACE
LANDSCAPE

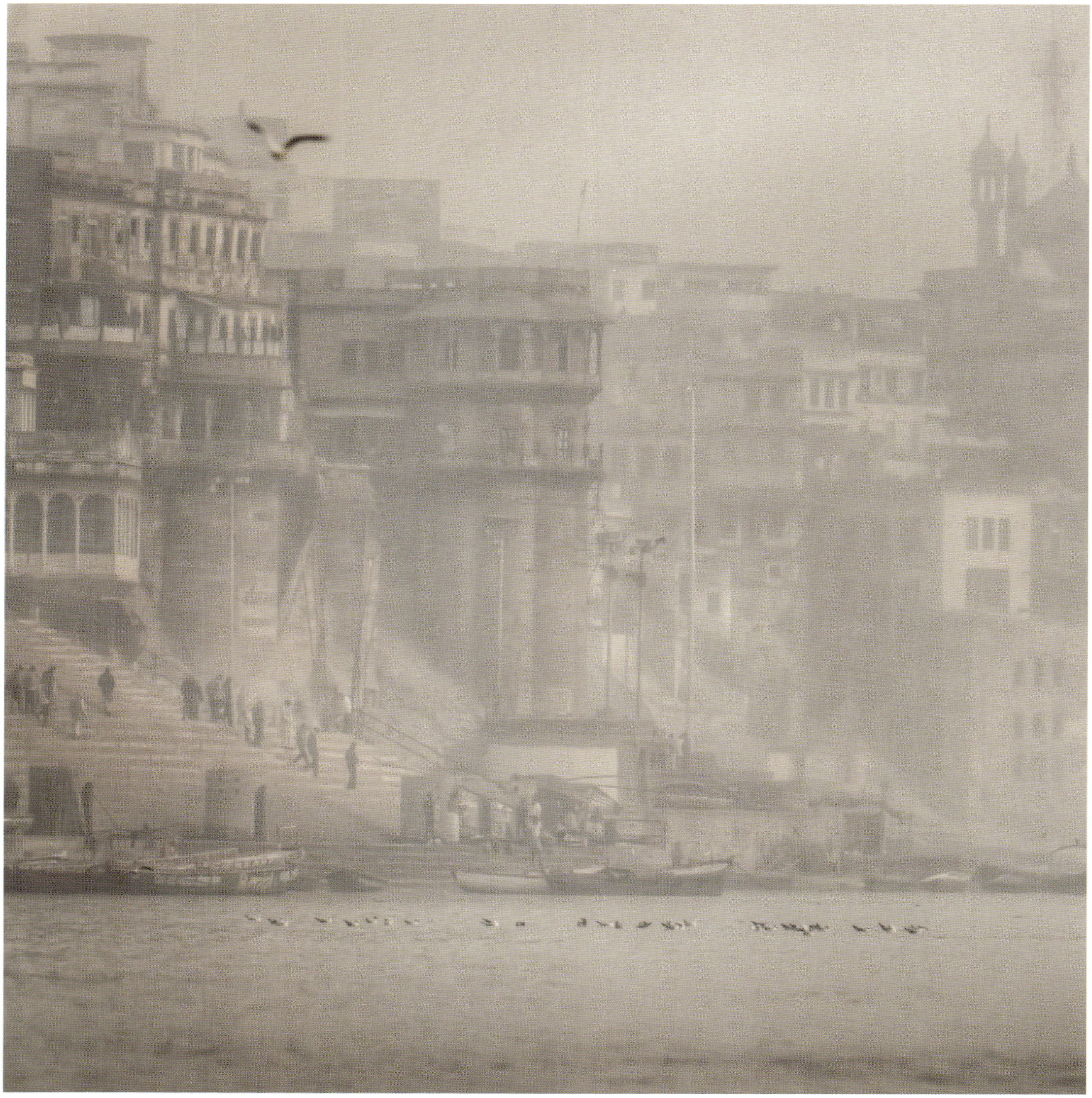

Millenniums of millions gods. A series on the landscapes made not by millions of years of tectonic activity, but by millennia of men and monsoons. Here, hundreds of generations have been born and died, while tropical rains gnawed at the stones. Benares is one of the holiest cities in India, a place seen as the house of the God Shiva. And if some brick crumbles in your hands, if the wood rots, these just contribute to a new stratum on which the city stands. The particular tones of this series come from the fact these photos were made in a dense fog. The mood as it appears is close to what I felt: an eternal land, eroding every second.

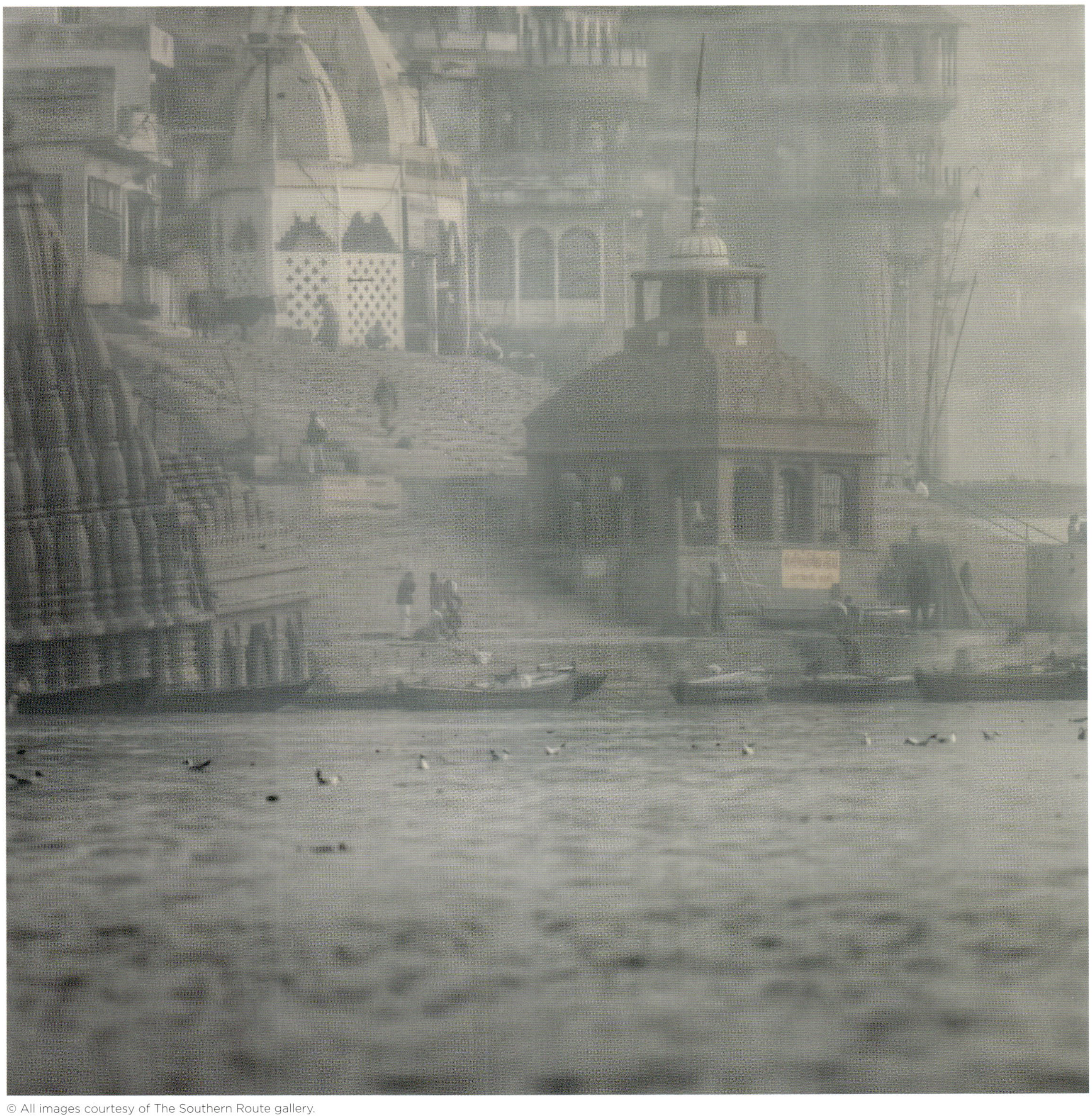

ARJEN SCHMITZ NETHERLANDS

3RD PLACE
LANDSCAPE

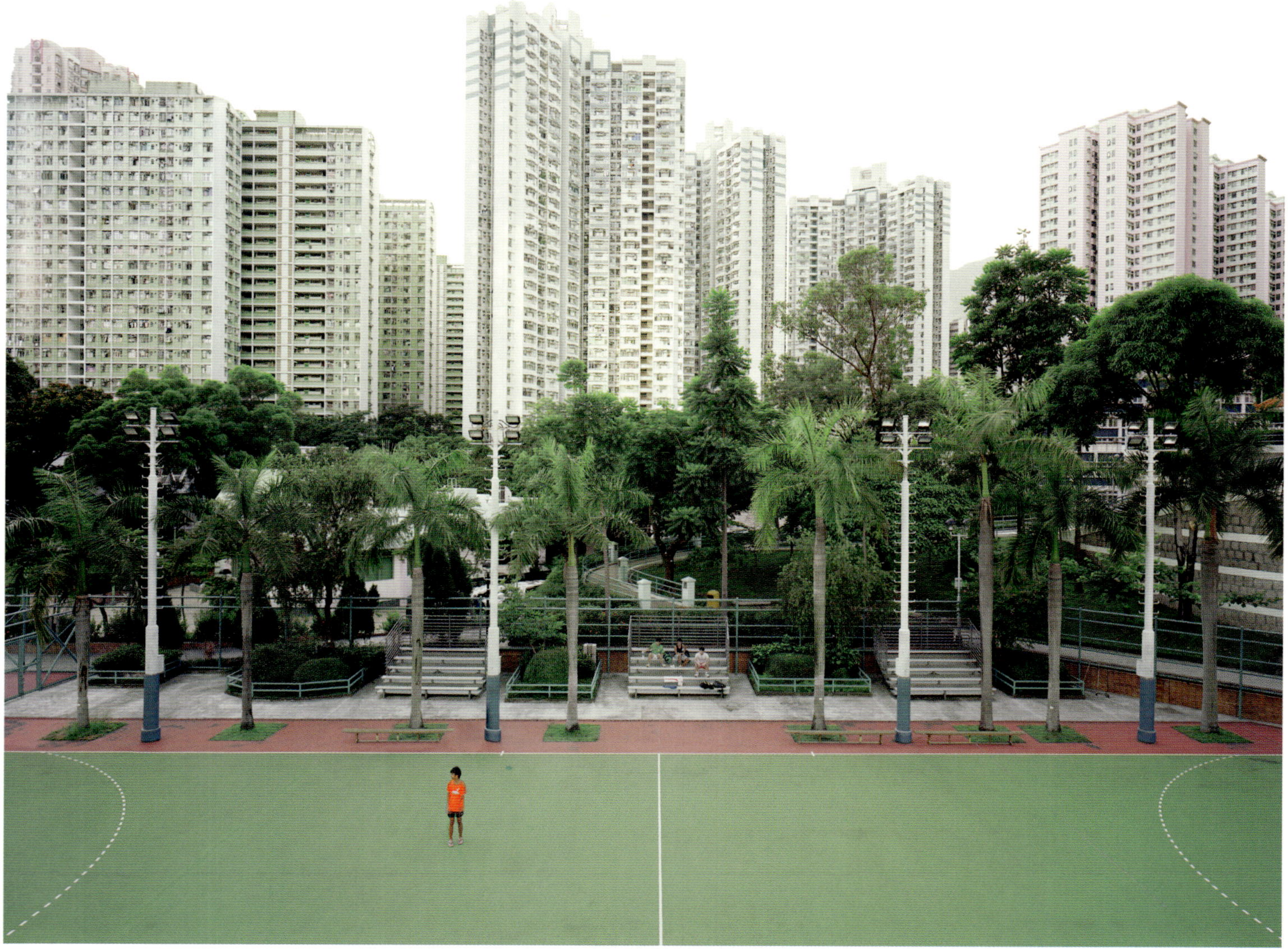

Hong Kong. All these photographs were taken in Hong Kong. This is my first series of independent work. The images concern living places and the way that we deal with public space.

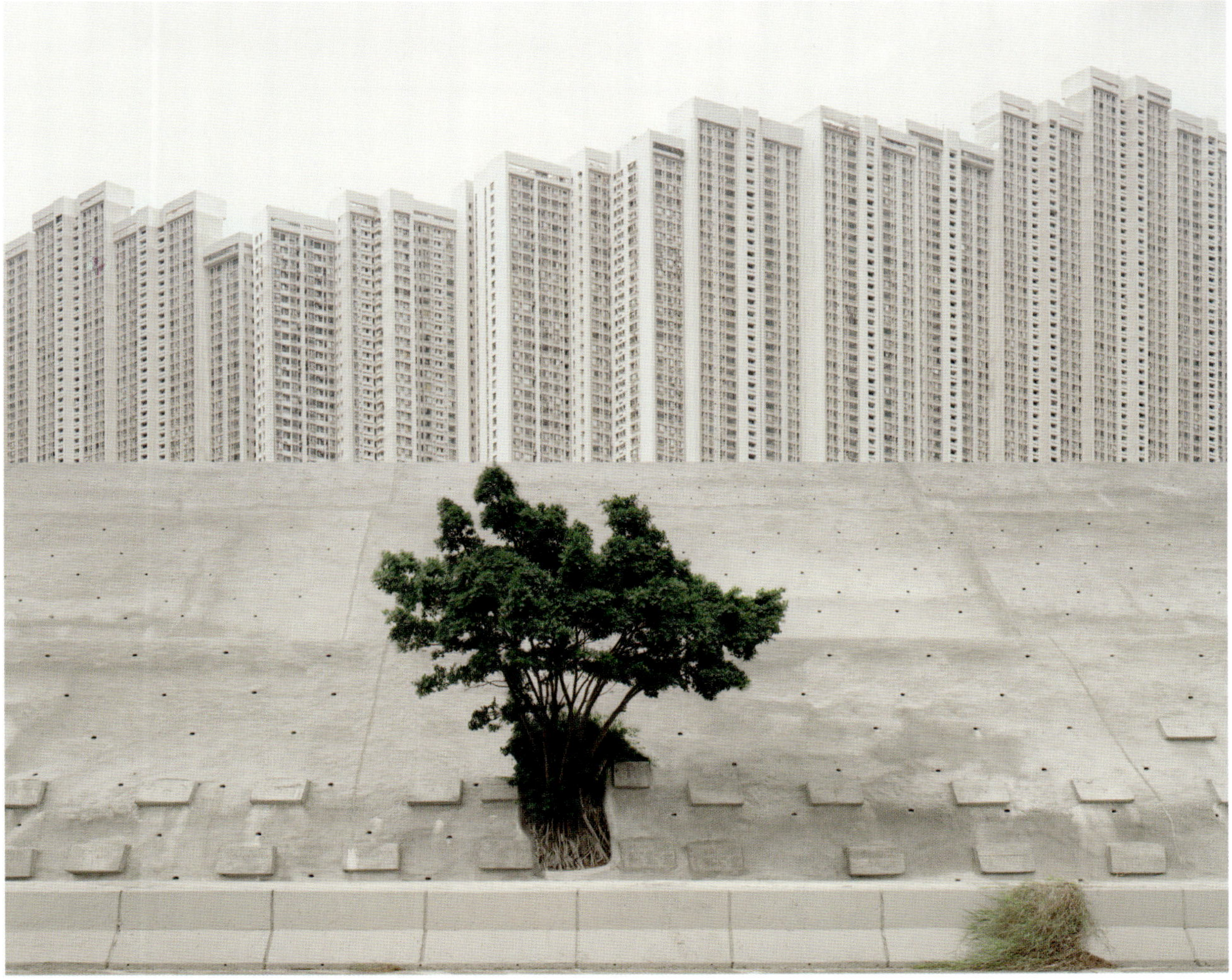

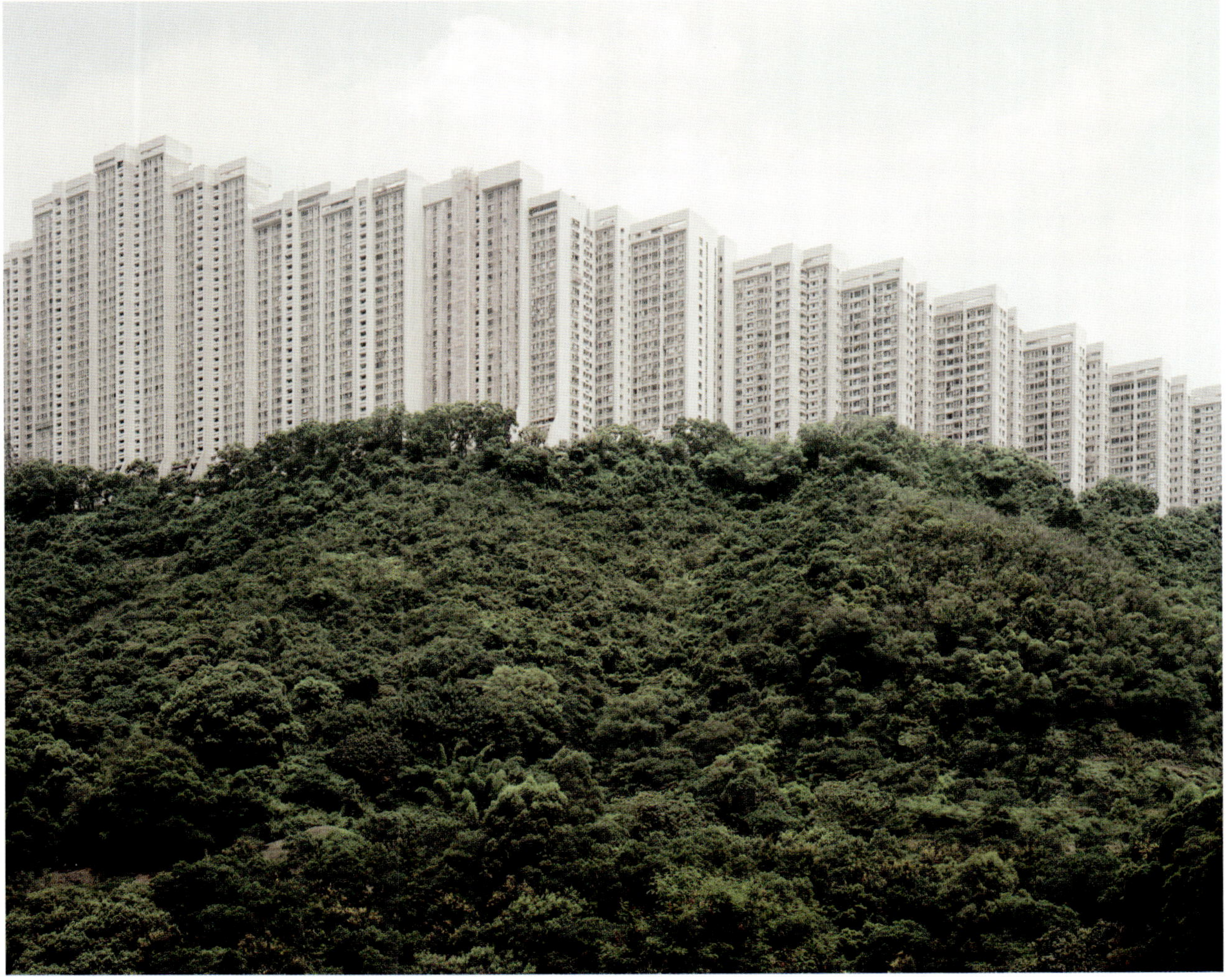

ALICE CAPUTO ITALY

1ST PLACE
LIFESTYLE

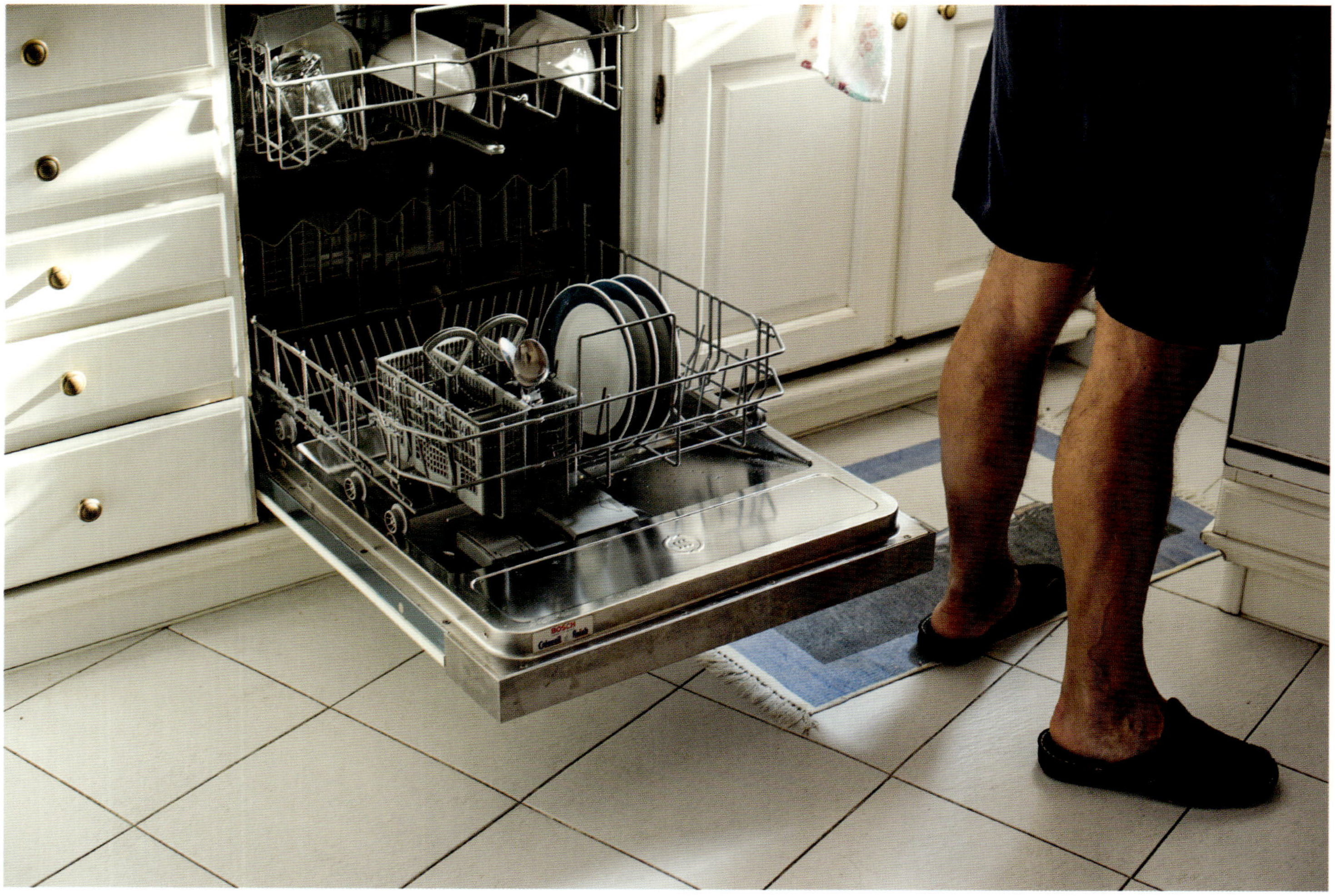

Summer Family. It's very normal for me to look at things as though they were on film.

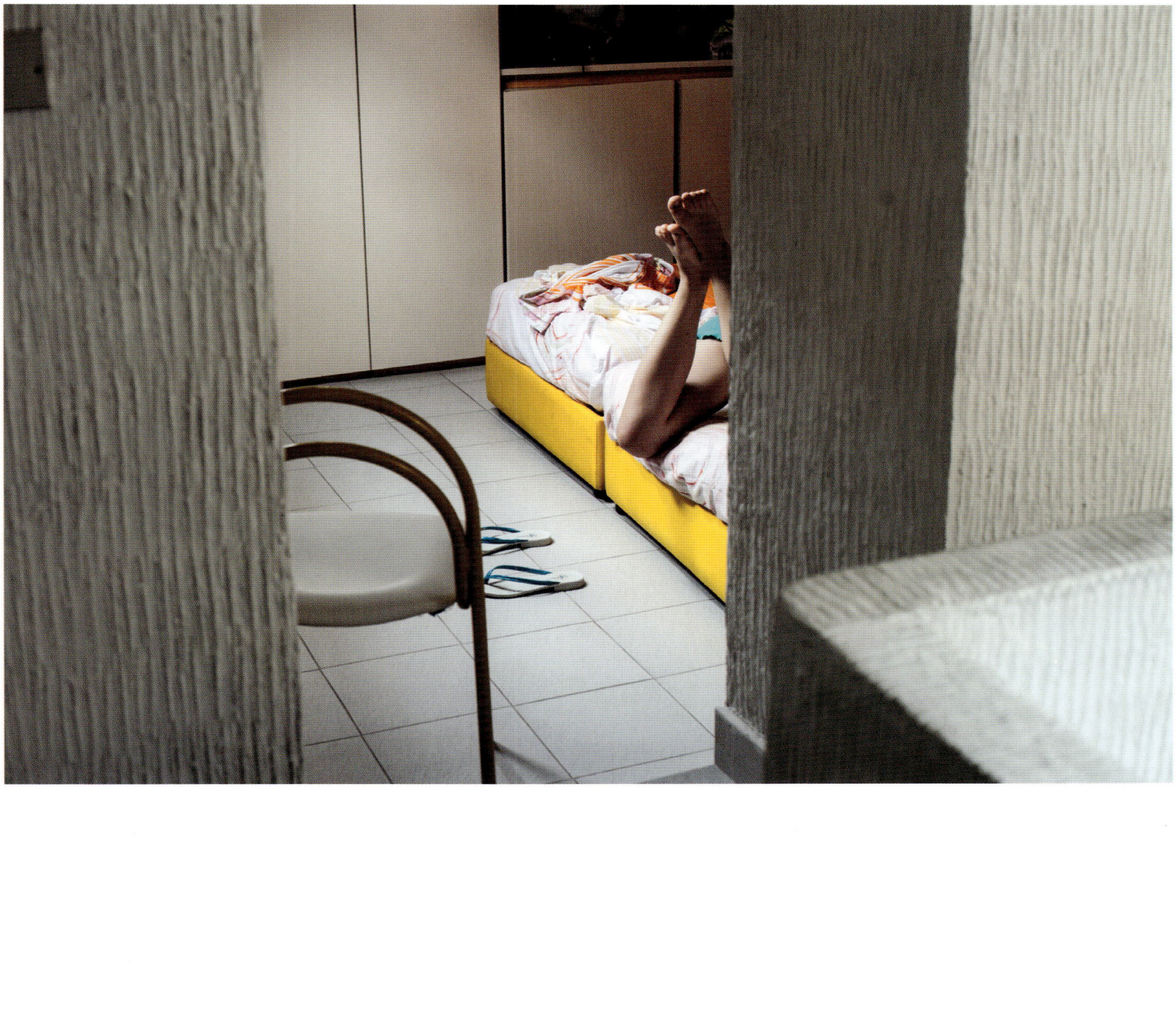

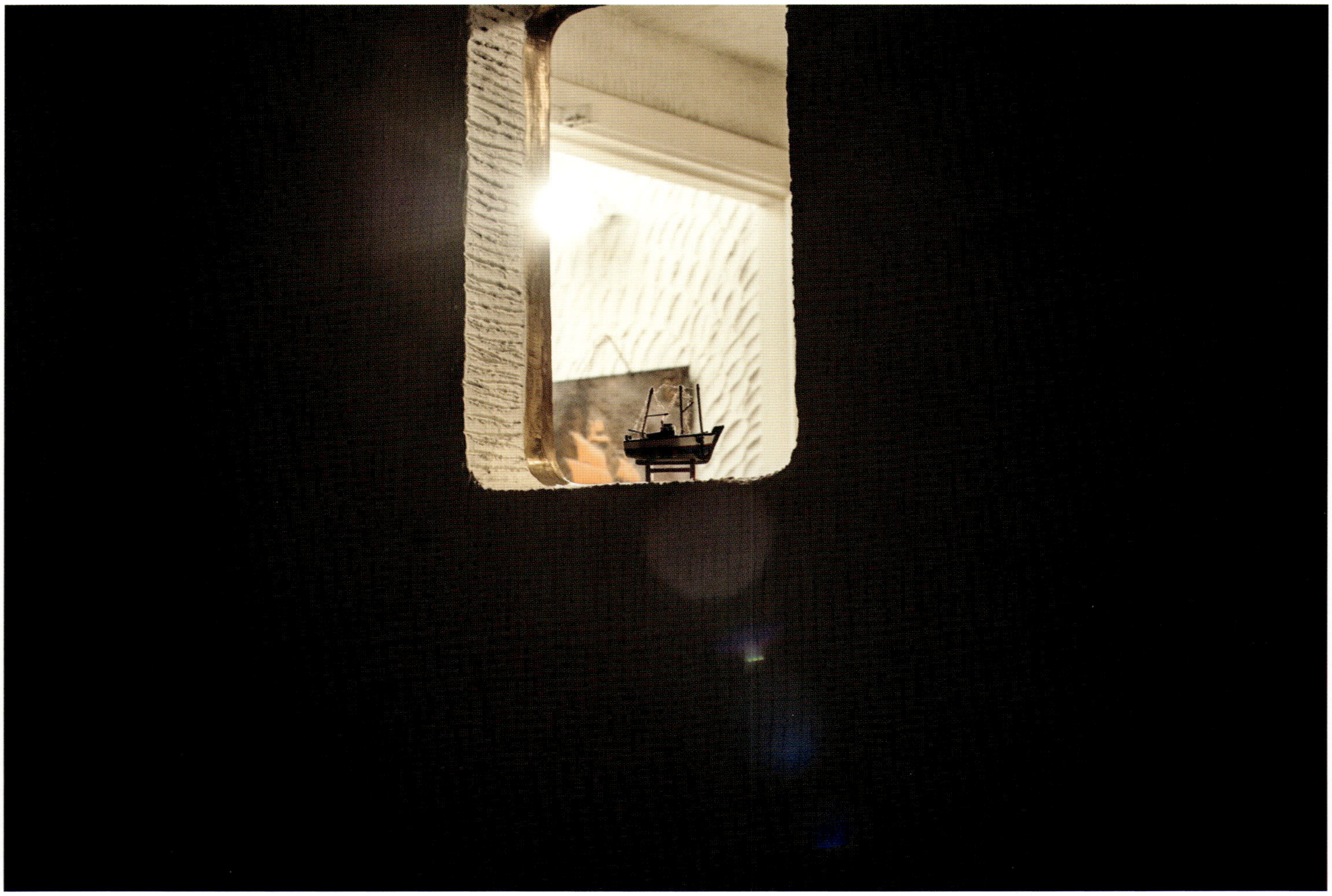

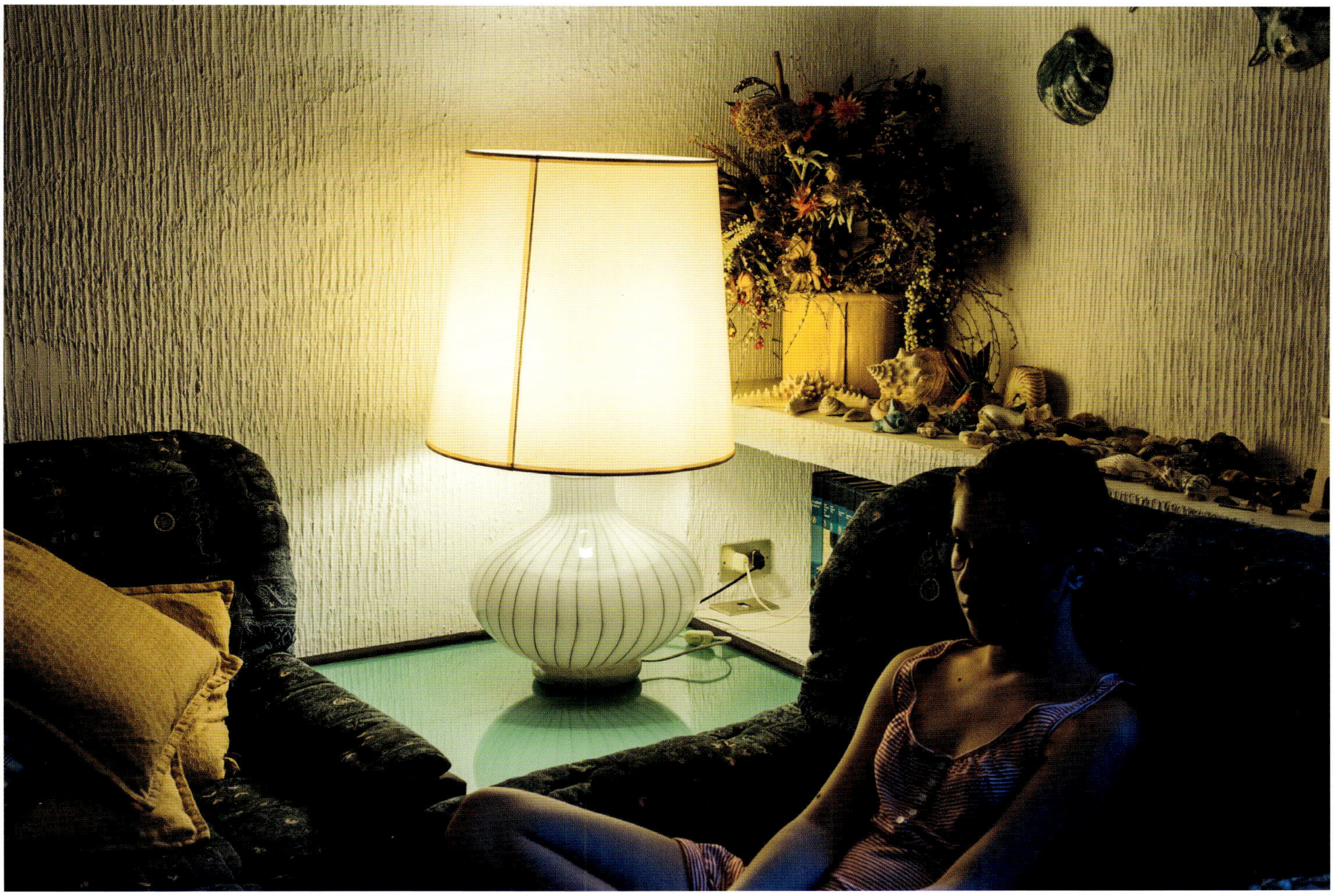

KUNI TAKAHASHI JAPAN

2ND PLACE
LIFESTYLE

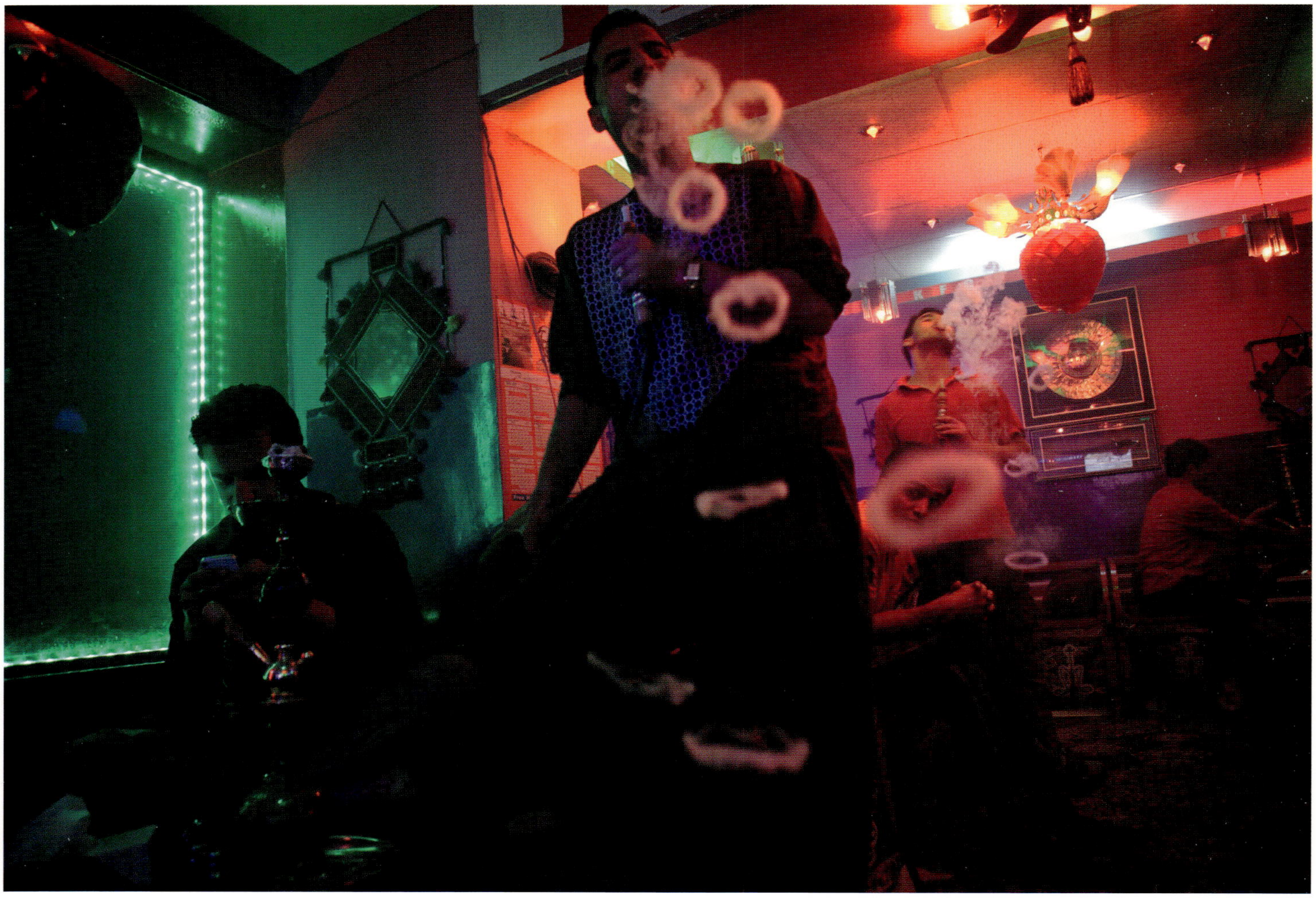

Life goes on – Afghanistan. Over the past three decades, Afghanistan has been a battleground for strategic wars by larger external powers, and internal conflicts between ethnic groups. Despite fragile security and the constant threat of violence, with NATO and U.S. troops scheduled to withdraw in 2014, life in the country goes on, and Afghans try to make the most of it.

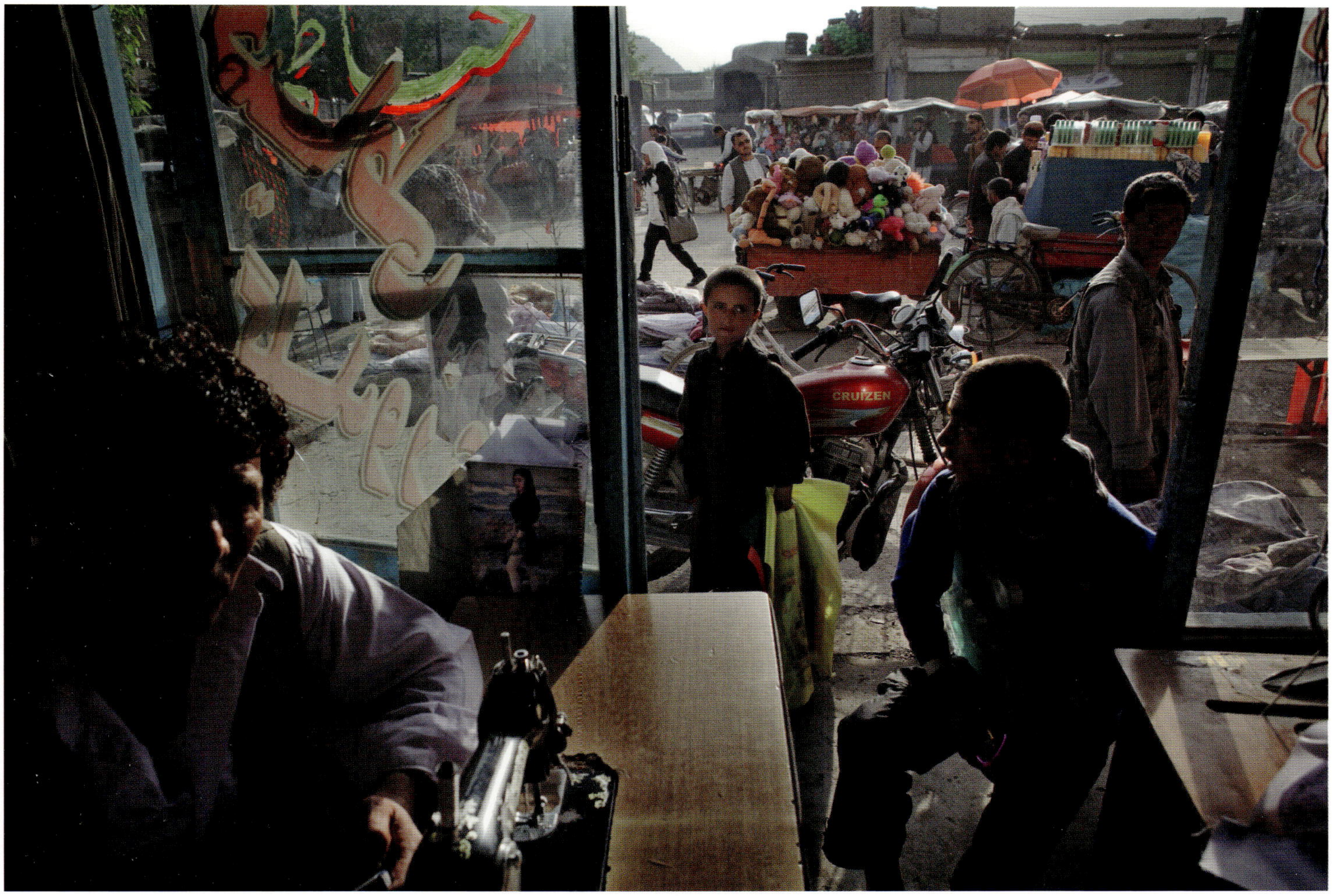
CRUIZEN

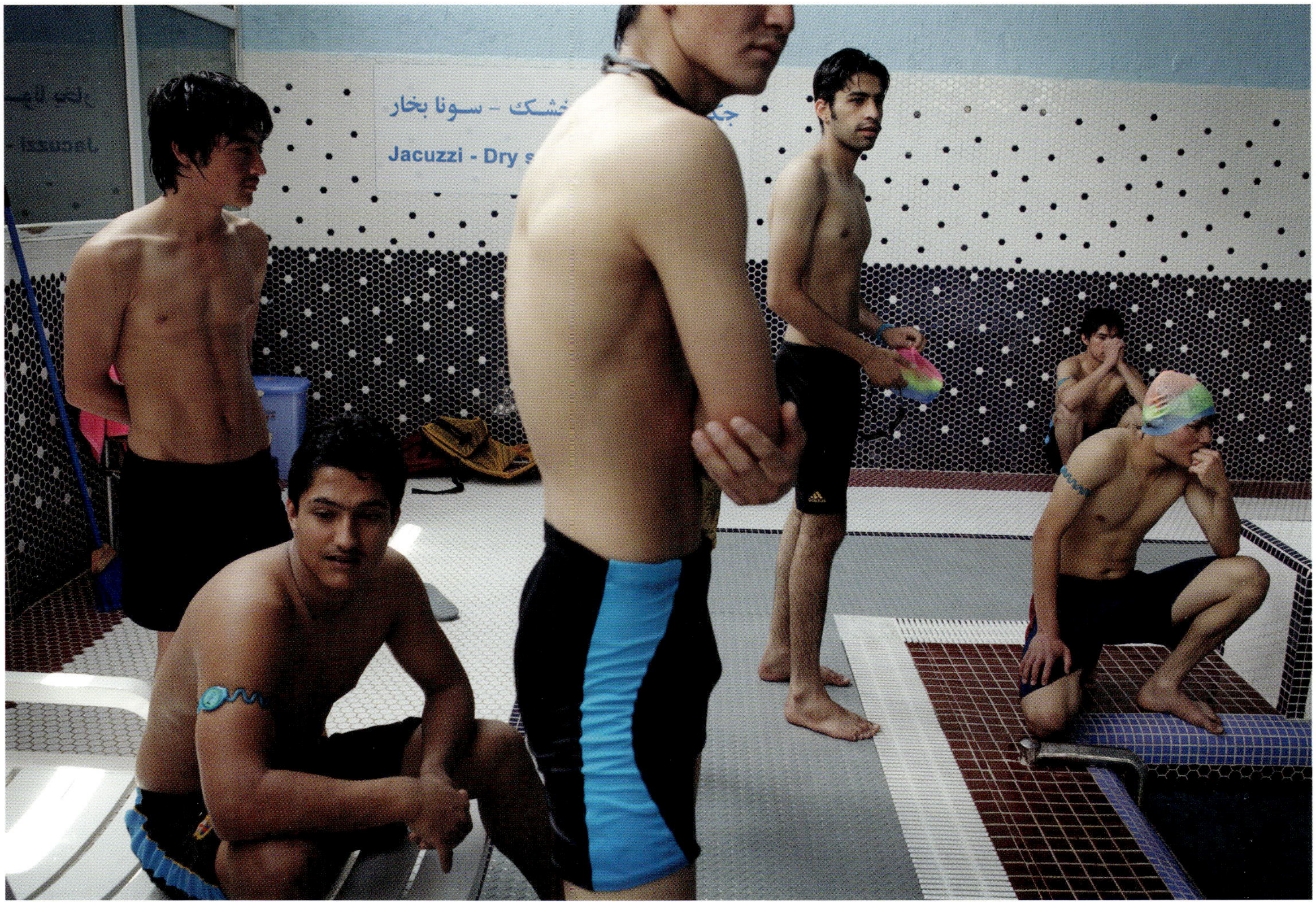
خشک - سونا بخار
Jacuzzi - Dry s

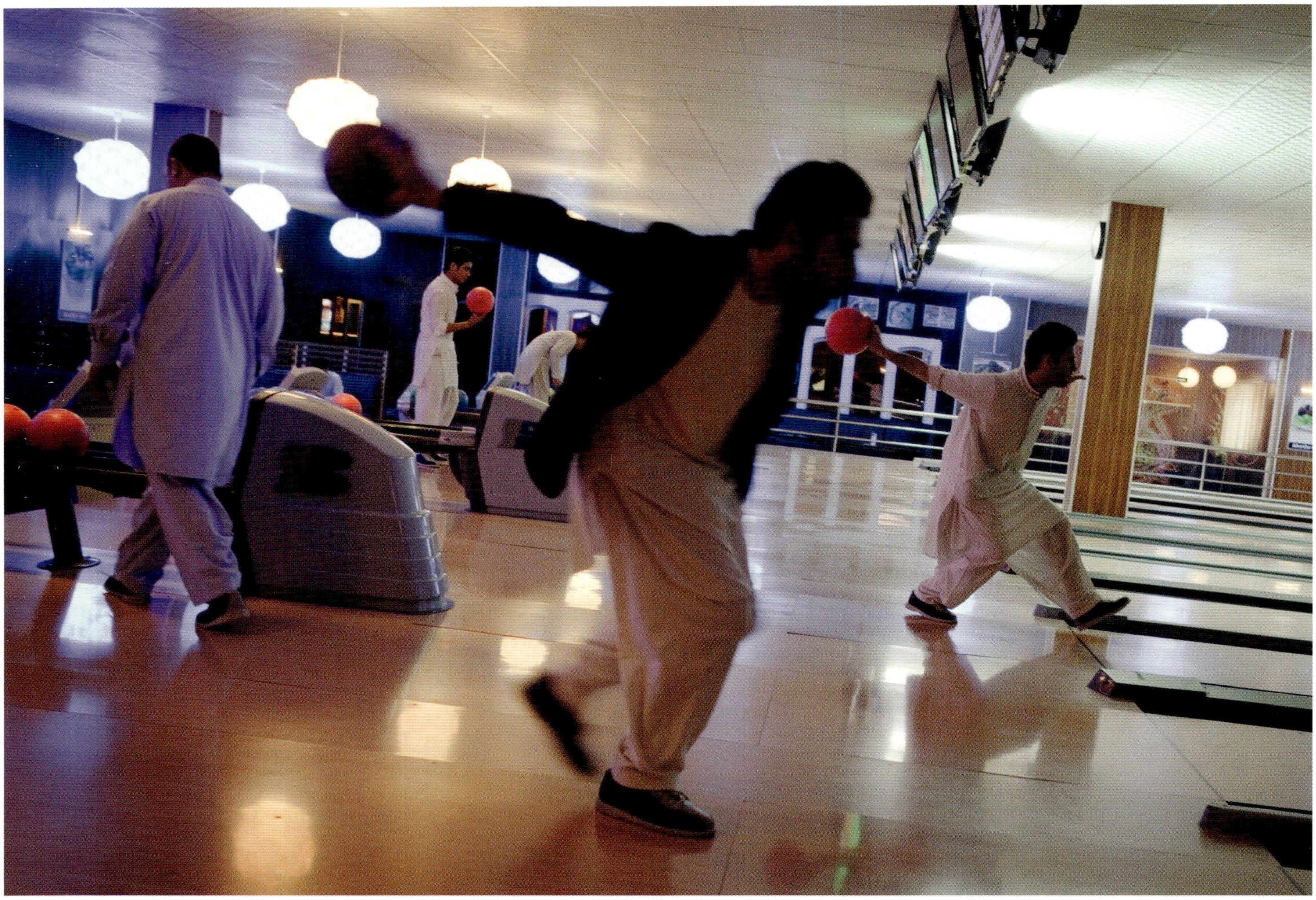

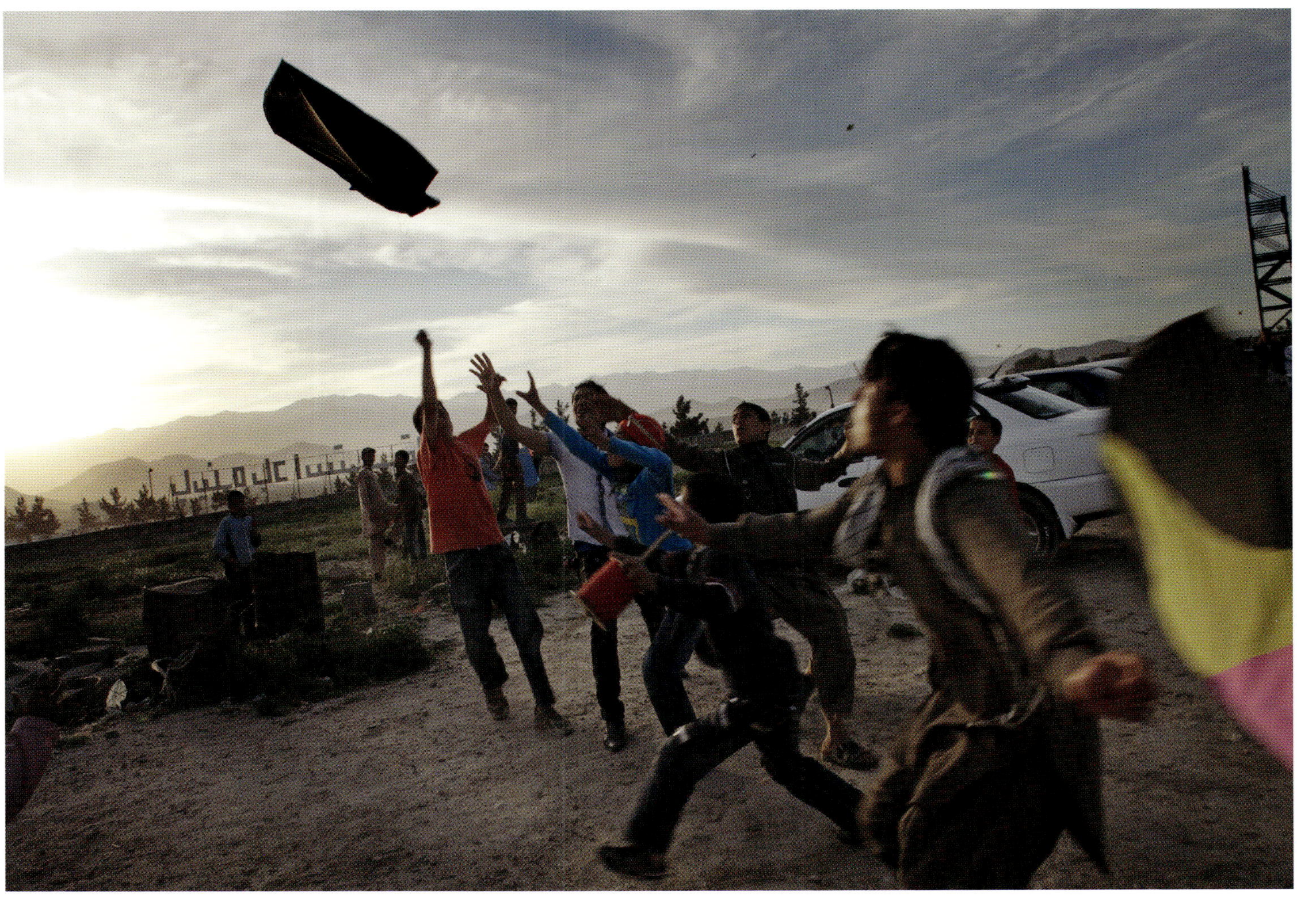

FAUSTO PODAVINI ITALY

3RD PLACE
LIFESTYLE

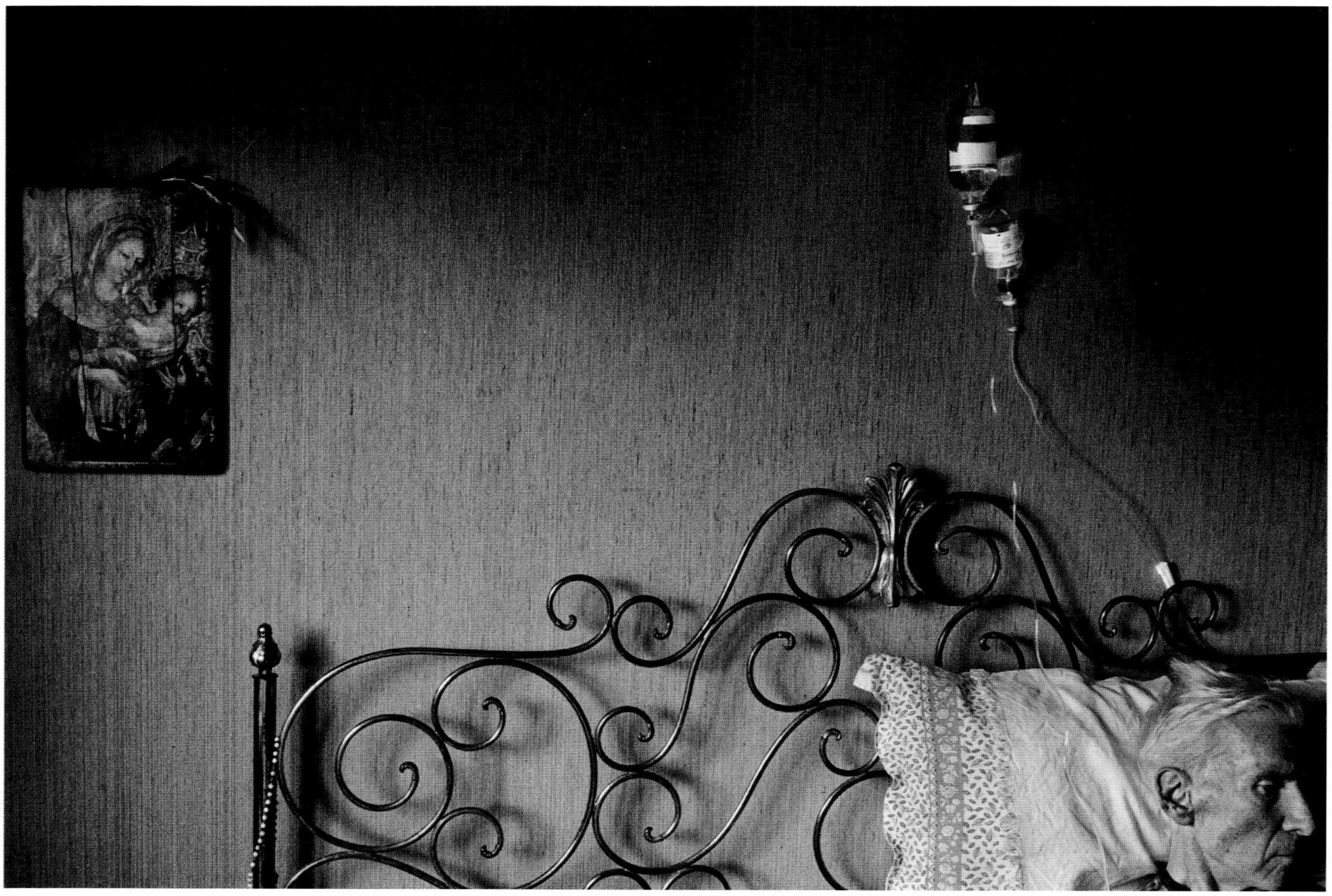

Mirella. Mirella is 71, and has spent 43 years of her life with the man she loves, years of difficulties overcome together, of laughter and good times, of family values passed on. When her husband developed Alzheimer's disease, she cared for him with strength and devotion, trying to look ahead, trying to believe that where there is life there is hope. His death brings immeasurable sorrow and loneliness, and she is left to face the biggest challenge of her life, racked by disbelief, anguish, resignation and helplessness. This is the story of a woman's love for her husband.

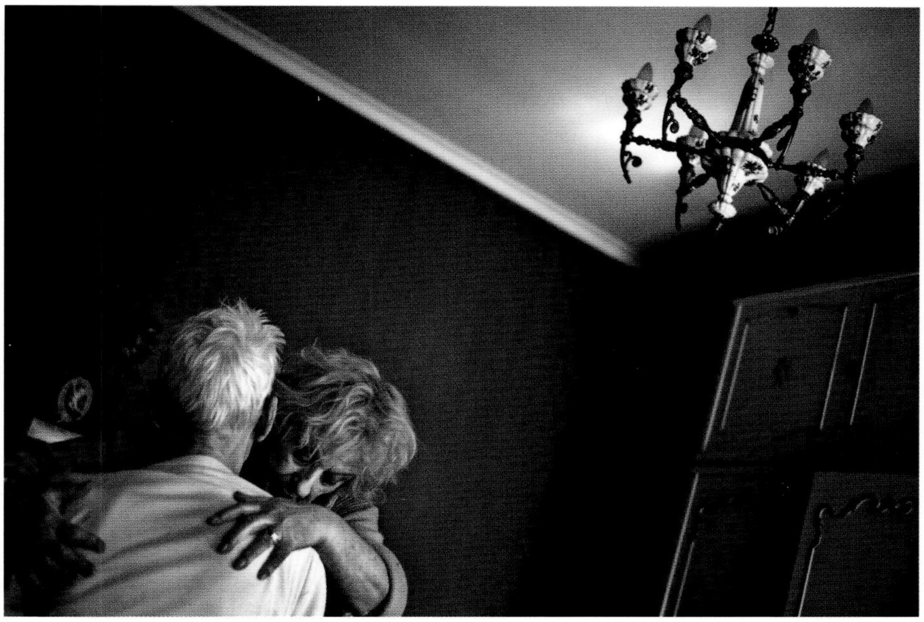

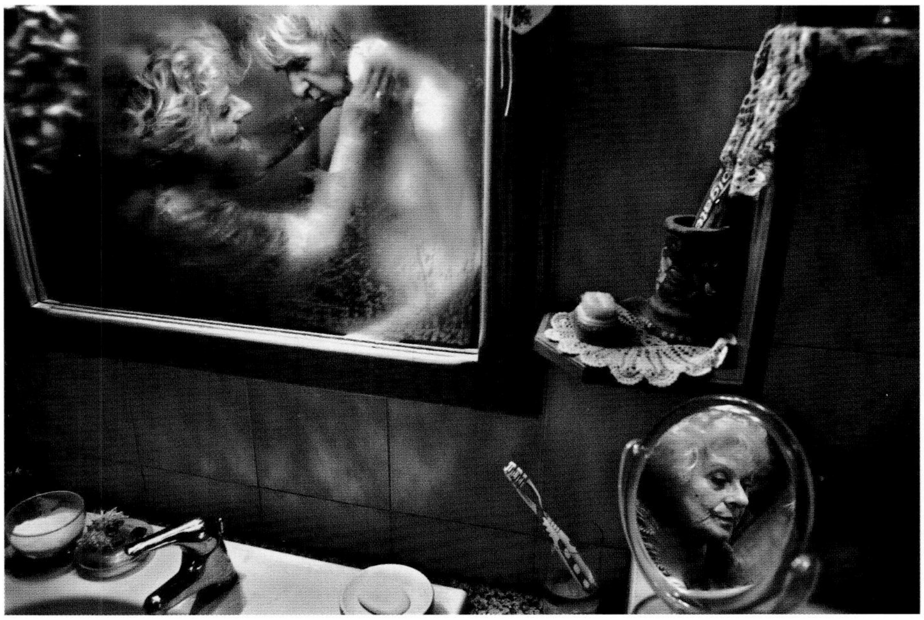

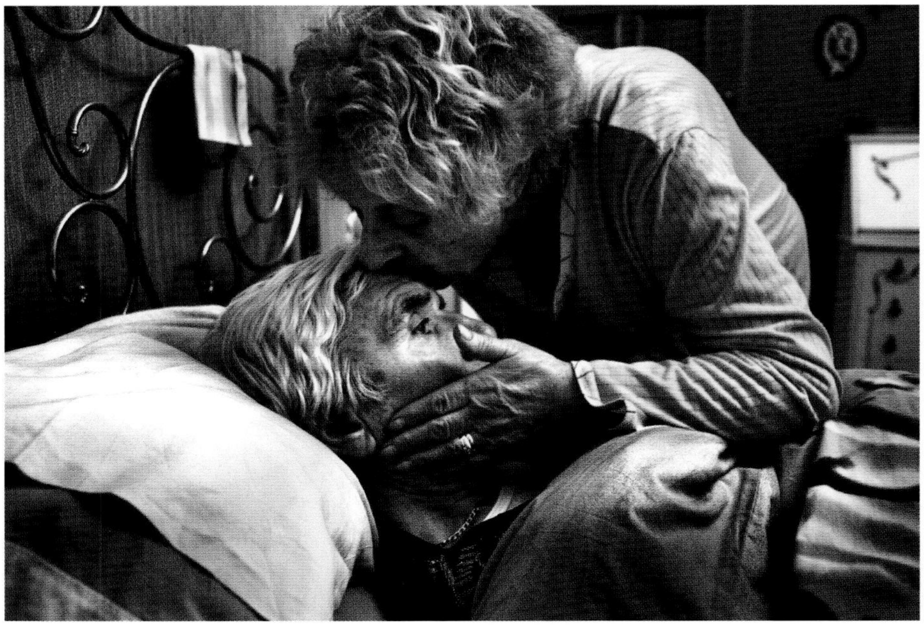

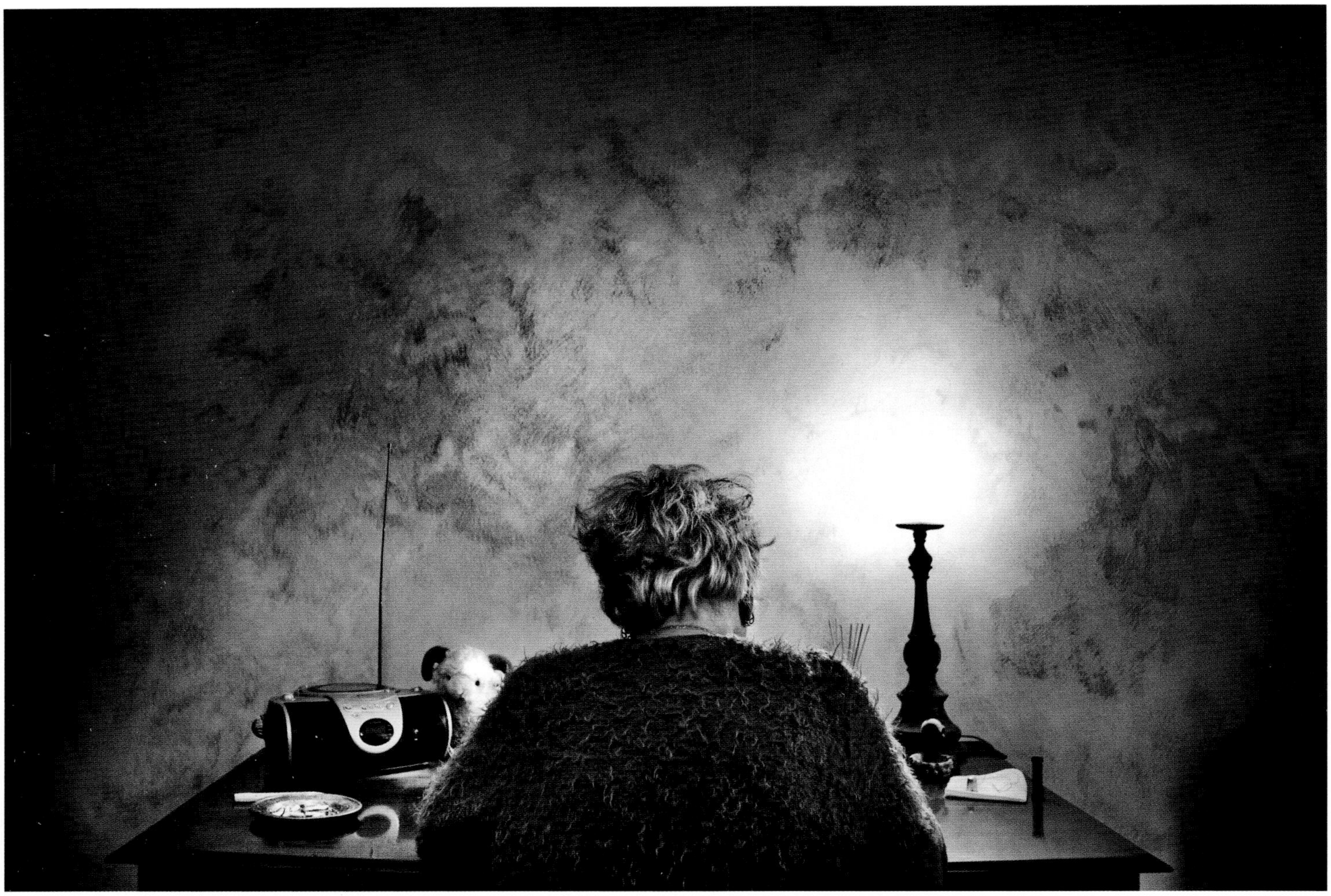

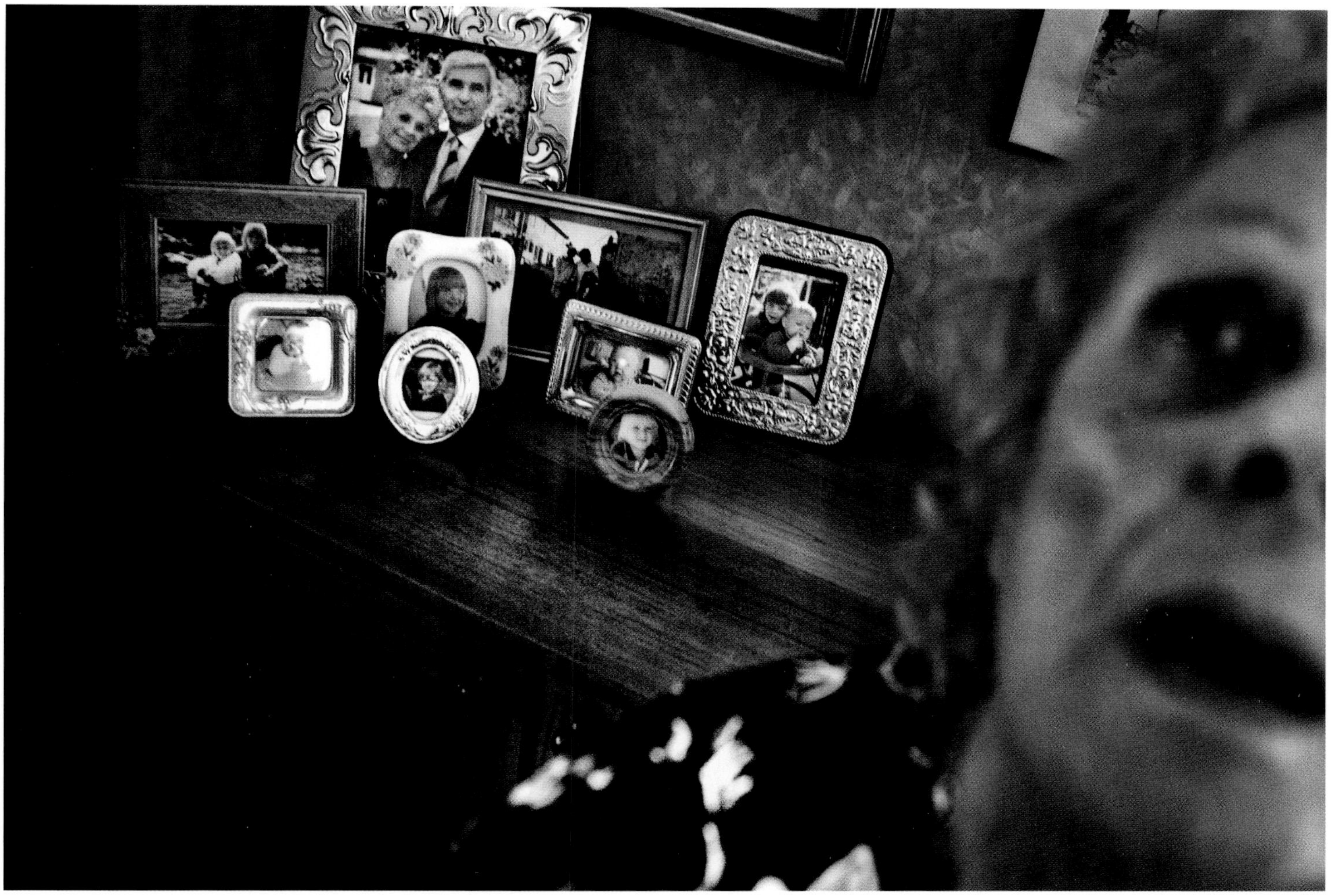

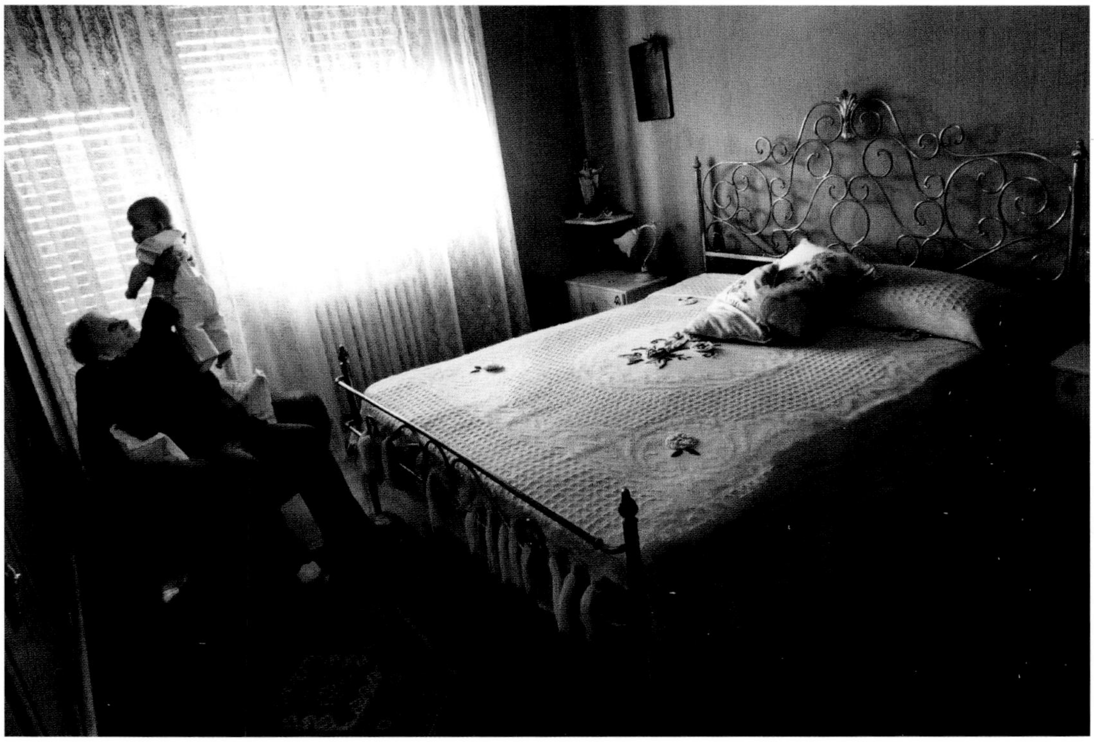

SATORU KONDO JAPAN

1ST PLACE
NATURE & WILDLIFE

Moment. A flower is not a flower. It's like a woman. A flower's life is transient, but beautiful.

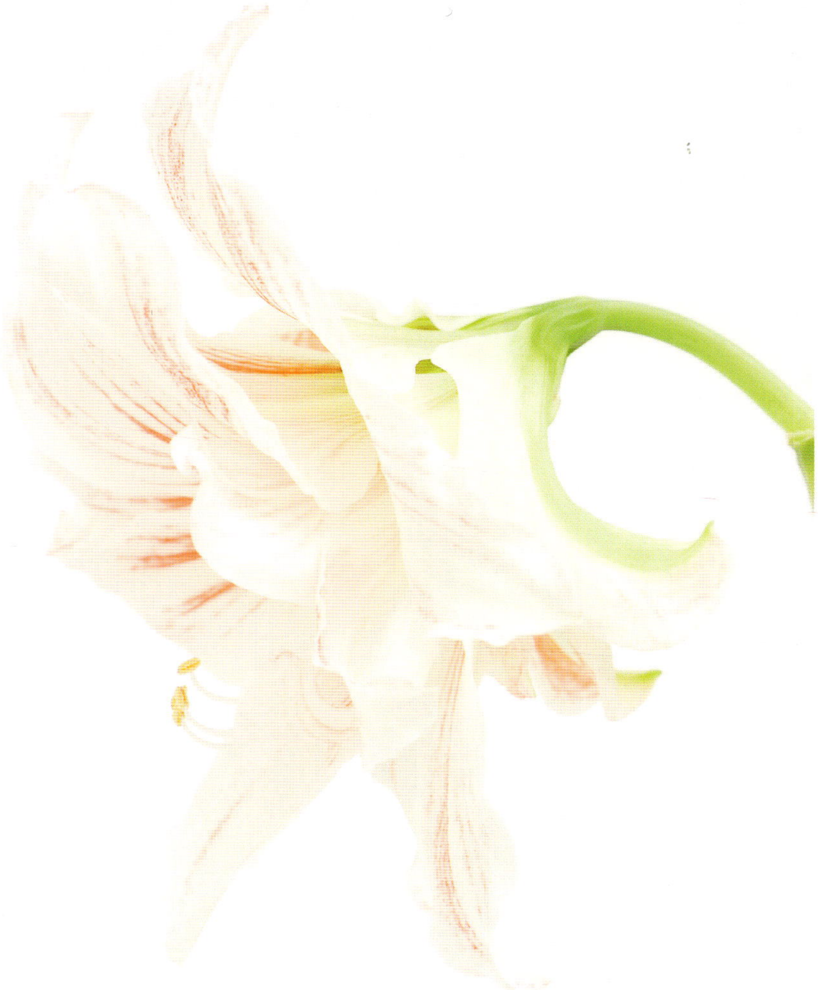

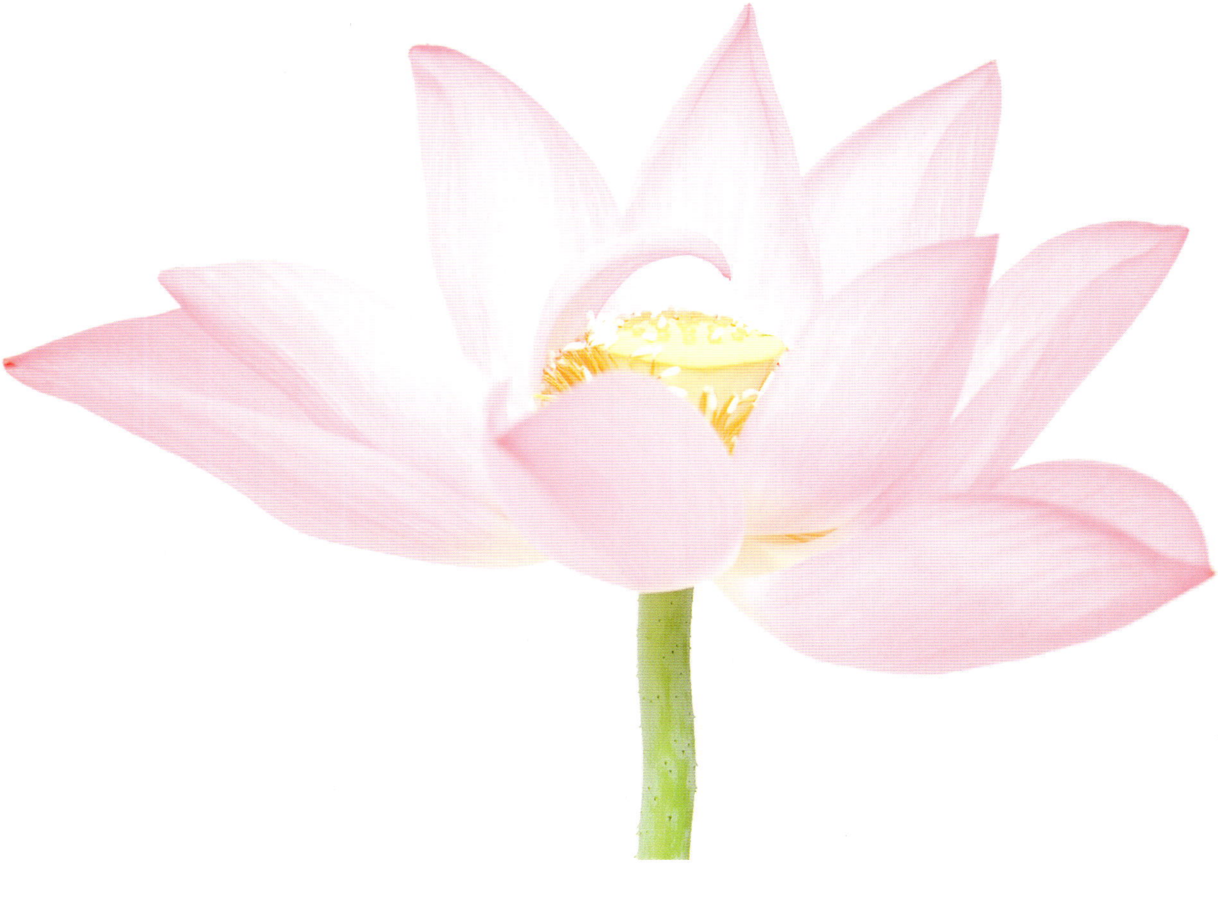

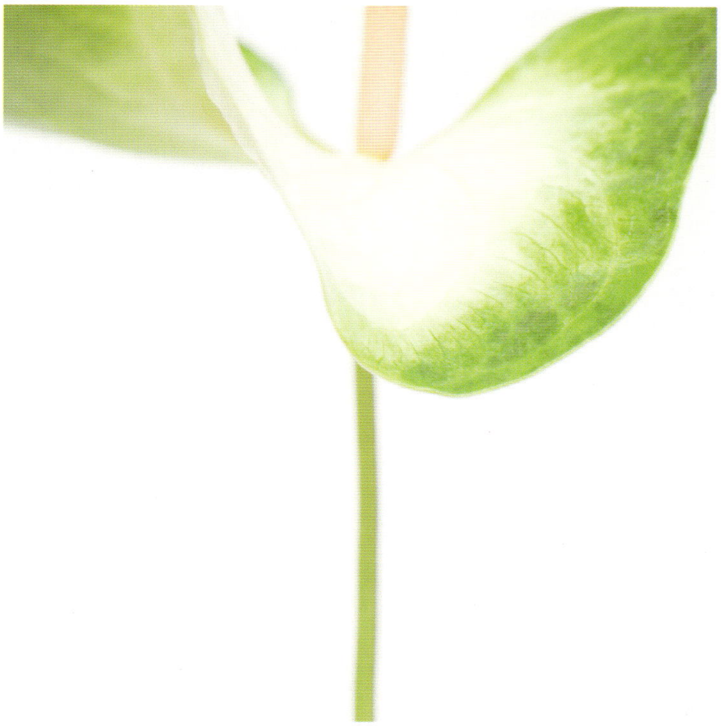

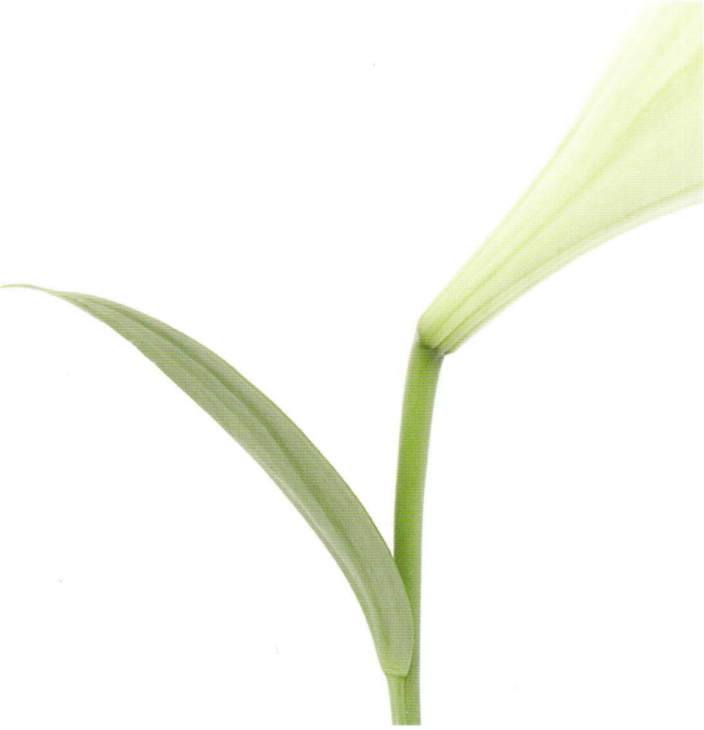

ERNEST GOH SINGAPORE

2ND PLACE
NATURE & WILDLIFE

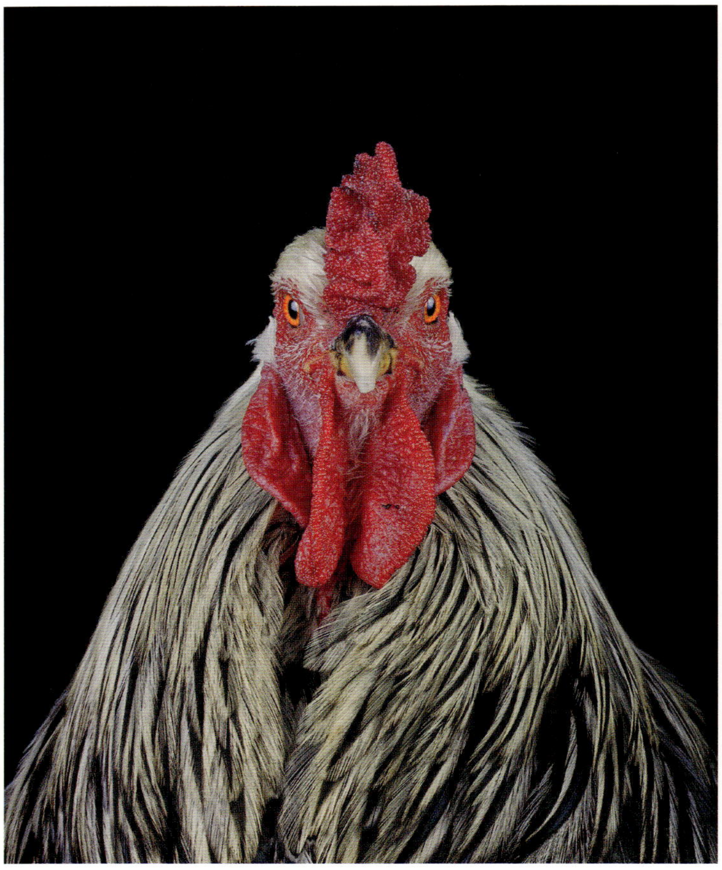

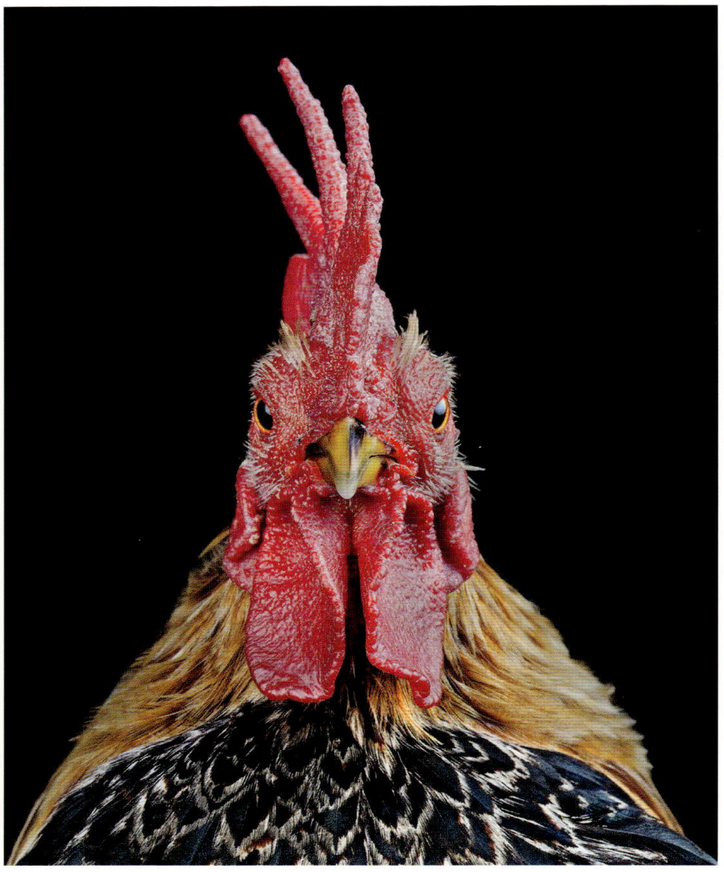

Cocks! Ornamental chicken breeding clubs have emerged in Indonesia, Thailand, North America and even in the UK and France. Malaysia, however, is the epicentre of this cultural phenomenon, and beauty contests, as they are often described, are held routinely in Malaysian villages. Judges sit around a square table inspecting each chicken for a few minutes, trying to determine a champion specimen in each weight class; based on its stance, temperament and physical assets. Owners often regard their pets as warriors or soldiers ready for battle, and it is this image of strength and grace that intrigues me.

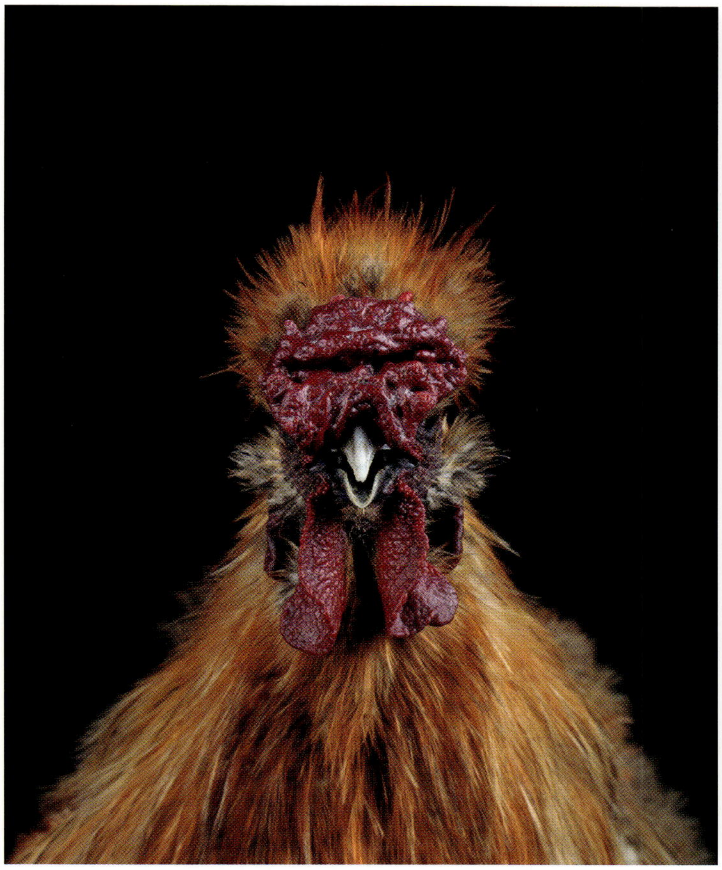

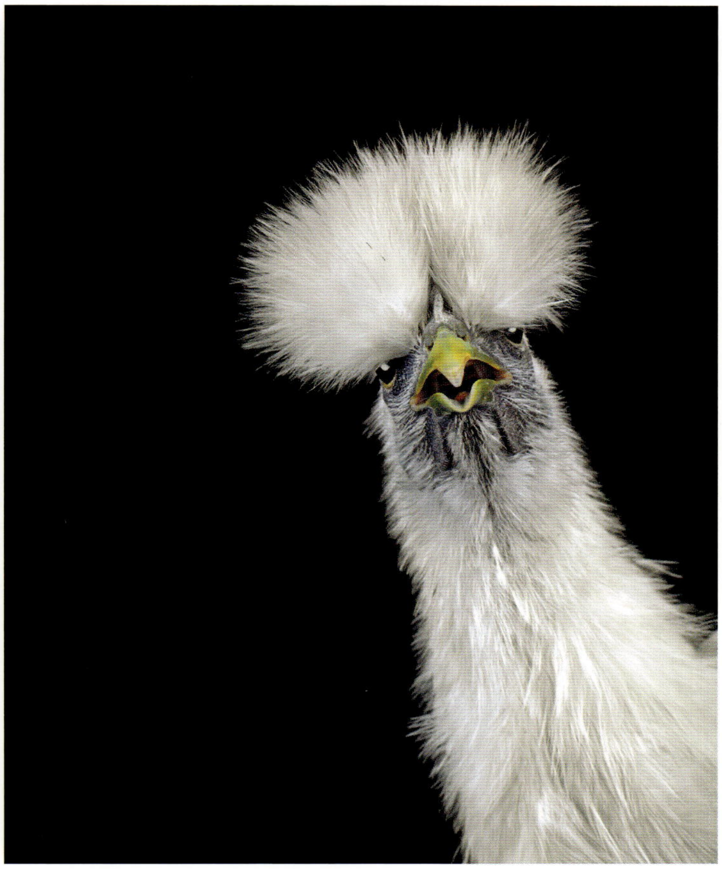

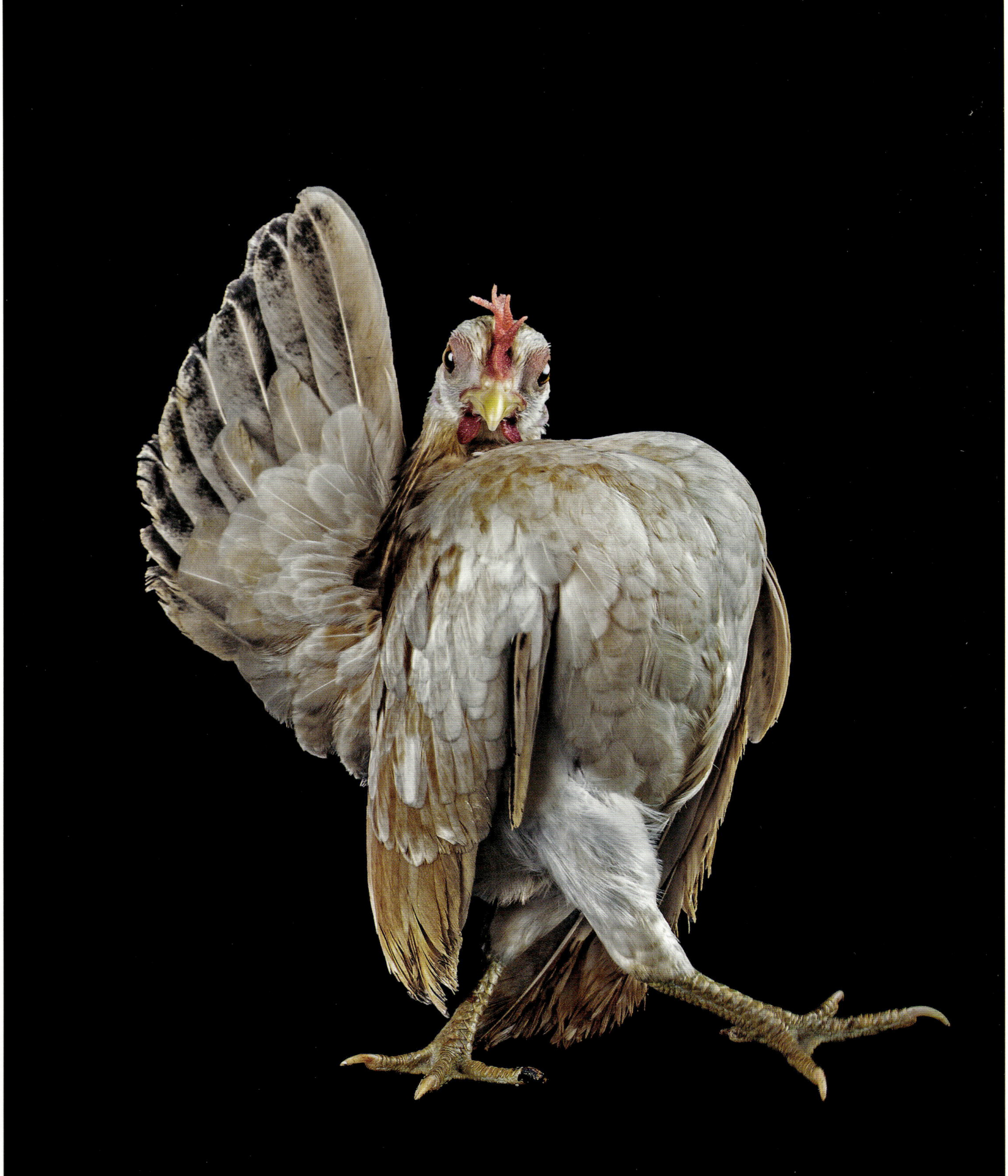

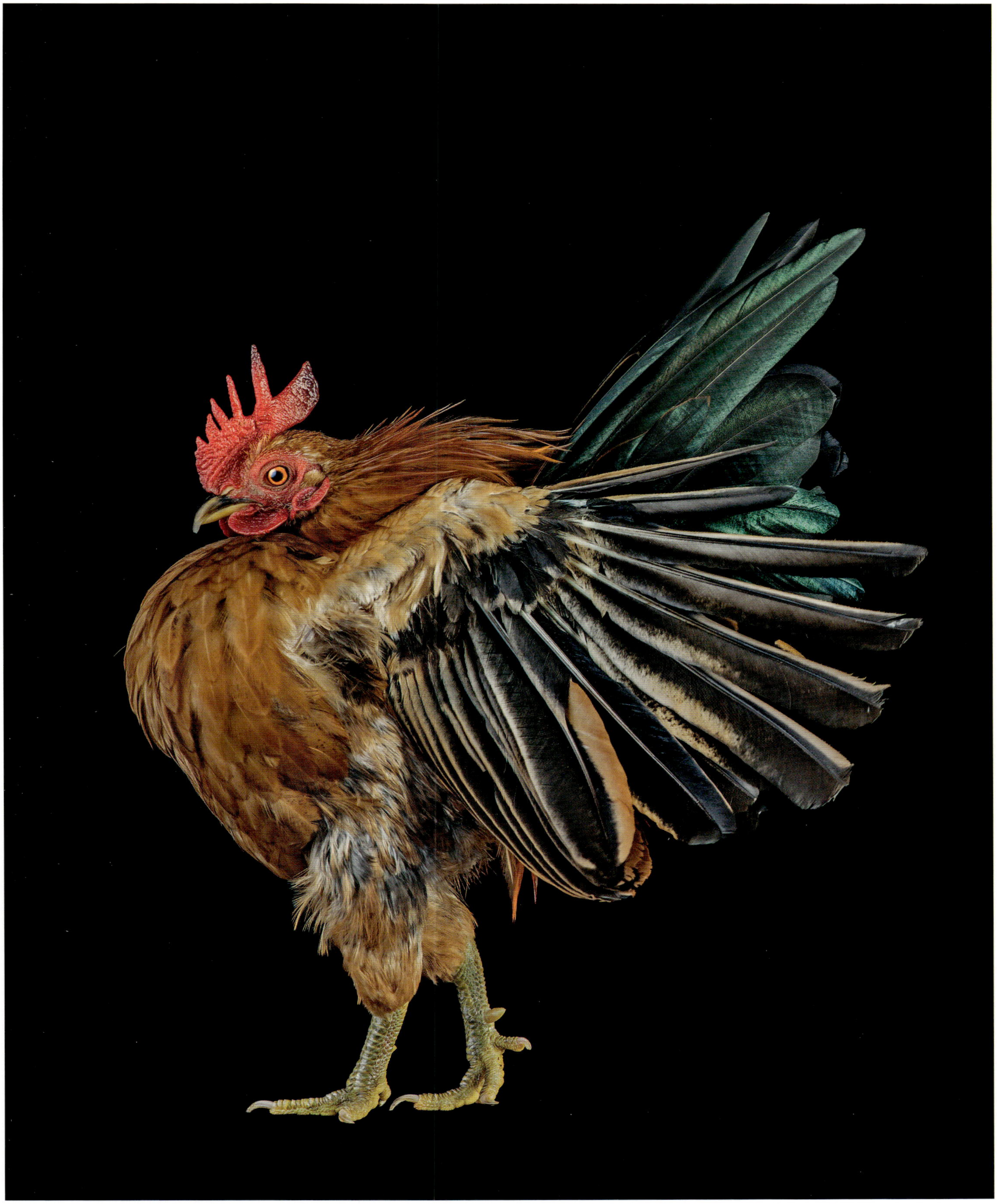

HUDSON GARCIA BRAZIL

3RD PLACE
NATURE & WILDLIFE

Designed to Jump. A series of two species of treefrog in southern Brazil. These amazing animals jump to escape predators and catch their prey.

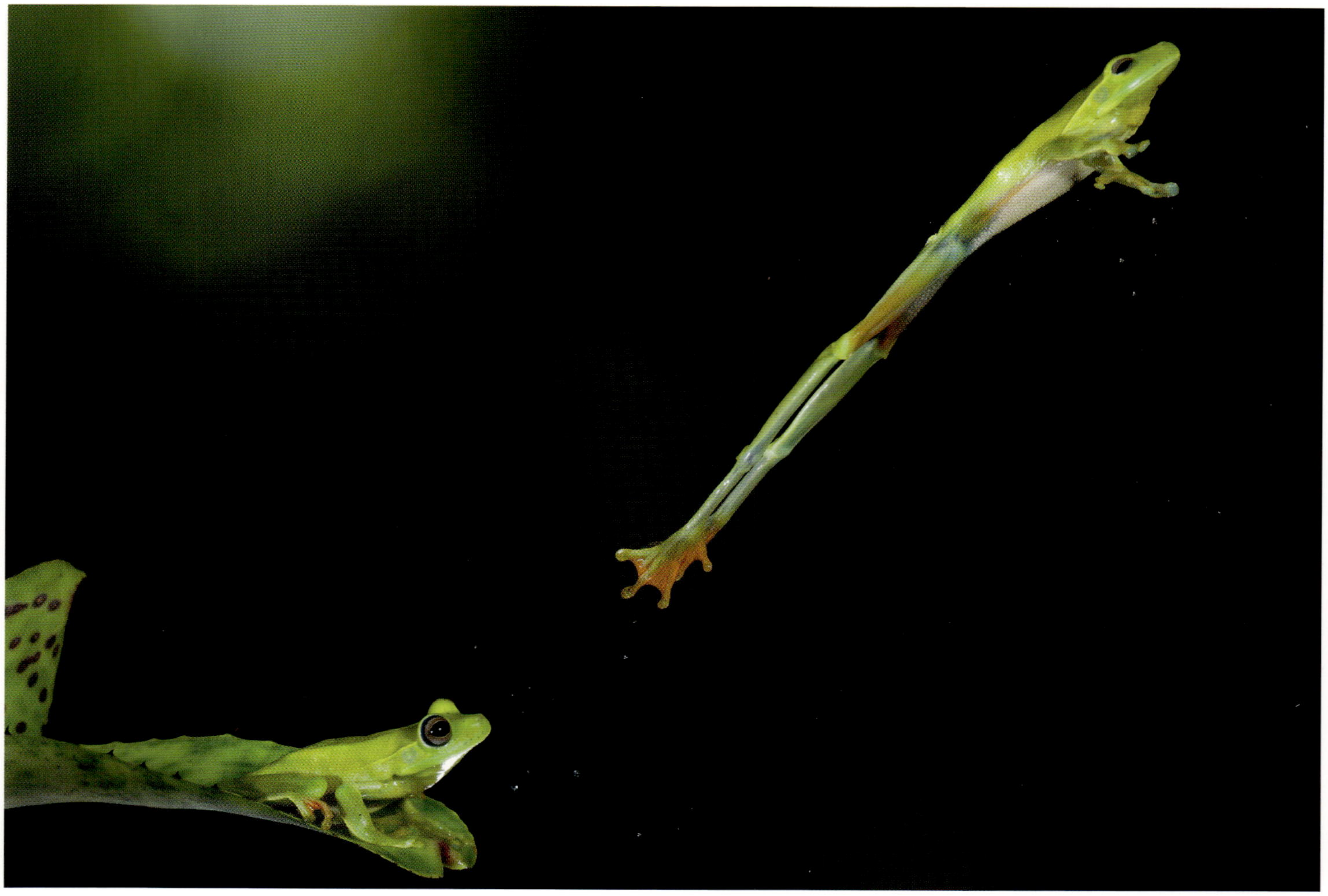

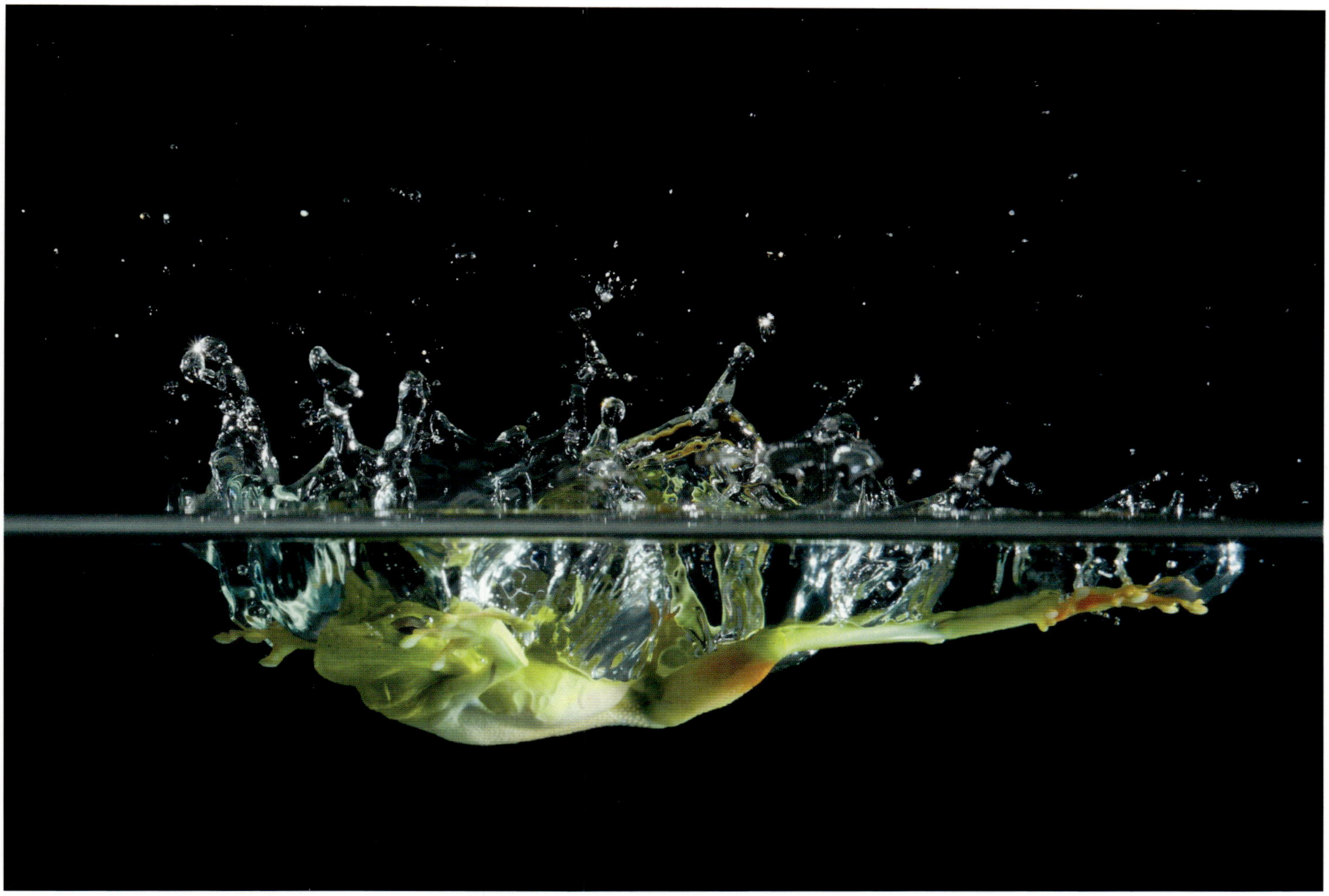

ANDREA GJESTVANG NORWAY

1ST PLACE
PEOPLE

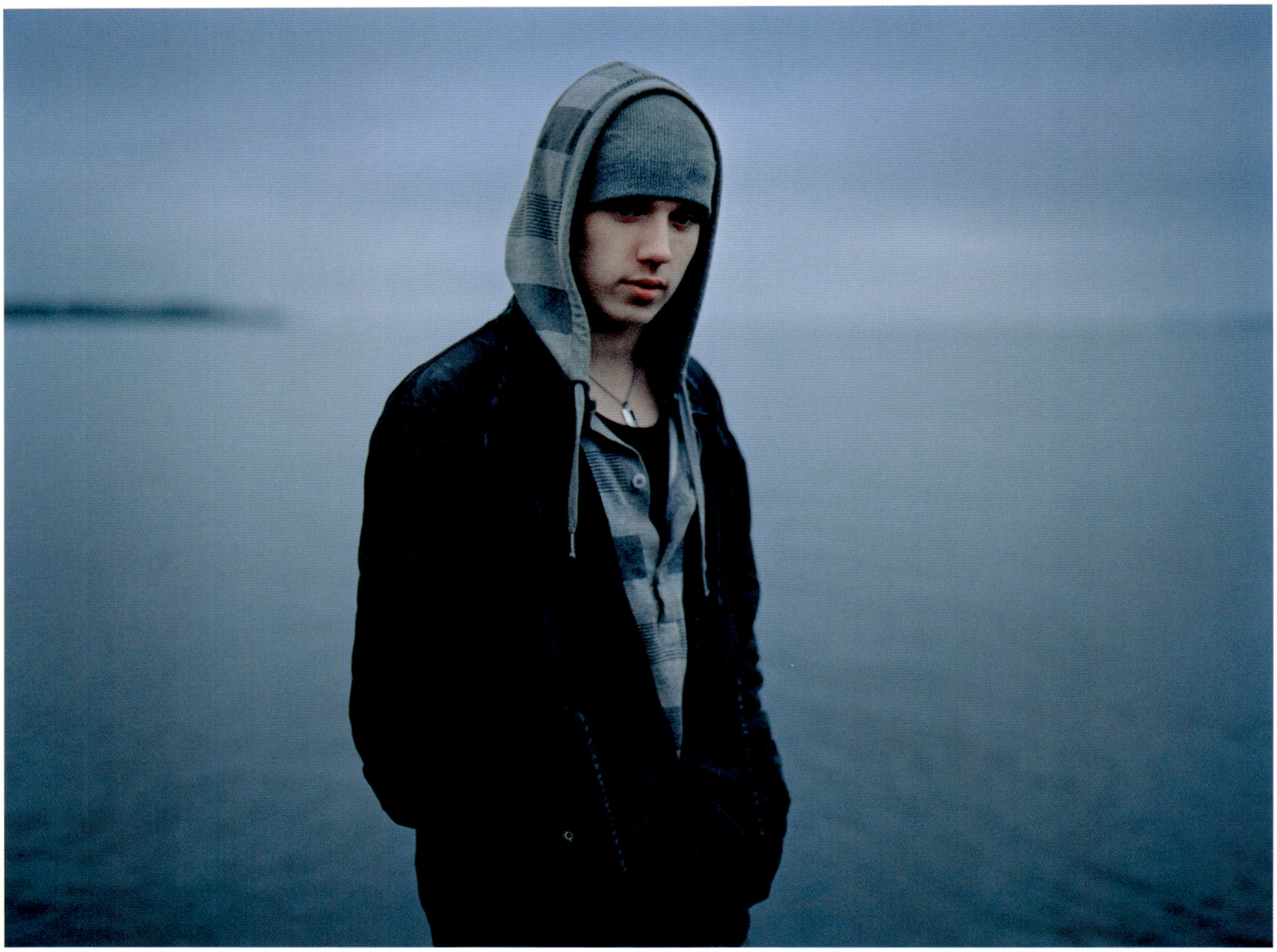

Marius Hoft (18) was hiding on a ledge to avoid the shooting. His best friend fell down and died in front of his eyes.

One Day in History. Portraits of children and youths who survived the massacre on the island of Utøya, outside Oslo, on 22 July 2011.

Cecilie Herlovsen (17) hid at the south end of the island, where she was shot in her arm, her shoulder and chin.

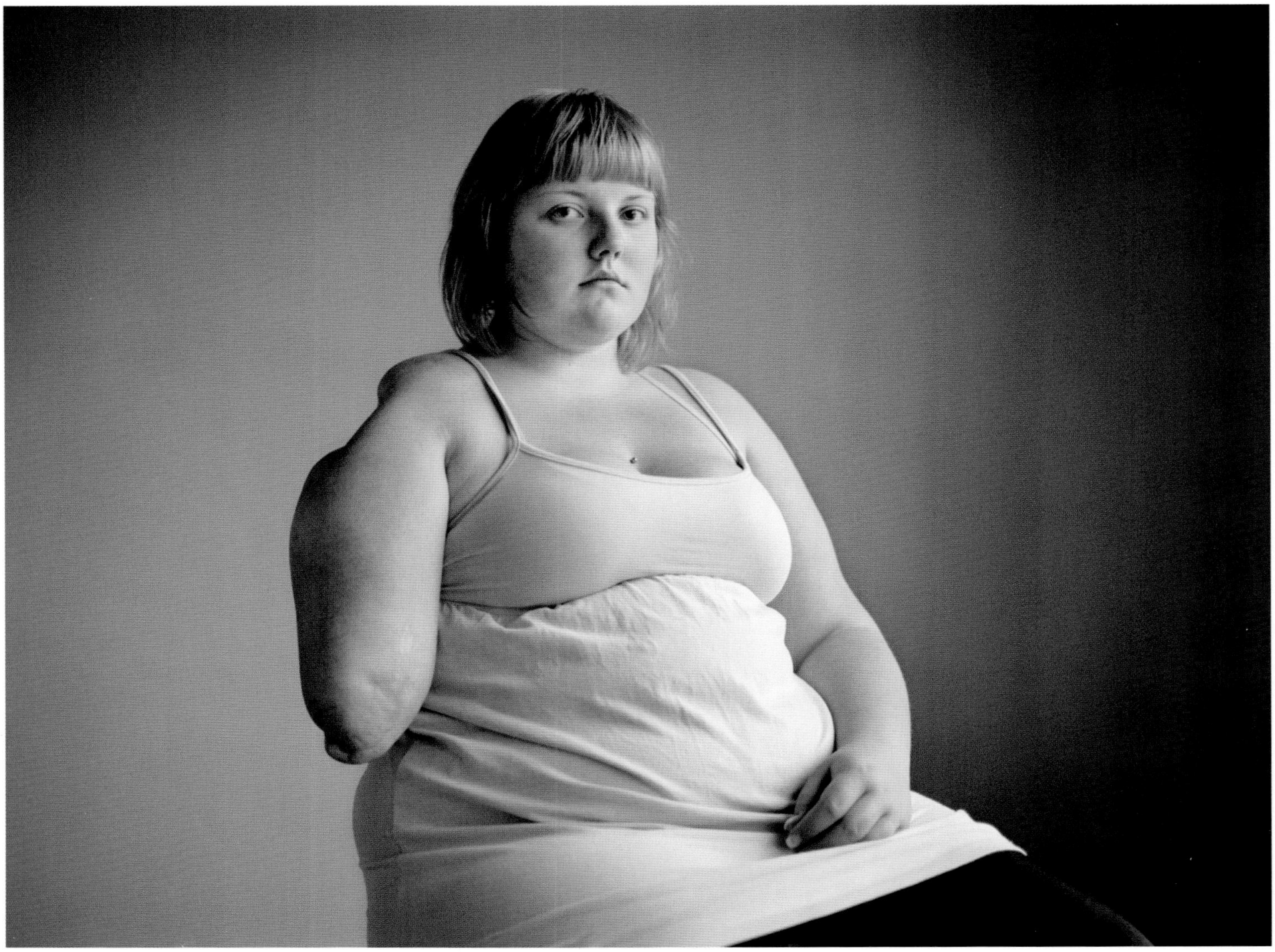

BALAZS GARDI HUNGARY

2ND PLACE
PEOPLE

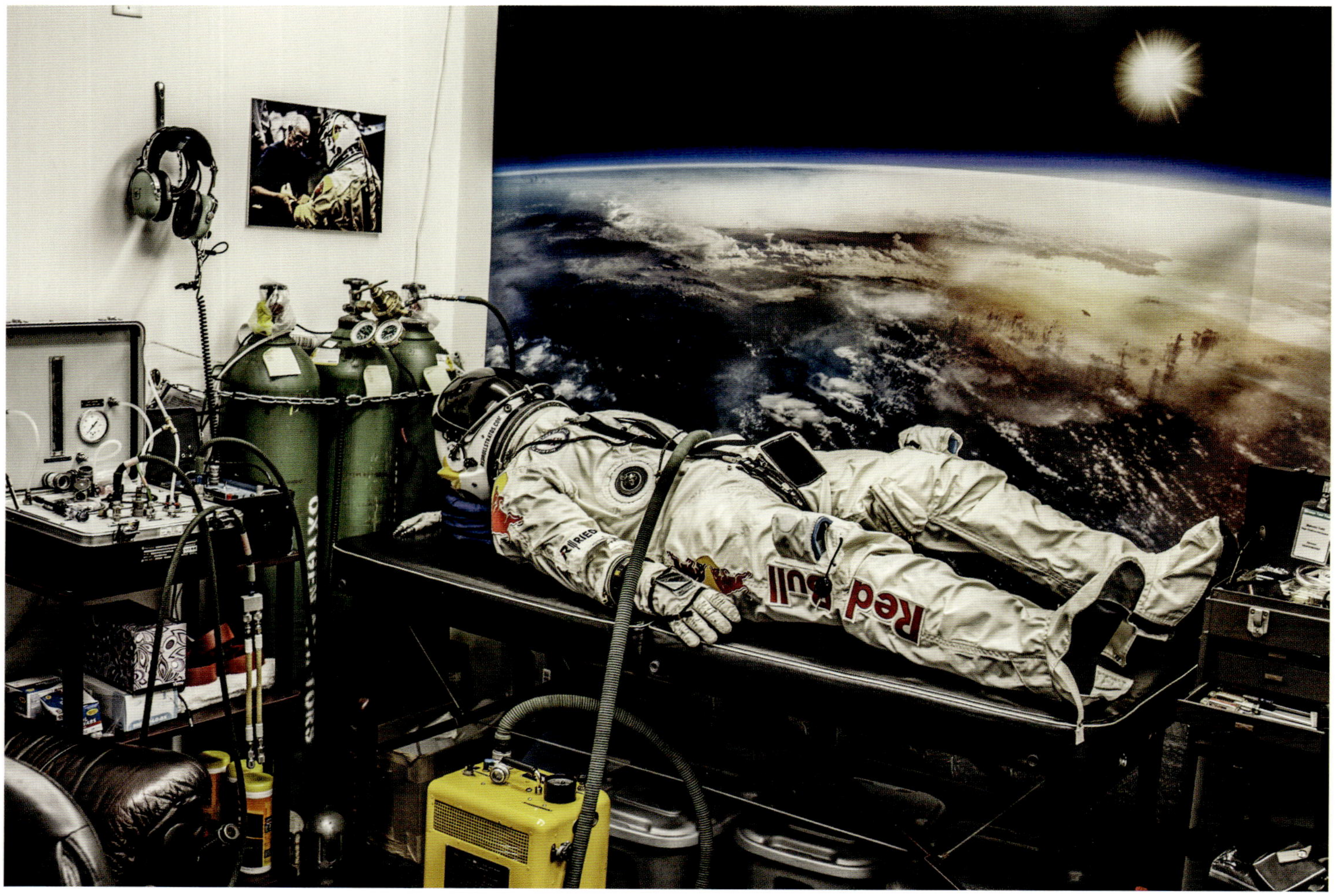

Felix Baumgartner: Faster than the speed of sound. On 14 October 2012 Austrian skydiver Felix Baumgartner broke the world record for manned balloon and freefall height and became the first person to break the sound barrier without propulsion. After jumping from a capsule underneath a helium balloon over 39 kilometres into the stratosphere, his freefall reached a speed of 1,342 kilometres per hour. The images in this set were taken over a 10 month period following Felix from the early preparation phase to the end of this record-breaking mission.

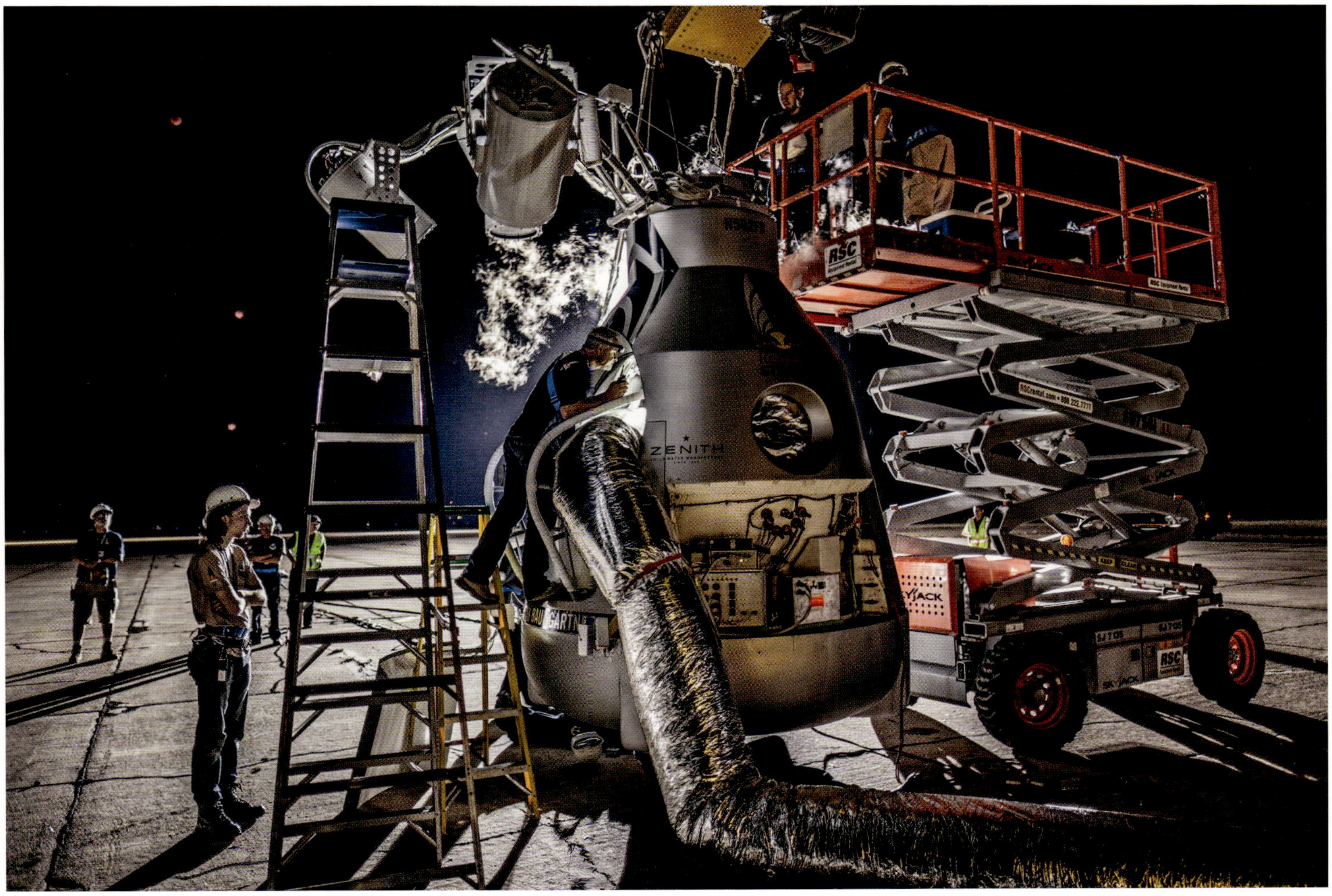
ZENITH
RSC

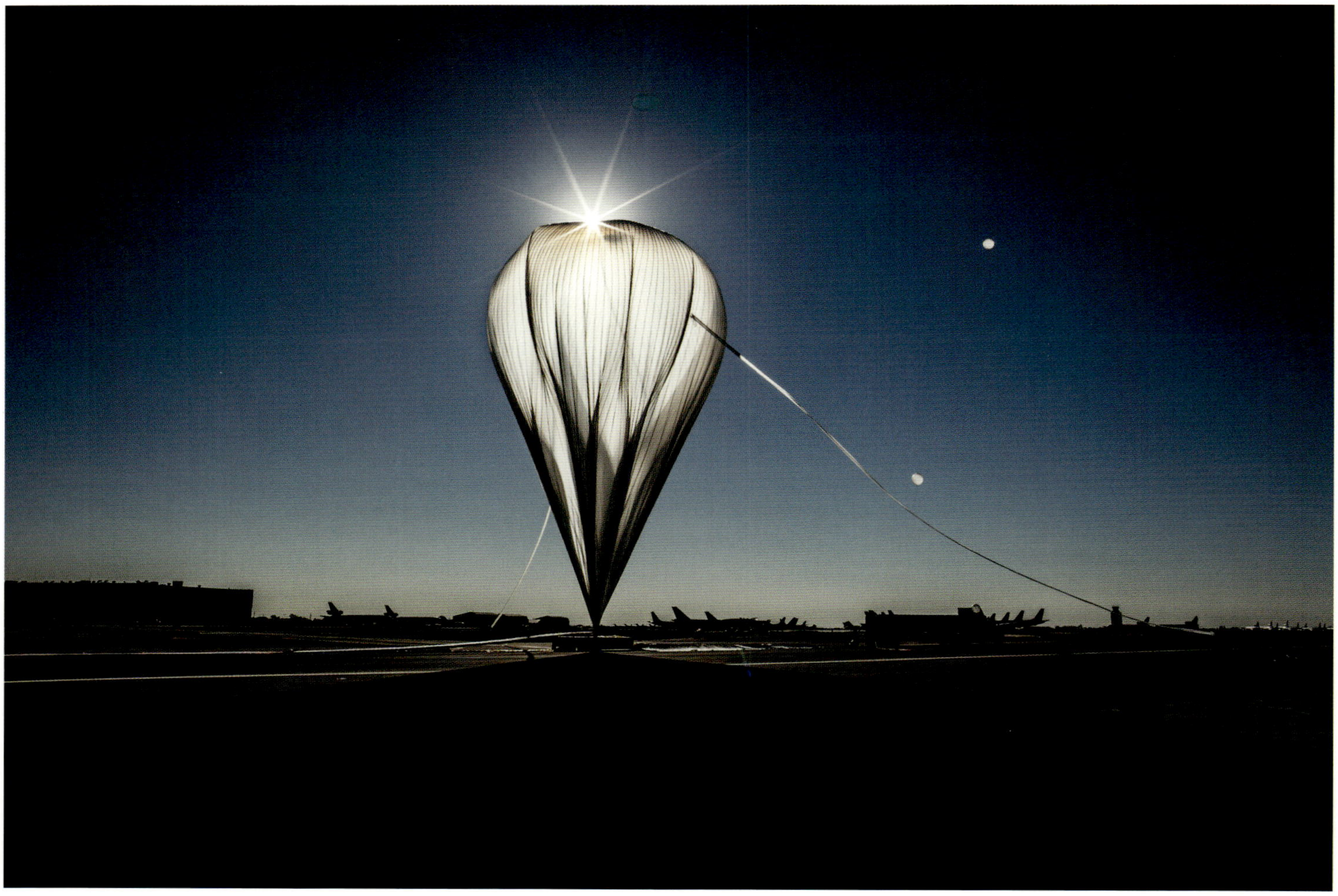

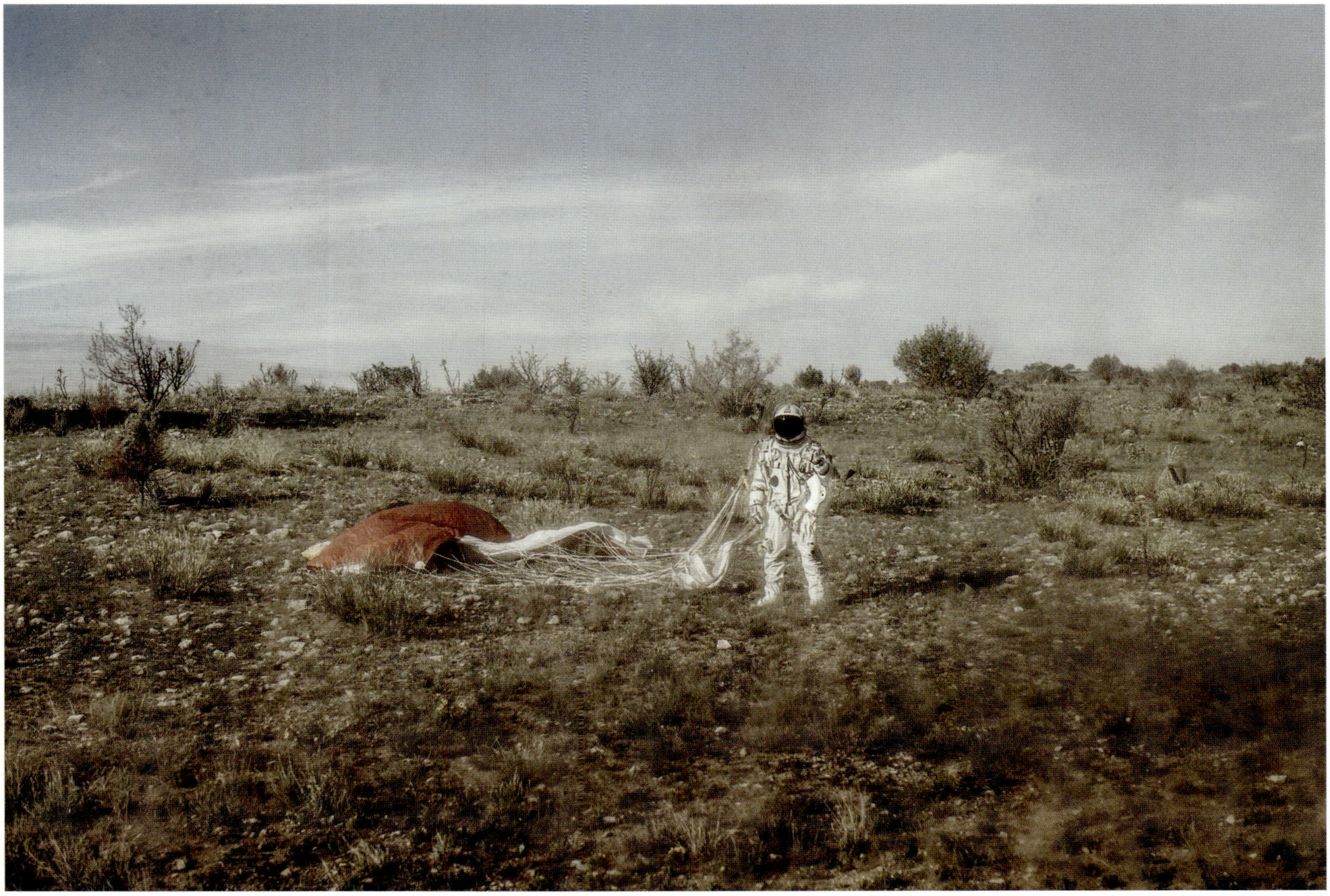

© Balazs Gardi for Red Bull.

PETE MULLER USA

3RD PLACE
PEOPLE

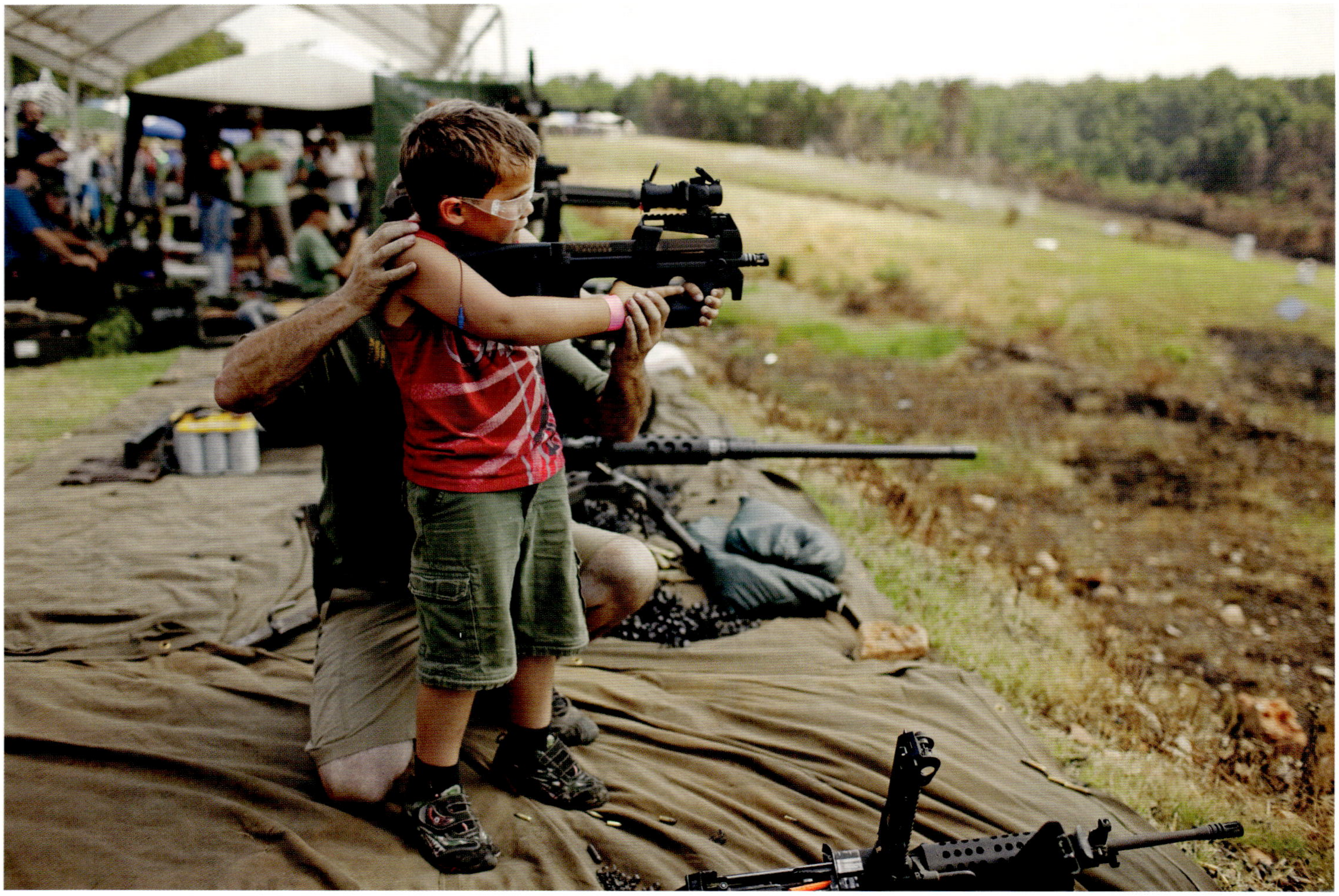

Machine Gun Americana. On the edge of Oklahoma's Ozarks, where prairies ascend to rolling hills, an outgrowth of American tradition thunders in the air. Under a summer sun, gun enthusiasts peer down the sights of devastating weapons at the annual Oklahoma Full Auto Shoot and Trade Show, one of the country's largest fully automatic machine gun expos. Husbands and wives, often with children in tow, make a weekend of firing a vast array of fully automatic weapons, riding in tanks, and flying in military helicopters. In wild and hostile environments, where no police are in sight, the civilian-owned weapon is sacrosanct.

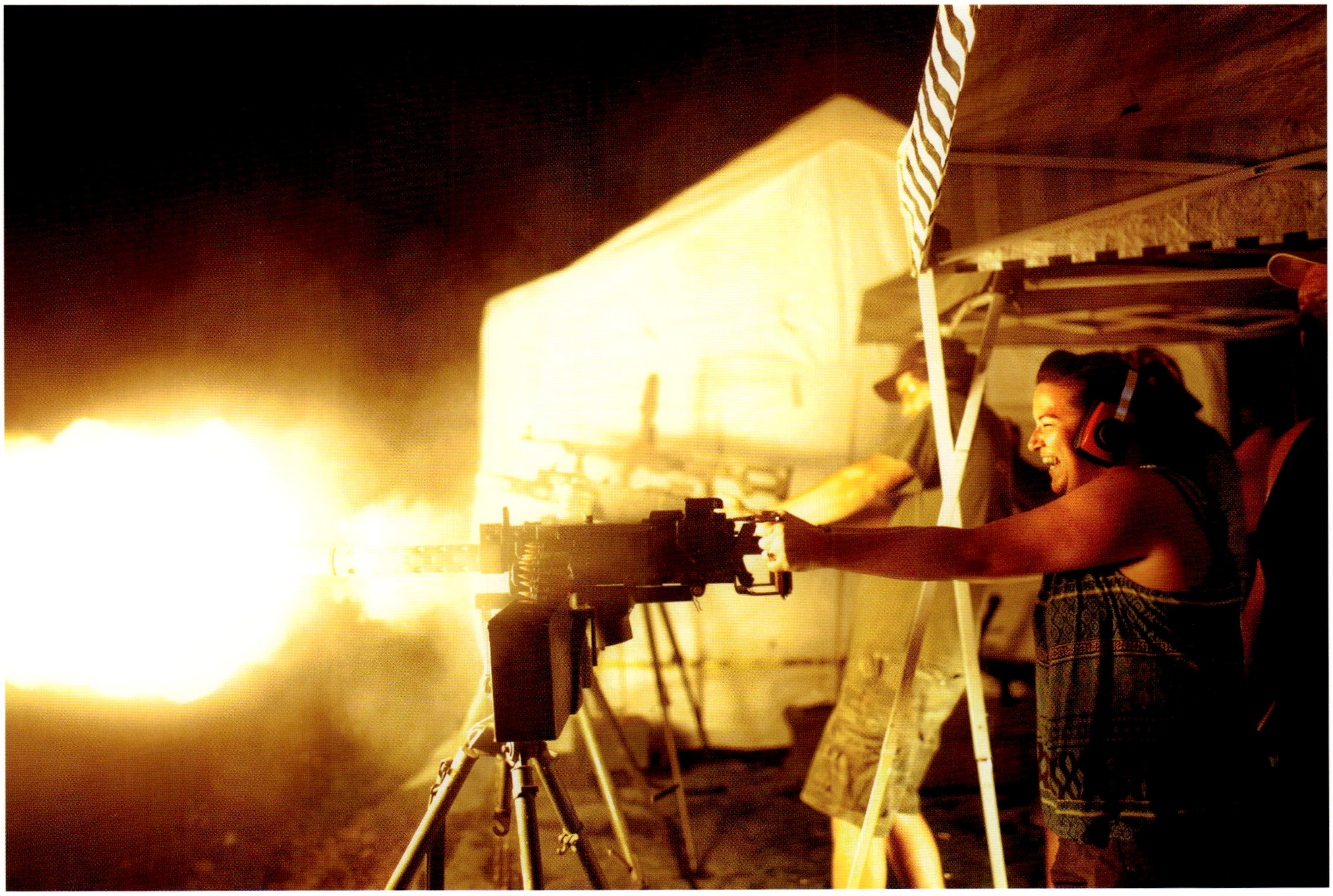

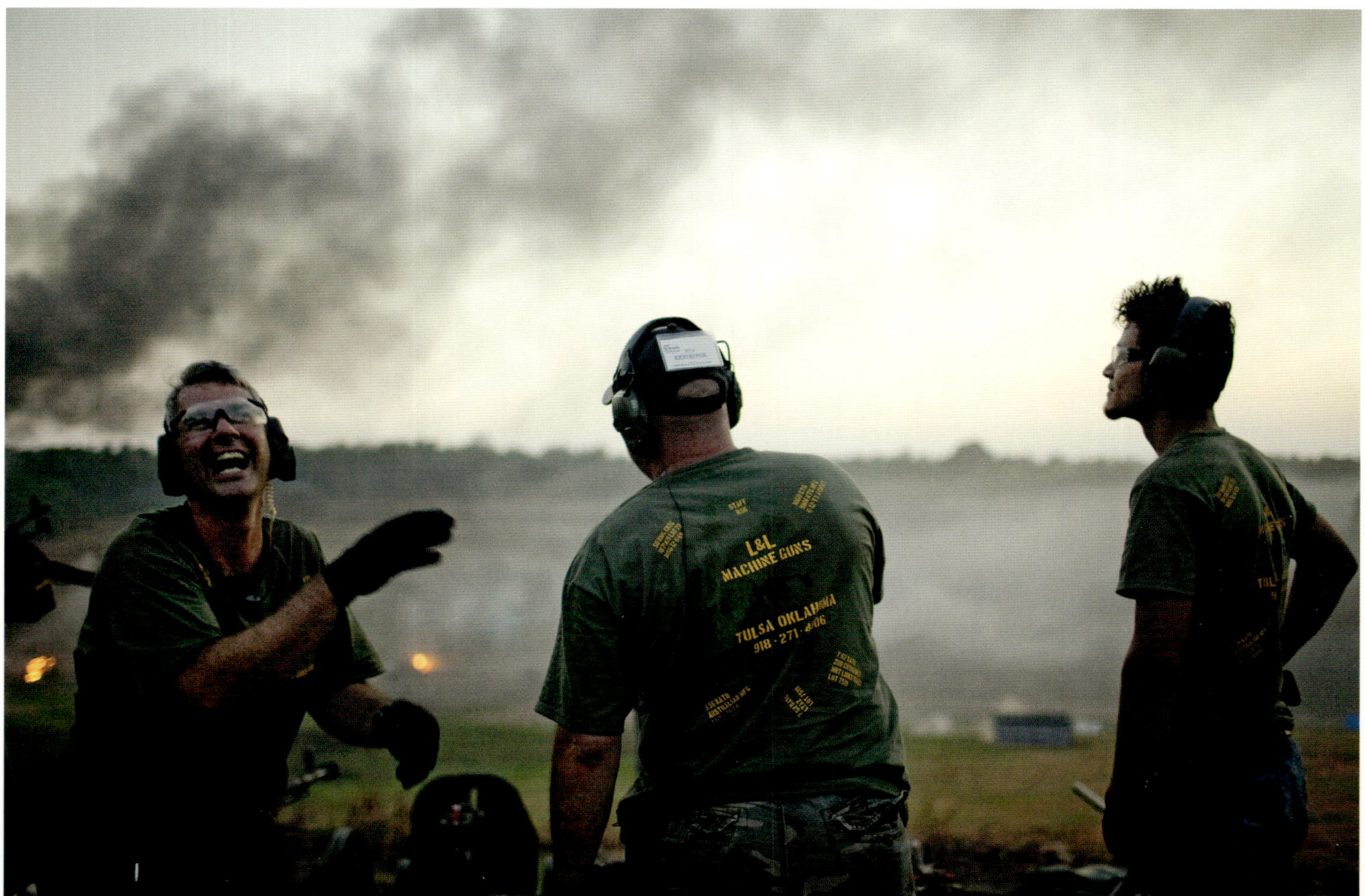
L&L
MACHINE GUNS
TULSA OKLAHOMA

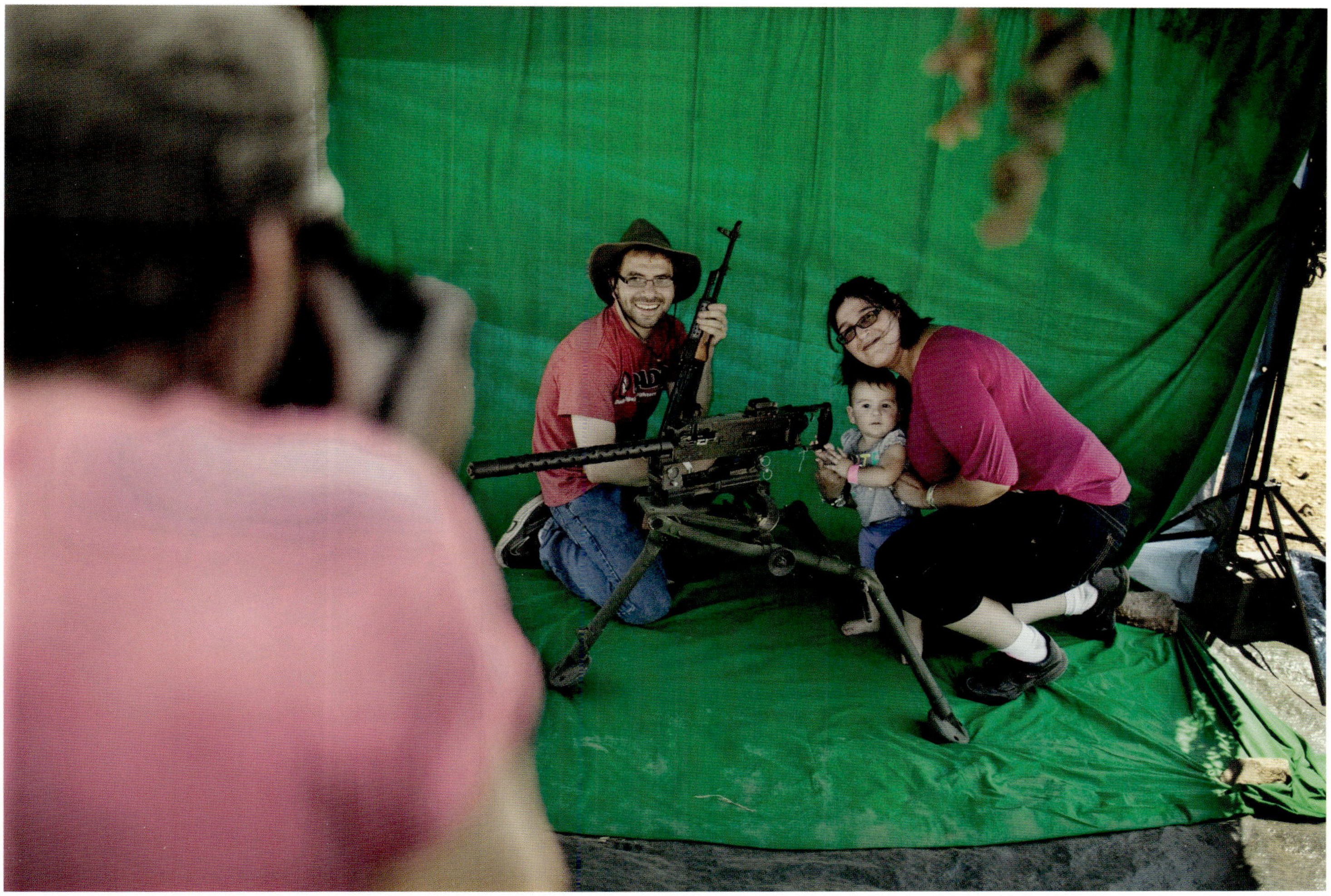

JENS JUUL DENMARK

1ST PLACE
PORTRAITURE

Six Degrees of Copenhagen. Taking its point of departure from the idea that every person on Earth is connected by only six degrees of separation, this series of photos depicts human connections through the city of Copenhagen. The set up is that I portray random people that I engage with in the streets, and that these chance meetings end up with me taking highly personal photos of these people, who then each send me on to another person in their network, who I can portray, who then gives me the name of another person.

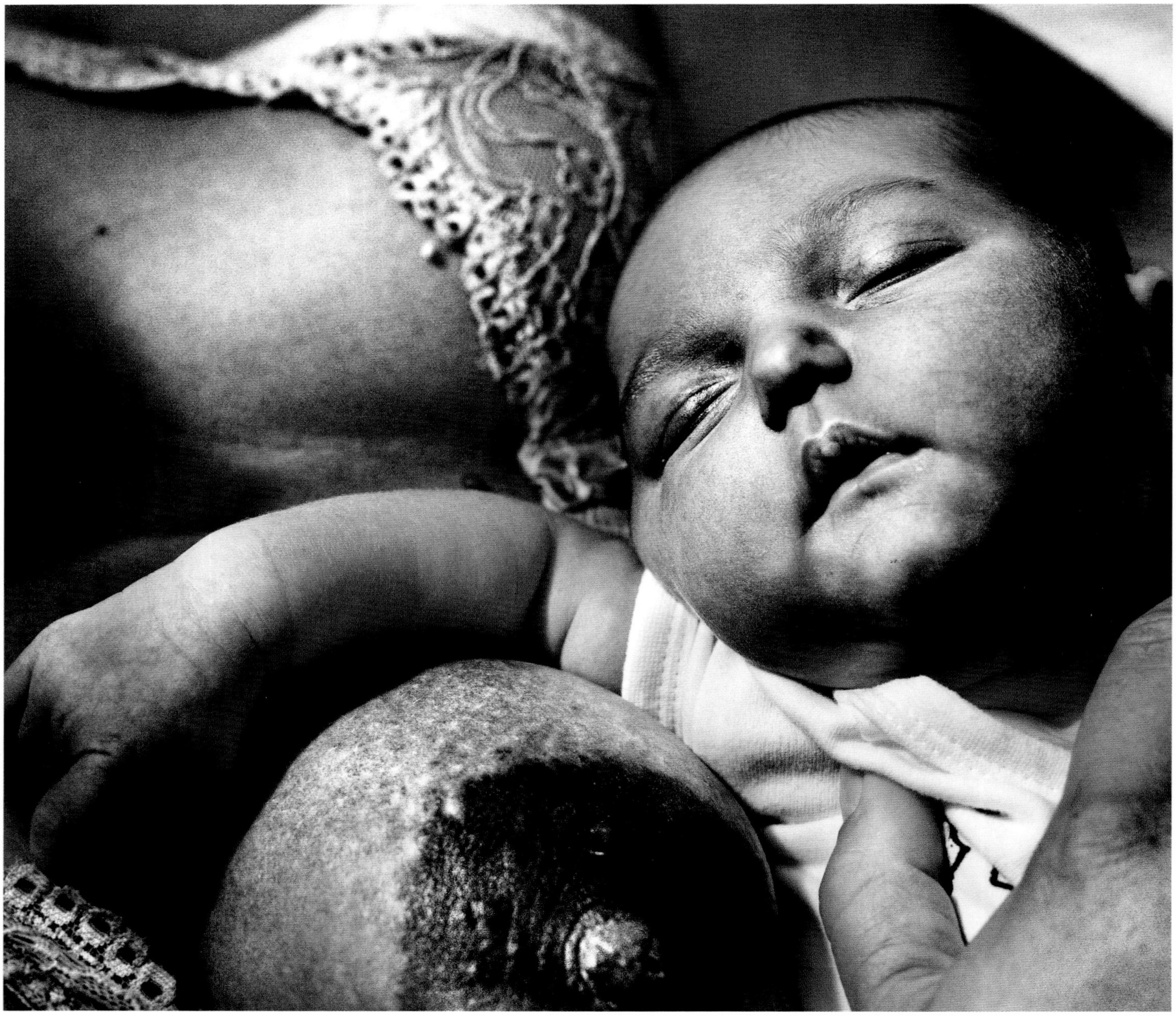

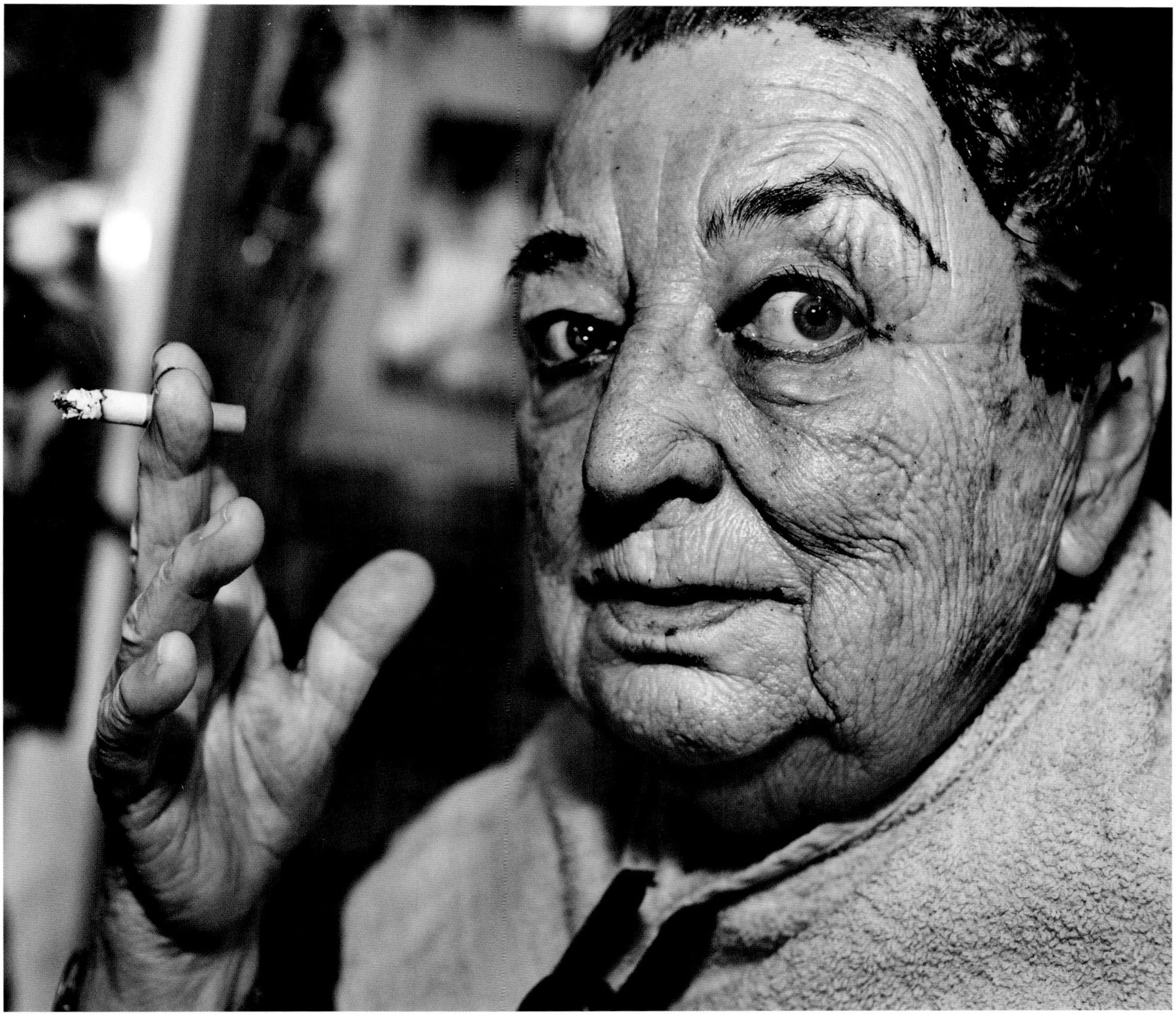

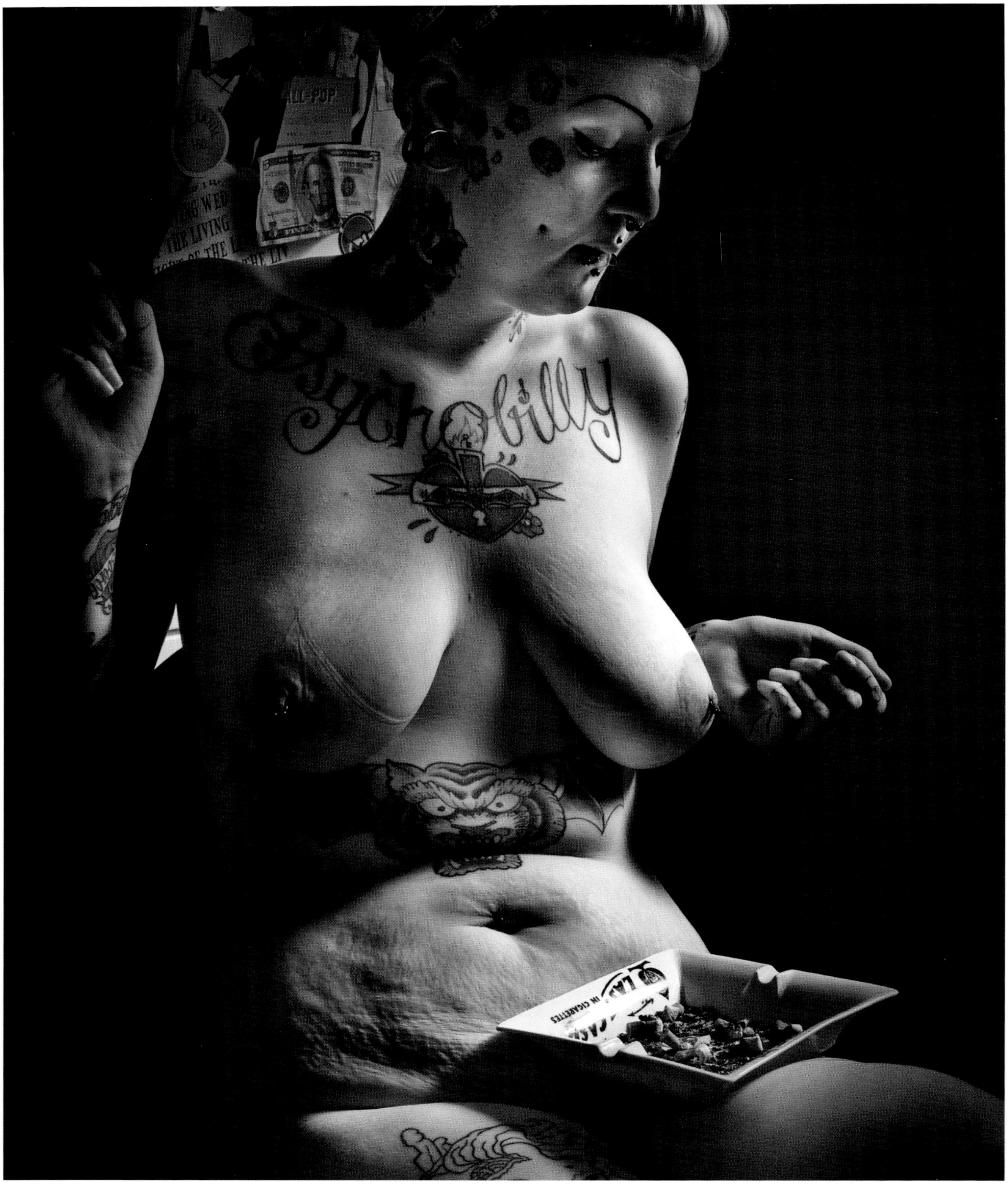
ALL-POP
Psychobilly

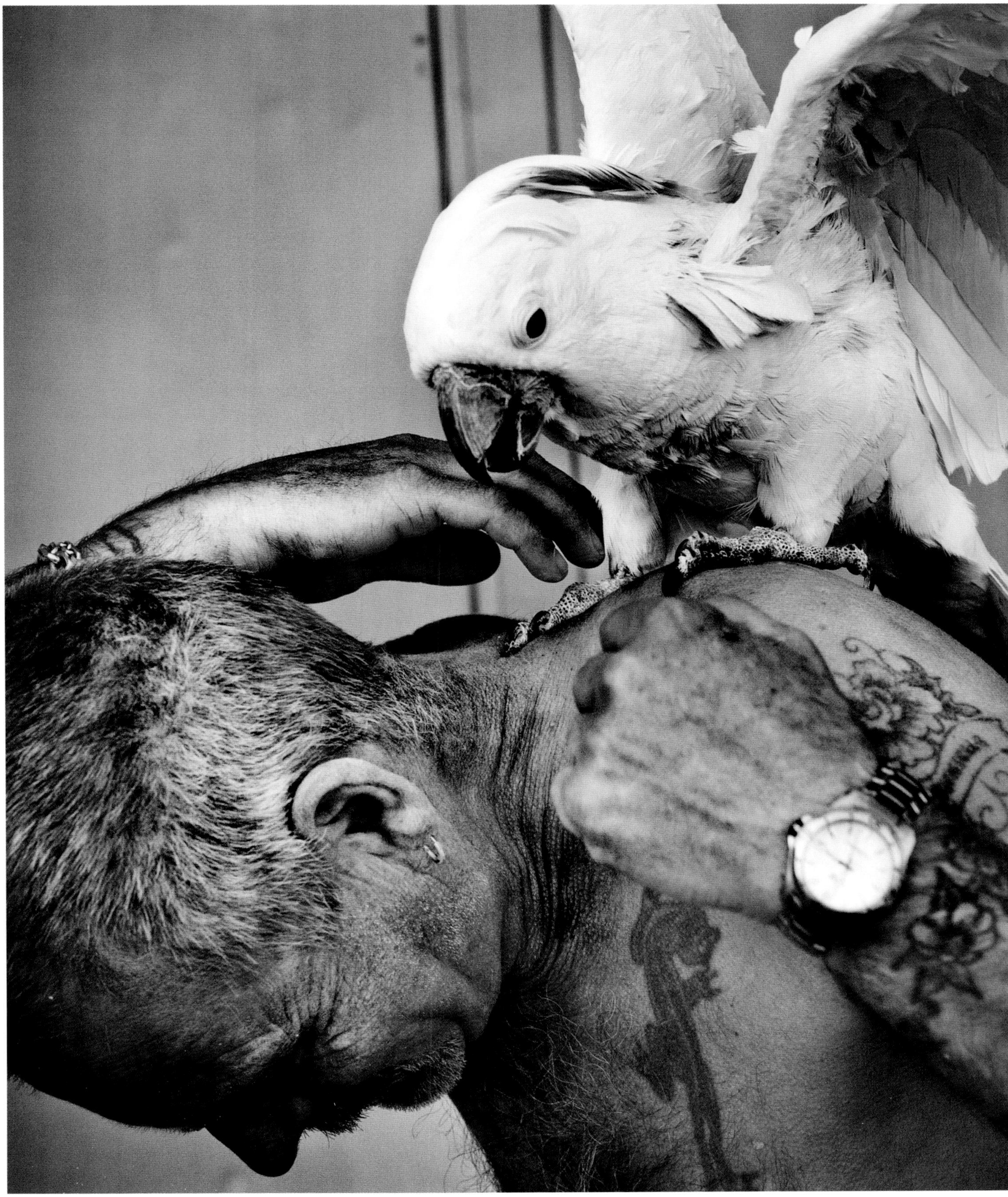

ADAM PRETTY AUSTRALIA

1ST PLACE
SPORT

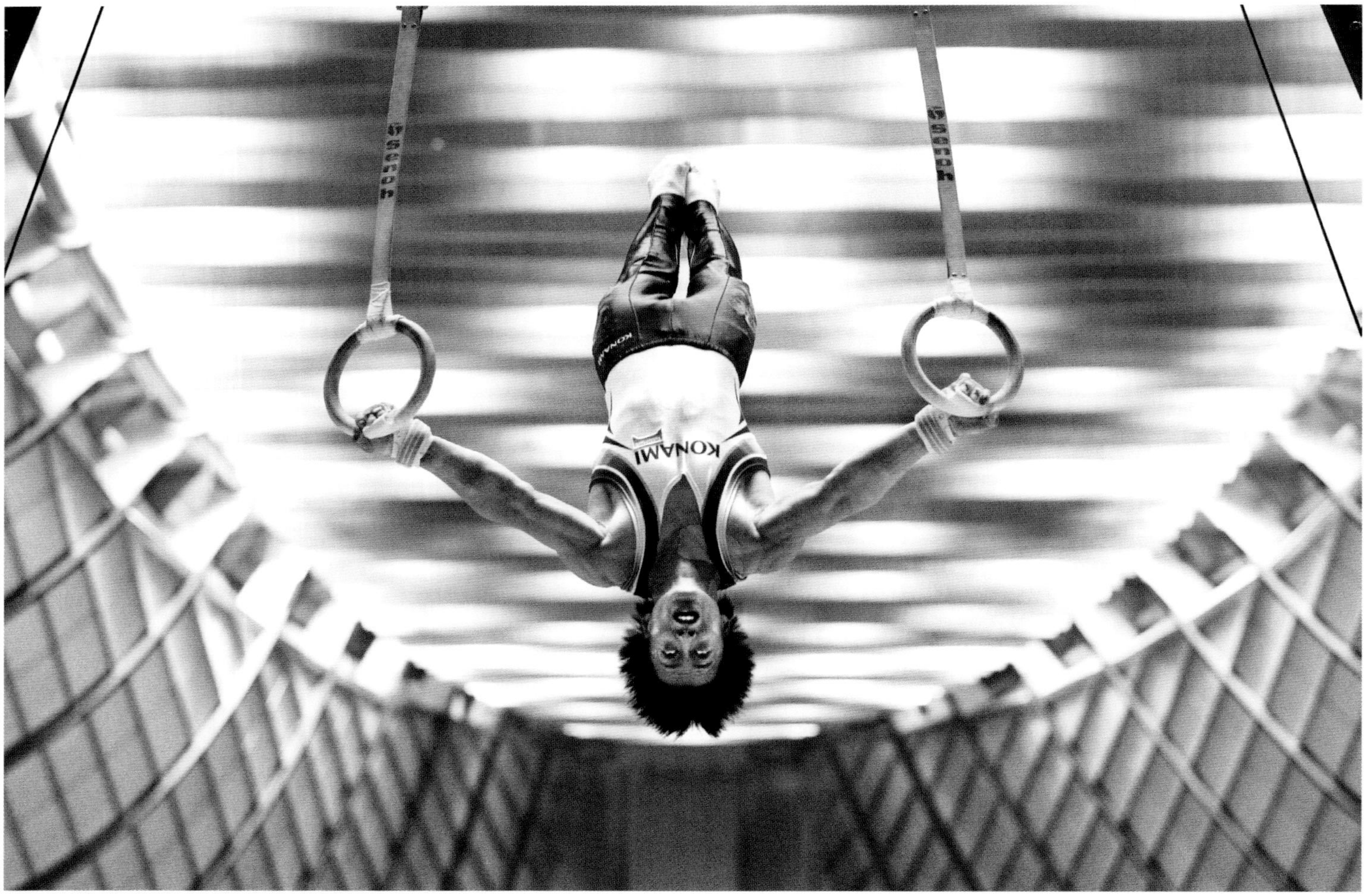

Olympic Journey 2012. A series of sports imagery from Olympic qualifying events and the London 2012 Olympic Games.

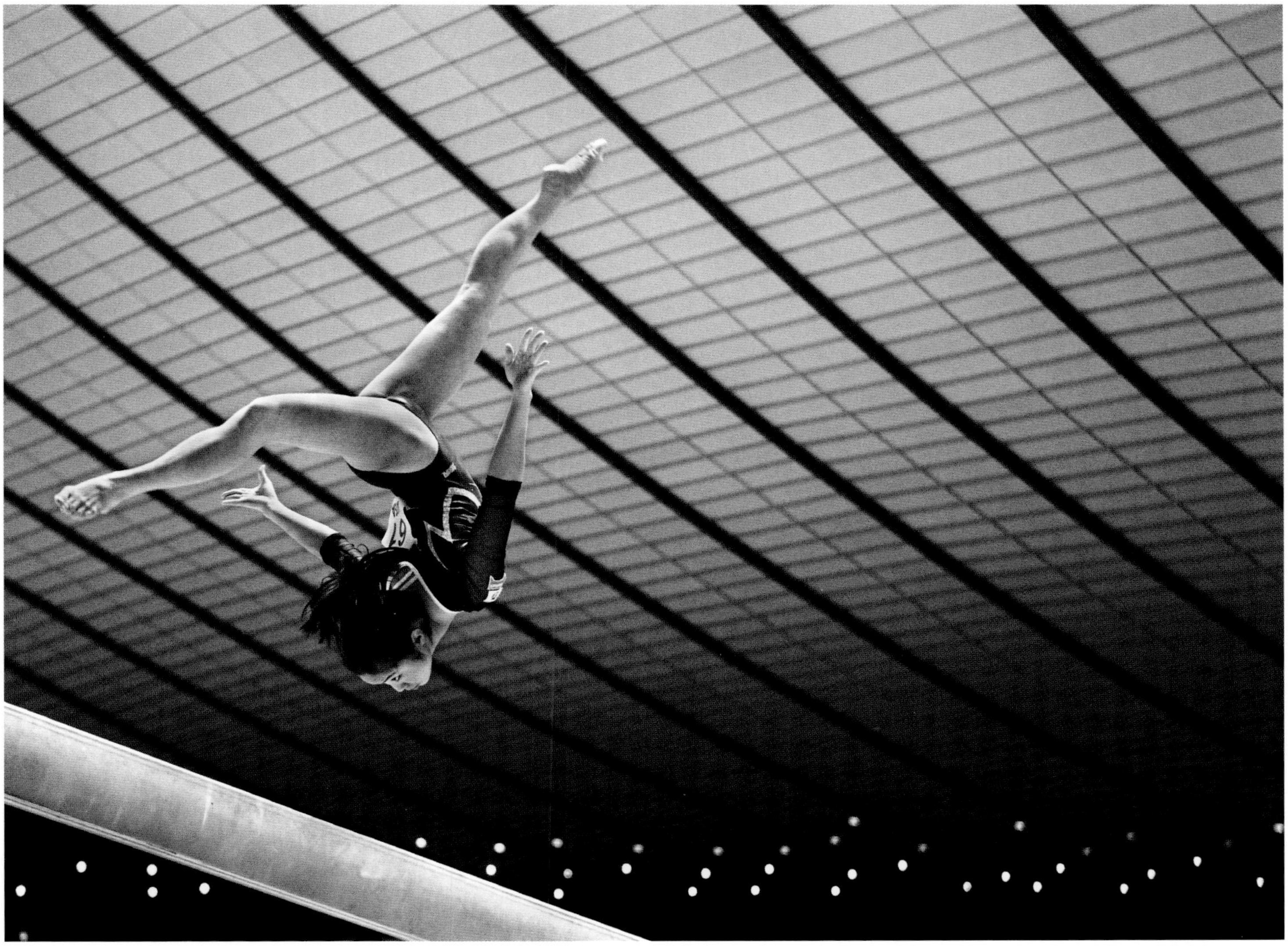

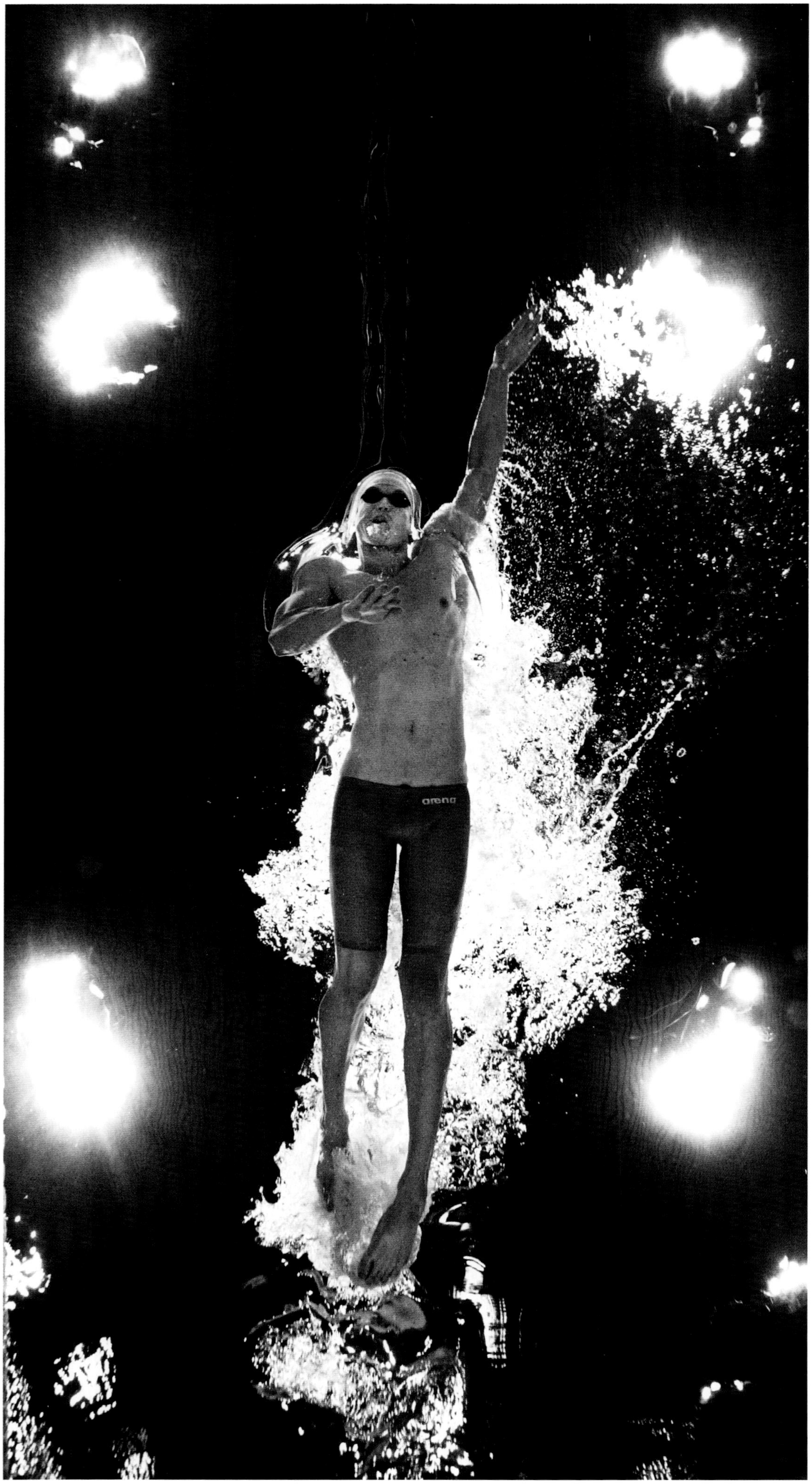
arena

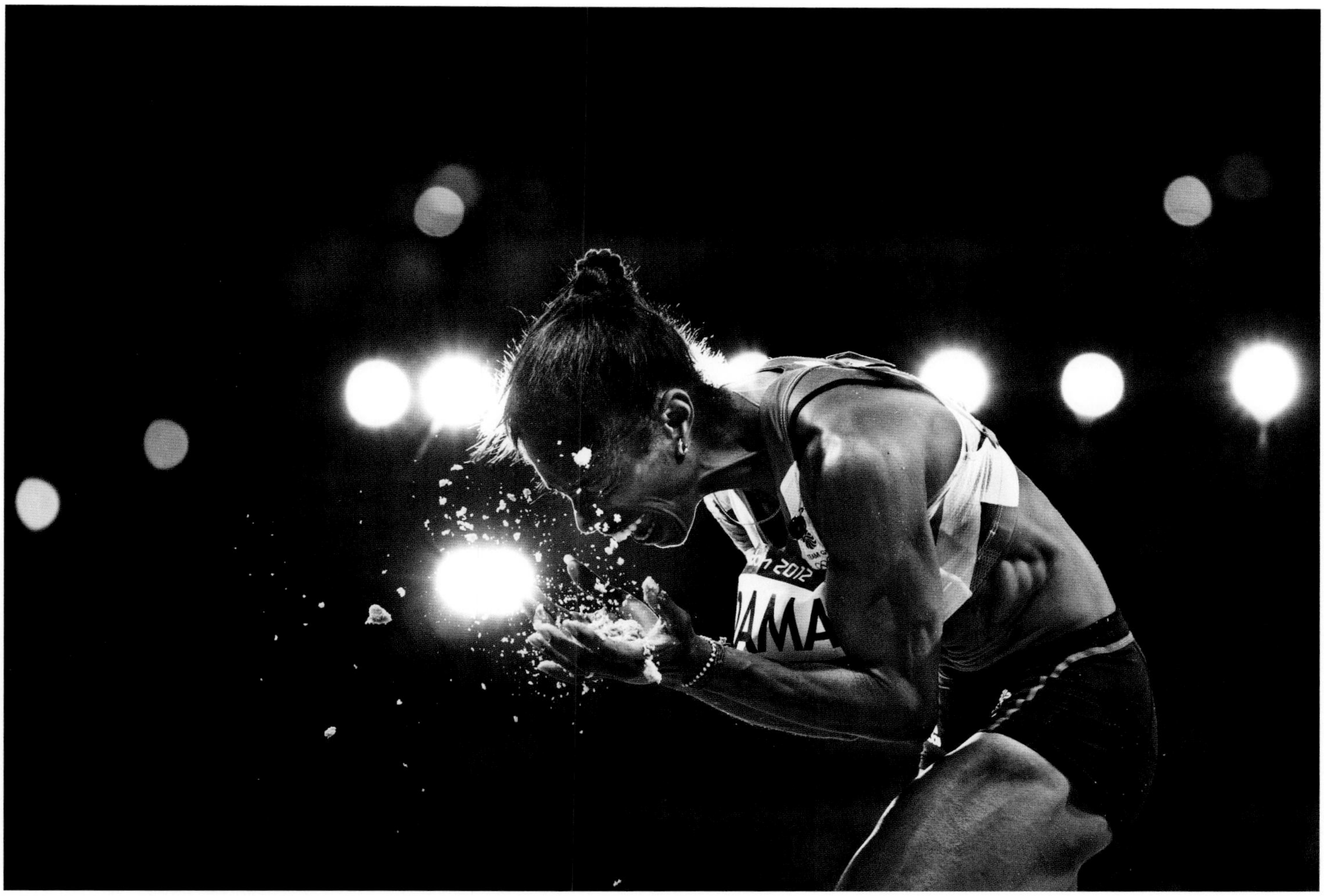

© All images courtesy of Getty Images.

RYAN PIERSE AUSTRALIA

2ND PLACE
SPORT

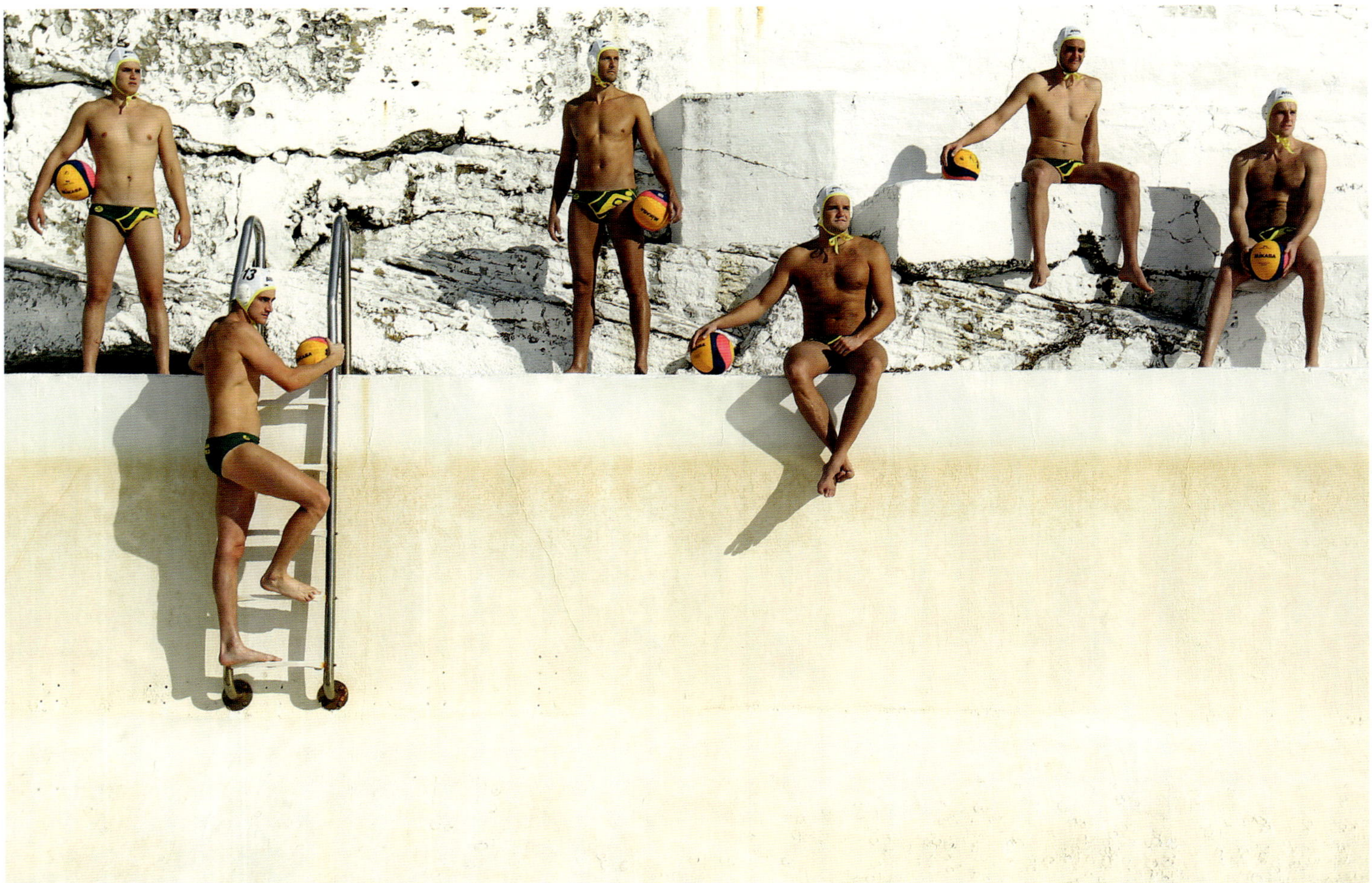

Fish out of Water. The Australian Men's Olympic Waterpolo Team are photographed in an empty Bondi Icebergs pool at Bondi Beach on 31 May 2012 in Sydney, Australia. The Aussie Sharks, as they are known, were finalising their preparations for the London 2012 Olympic Games when I asked them to pose in this famous ocean pool...with the twist of it being empty.

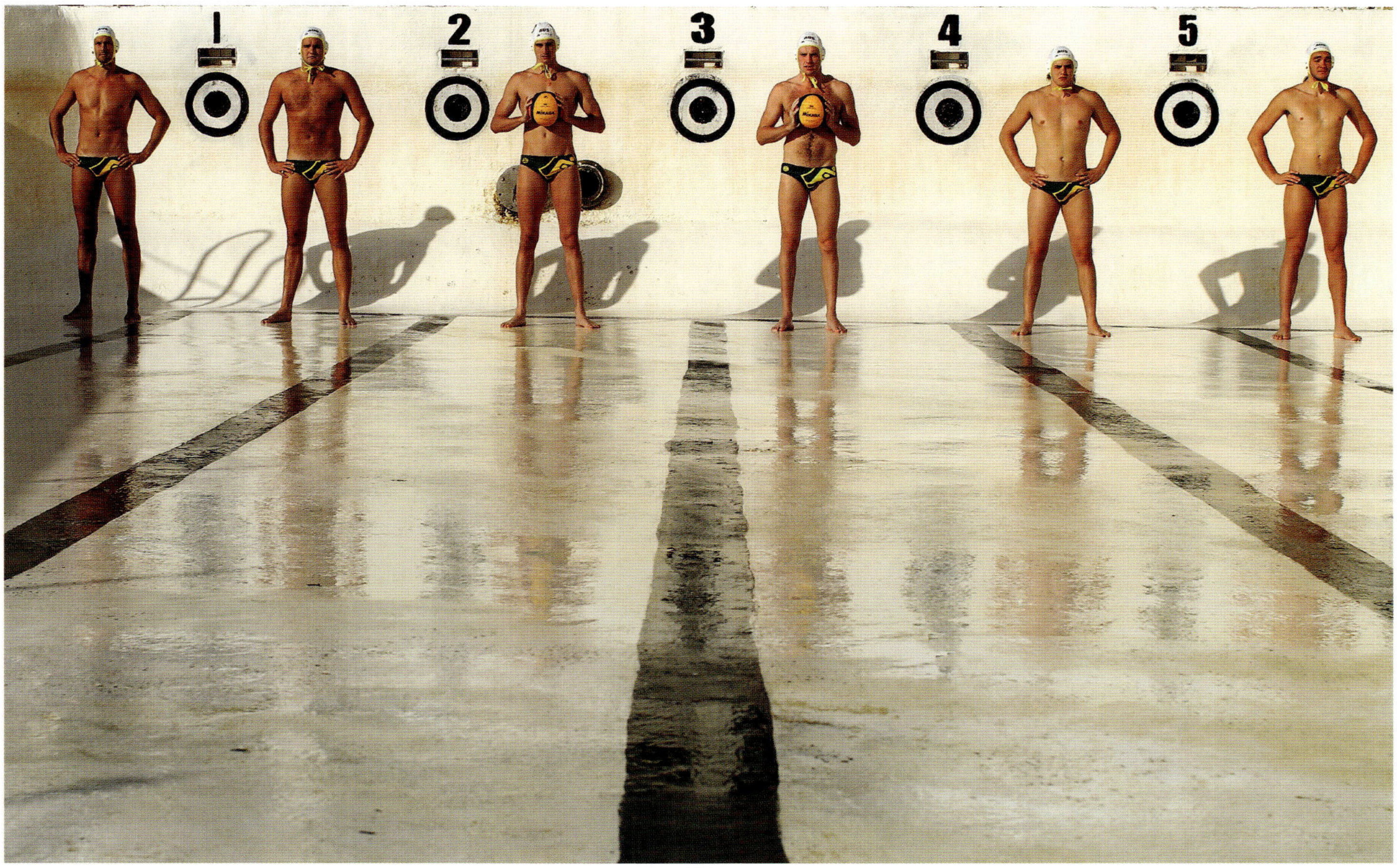
1
2
3
4
5

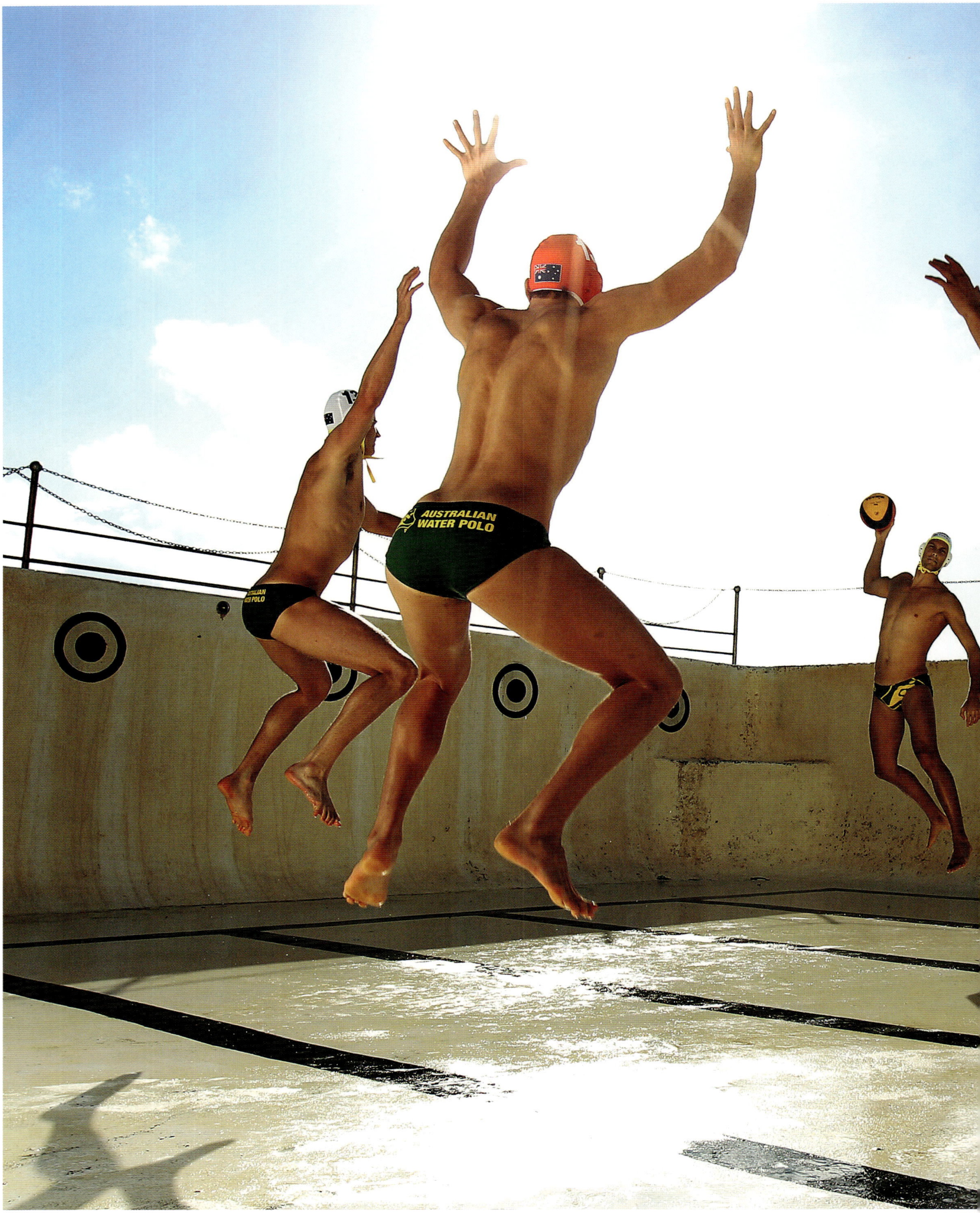
AUSTRALIAN
WATER POLO

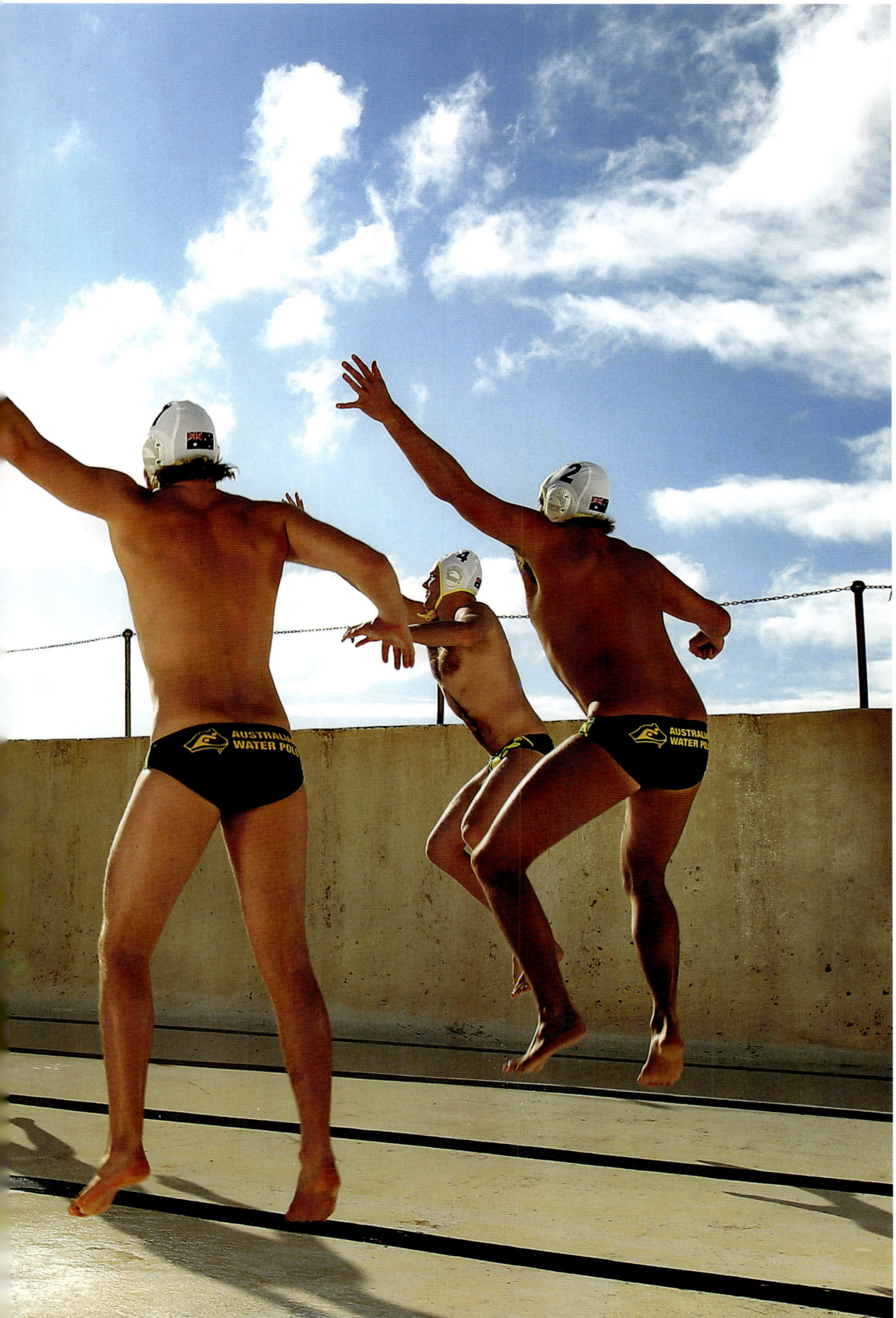
AUSTRALIA
WATER PO
AUSTRALIA
WATER POLO
4
2

ISABELA PACINI BRAZIL

3RD PLACE
SPORT

Naadam festival in Mongolia. The Naadam Festival is the traditional Mongolian Olympic Games featuring three sports: wrestling, archery and horse racing.

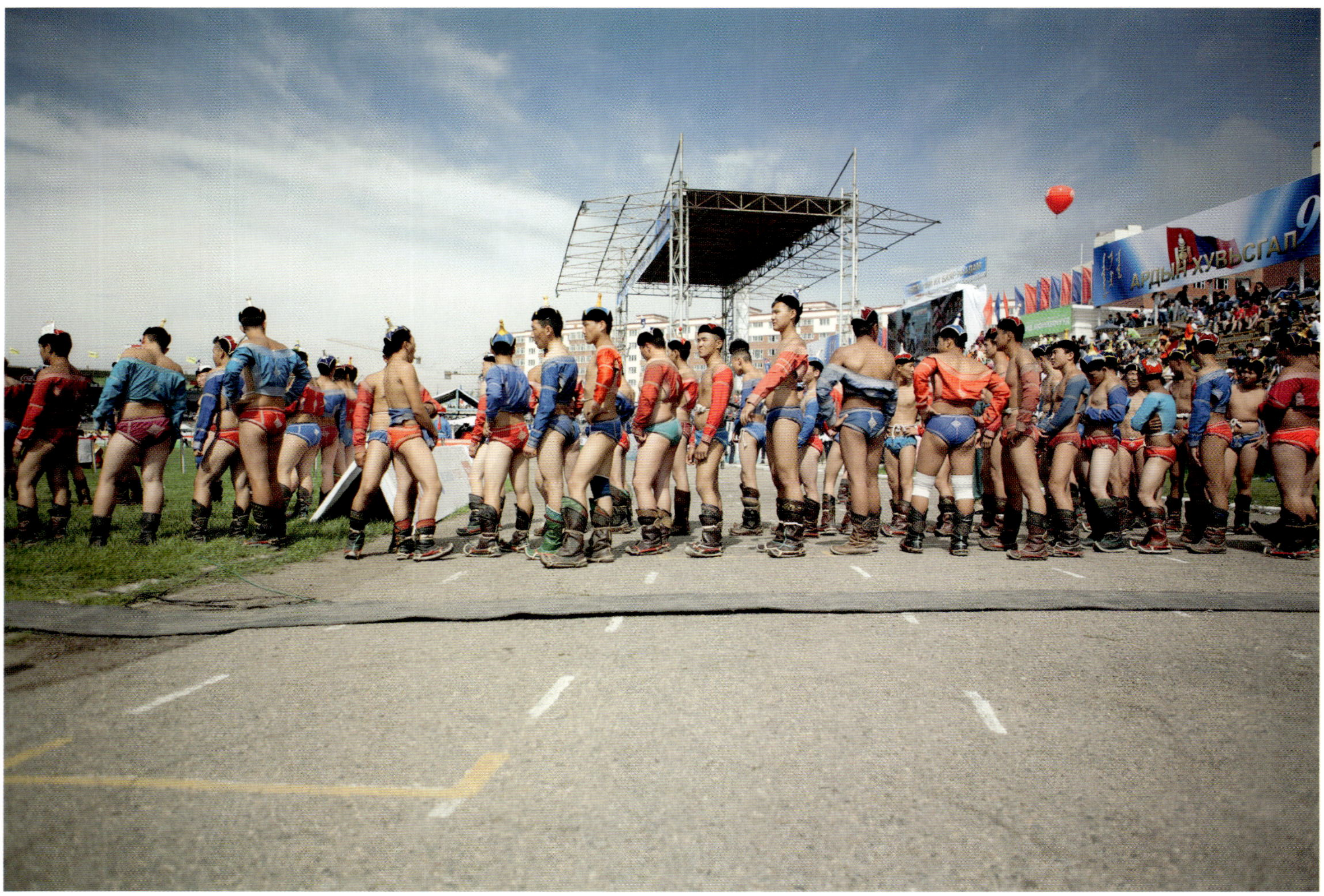

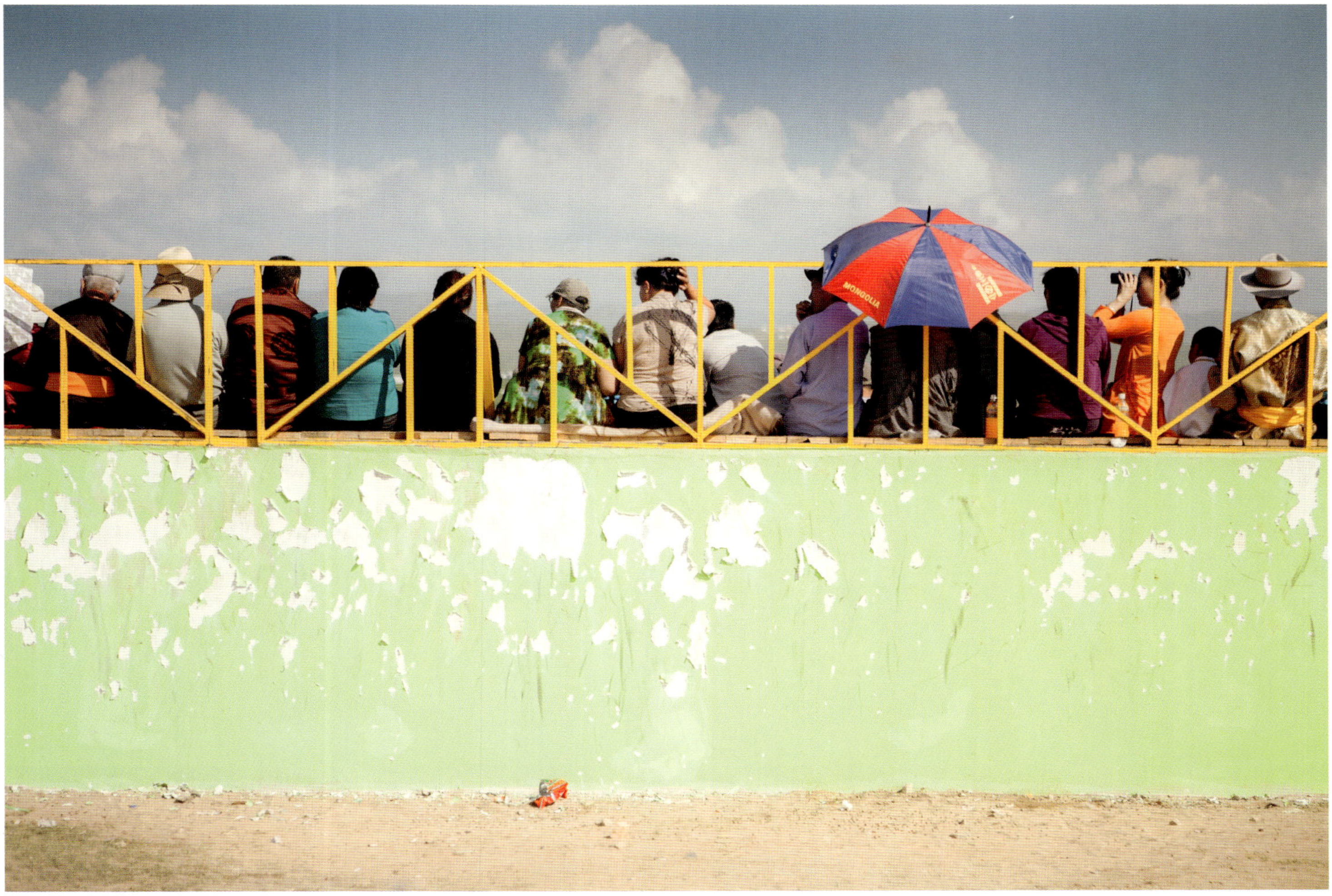
MONGOLIA

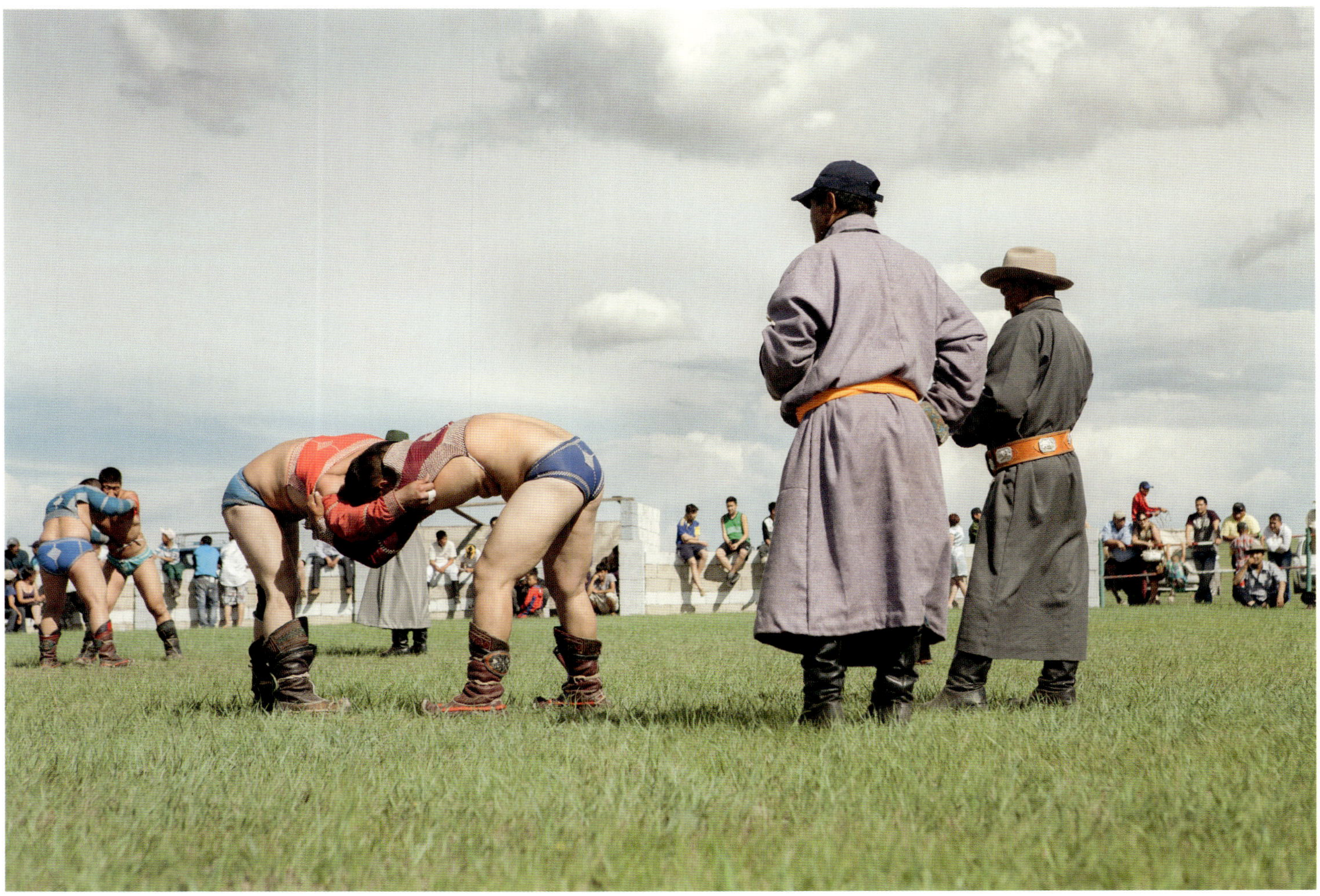

VANESSA COLARETA PERU

1ST PLACE
STILL LIFE

Migrant. Migrant is a photographic series based on the reinterpretation of Spanish Still Life of the 17th to 19th centuries from the collection of the Prado Museum. Multiculturalism is the main theme of the images that make up the series; they are based on texts and testimonies on female migration experiences in Valencia.

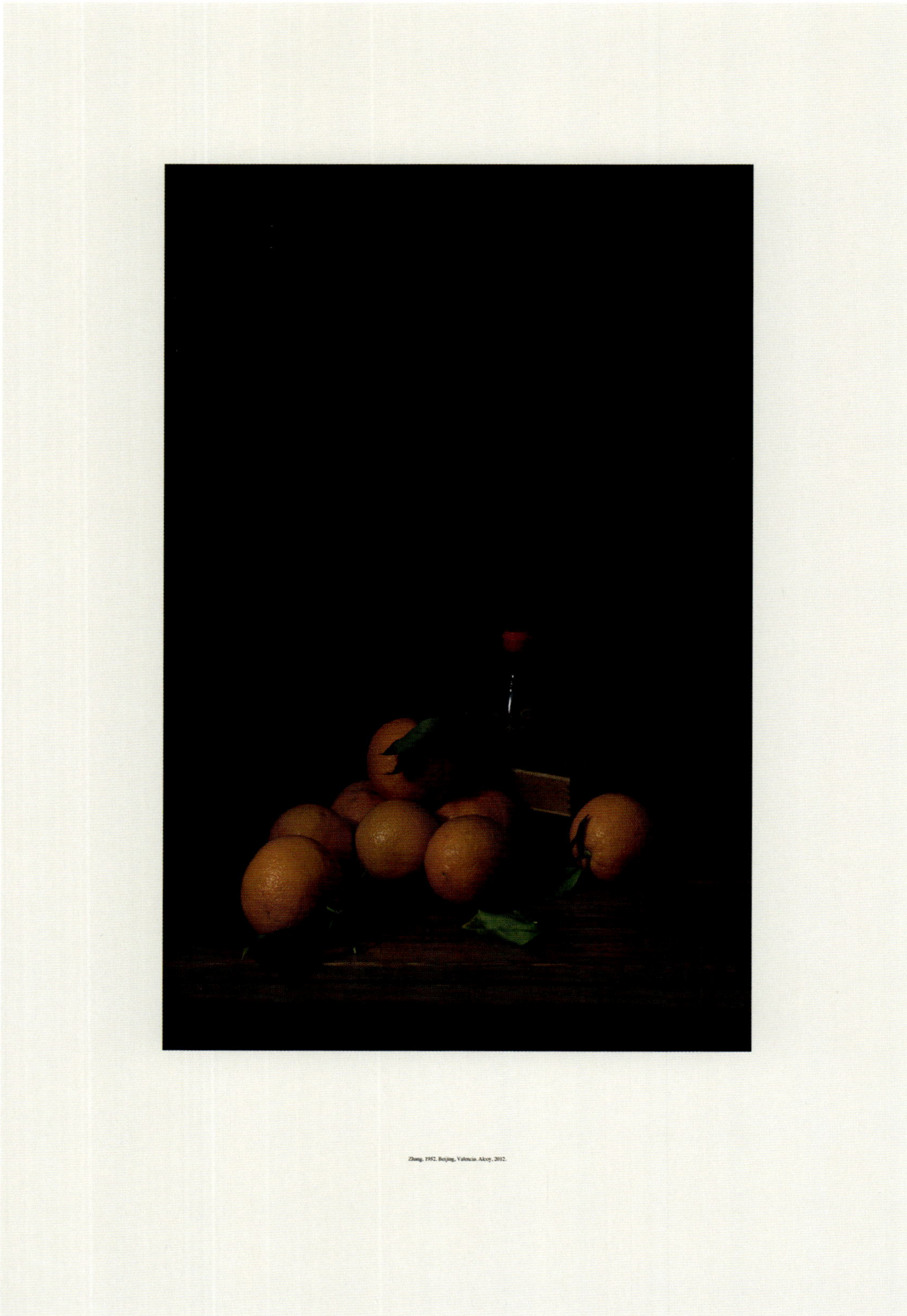

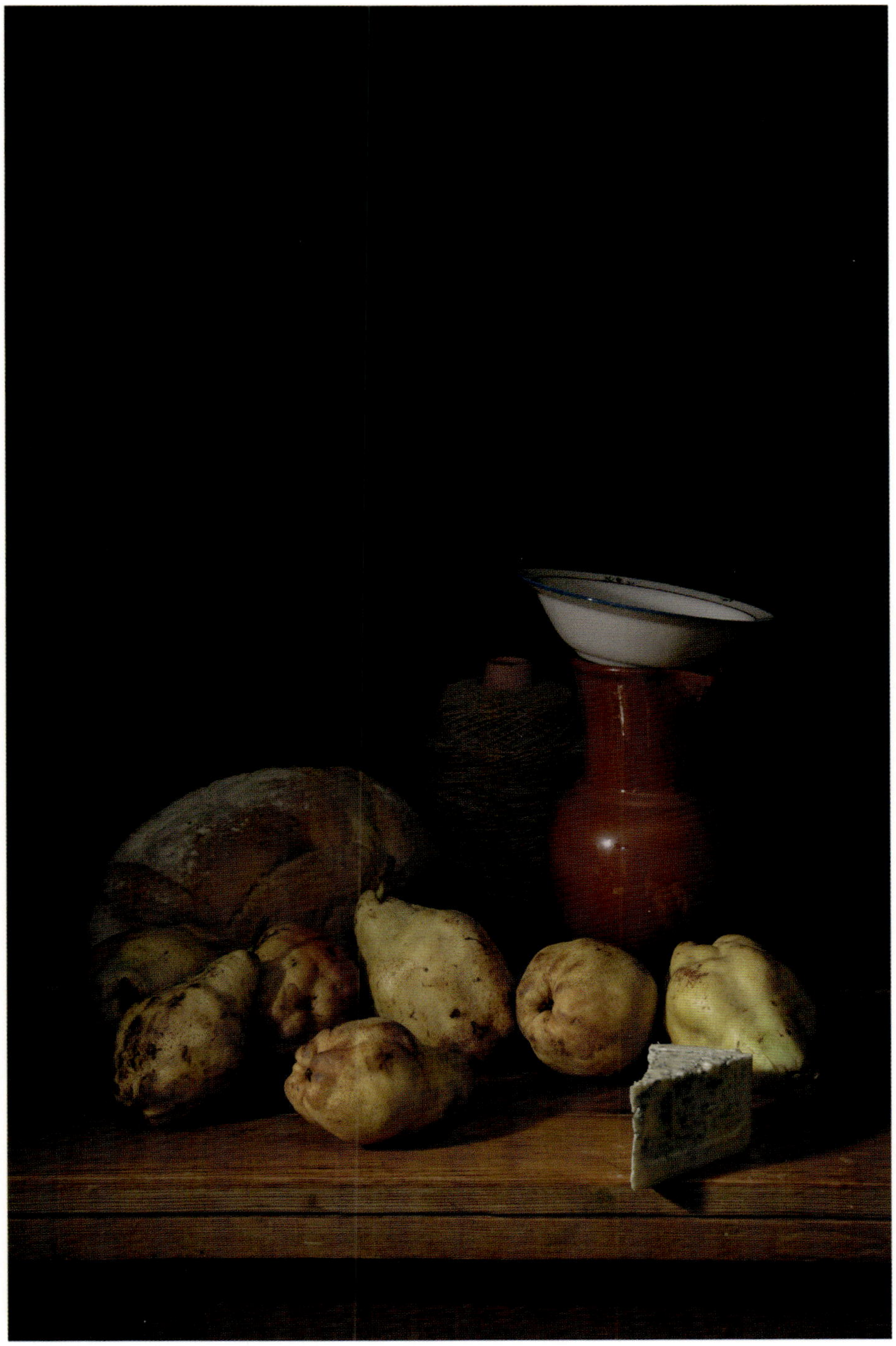

Maru, 1956. Alcoy, Paris. Alcoy, 2012.

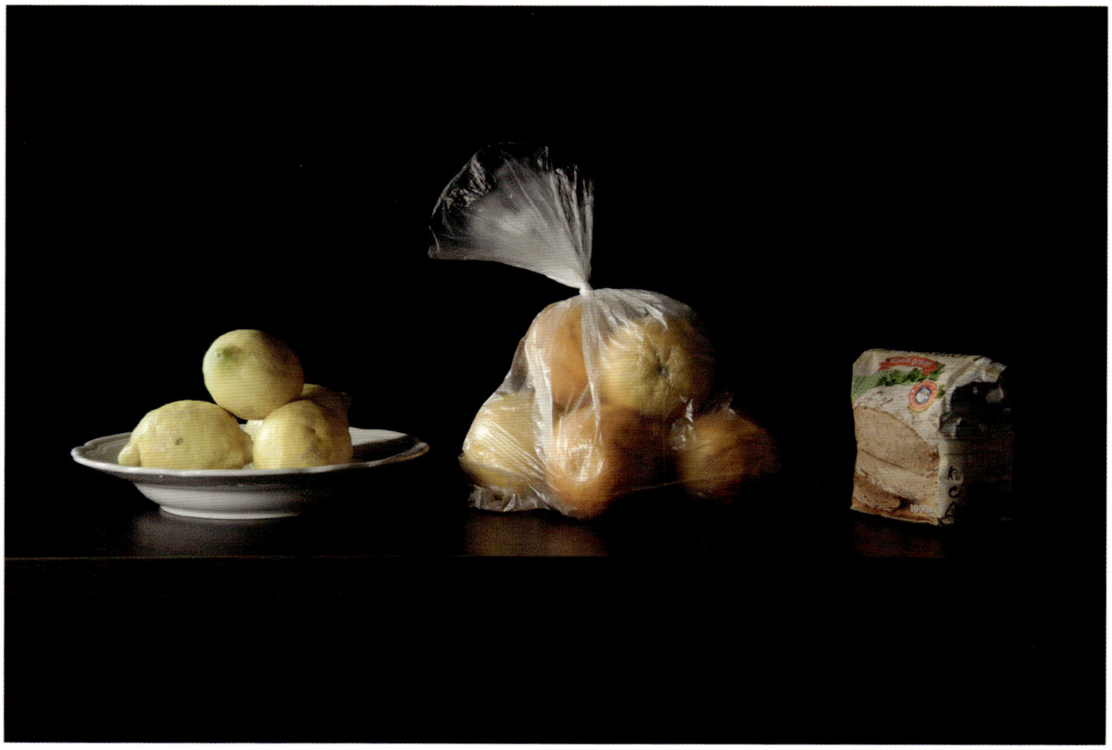

Alemania estaba veinte años más adelantada en todo. Recuerdo mucho la nieve, hacía mucho frío y los días eran cortos.

Germany was more developed in every sense, by twenty years or so. It was very cold, the days were short and I always remember the snow.

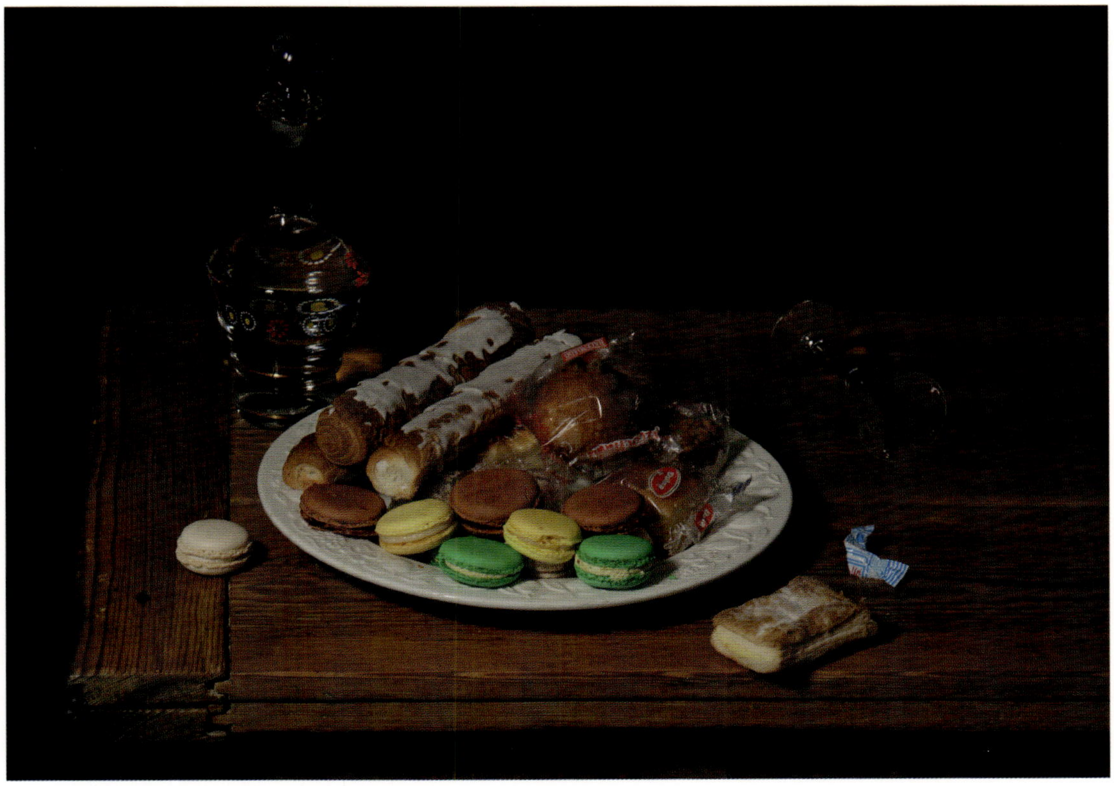

Emigramos porque mi padre fue a buscar trabajo y en Francia buscaban mano de obra. Él fue primero y pasado un año nos reunimos con él.

We emigrated because my father was looking for work and France had opportunities. He left first; we met him a year later.

GALI TIBBON ISRAEL

1ST PLACE
TRAVEL

Bottom image: Pilgrims gather around the crossed-shaped church of Bet Giyorgis as a dove flies over. **Top right image:** A hermit reads verses from the bible as he sits in a cranny in the red volcanic rock surrounding the Lalibela churches. **Bottom right image:** An infertile woman is baptized by priests; according to faith the water has fertility powers that will allow her to conceive.

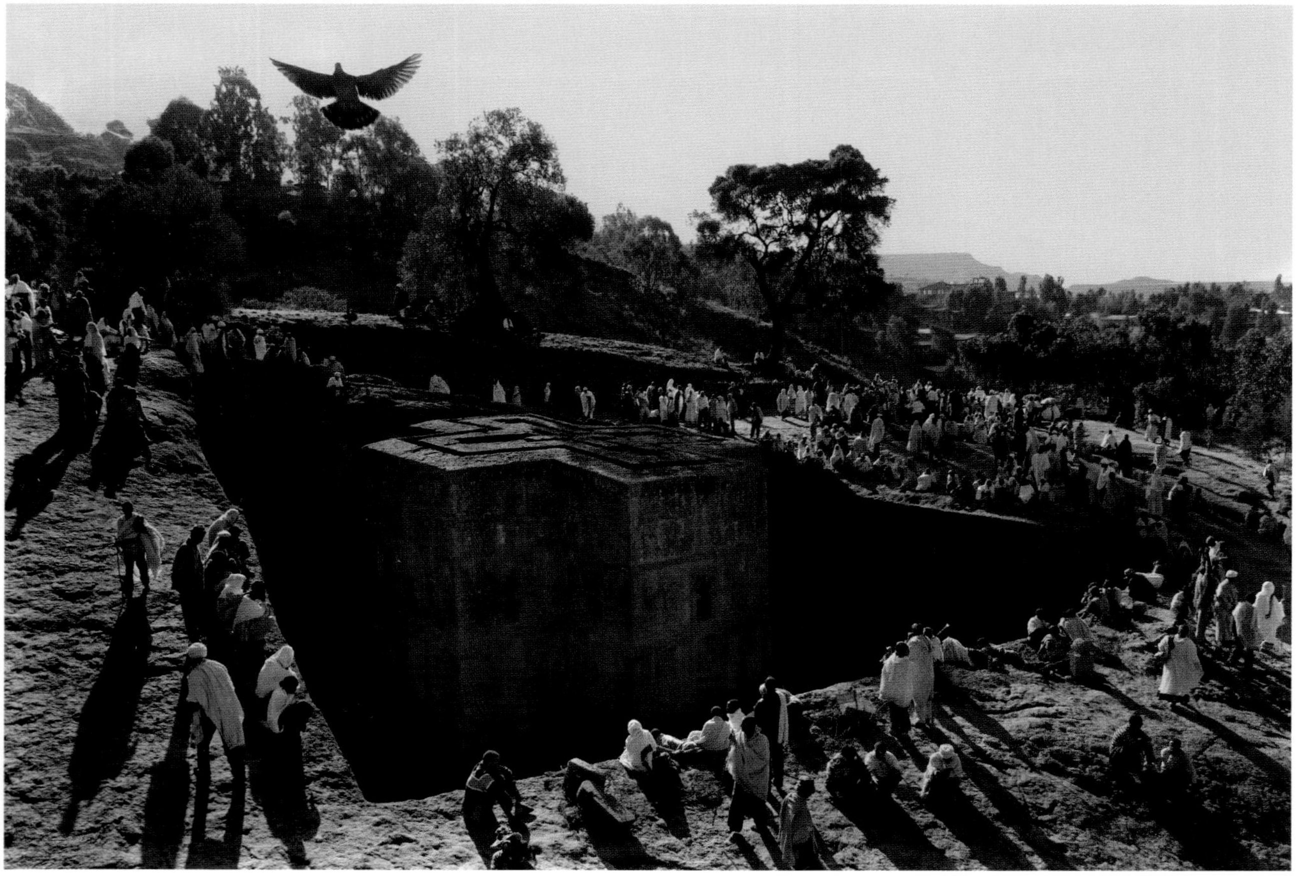

Journey to the Jerusalem of Africa – Lalibela, Ethiopia. Every year, just before Christmas day (Julian calendar) thousands of pious Christian orthodox worshippers make the pilgrimage to Lalibela, a small town in Ethiopia's highlands, known as the Jerusalem of Africa, or Black Jerusalem. Lalibela is famous for its 13th century monolithic churches, carved out of the living rock, one of the great wonders of the world.

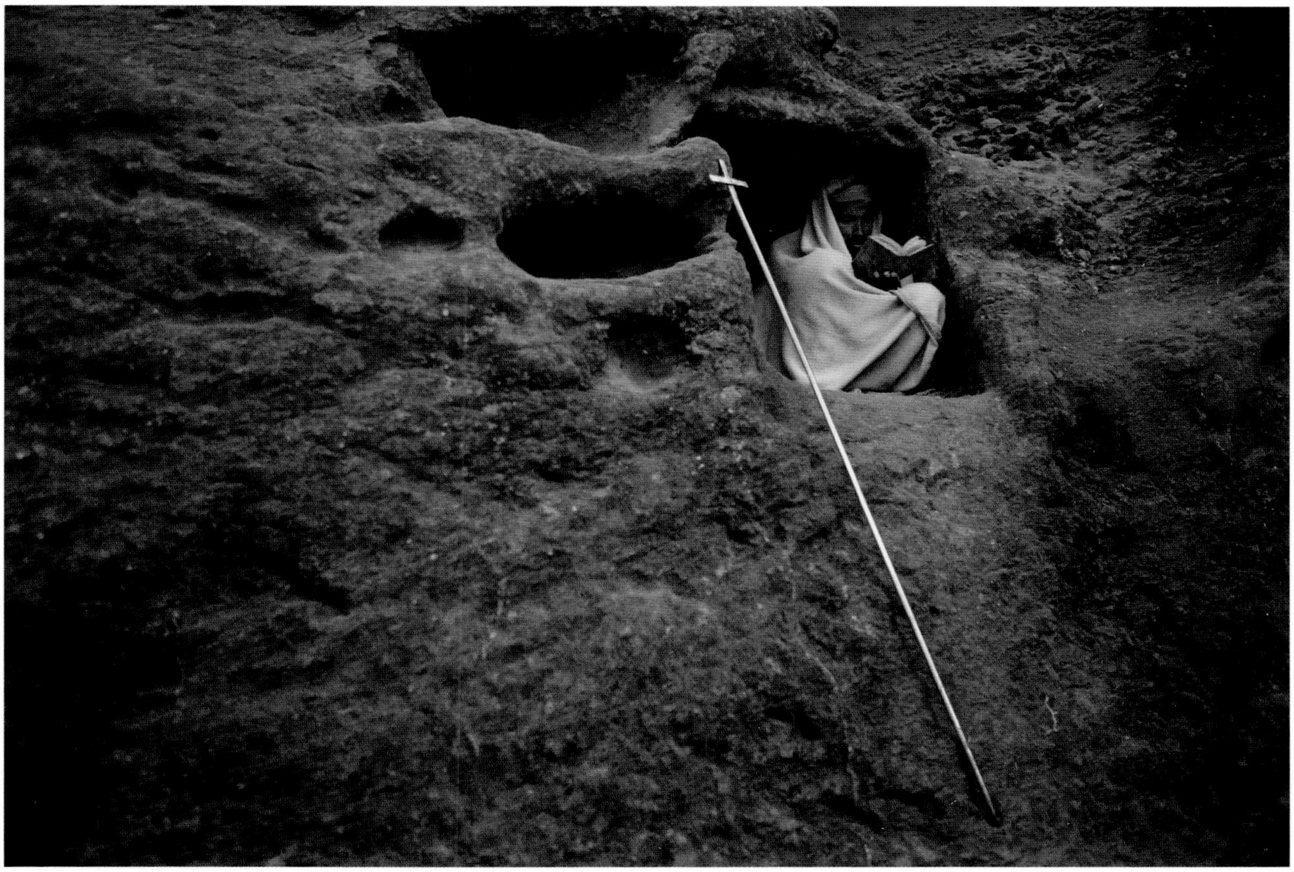

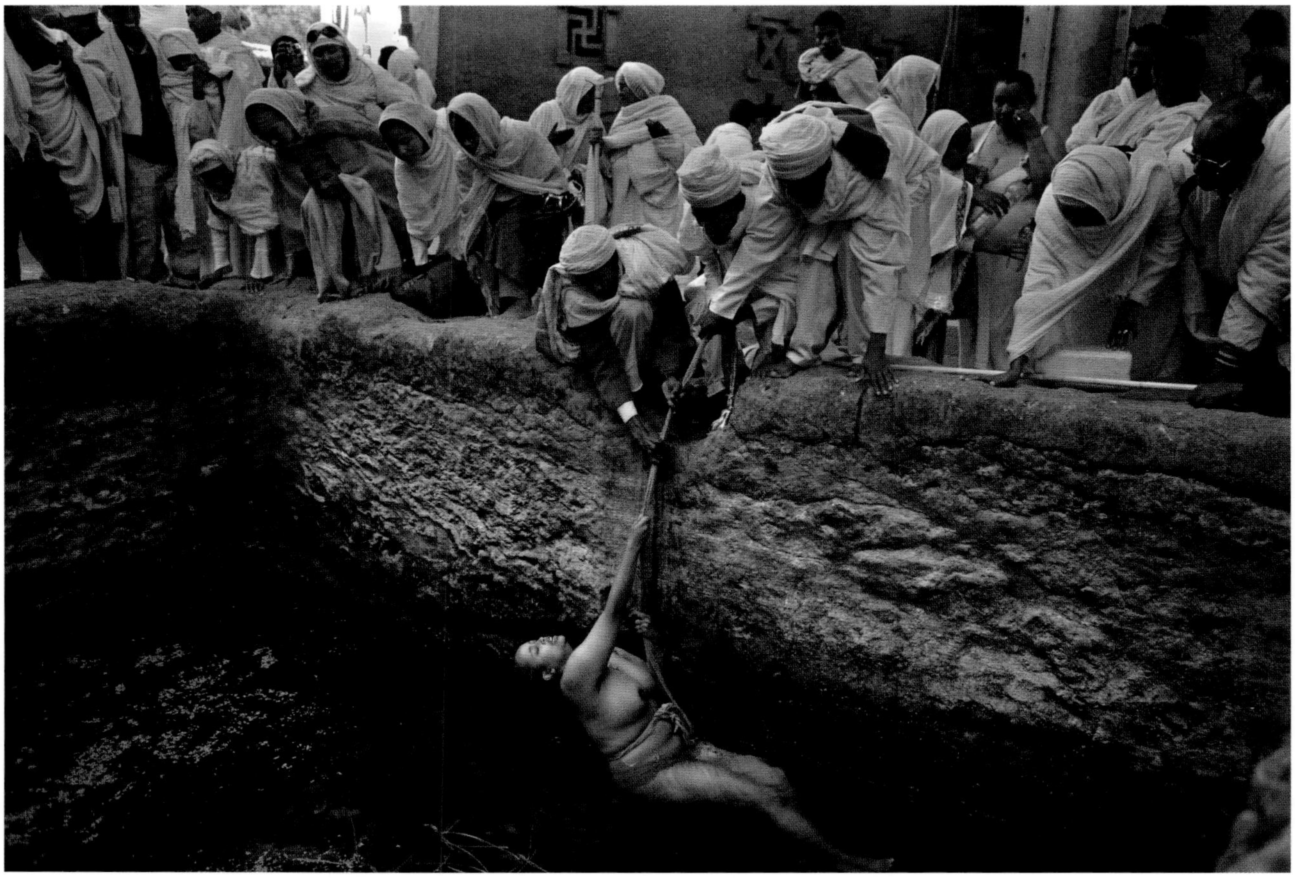

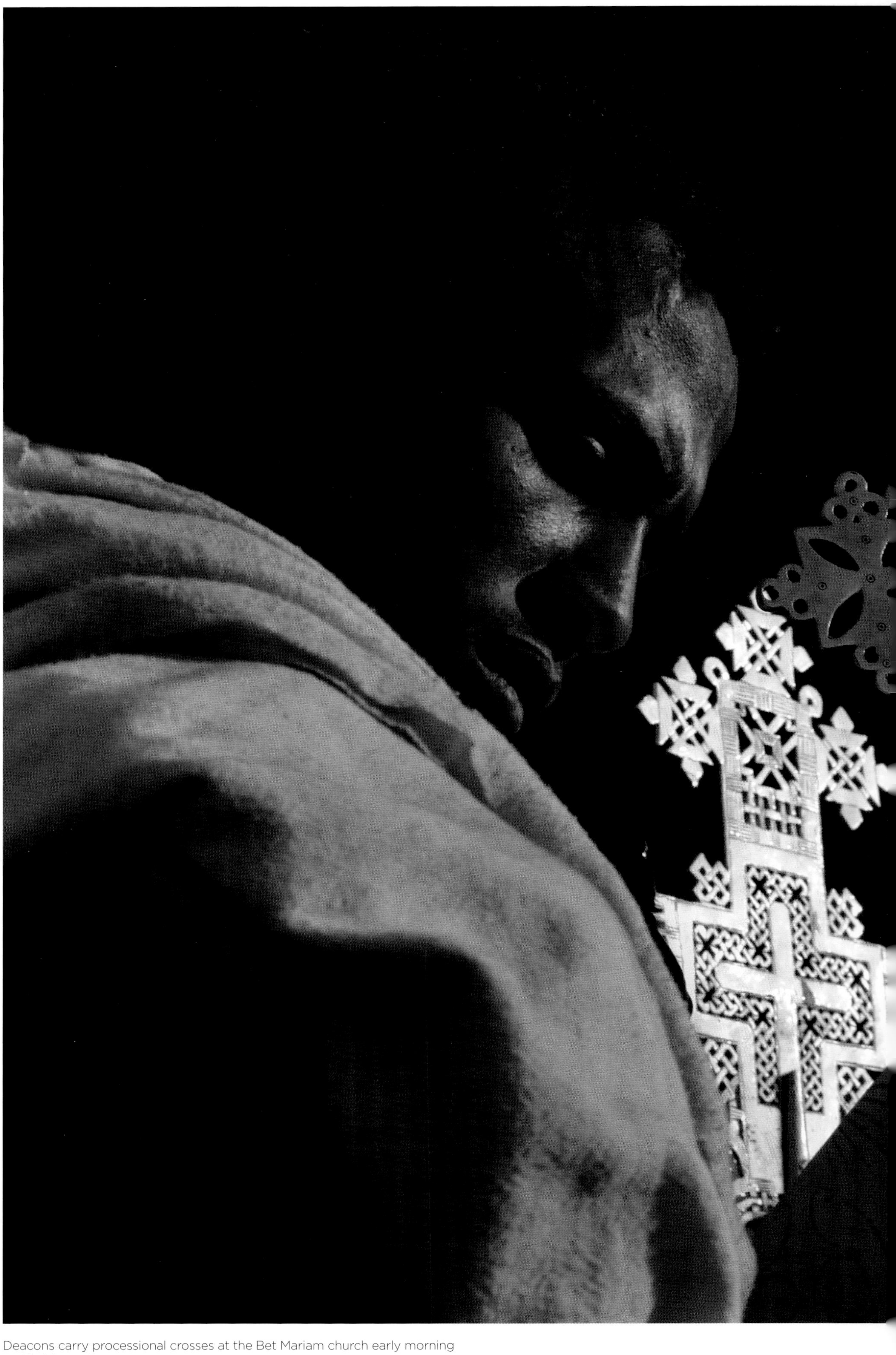

Deacons carry processional crosses at the Bet Mariam church early morning on Christmas day.

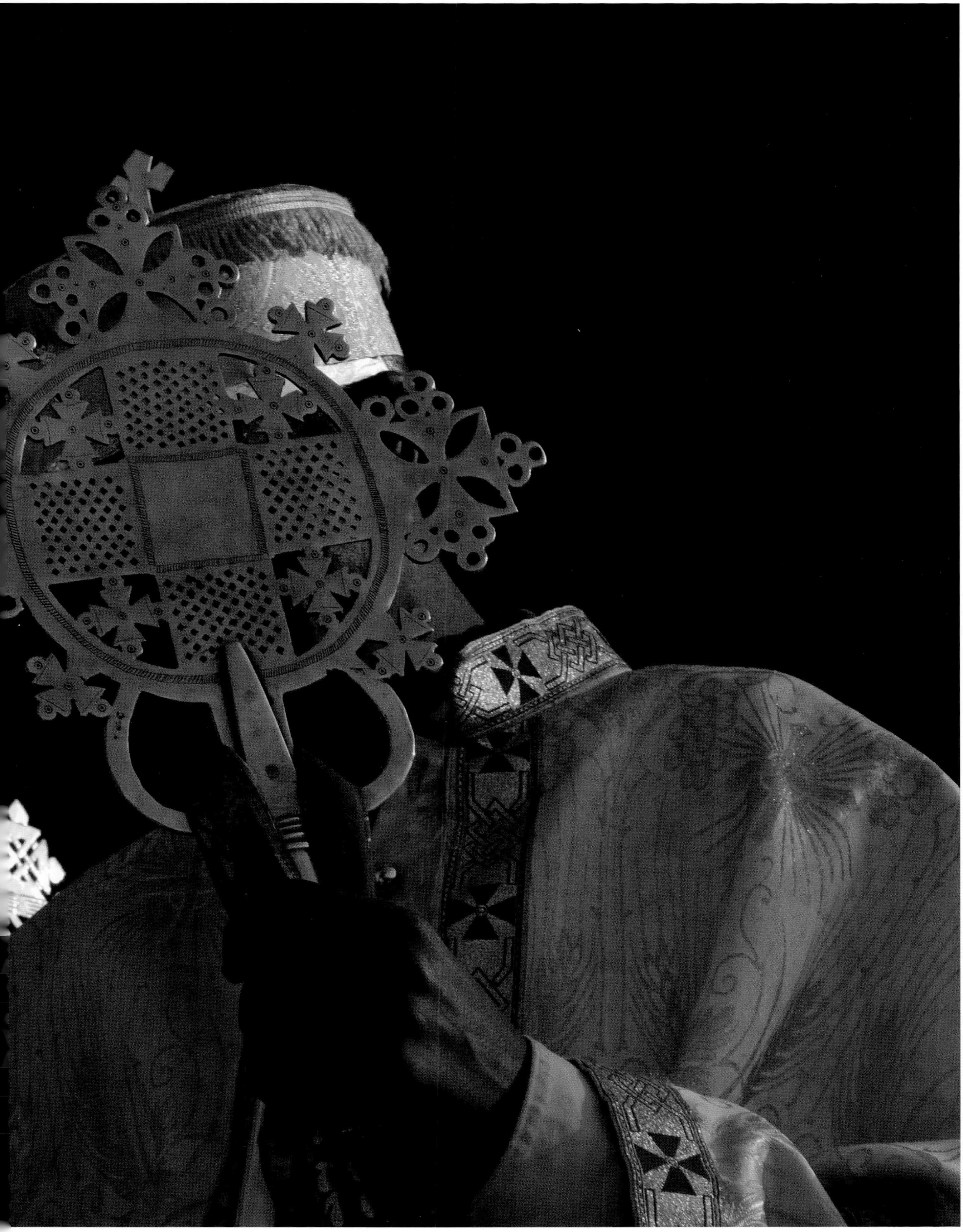

DANIEL DUART SPAIN

2ND PLACE
TRAVEL

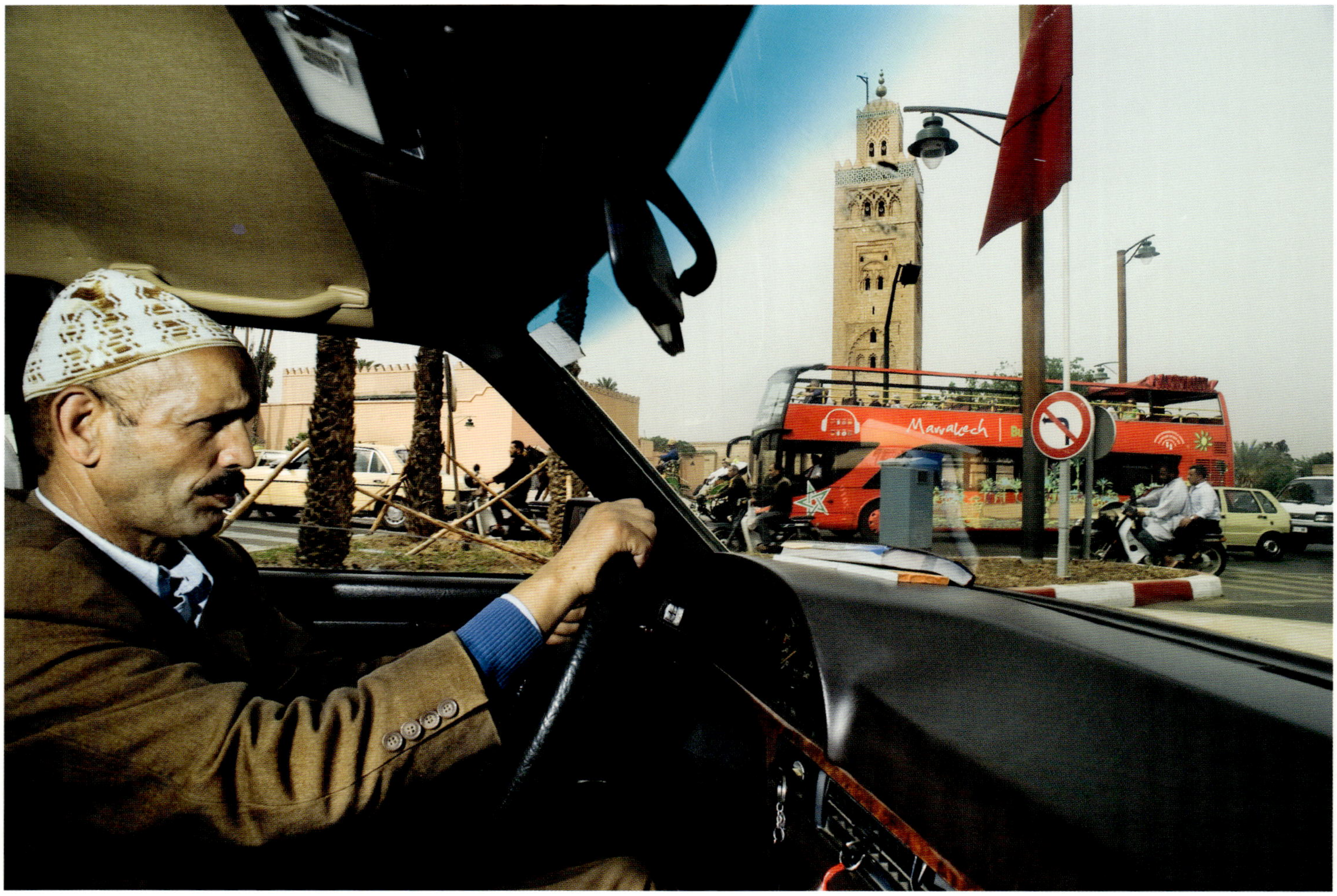

Views of different cities seen from the inside of a taxi – a new kind of tourism?
How often we arrive in the airport of an unknown city, ask for a taxi and go in the search of our hotel. That route is the first impression we get, quick glances at the locals, at streets with no names. In this new project, I capture these ephemeral sights. New York, Paris and Marrakech are the first cities I chose, because they represent three continents and three cultures. I don't direct the taxi driver; I simply let myself be carried, aware of what's happening outside. I shoot left and right, back and forth, with the avidity of a tourist, always within a frame: the car window.

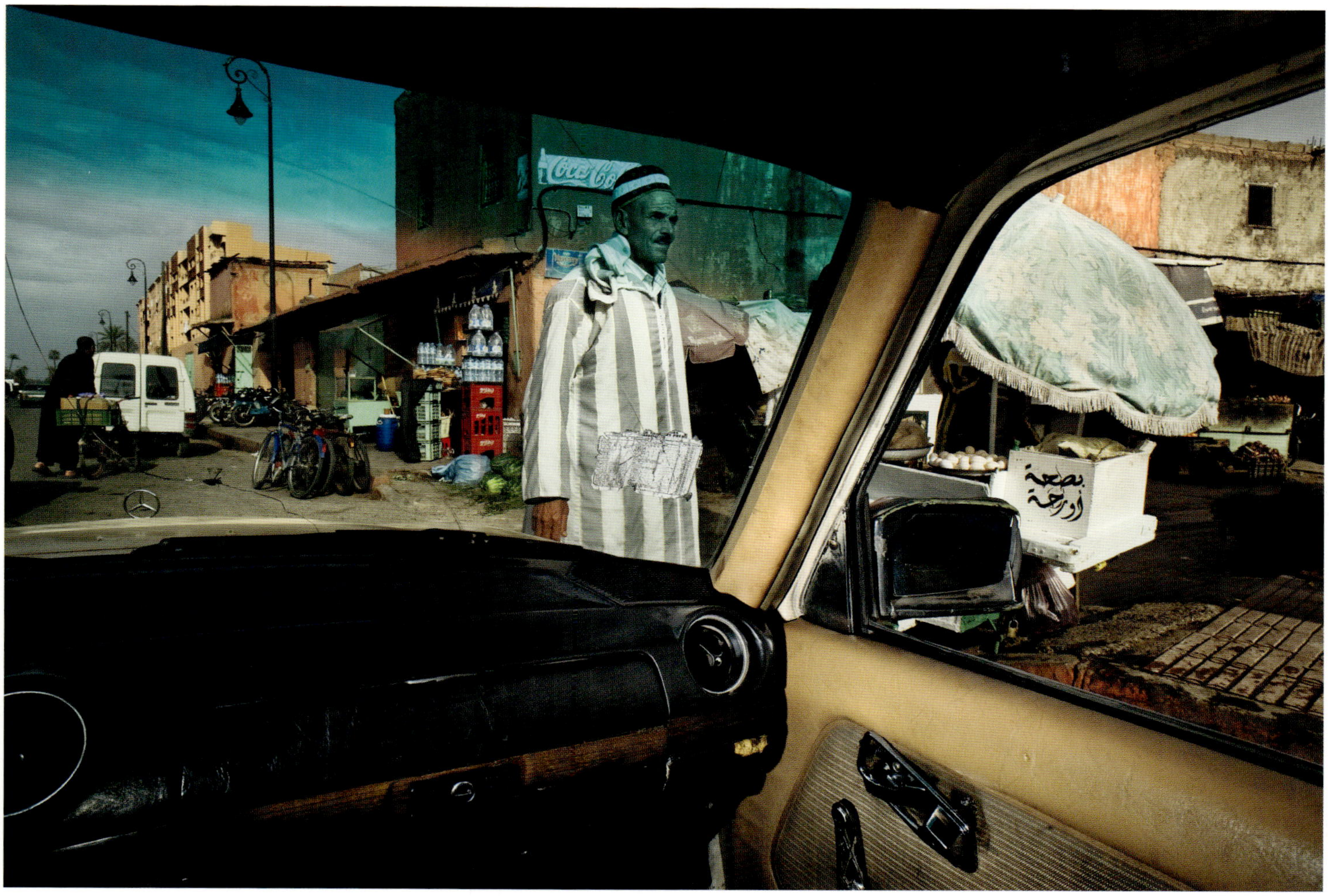

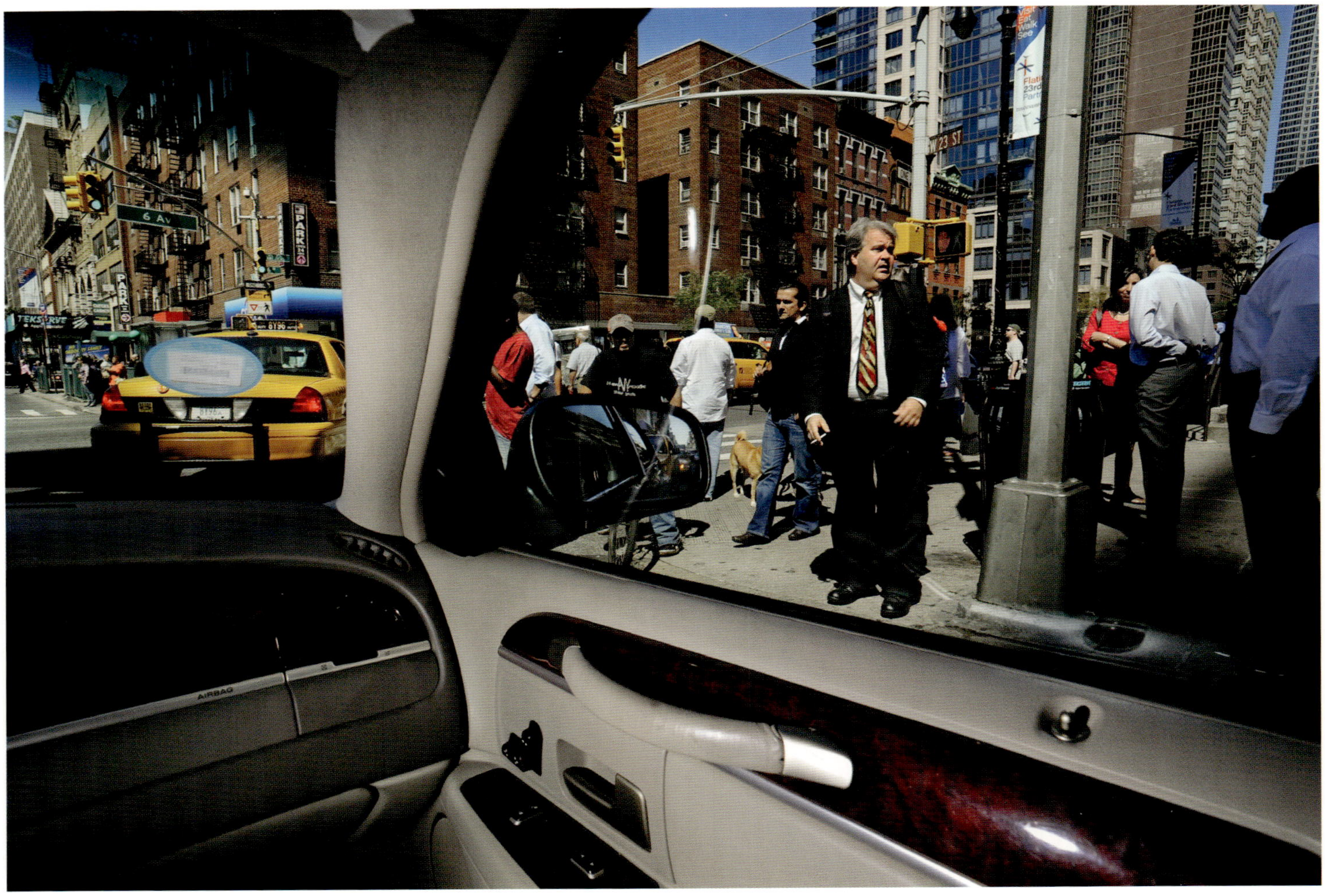
6 Av
PARK
W 23 ST
AIRBAG

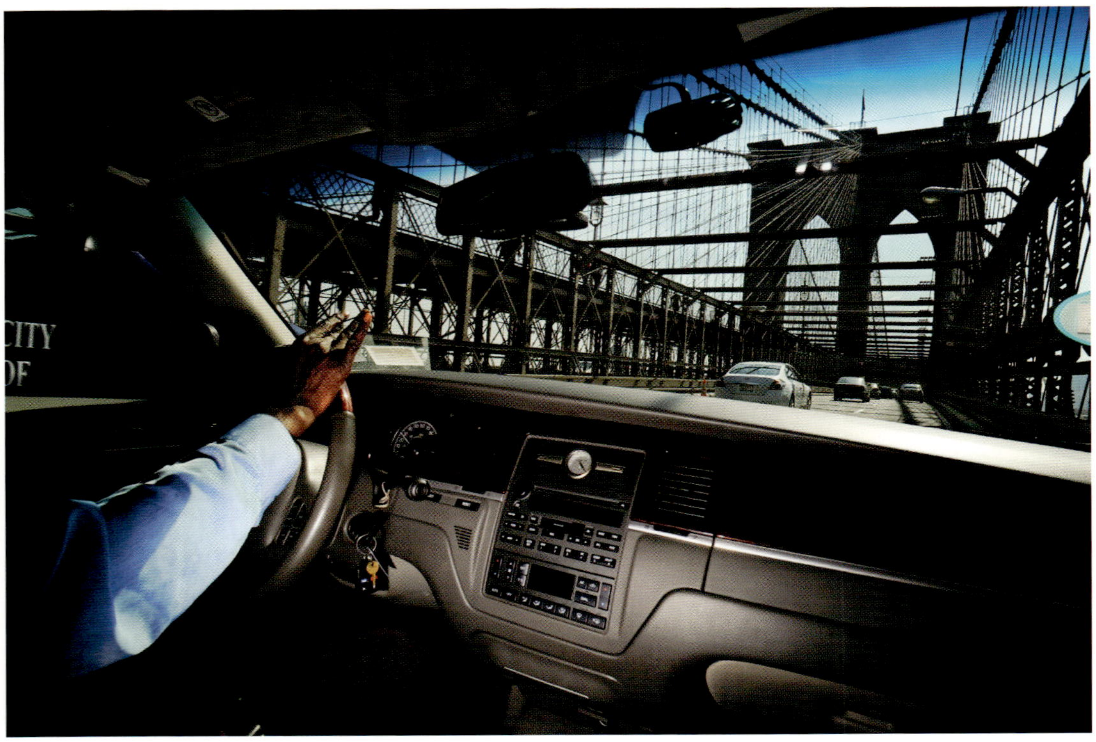
CITY
OF

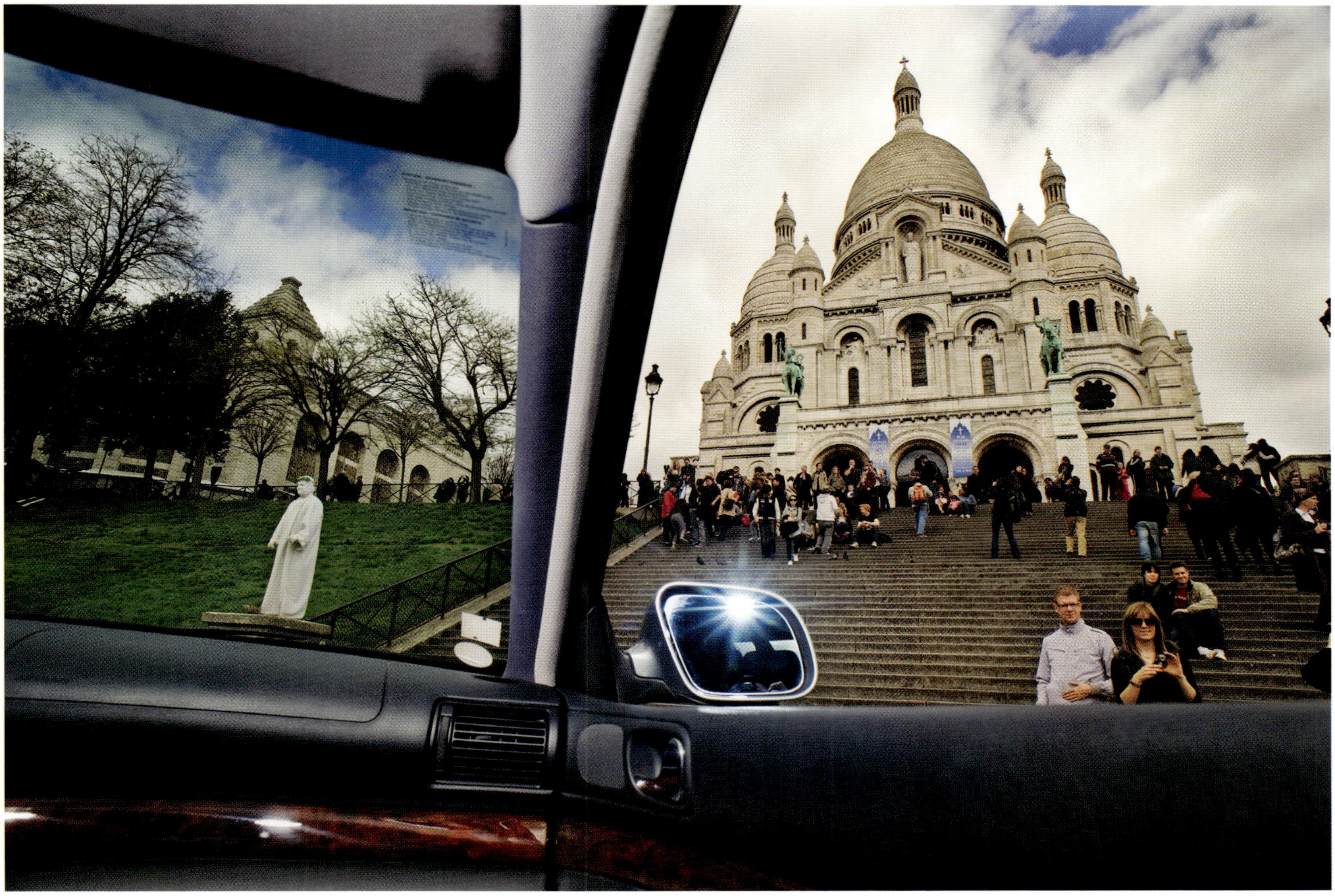

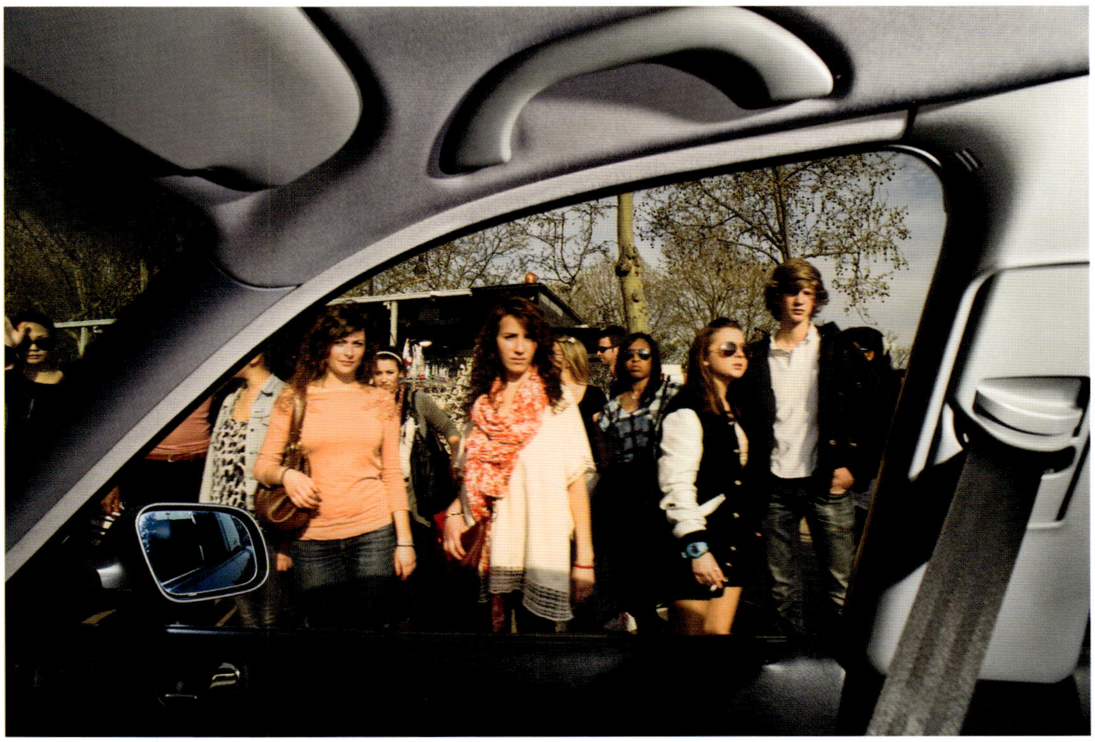

JOHANNES HEUCKEROTH GERMANY

3RD PLACE
TRAVEL

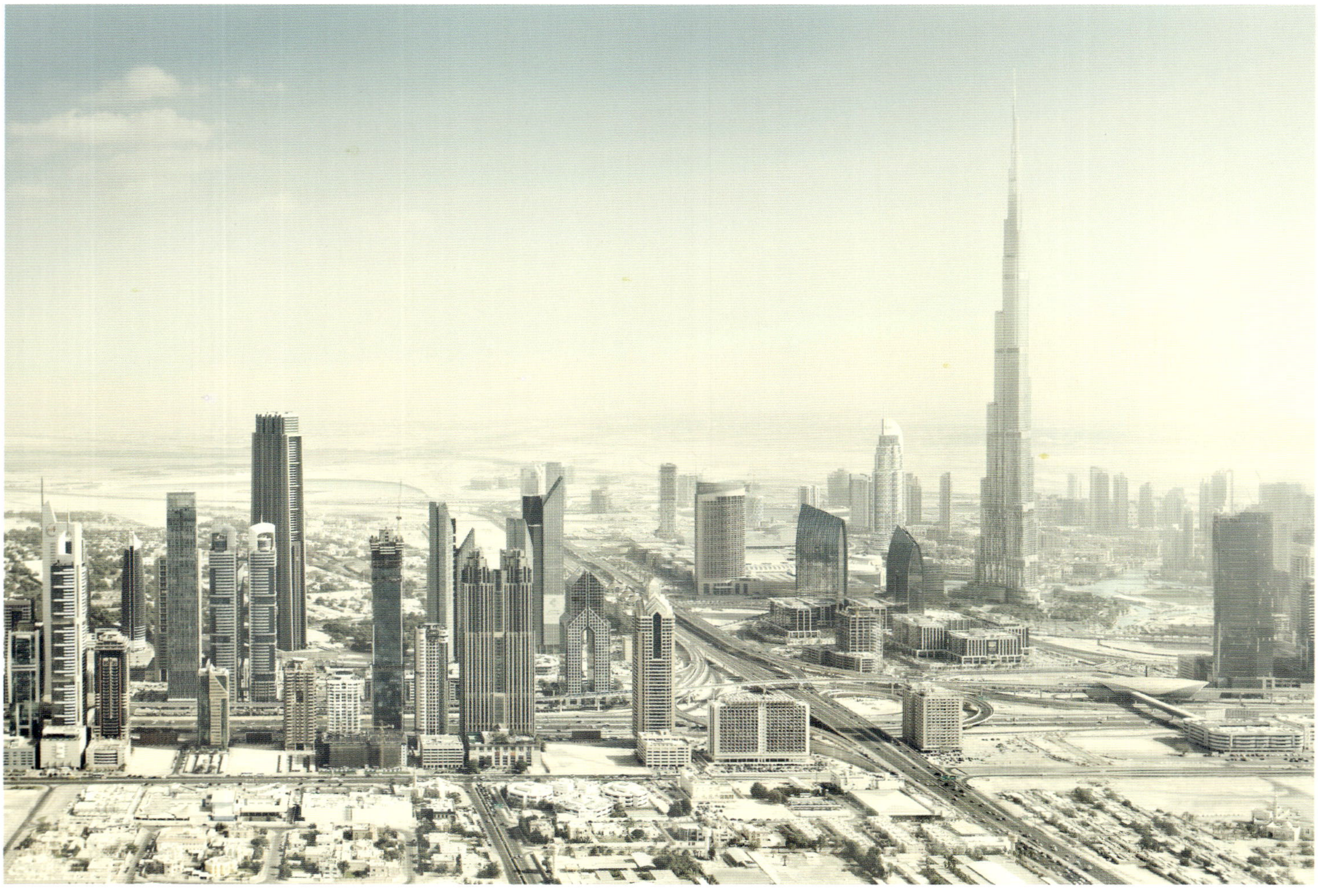

Dubai Aerials. 'Come, let us build ourselves a city, with a tower that reaches to the heavens, so that we may make a name for ourselves.' This biblical description of the building of the Tower of Babel became reality in the 21st century. In 2010 the Burj Khalifa, the highest building in the world, was opened in this small desert country. It rises out of the desert to 828 metres, like a mirage. The tower has only one purpose: to focus the world's eyes on Dubai. In my work I show these gigantic landmarks and surreal cityscapes from above.

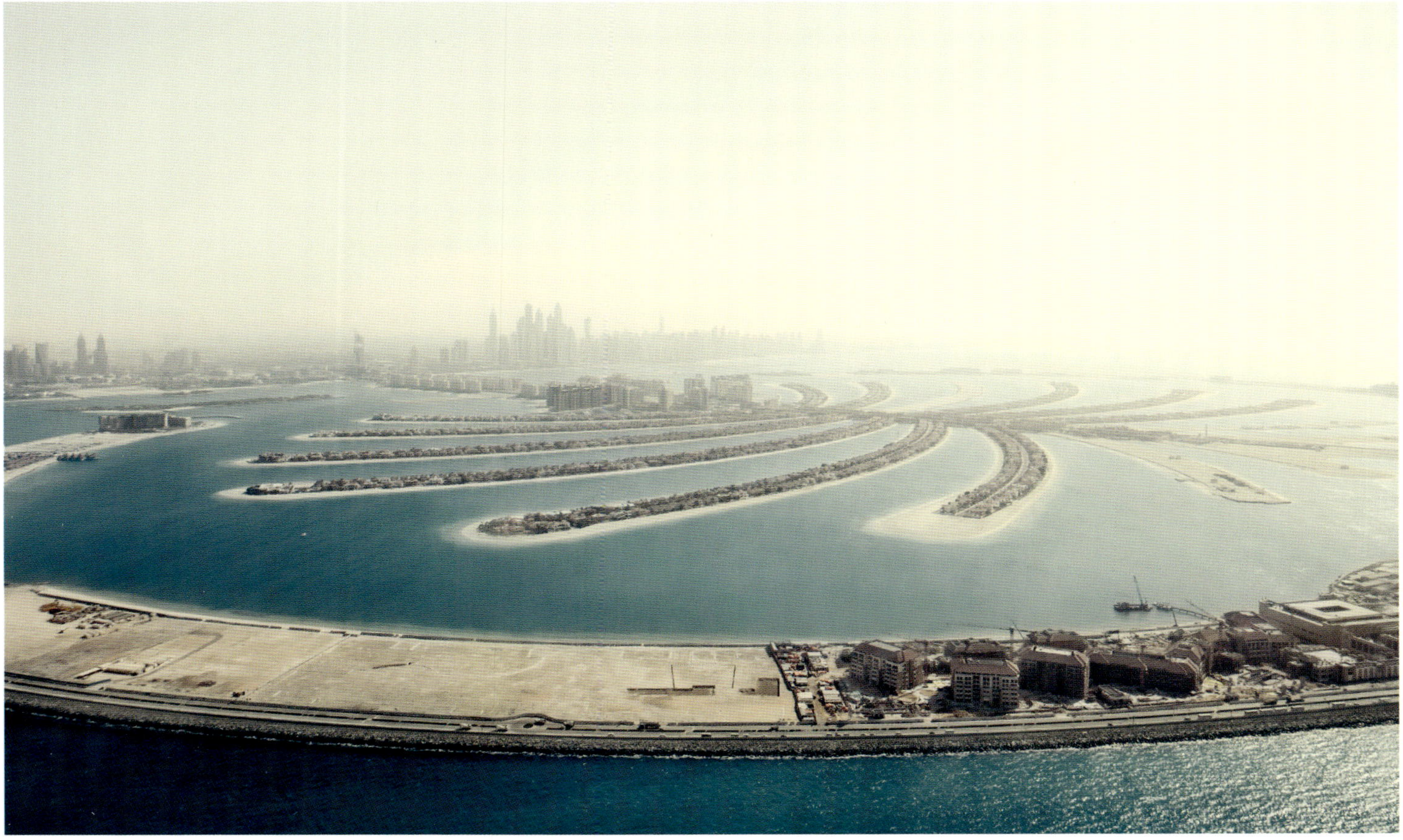

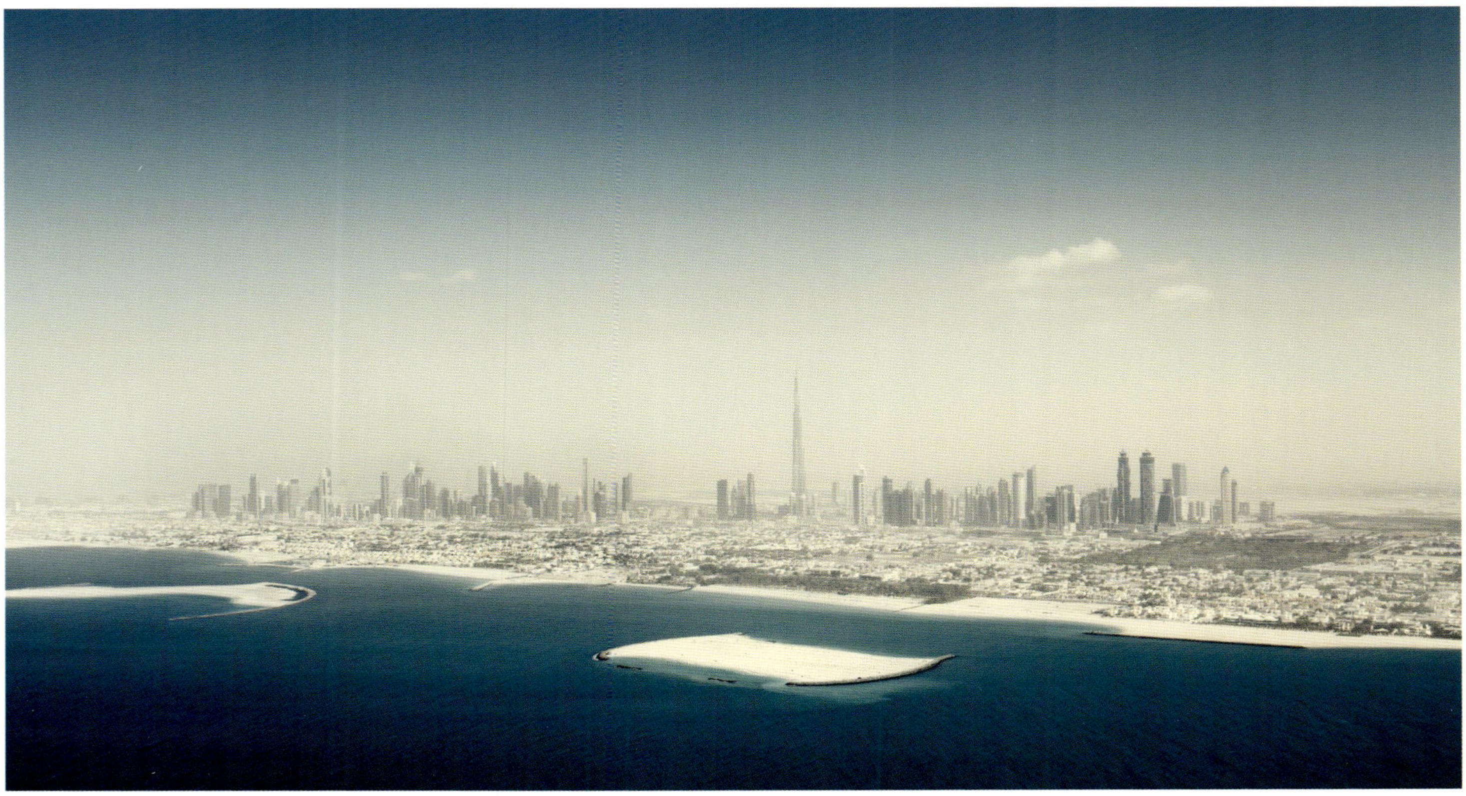

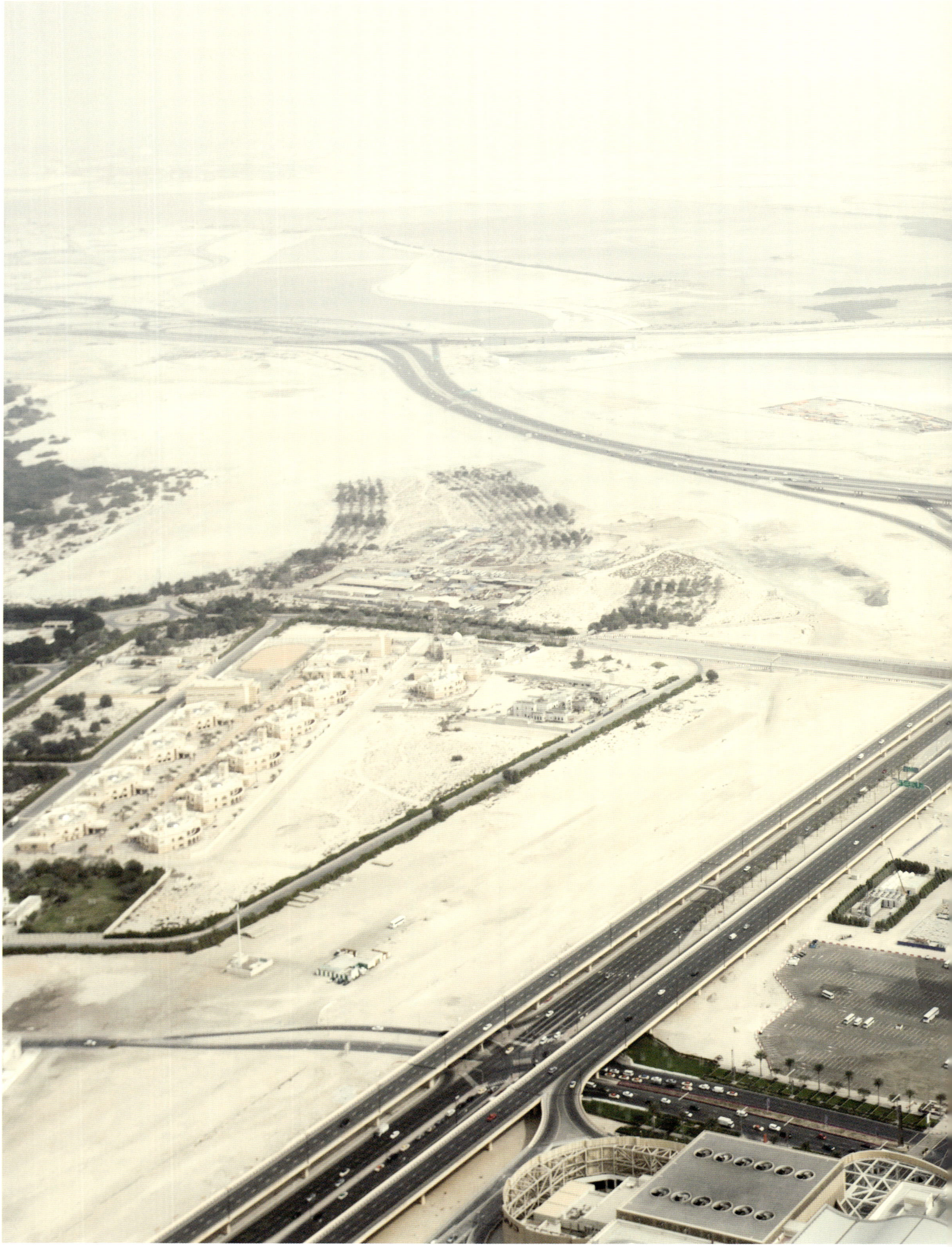

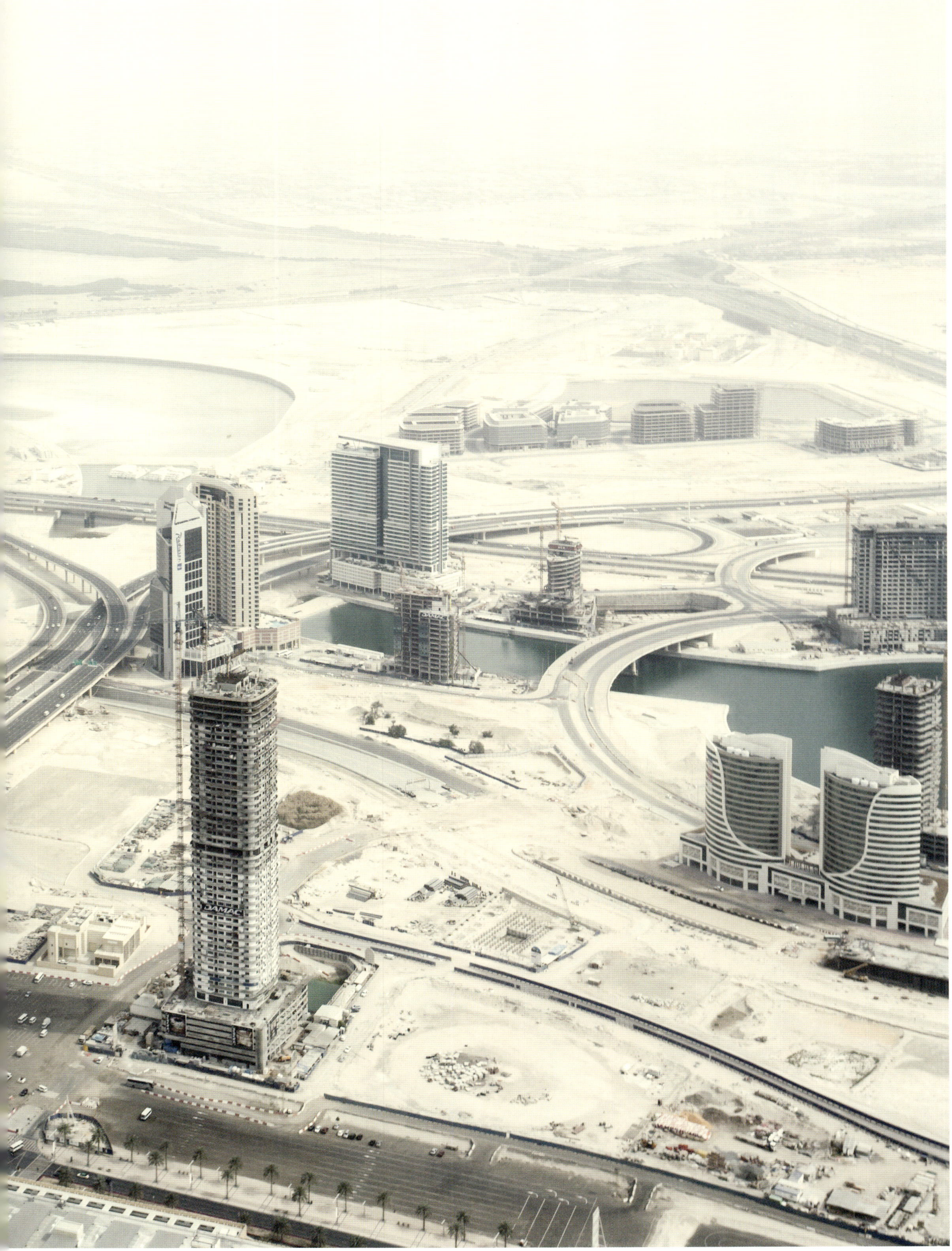
DAMAC

A SINGLE SNAPSHOT
WINNERS

OPEN COMPETITION WINNERS

"It takes will, determination and enthusiasm."

DAMIEN DEMOLDER (UK)
EDITOR, AMATEUR PHOTOGRAPHER MAGAZINE
PRESIDING CHAIR OF JURY

There really is no purer form of photography. Not in it for the cash, the amateur shoots what he likes, when he fancies it and when he has the time. And that time is his own.

In those spare moments, he chooses to take pictures above all other activities. It takes will, determination and enthusiasm - an internal drive.

For so many people around the world, photography provides the antidote to a nine to five graft, a release of pent-up expression, emotion and creativity that can't be tapped during the working day - a few hours of contemplative relaxation that balance the stresses of everyday life. That's what makes this Open section of the Sony World Photography Awards competition so special: it represents the finest fruits and loves of Everyman's liberated imagination.

Whoever your god is, he gave you photography to make your heart sing, to make your eyes see, to lend your soul a firm anchor and to make your life full. Relish it.

DAMIEN DEMOLDER (UK)
EDITOR, AMATEUR PHOTOGRAPHER MAGAZINE
PRESIDING CHAIR OF JURY

NGUYEN HOANG HIEP VIETNAM

OPEN PHOTOGRAPHER OF THE YEAR
1ST PLACE ENHANCED

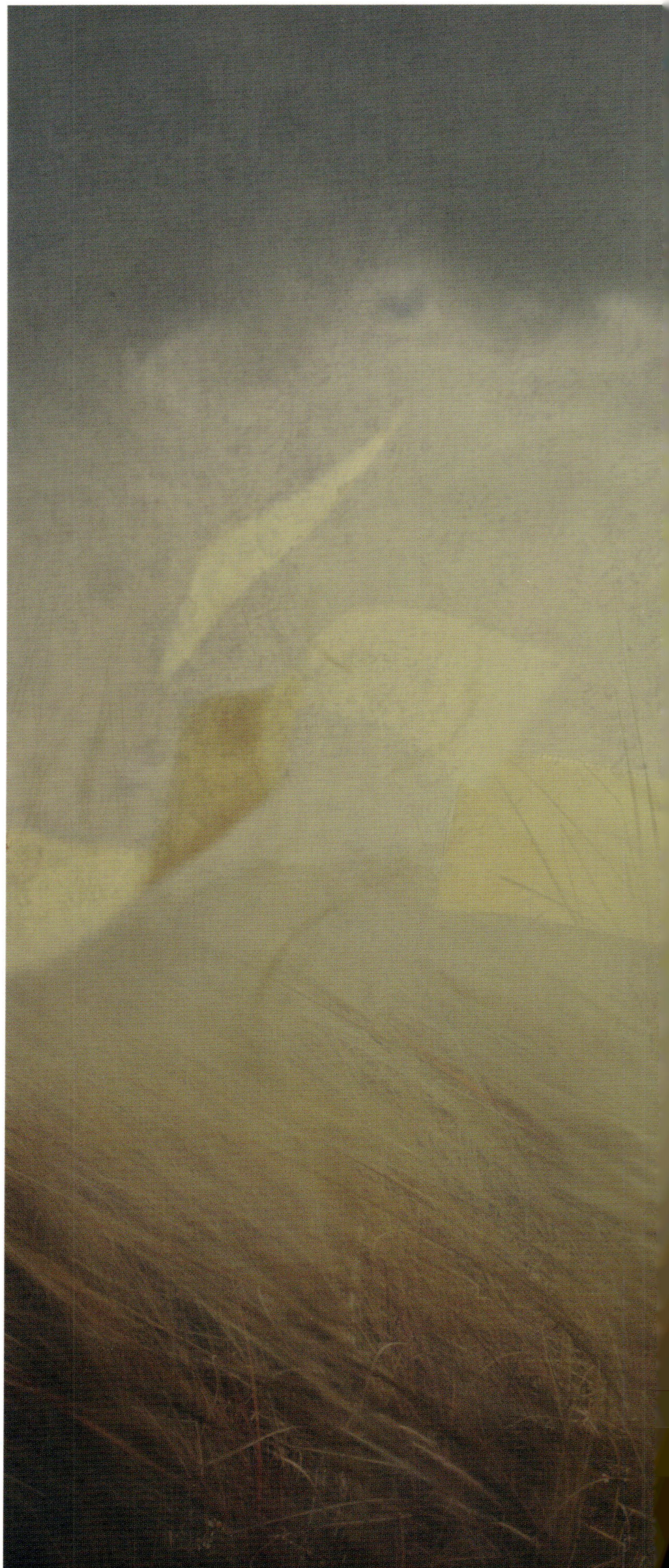

Storm. The girl alone in the storm. When the storm comes, she will not run away.

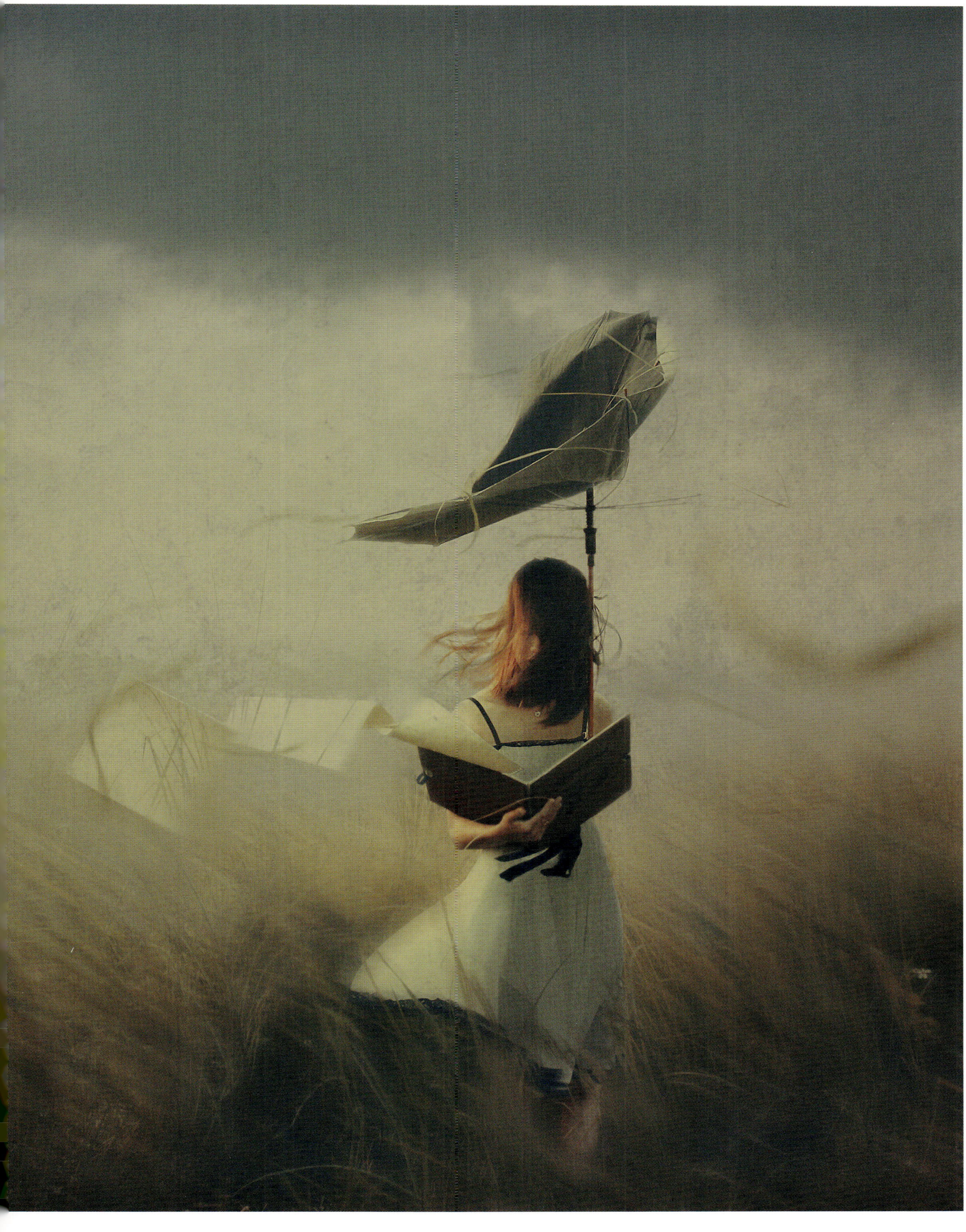

MARTINA BICCHERI ITALY

1ST PLACE
ARCHITECTURE

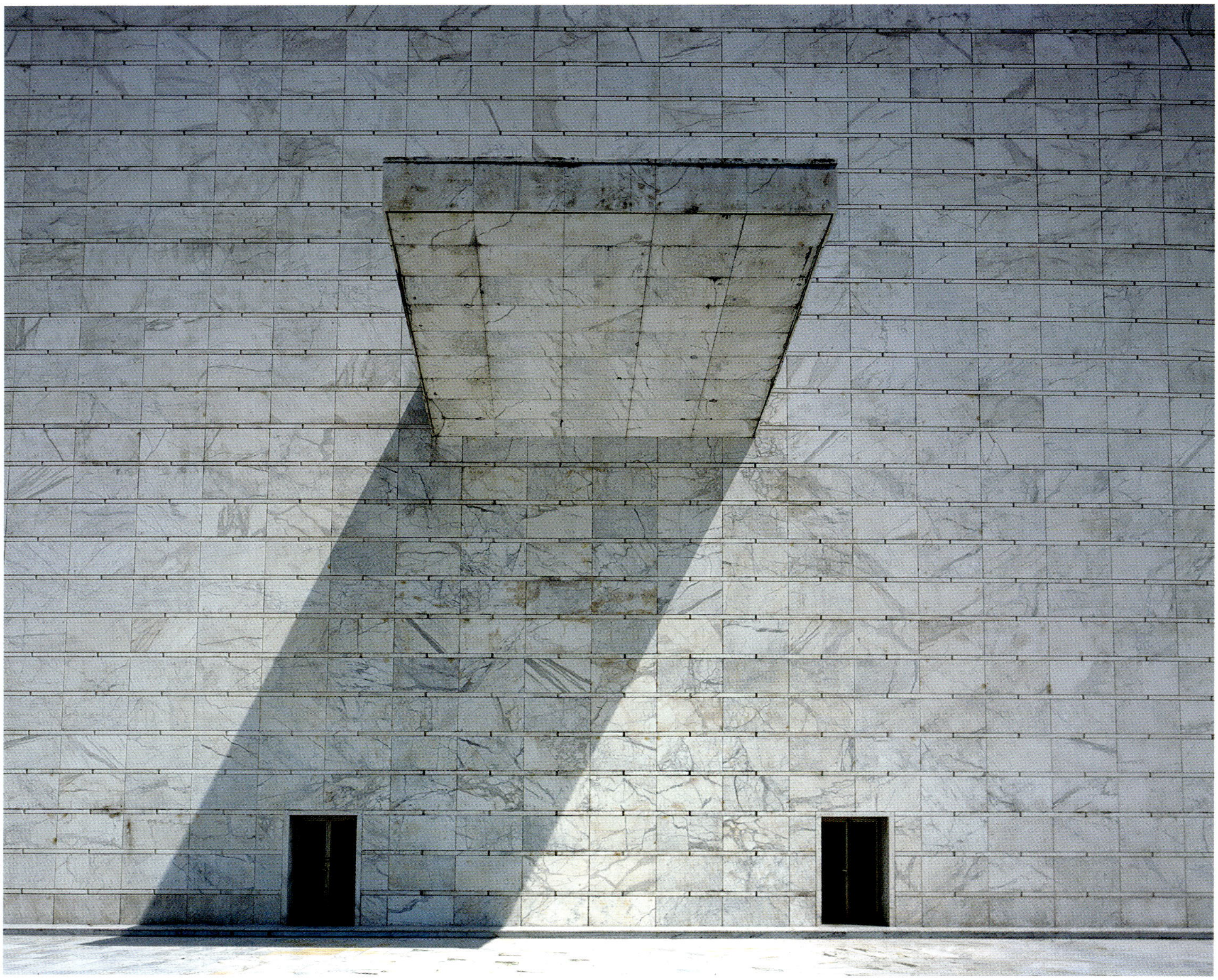

2pm. I took this photo in spring 2012 in Rome, my hometown. It was taken with a monorail view camera (5x6 film), manually developed, then scanned and post-produced to achieve the perfect shadow and exposure. I had to go back to the location several times, always hoping it would be sunny enough. Once I spent the whole day in front of that wall, just to check at which time of the day the shadow appeared at its most geometrical; it transpired that this was at 2pm.

GILBERT YU HONG KONG

1ST PLACE
ARTS & CULTURE

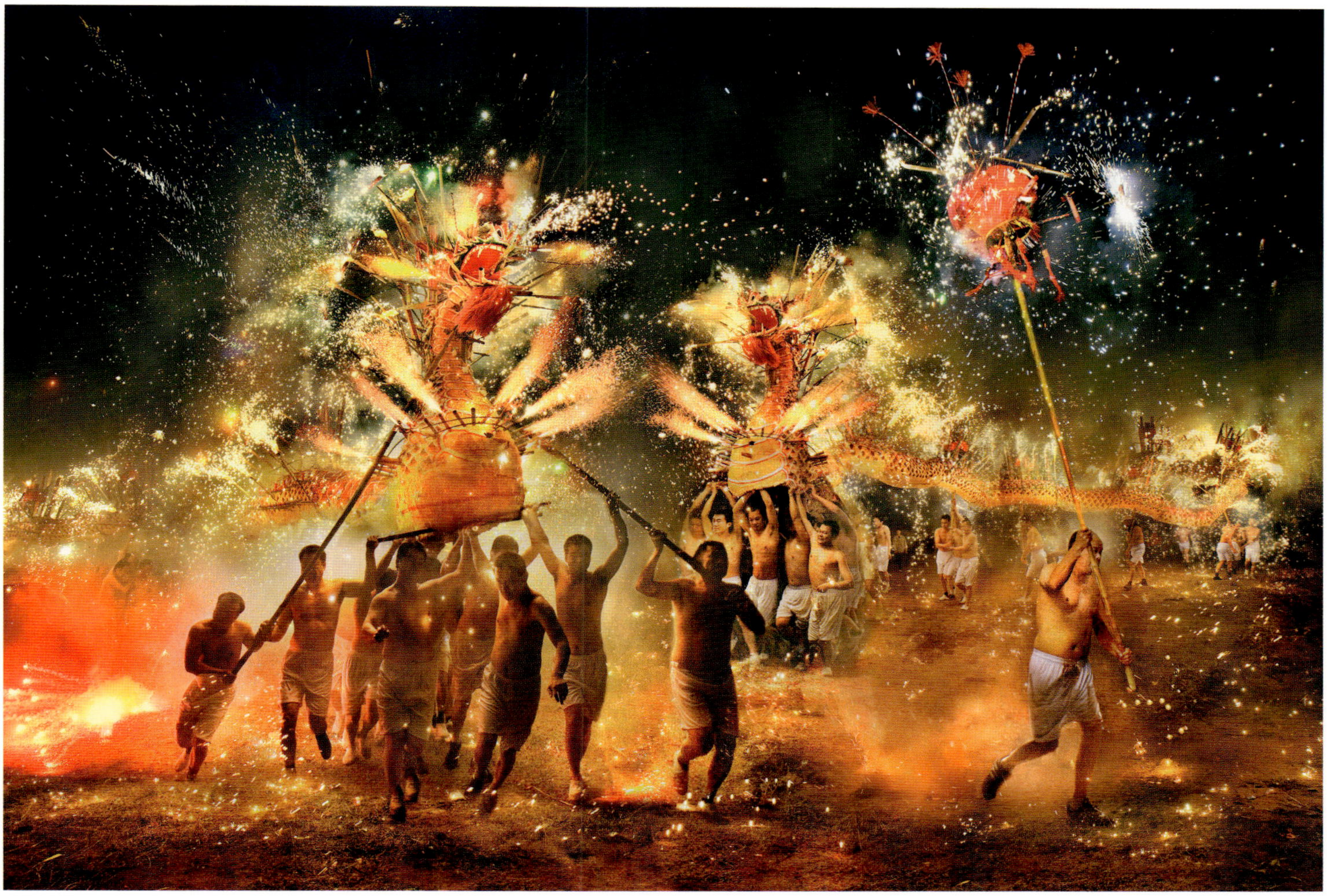

Fire Dragons of "Fung Shun". The "Fung Shun" fire dragon dance is a 300-year old traditional ceremonial event held on the 15th day of the Lunar New Year in southern China. The dragons are hand-made each year by local artists, each over 30m long and heavily decorated with fireworks, firecrackers and fire arrows.

ELMAR AKHMETOV KAZAKHSTAN

1ST PLACE
LOW LIGHT

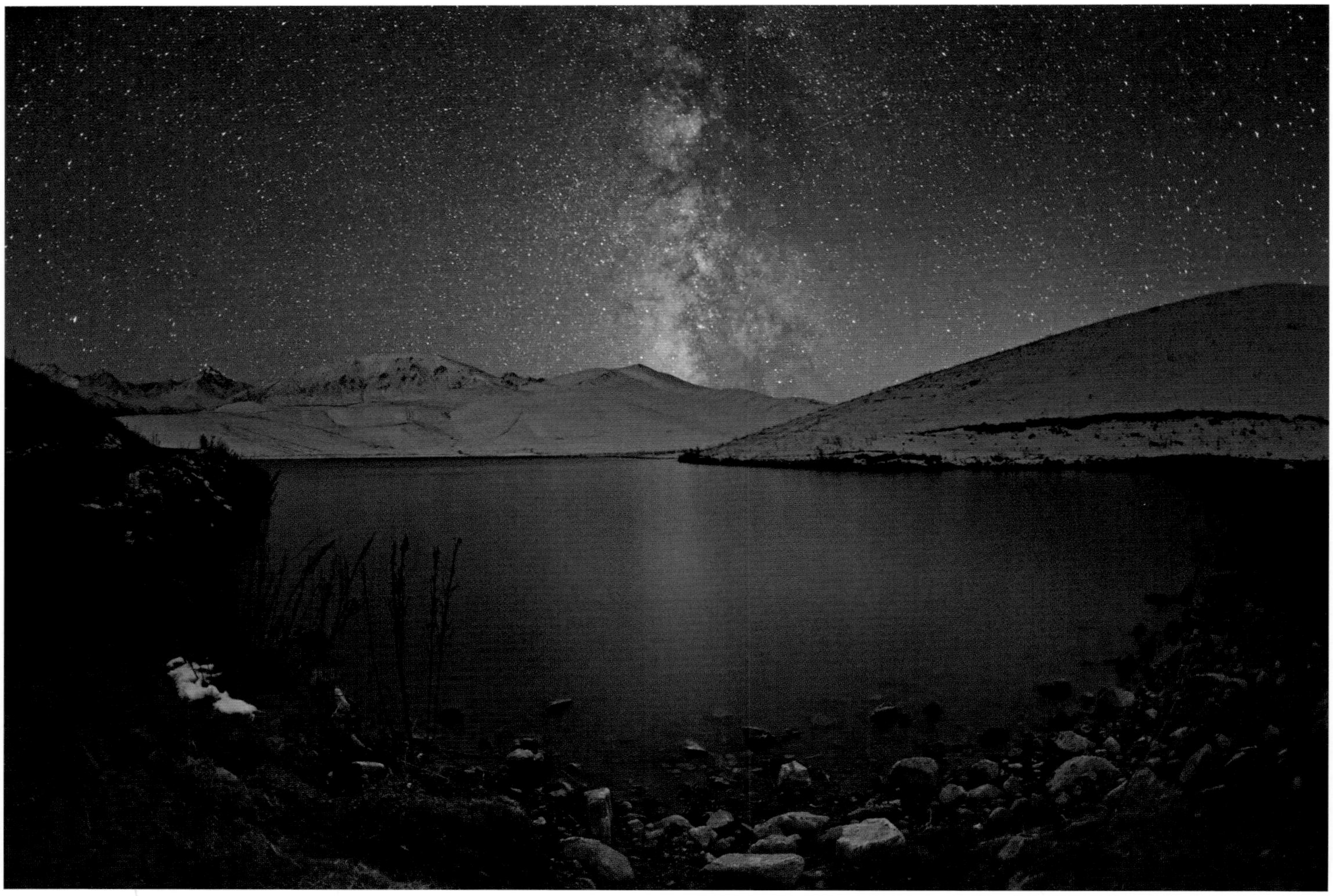

Starry Tree. This image was shot in the Almaty region of Kazakhstan, on the plateau of Ush Konyr, with a Fisheye lens. I kept the horizon in the middle of the frame to minimize the distortion. In this single shot I exposed the sky for 25 seconds, while the bottom of the frame was exposed for almost 100 seconds.

KRASIMIR MATAROV BULGARIA

1ST PLACE
NATURE & WILDLIFE

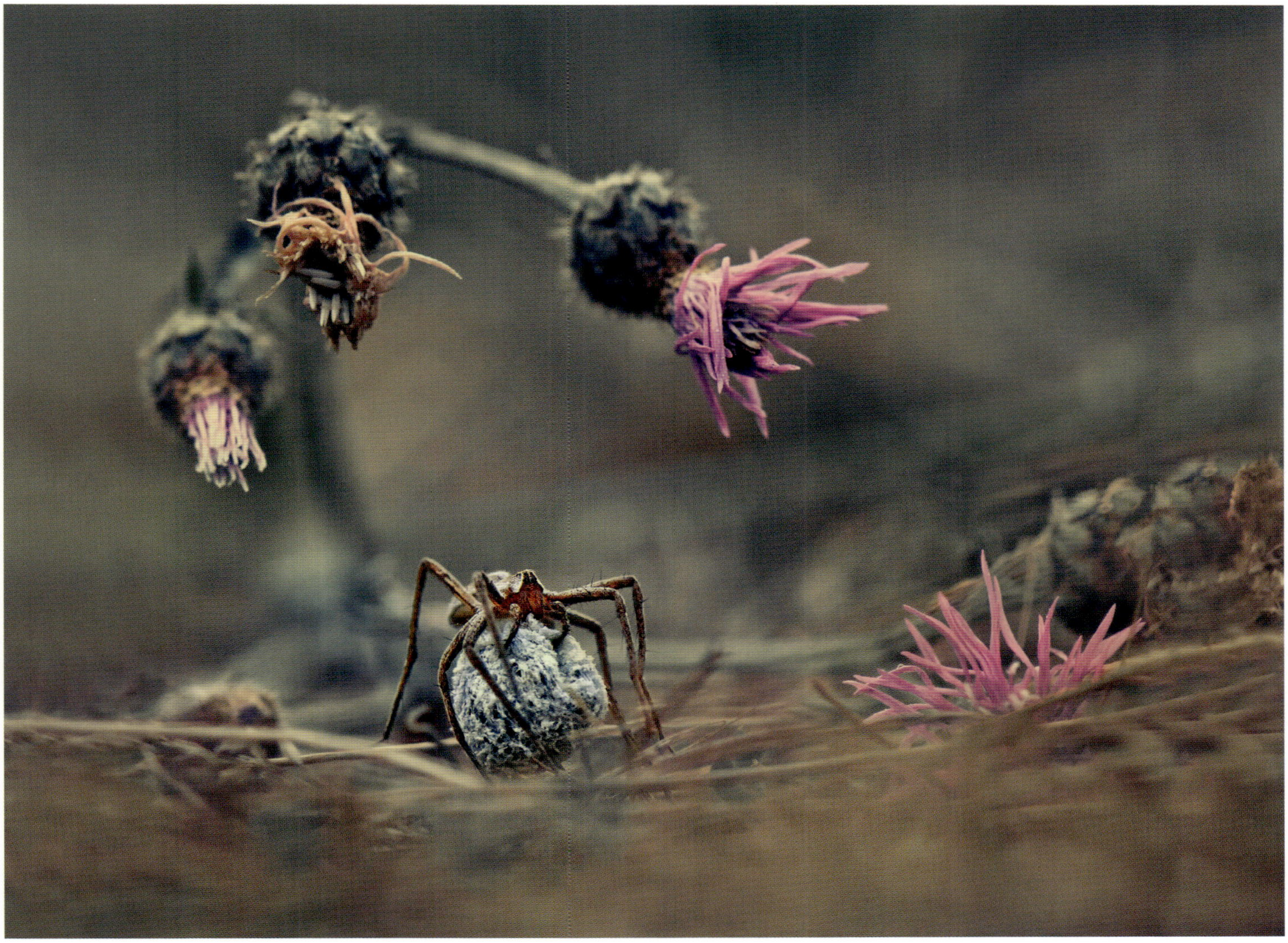

Welcome to the world of the spider. Welcome to the world of the spider.
It is like a spider from another world.

YEOW-KWANG YEO SINGAPORE

1ST PLACE
PANORAMIC

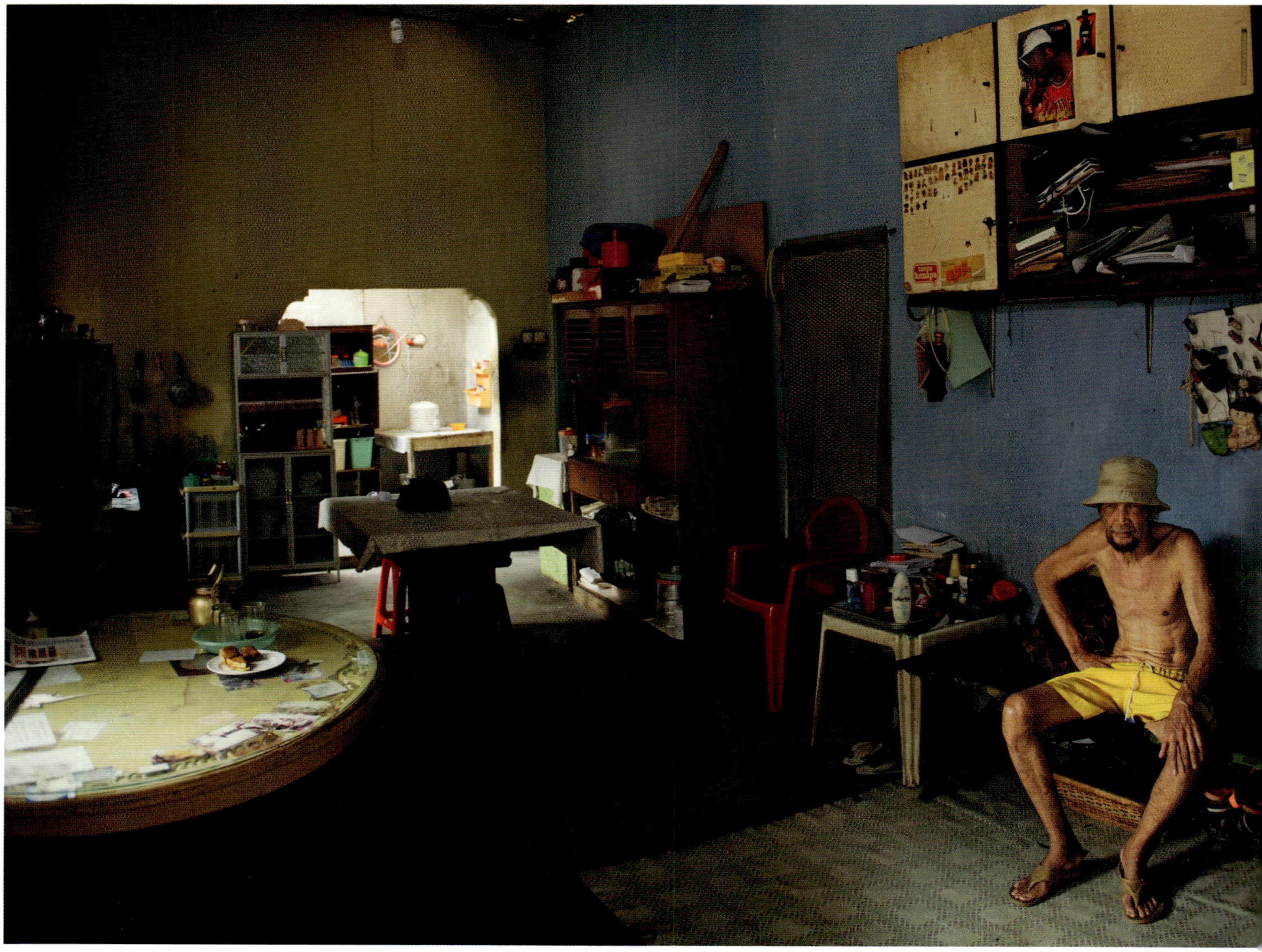

My Old House. In a small village outside Jakarta, I met this old man who has lived here since he was a boy. He was very hospitable and showed me around his house. I took several photos and created this panoramic image in Photoshop.

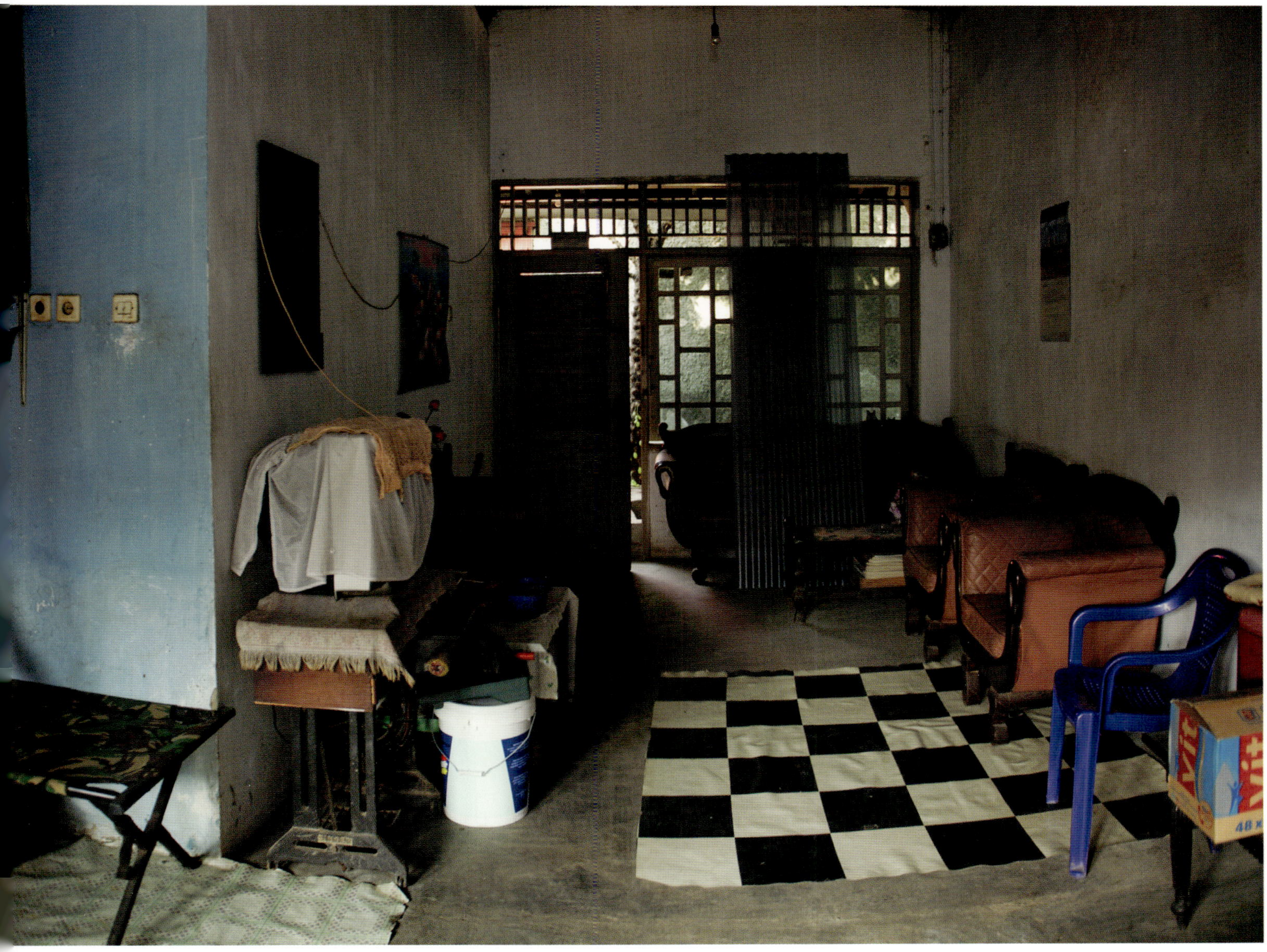
Vit

HISATOMI TADAHIKO JAPAN

1ST PLACE
PEOPLE

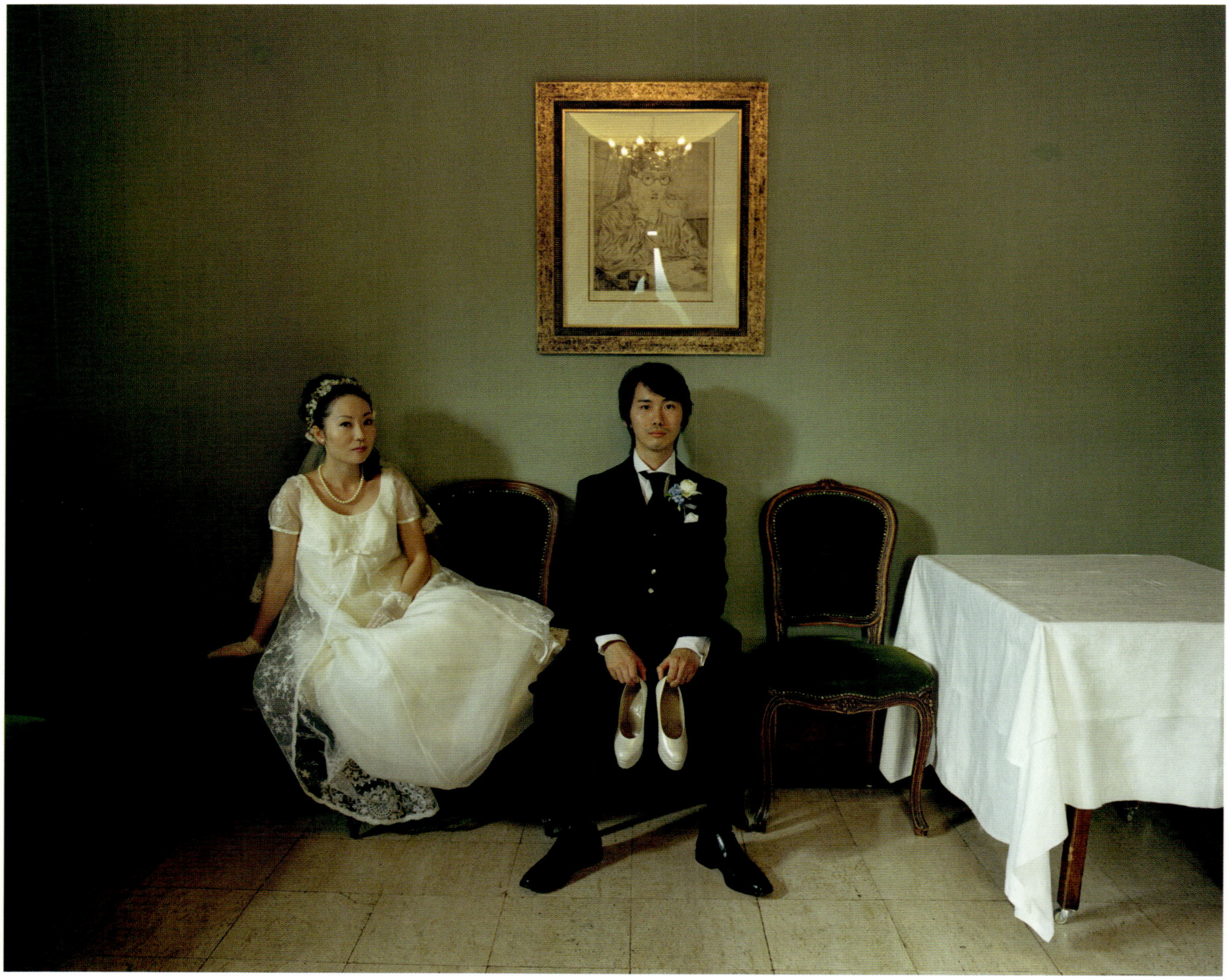

Wedding. The most precious moment - marriage. The hands holding the shoes promise honesty and eternal love.

MING HUI GUAN CHINA

1ST PLACE
SMILE

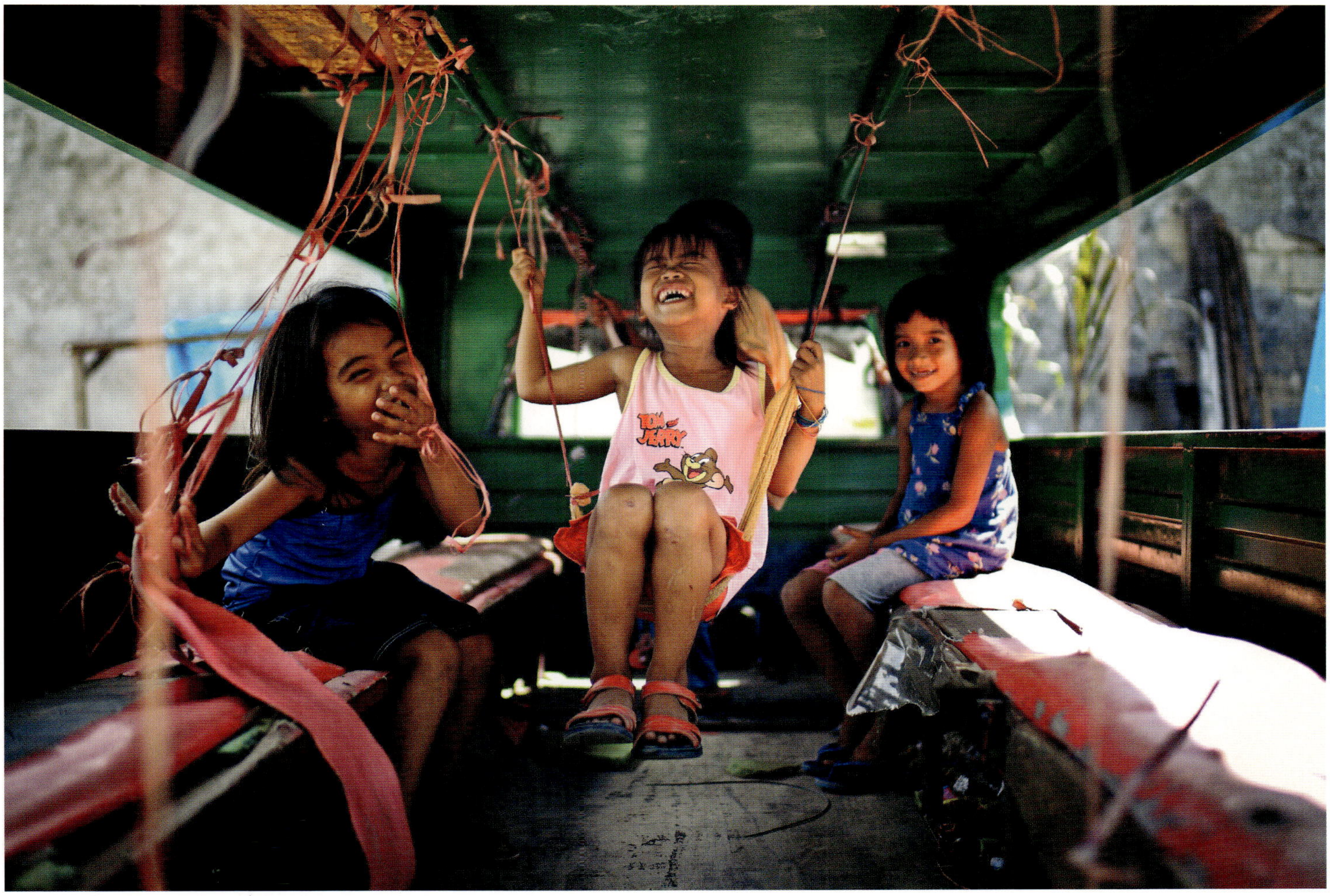

Cebula. Smiles which I will never forget.

MATÍAS GÁLVEZ CHILE

1ST PLACE
SPLIT SECOND

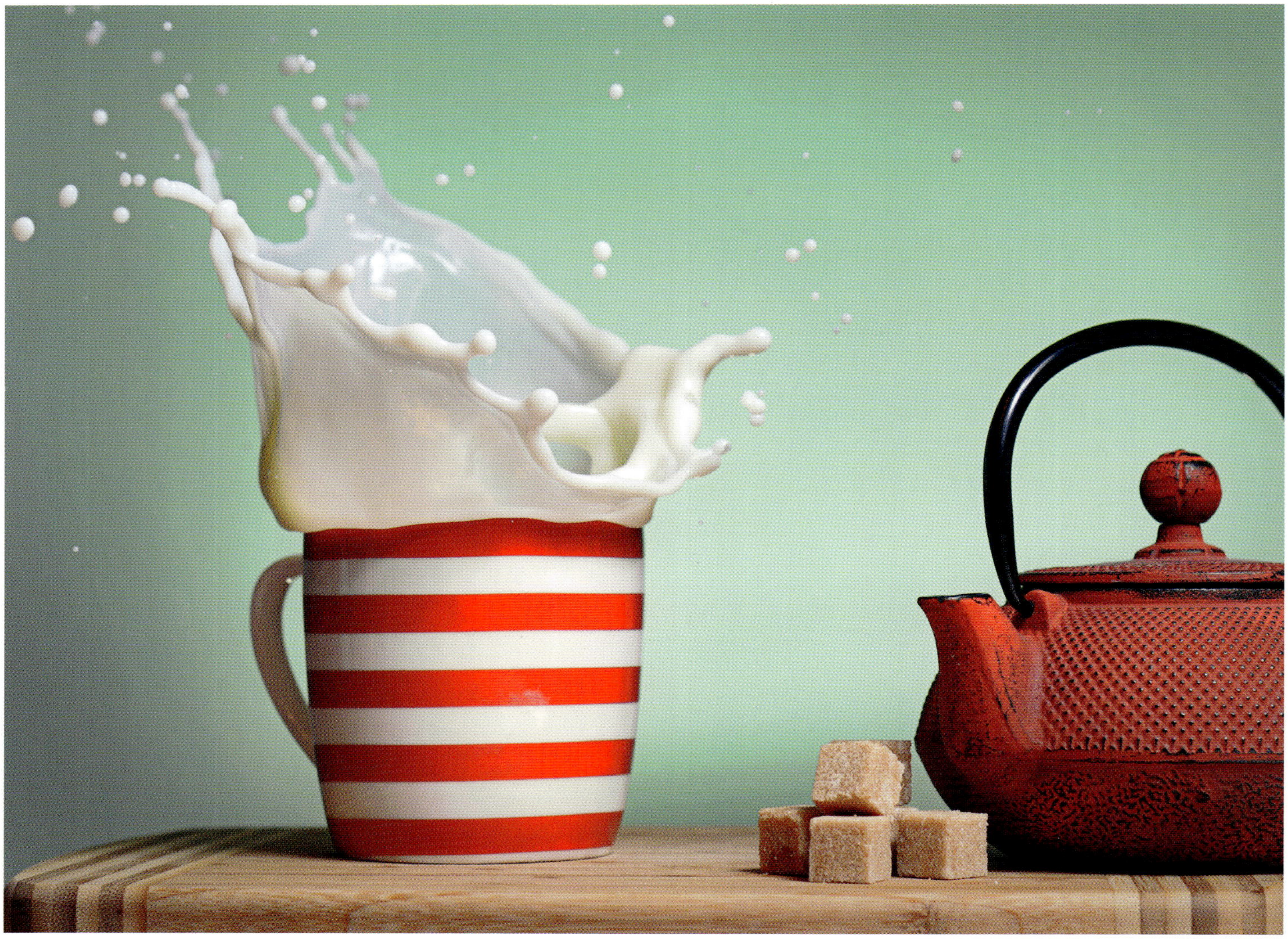

Splash! An explosion of milk.

MANNY FAJUTAG PHILIPPINES

1ST PLACE
TRAVEL

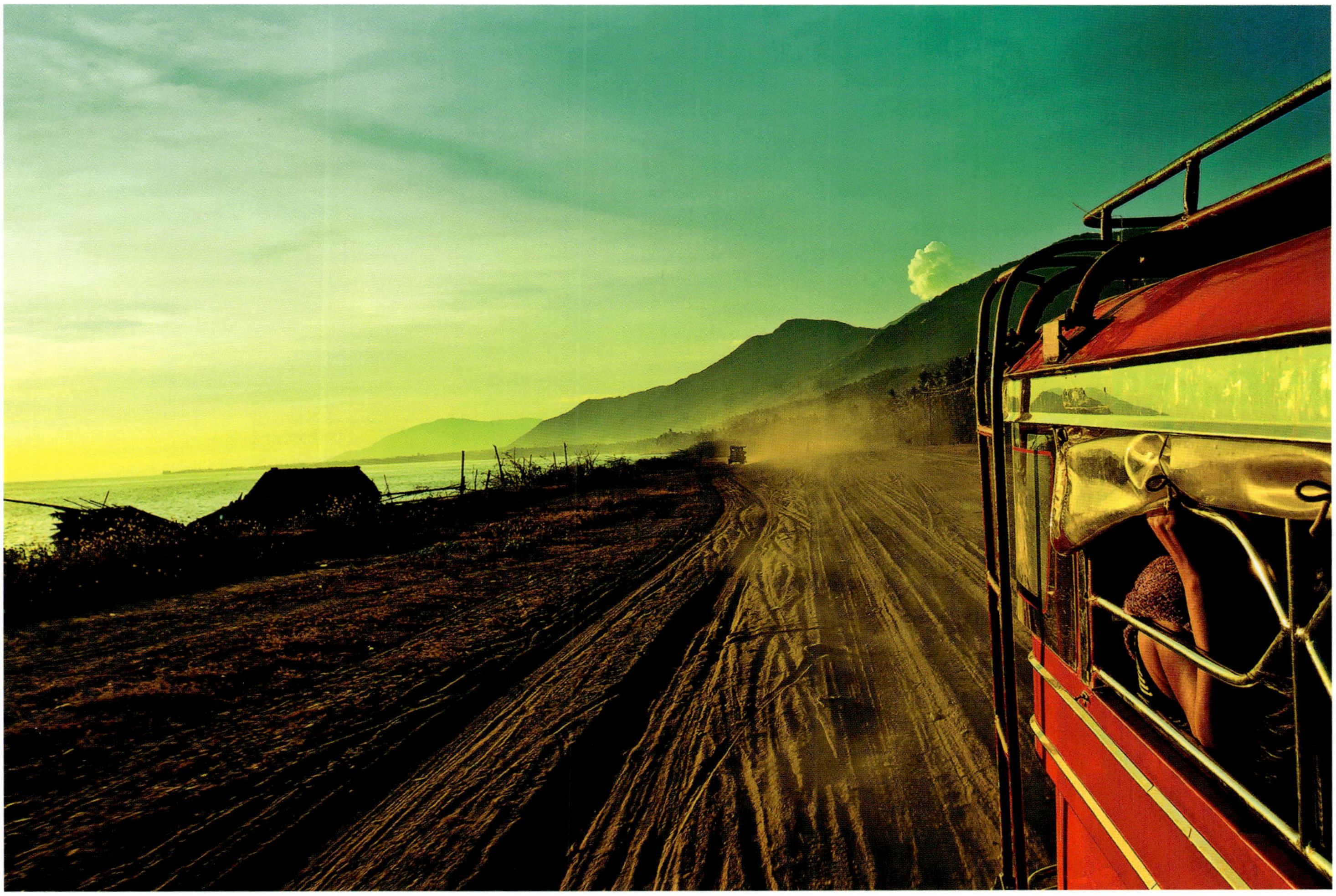

Rush hour. Taken at Sibuyan Island, the Philippines. A group of people riding a jeep returning home from the beach.

"The work itself was inspiring, it reminded me of first wanting to become a photographer twenty years ago and setting out on that journey. I have met so many wonderful photographers working alongside the World Photography Organisation this year as a result of being involved in the Student Focus programme and it makes me very glad that I did."

JONATHAN WORTH

PHOTOGRAPHER AND AUTHOR OF THE OPEN PHOTOGRAPHY CLASSES #PHONAR AND #PICBOD

STUDENT FOCUS

JUDGES

W.M. HUNT (USA)
PHOTOGRAPHIC CONSULTANT

LÉONIE HAMPTON (UK)
PHOTOGRAPHER

JONATHAN WORTH (UK)
PHOTOGRAPHER AND AUTHOR OF THE OPEN PHOTOGRAPHY CLASSES #PHONAR AND #PICBOD

Student Focus is the WPO global education programme incorporating over 230 universities around the world. One of the WPO's key aims is to discover and support emerging photography talent, and the Student Focus programme is vital to achieve this.

The 2013 Student Focus competition asked photographers to enter a single image to capture the spirit of a celebration.

The judges - photography collector, curator and consultant W.M. Hunt, plus British photographers Jonathan Worth and Leonie Hampton - were asked to select an image from each of the six continents, along with their four favourites from anywhere in the world, to make a list of 10 finalists from the entries.

The 10 finalists are then provided with new DSLR cameras, courtesy of Sony, and asked to complete an assignment, with the overall winning university being awarded over €30,000 worth of photographic equipment.

Photography education is equally important to us, and in 2012 we hosted the first WPO Educators' Symposium in Germany. Twenty professors from leading photography institutions in Europe were invited to join a discussion led by Virginia Morrison, US, Director of the Society for Photographic Education. The points arising from the discussions have been collated into a white paper on photographic education incorporating core competencies, and this has been distributed to all 230 participating institutions.

NATALIA WIERNIK POLAND

JAN MATEJKO ACADEMY OF FINE ARTS, KRAKOW

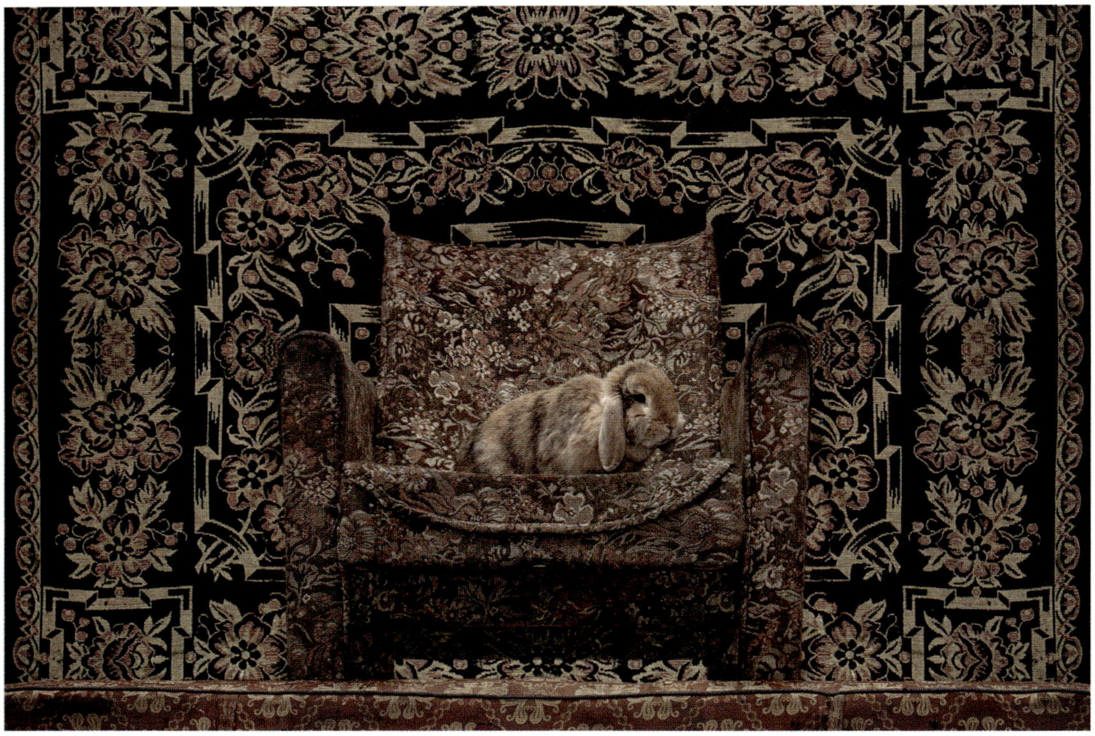

Thanksgiving. The rabbit – a symbol of fertility.
Here is revealed a place of worship, touched by the songs of the passing time, a natural altar, a piece of furniture adapted for the requirements of ceremony. Among the baroque splendour of forms the profane becomes the sacred. Fertile nature is temporarily subdued for the purposes of ritual. The image becomes an Icon. The animal is exalted by the author, taking on the role of either sacrificial victim an object of adoration.

ANSHUL MEHROTRA INDIA

JAMIA MILLIA ISLAMIA

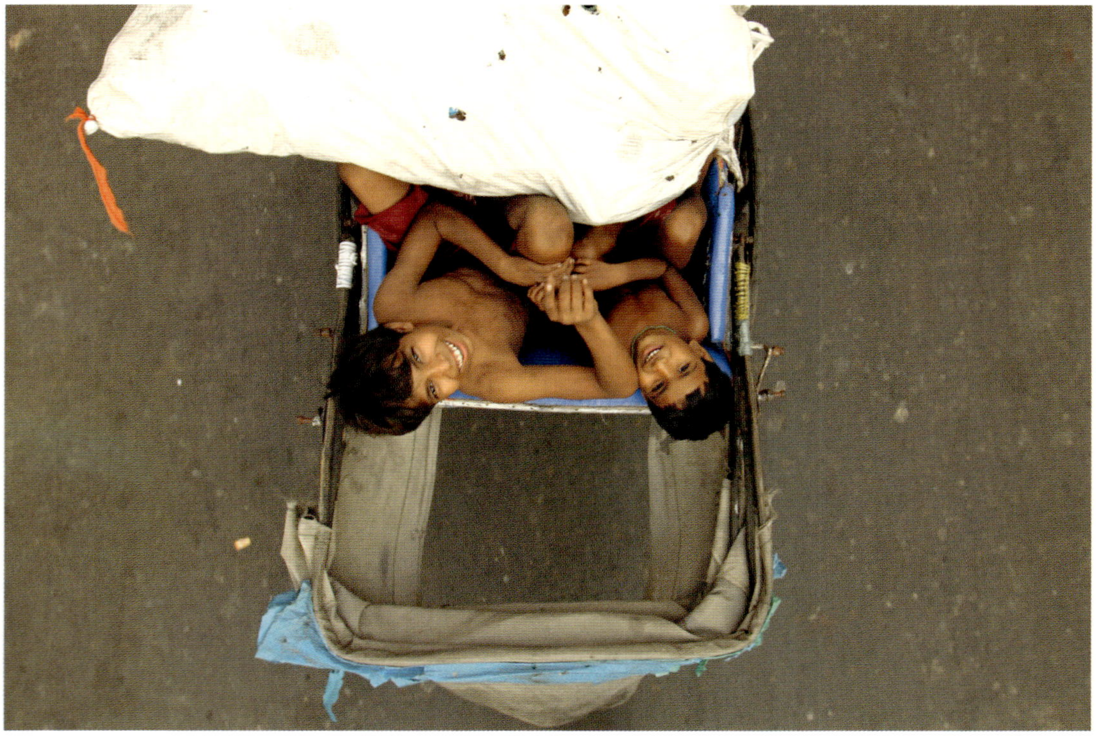

Over The Top. This image marks the celebrations of the Chhath Puja, an ancient Hindu festival dedicated to the healing energies of the Sun God Surya. Chhath Puja is celebrated in Bihar and Uttar Pradesh, and also in New Delhi, by a large migrant population. It is a time when this fleeting population comes together in a foreign land, and seeks warmth amidst the community. On a winter morning I saw these two boys sitting on their father's rickshaw. Their parents had been fasting for the last four days; other rigorous rituals include long periods of standing in ice cold water, hands folded, bowing to the Sun god, followed by offering water to the setting Sun in the evening. These two boys signify for me this celebration of life and joy and faith, and that fleeting moment which happiness is.

KIM ANNAN NEW ZEALAND

THE UNIVERSITY OF AUCKLAND

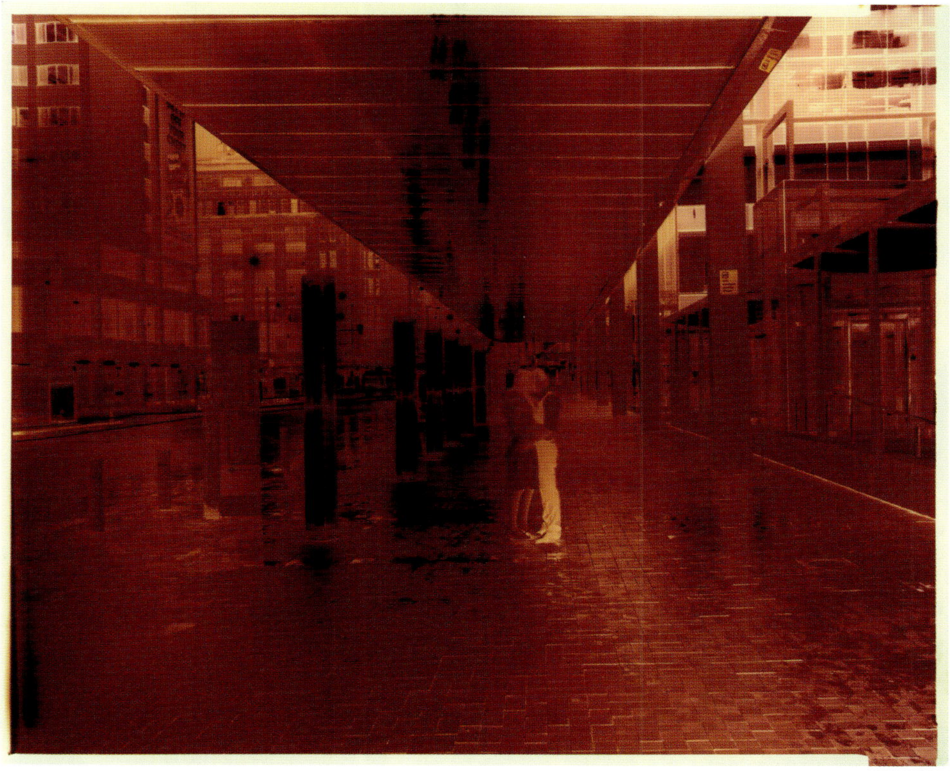

Welcome Home. Welcome Home is a classical scene of celebration between two lovers reunited.

In this globalised world it has become common for people to travel for work. Such travel strengthens economies, and allows cultural practices to be exchanged and acquired. However, people always leave a part of themselves behind: their home. There are many wonders of the world, places to be seen, but nothing quite so cherished as being with the people you love.

This staged pose was inspired by candid photographs of men returning home from war to be passionately greeted by their soulmates. Welcome Home captures the essence of a moment that is universally treasured.

MARCELO SÁNCHEZ MEXICO

TECNOLÓGICO DE MONTERREY

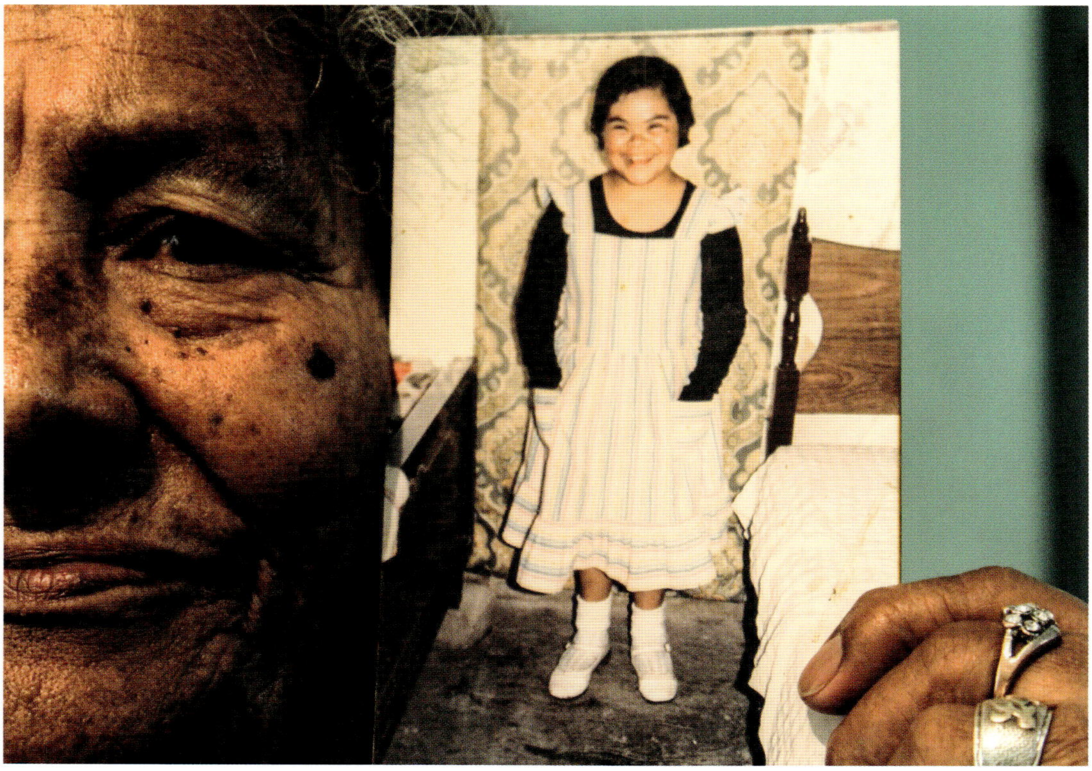

Reina. The happy little Reina appears in a small photograph taken by her mother. She has lovingly cared for her daughter, who suffers from Down's syndrome, throughout her life.

ANDRÉA AZÉMA BELGIUM

ÉCOLE NATIONALE SUPÉRIEURE DES ARTS VISUELS DE LA CAMBRE

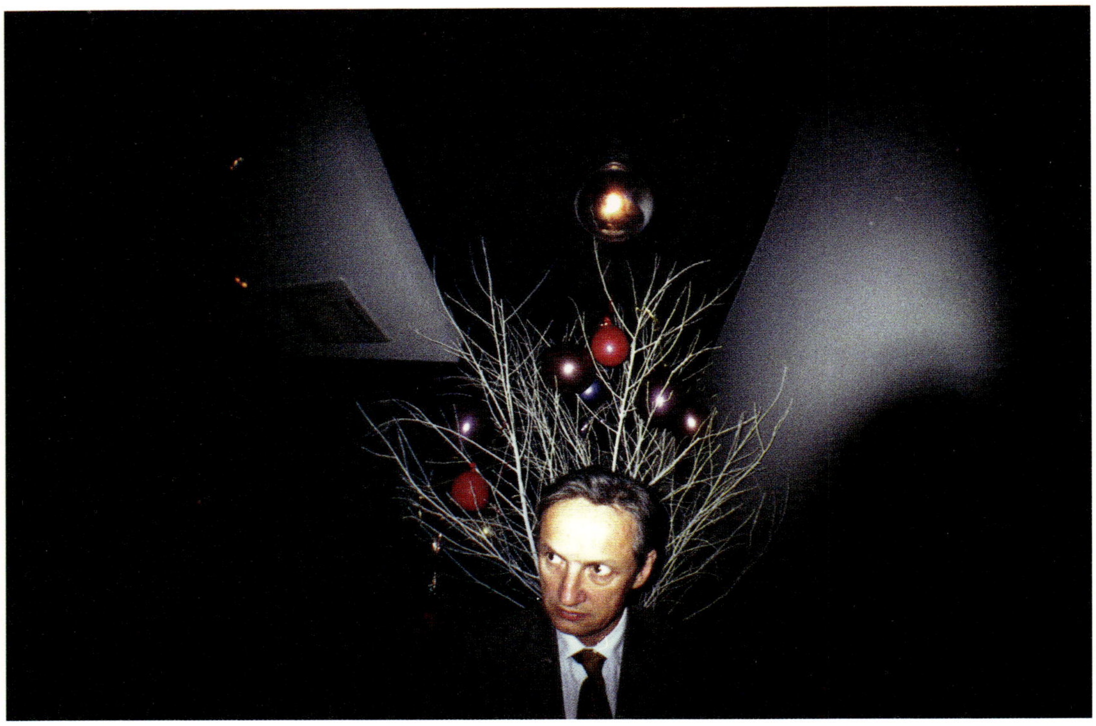

Dad, 2012. We love to celebrate! And the photographic image is there to solemnize and immortalize those collective moments. It is photography's ability to capture for eternity the instant, the event, the people that have been brought together. There is no Christmas, no wedding, no birthday without a picture. People, places and cultural traditions are very diverse, yet vernacular photography is often excessively conventional and codified. This image, however, is a kind of in-between; an unexpected moment - the author's dad had just found time in his busy schedule for a dinner with her in a restaurant - recorded in an unconventional way. This image is able to convey strong emotions beyond what is visible. As the author would say, 'not your usual holiday picture'.

AIMEE TURNER UNITED KINGDOM

COLEG SIR GÂR, CARMARTHEN

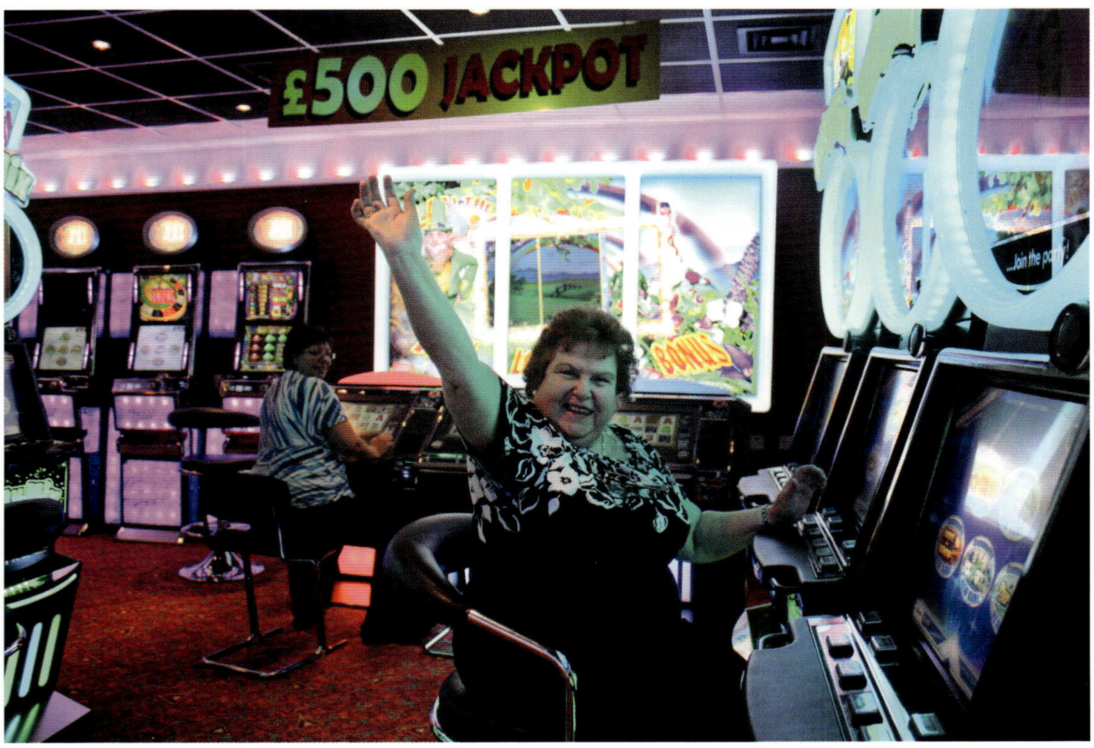

Jackpot. Grandmother on a slot machine.

Many people strive for different things in life - such as an education, health or fame; others are content with what they already have, happy to celebrate being lucky.

MARIA CANDELARIA RIVERA GADEA ARGENTINA

ESCUELA MOTIVARTE

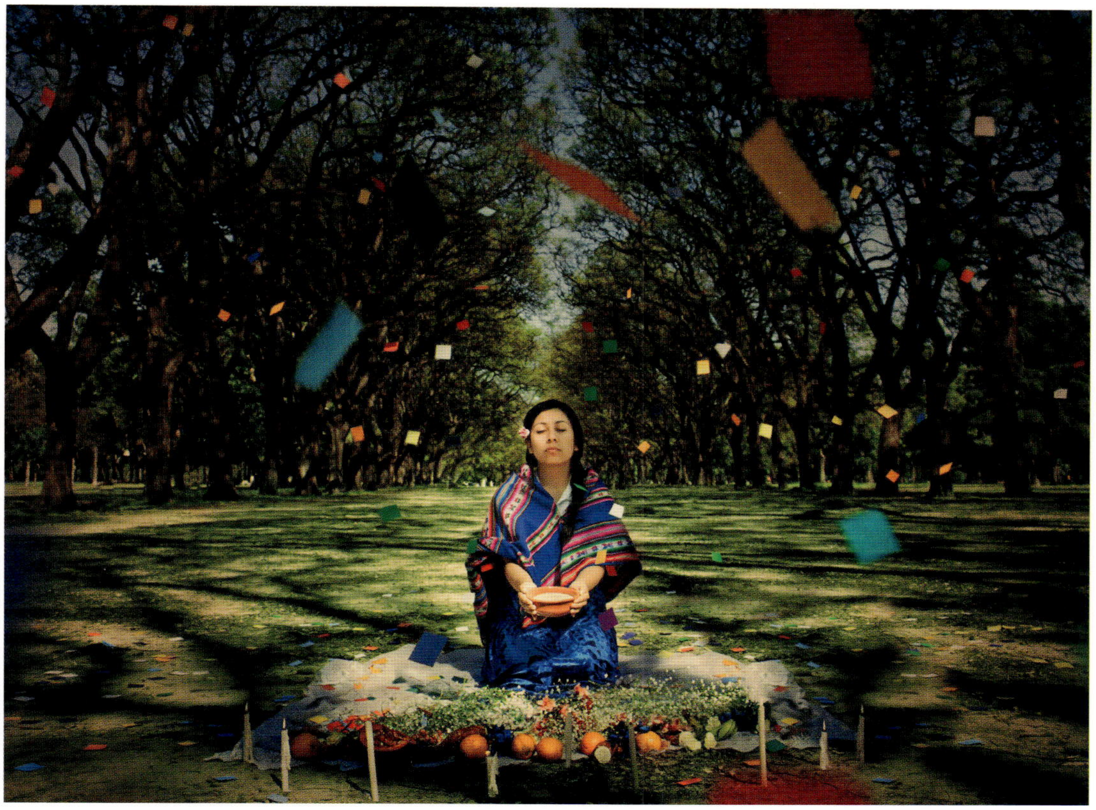

Offering Colours to Pachamama. In this picture I wanted to capture the celebration of Pachamama. It is a very beautiful festival celebrated by the Andean peoples of Latin America in honour of the fertility of the land.

The purpose of this great celebration is to joyously thank Mother Earth for all that nature gives us, and to make offerings signifying gratitude and devotion.

With the colours I wanted to represent the flag of the Andean peoples and the joy that pervades their culture. I was inspired by their fervent devotion, which produces in us the desire to share in this celebration of the greatness of Nature.

SARAI RUA FARGUES SPAIN

IEFC - INSTITUT D'ESTUDIS FOTOGRÀFICS DE CATALUNYA

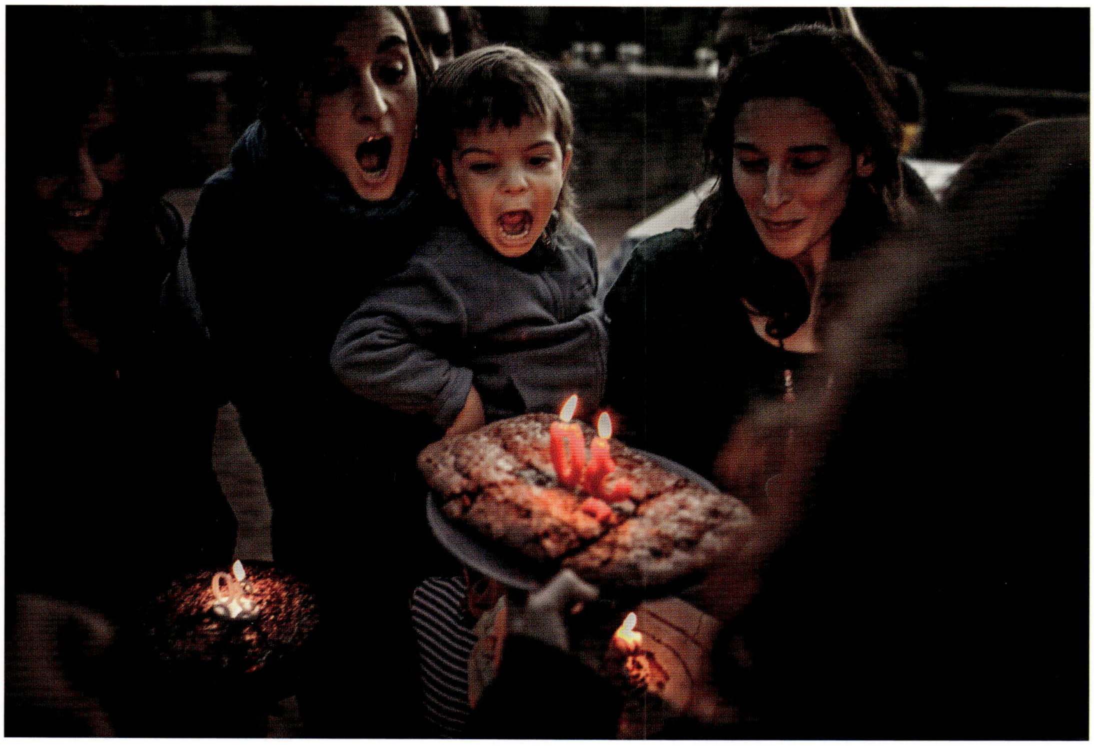

Turning 30 . Three childhood friends celebrate their 30th birthday in a farmhouse on the outskirts of Barcelona with family and friends. They grew up together and every day they feel the ties that bind their lives. This is the celebration of a friendship that can change, evolve, but it's always there.

EUGENE SOH SINGAPORE

NANYANG TECHNICAL UNIVERSITY

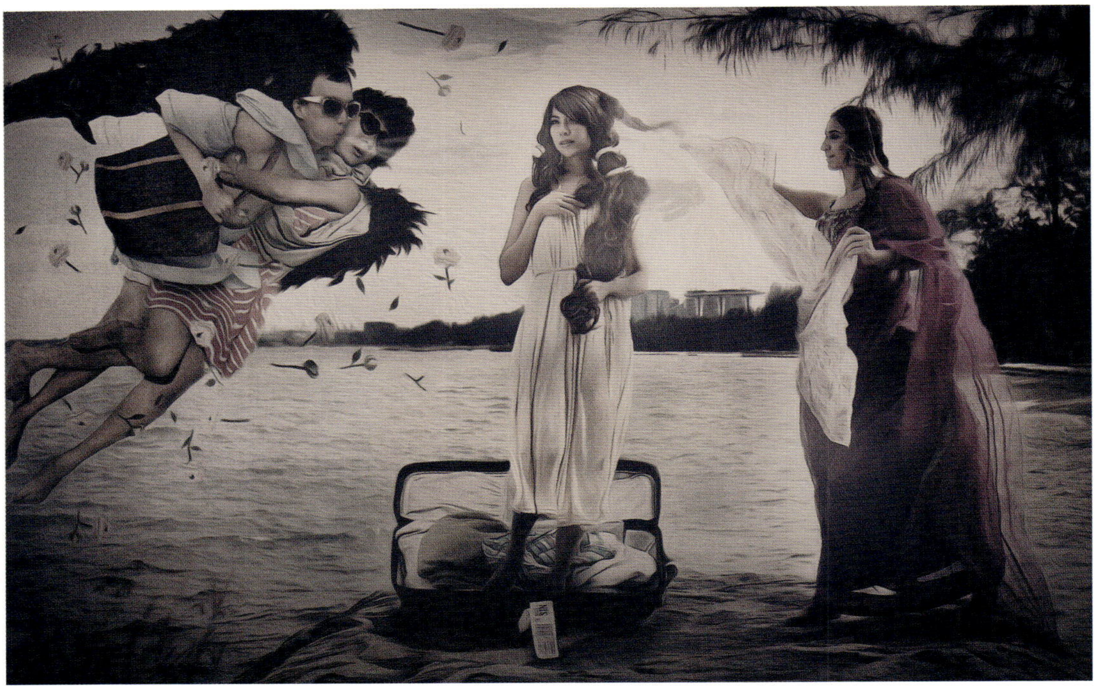

Celebrating the Birth of Venus. Here, in collaboration with *Campus Magazine*, the artist turns his attention to Botticelli's masterpiece, *The Birth of Venus*. Singapore attracts talent from across the world, with its youth and inherent possibilities. Here the 'birth' of Venus becomes the 'arrival' of Venus. The Goddess of Love, in the form of a beautiful foreign woman, symbolising hope, has crossed the rough seas on a suitcase with few possessions to reach Singapore. But the fledgling city, dominated by anxiety, does not welcome her. A local maiden seeks to turn the Goddess away; the disintegrating petals of the flowers of Spring represent the antipathy of the local people towards such foreign talent. But the Angel of Grace welcomes Venus with an exquisite shawl, symbolising what the city still has to offer.

ZANELE PLAATJIE SOUTH AFRICA

VAAL UNIVERSITY OF TECHNOLOGY

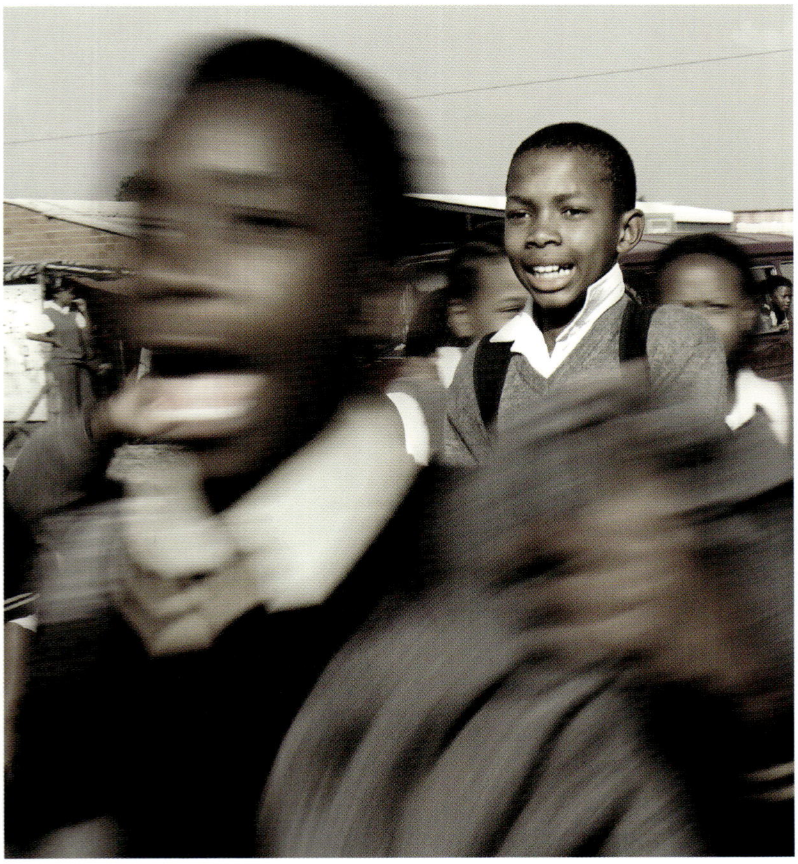

Youth Day. This image was taken in Sharpeville during the annual Youth Day celebrations of 16 June. This event commemorates the Soweto uprising of 16 June 1976. An estimated 20,000 students protested in response to the introduction of Afrikaans, which they saw as the language of the oppressor, as the medium of instruction in local schools. The decree was intended to forcibly reverse the decline of Afrikaans among black Africans. Many students died as a result of clashes with the police.

YOUTH AWARD

In search of the next generation of talented young photographers

Ages 12—19

At WPO we are constantly searching for new talent and these days, talent starts at a very young age.

Youths all over the world are experimenting with cameras and snapping photos daily as part of their social culture. We wish to discover those photographers and provide a programme that helps them channel their creative energy into producing meaningful work, whilst at the same time providing them with the exposure to have their talent recognised by the industry.

Supporting this next generation of photographers is a fundamental part of the WPO and the Sony World Photography Awards.

ALECSANDRA DRAGOI ROMANIA

YOUTH PHOTOGRAPHER OF THE YEAR
1ST PLACE CULTURE

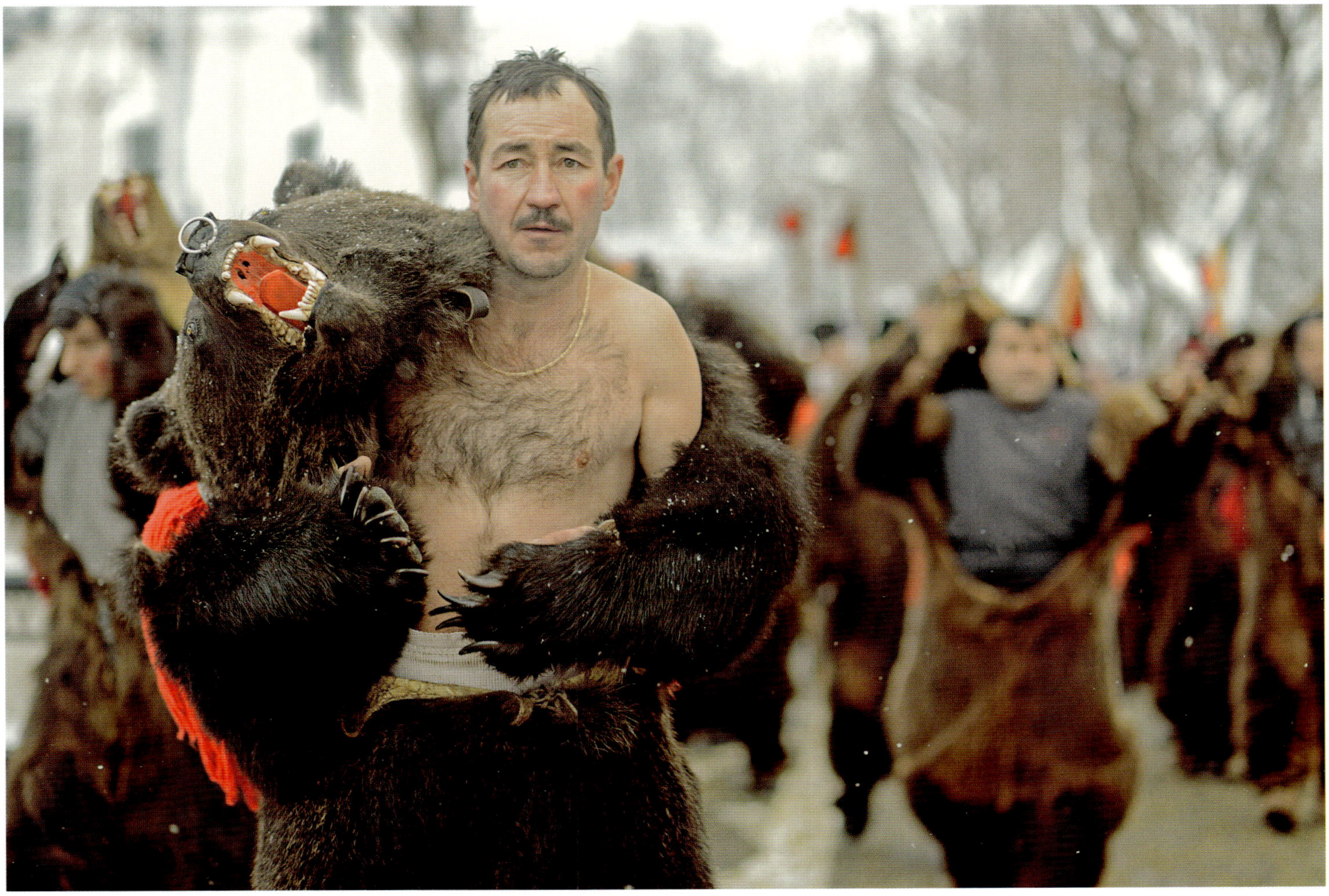

Traditions. New Year's Eve traditions in Romania.

XU WEI SHOU TAIWAN

1ST PLACE ENVIRONMENT

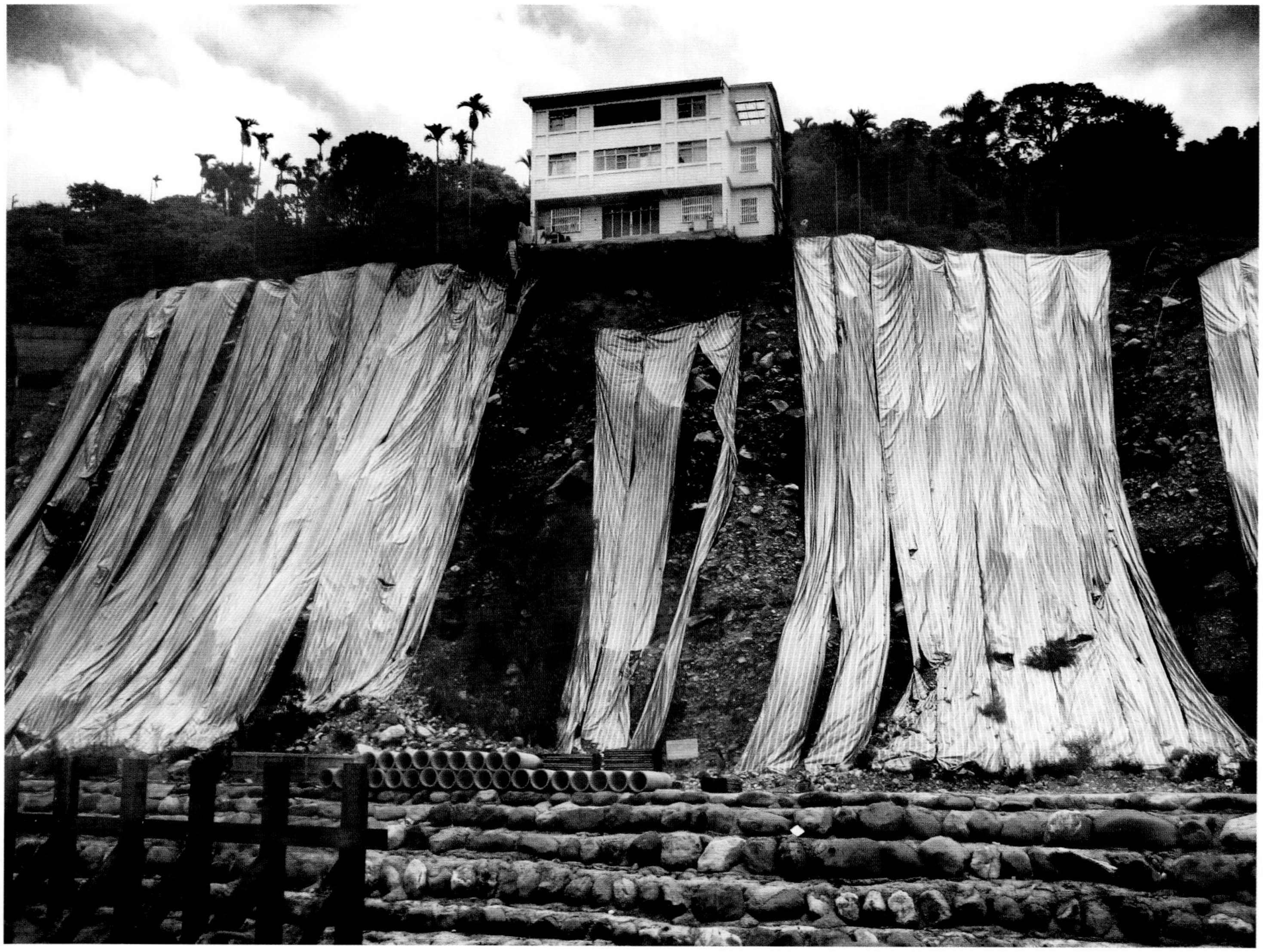

Nature fights back.

BERTA VICENTE SPAIN

1ST PLACE PORTRAIT

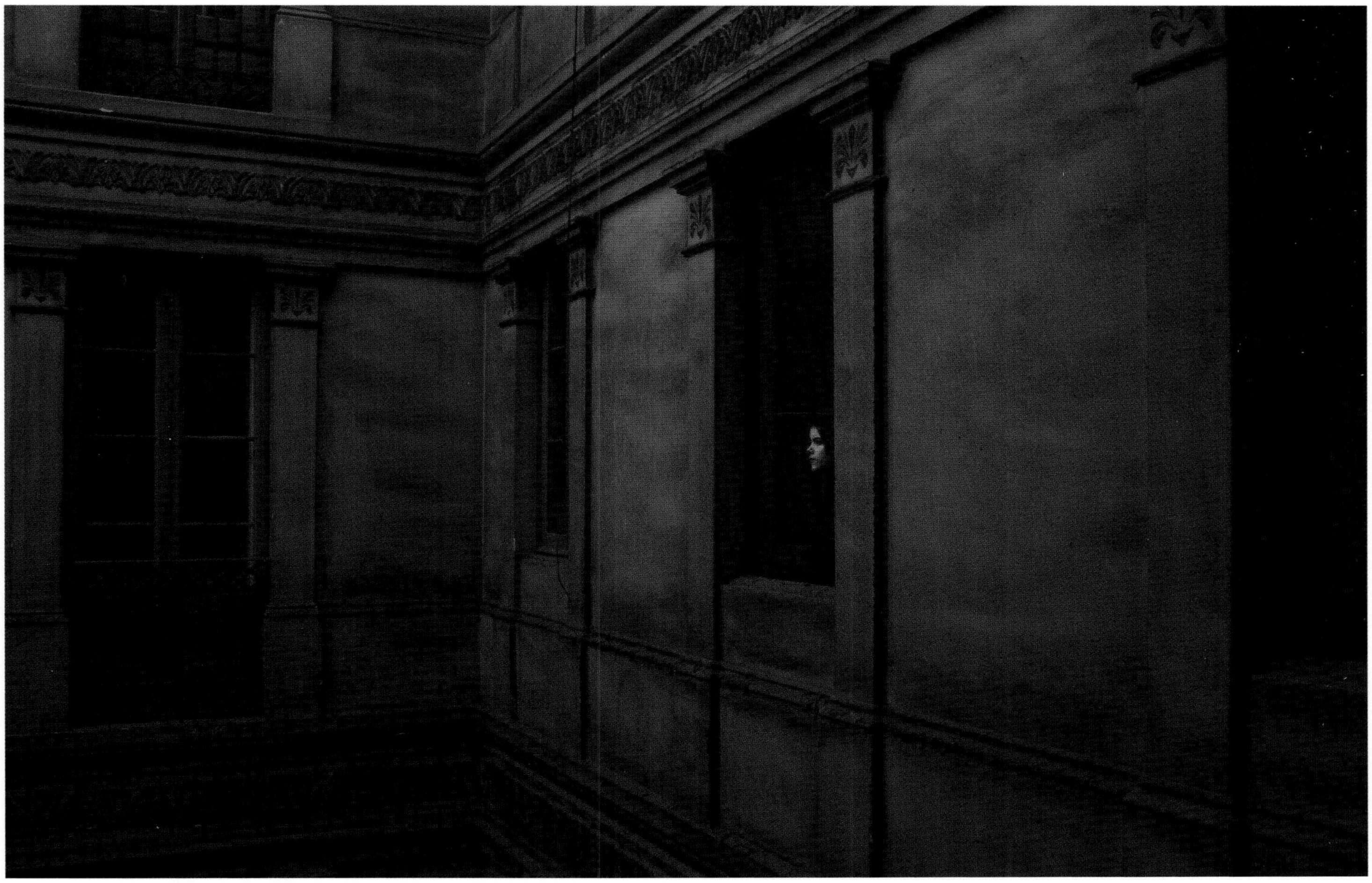

Ariadna in Urquinaona. One day I came across an uninhabited building. Once inside, I imagined a girl I used to meet on the bus and I made it come true.

"I have learnt about the people, the landscape and the importance of education for our youth."

LAURA SWART
STELLENBOSCH ACADEMY OF DESIGN AND PHOTOGRAPHY

YOUTH ON ASSIGNMENT

"Youth on Assignment" gives a live educational opportunity for students to experience the importance of documentation and communication in the field of social issues.

We are honoured that so many enthusiastic participants have joined from schools in Malawi and South Africa this year, to experience and document the activities we are conducting in each region.

We hope this young generation will continue to leverage the power of imaging to document efforts to safeguard the intangible heritage of traditional folktales in Malawi and to provide equal opportunities for primary education in remote areas of South Africa."

SHIRO KAMBE
CORPORATE EXECUTIVE
SENIOR VICE PRESIDENT
CORPORATE COMMUNICATIONS AND CSR, SONY CORPORATION

The Youth on Assignment project has been created by WPO in partnership with Sony to continue our commitment to students. The aim is for students participating in the Student Focus programme to experience the importance of documentation and communication in the field of social issues.

In each project, the WPO works with a chosen organisation and a local school to select students and create a brief.

Sony donates operational costs for shooting and the equipment for the students to use for each project. This is subsequently gifted to the school's photography department for use by all the students, providing ongoing opportunities for many students.

MALAWI

"Ever since I was a kid, I have had a keen interest in photography. Our journey into photography began in Llikuni, near the capital city Lilongwe where we spent three days photographing in several rural areas that I've never been to before. We produced some great pictures and we learnt a lot. I now see myself having a successful career in photography and film ahead of me."
Emmanuel Michael Mwanyongo, The University of Malawi – The Polytechnic

Sony and UNESCO established the project Folk Tales, which aims to document the tradition of storytelling using multimedia in Malawi, to help preserve this cultural heritage before it dies out in this age of mass communication.

Through the Sony World Photography Awards programme the Malawian Folk tales were filmed and the process documented by two students, Emmanuel Mwanyongo and Esnart Piriminta, who were supported and tutored by professional photographers, Arjen van de Merwe and Peter Mitunda from the University of Malawi – The Polytechnic.

Photograph: Emmanuel Mwanyongo, University of Malawi – The Polytechnic.

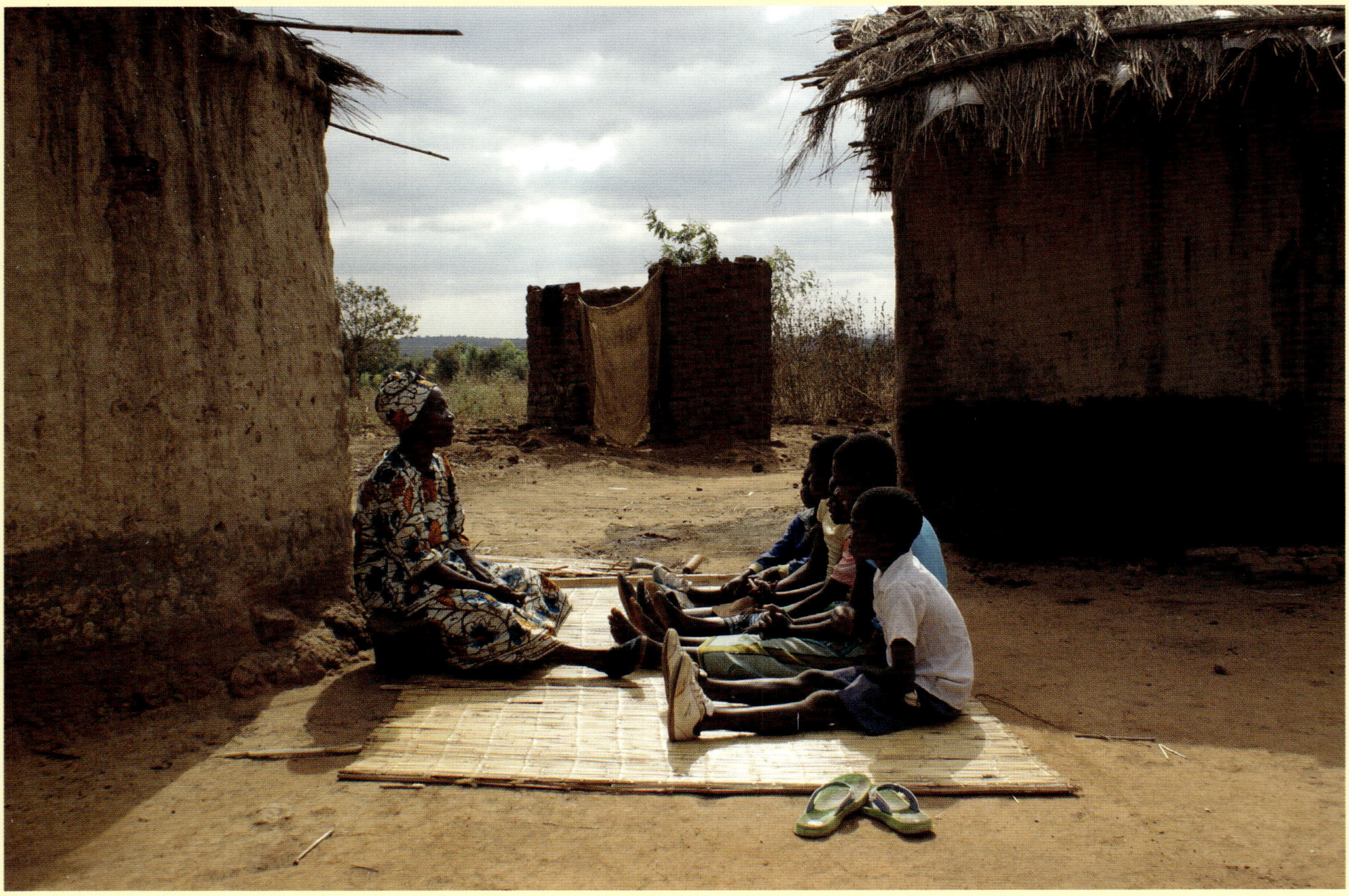

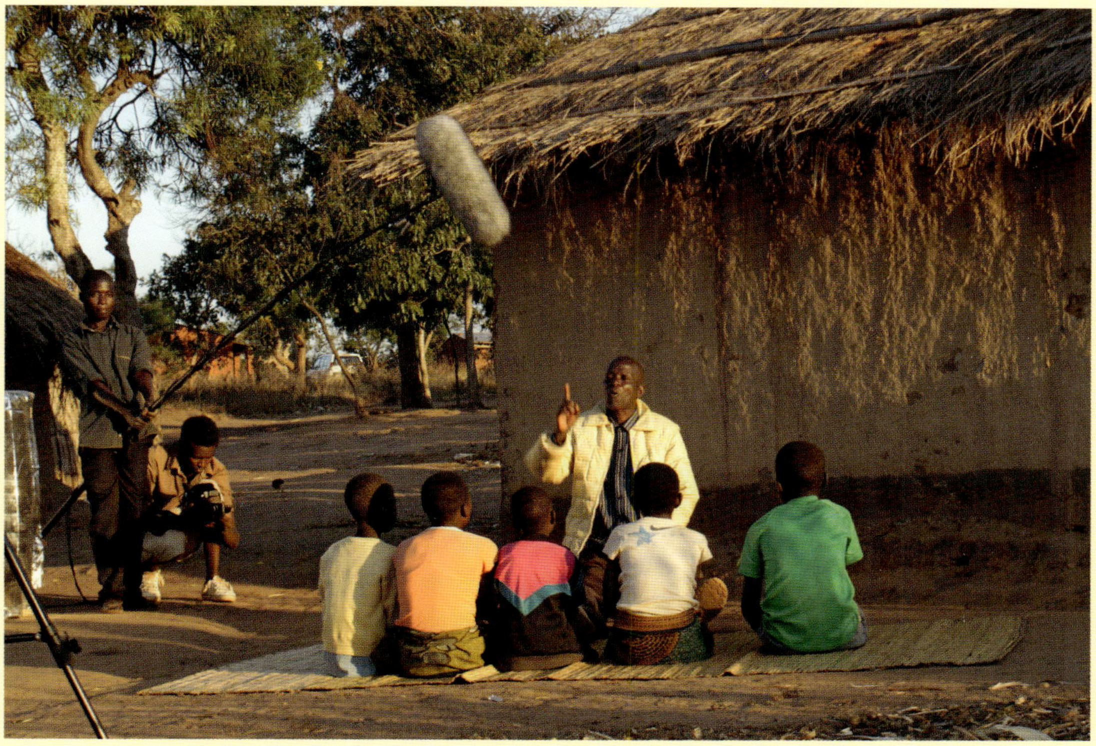

"I loved the trip and particularly enjoyed the in the field experience. I sharpened my media skills especially in photography as well as video shooting. as a media student, it was a very special privilege for me to take part."

Esnarth Priminta, University of Malawi – The Polytechnic

Photograph: Emmanuel Mwanyongo, University of Malawi – The Polytechnic.

Photograph: Esnart Piriminta, University of Malawi – The Polytechnic.

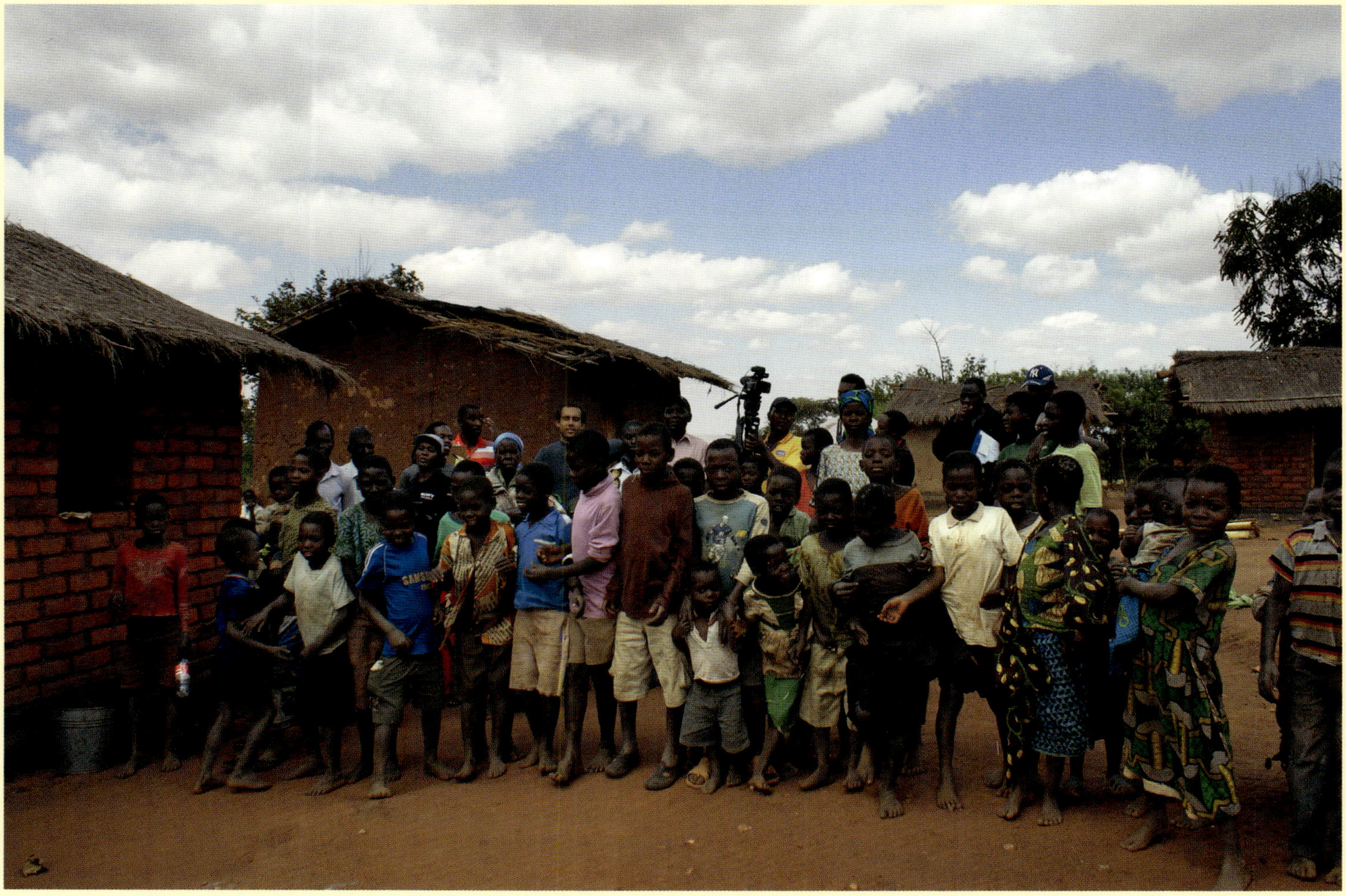

SOUTH AFRICA

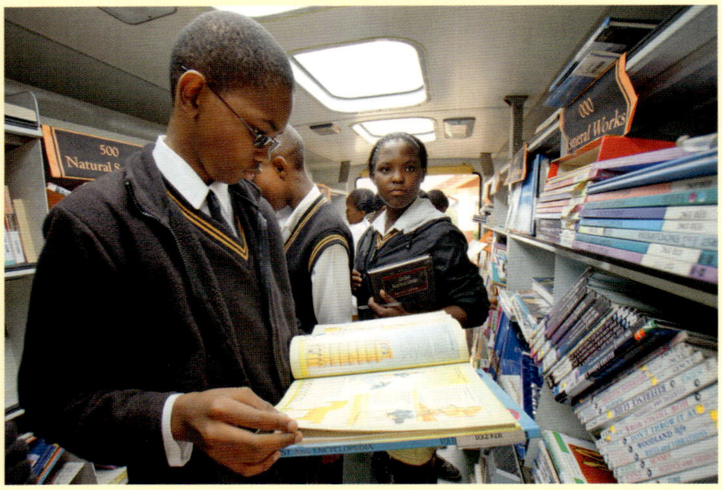

Photograph: Nina Lieska Grindlay, Rhodes University

Sony Group collaborated with SAPESI, an NGO based in South Africa, supporting the South Africa Mobile Library Project. Jointly launched by SAPESI and the South African Department of Education in 2005, the project aims to improve literacy levels by loaning books to schools across the country. Sony will make a financial contribution to SAPESI in support of the project's operations, and will also donate used children's book collected at eight Sony Group companies located in English-speaking regions.

WPO has teamed up with three schools to document this project throughout the year: Tshwane University of Technology, Rhodes University, and Stellenbosch Academy of Design and Photography.

"Mr. Khumalo is the librarian on the bus, a gentle man who is very caring with the kids. The panels of the bus open outwards and expose the masses of books within. Inside the bus the books are comprised of study material, the outside section is purely fictional books. For some of the kids, it was the first time they had taken possession of a book, whereby anticipation and intrigue follows."

Nina Lieska Grindlay, Rhodes University

Photograph: Nina Lieska Grindlay, Rhodes University

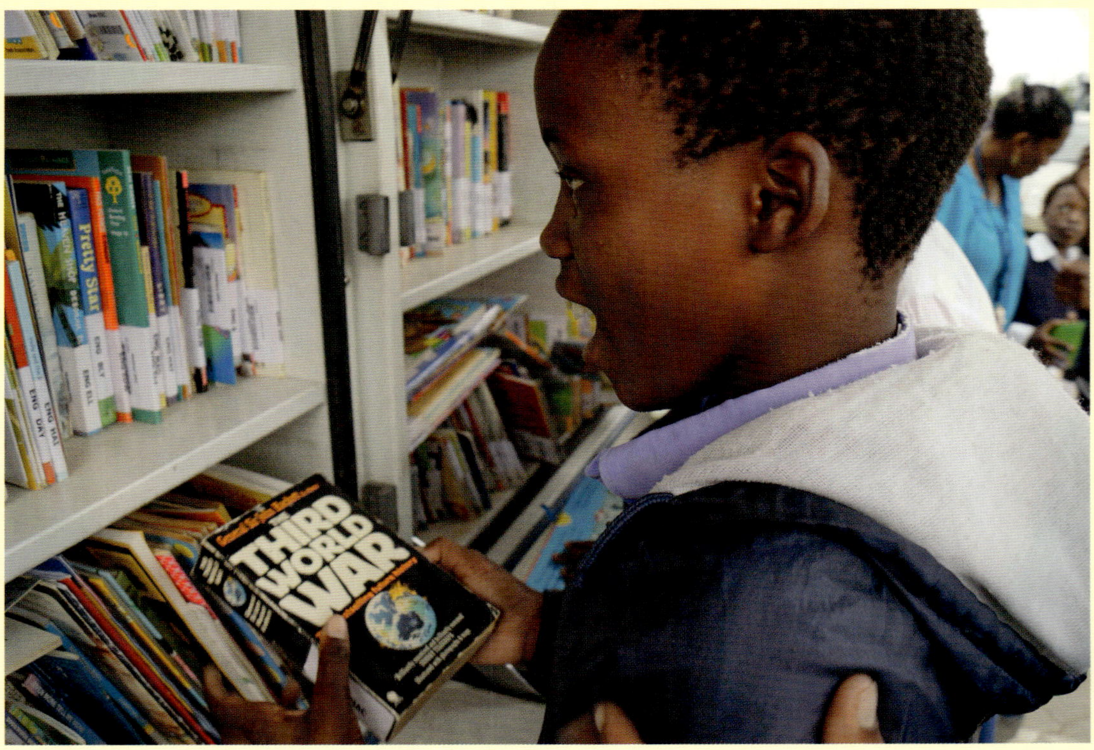

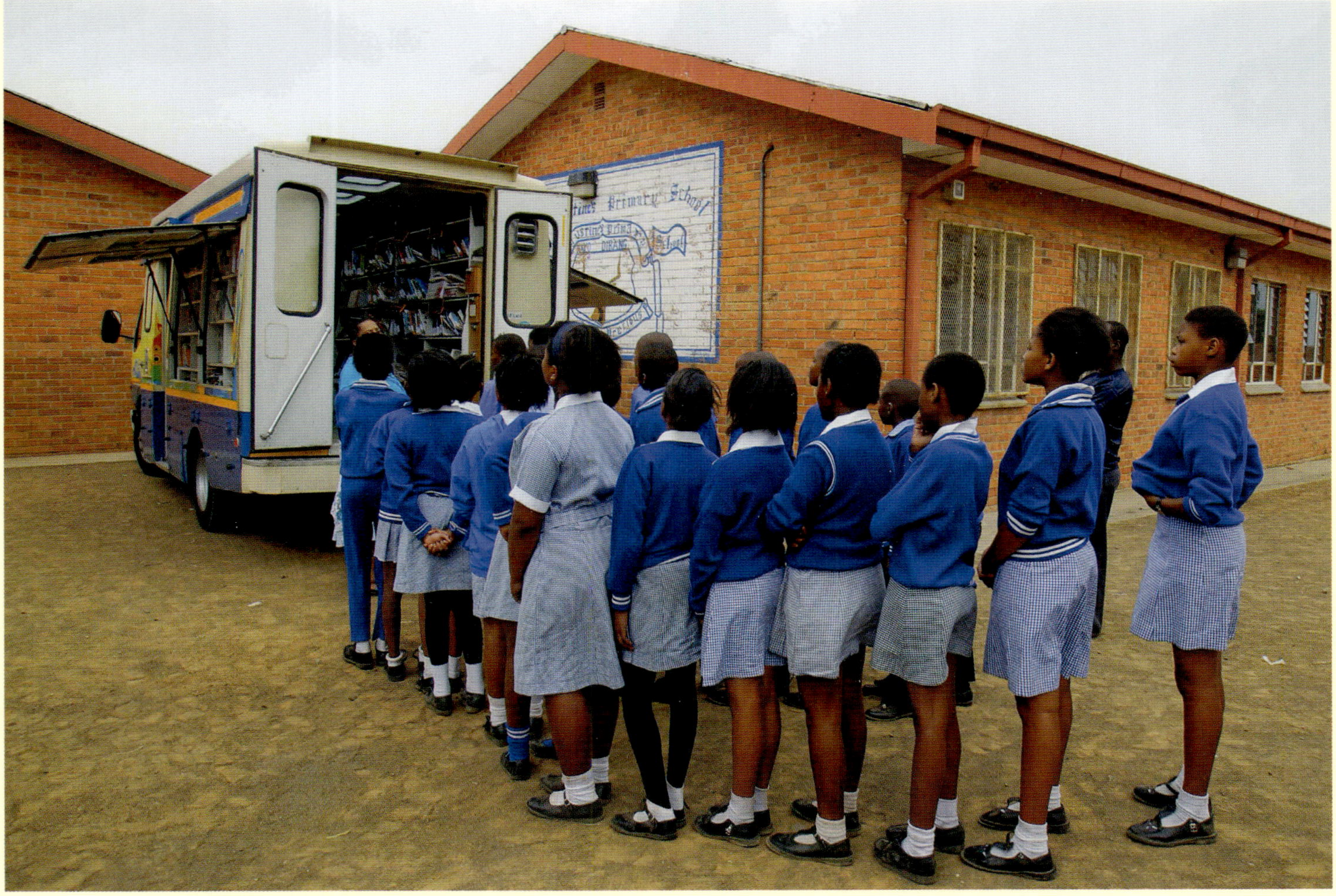

Photographs: Nina Lieska Grindlay, Rhodes University

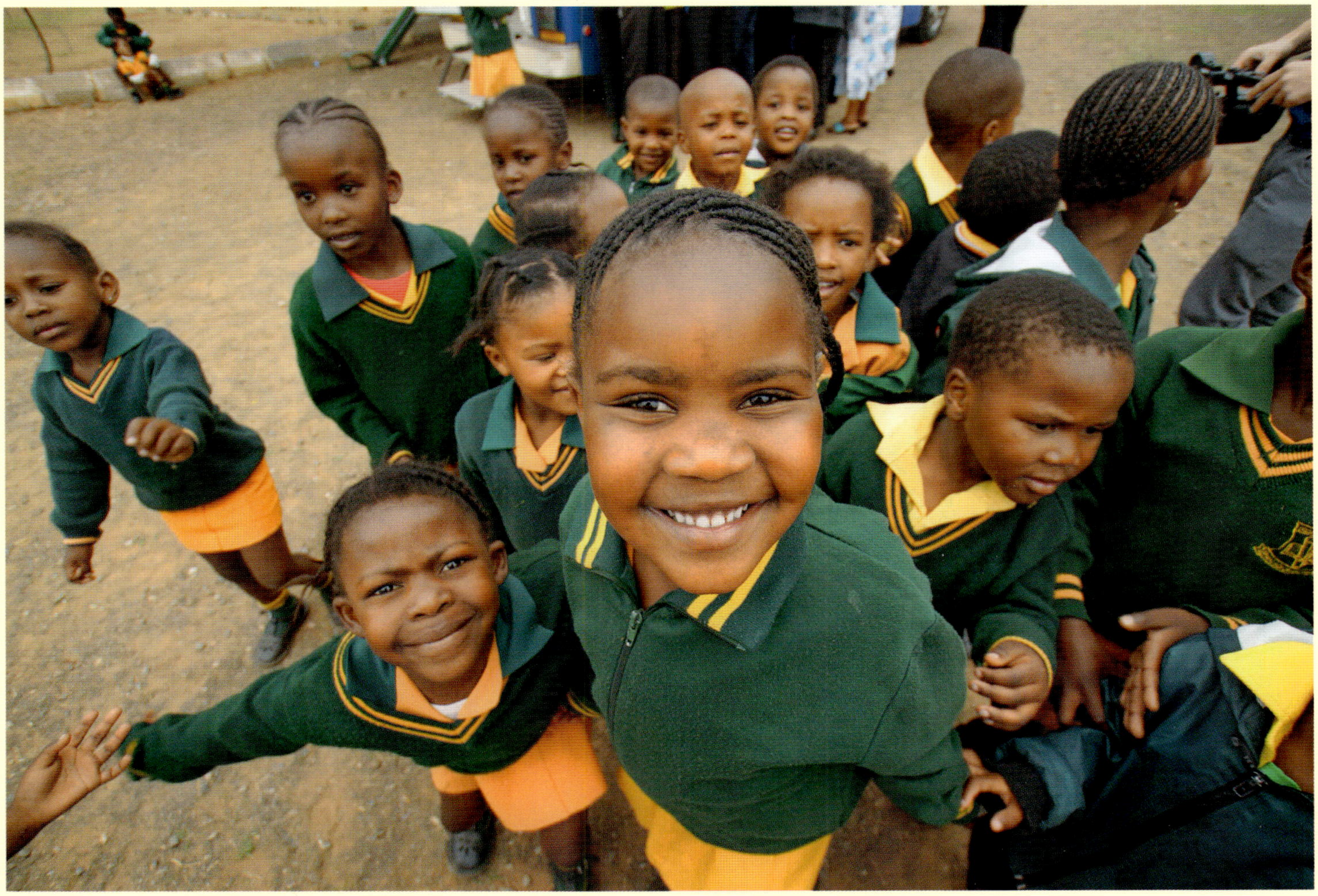

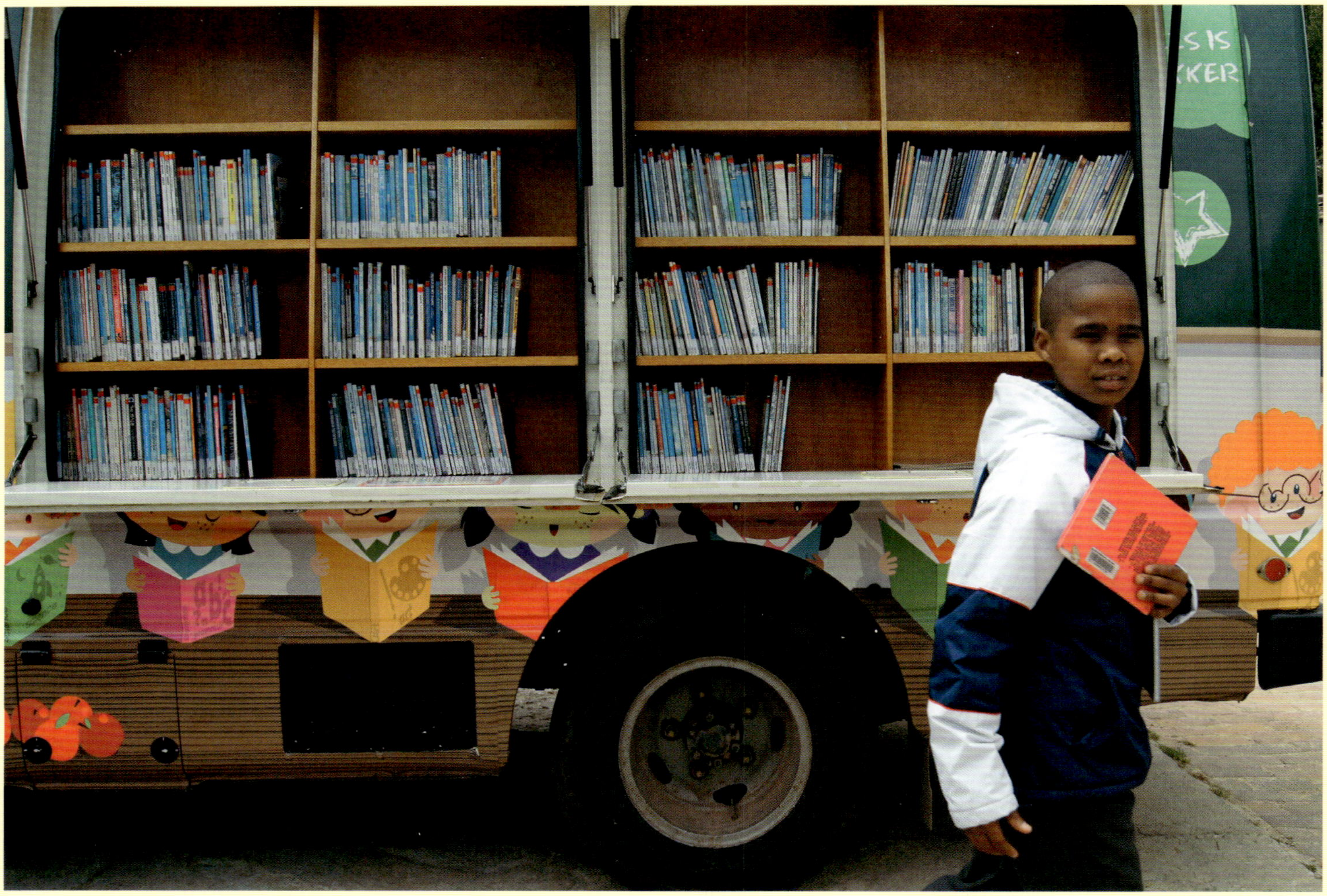

Photograph: Laura Swart, Stellenbosch Academy of Design and Photography

"I worked with truly inspiring people and met many kind little faces. These three days have taught me so much more in addition to photographic skills. I have learnt about people, the landscape and the importance of education for our youth."
Laura Swart, Stellenbosch Academy of Design and Photography

Photograph: Laura Swart, Stellenbosch Academy of Design and Photography

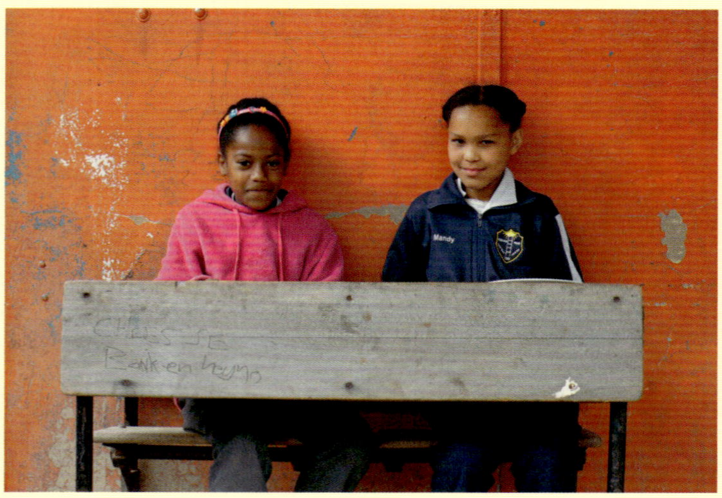

Photograph: Laura Swart, Stellenbosch Academy of Design and Photography

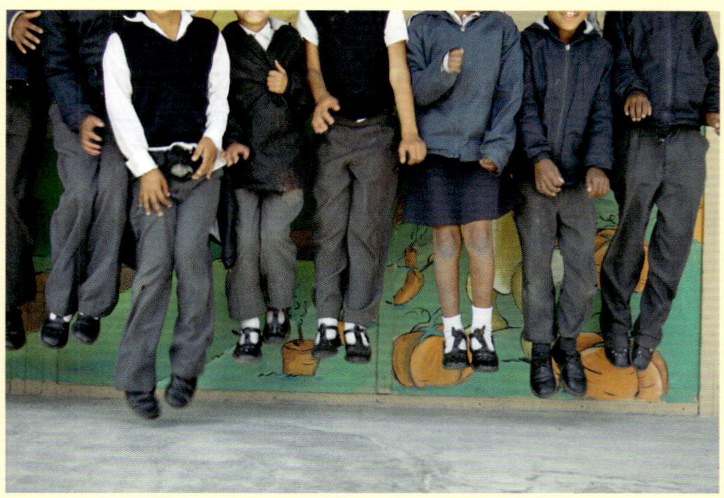

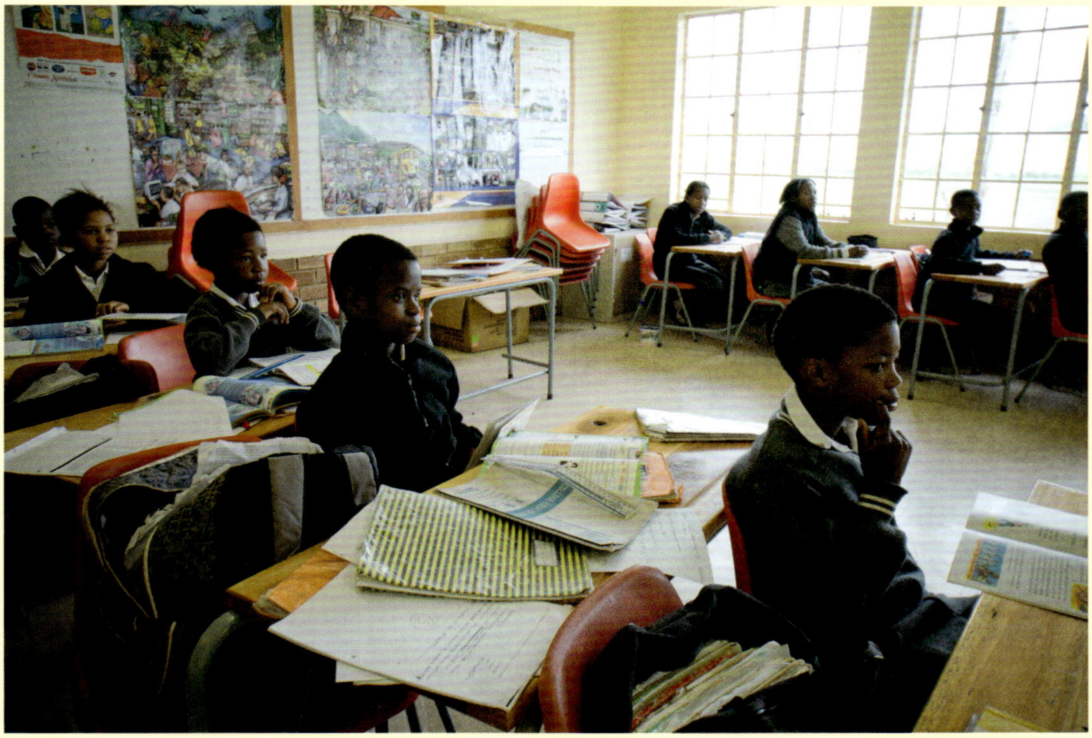

"When entering the smaller children's classroom they looked up in amazement, not really knowing what it was I had in my hands. After showing them the photos I took of them their faces lit up, pointing and almost screaming "That's me!."
Christiaan de Beer, Tshwane University of Technology

Photograph: Christiaan de Beer, Tshwane University of Technology

Photograph: Christiaan de Beer, Tshwane University of Technology

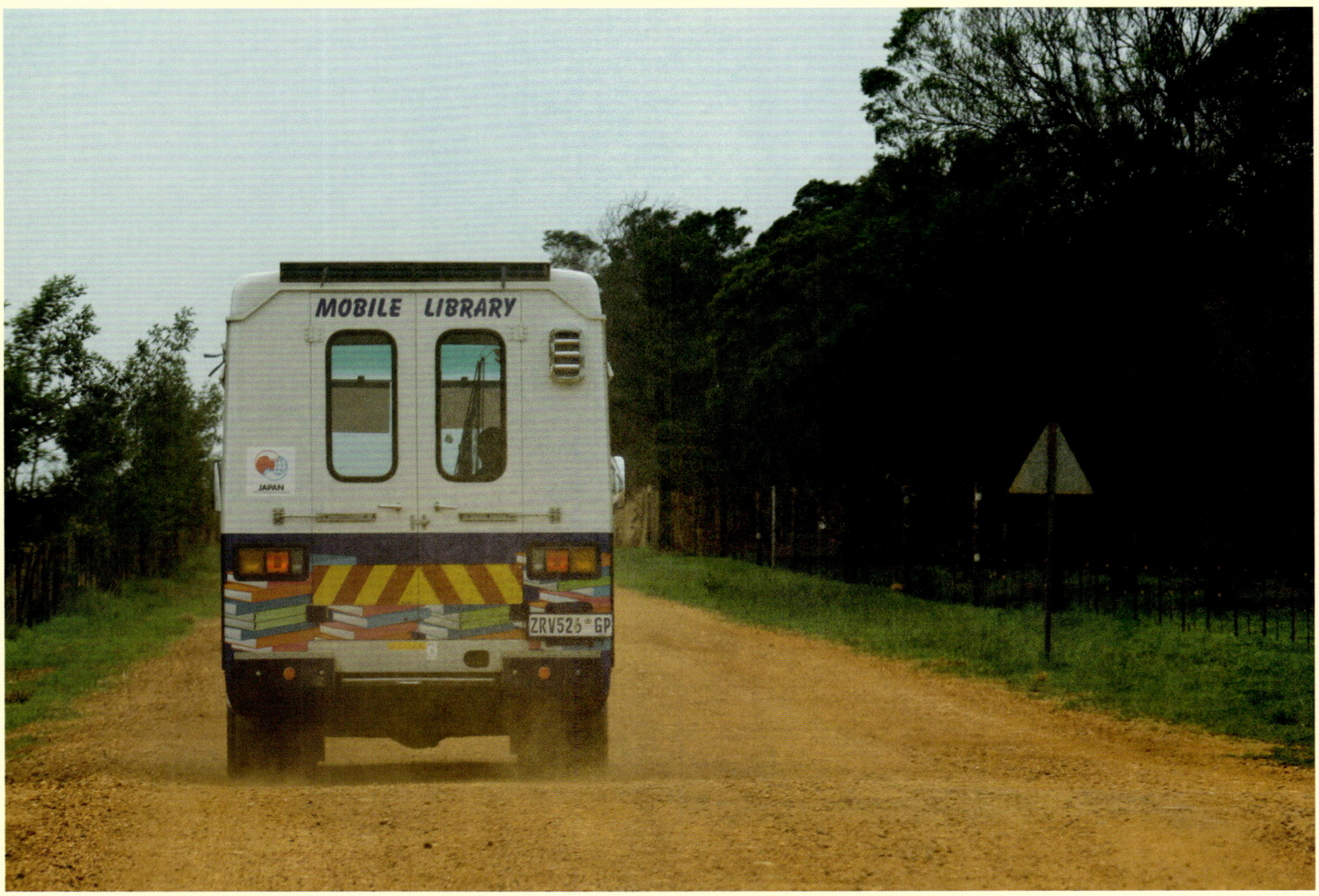

OPEN COMPETITION SHORTLIST

With the arrival of the digital age, we witnessed an explosion in image making which continues to accelerate. In a year that saw a record number of entries from across 170 countries, we feel it is important to acknowledge the true enthusiasts who come from all walks of life but share a love of photography.

While there can be only one winner in each category, we commend all the photographers who take the chance and submit their work to our awards. In the following pages, we celebrate those who reached the Open Competition shortlist and prompted our jury to pause to admire the imagery that has been captured by those who simply have a passion for photography.

ARCHITECTURE

SHORTLIST
OPEN COMPETITION

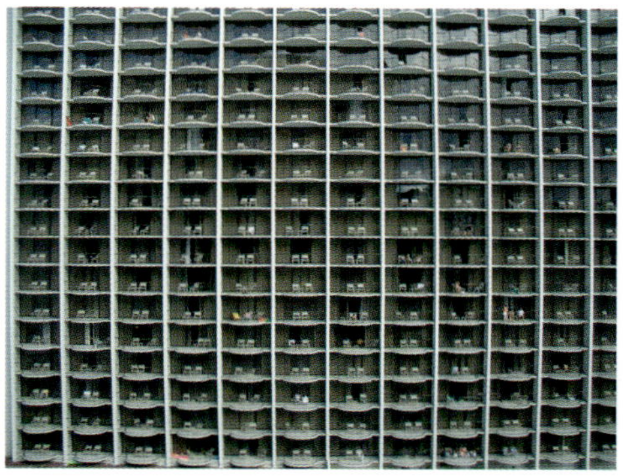
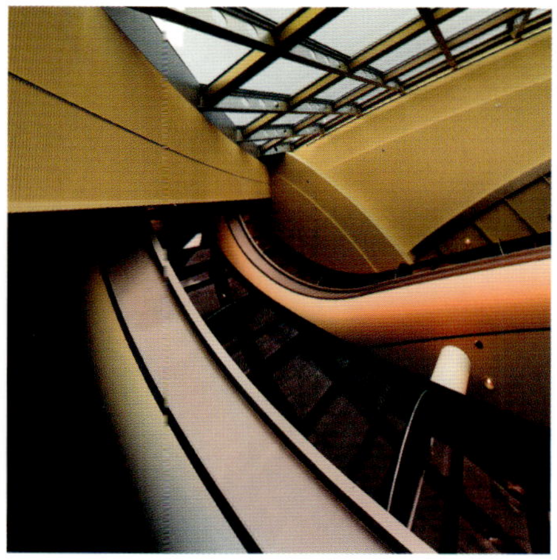
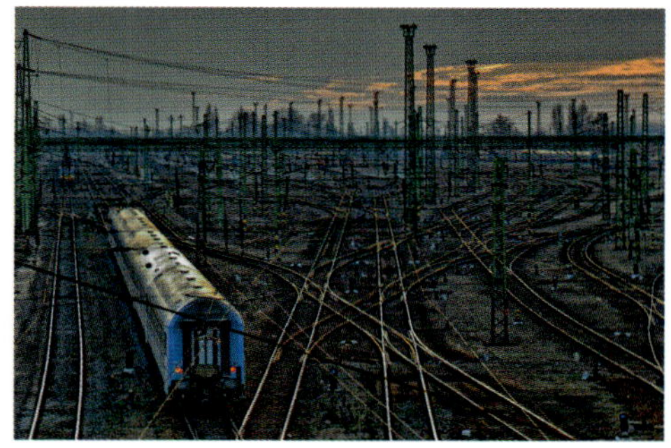
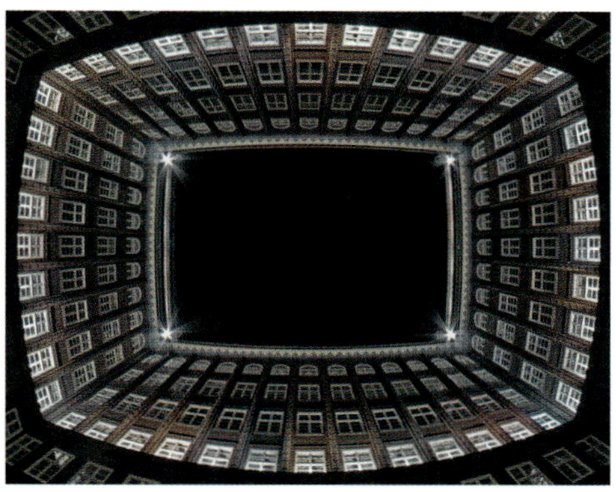
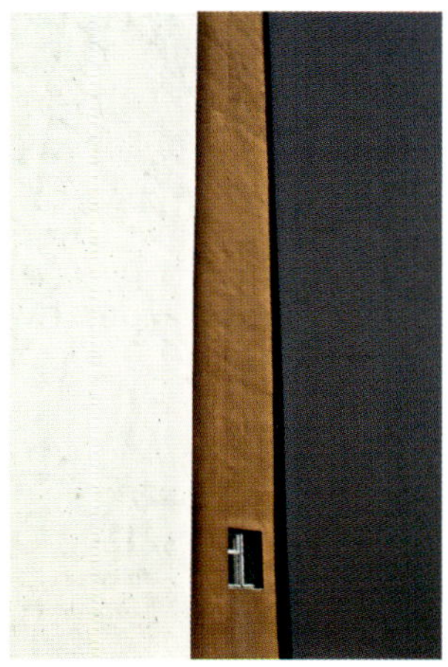
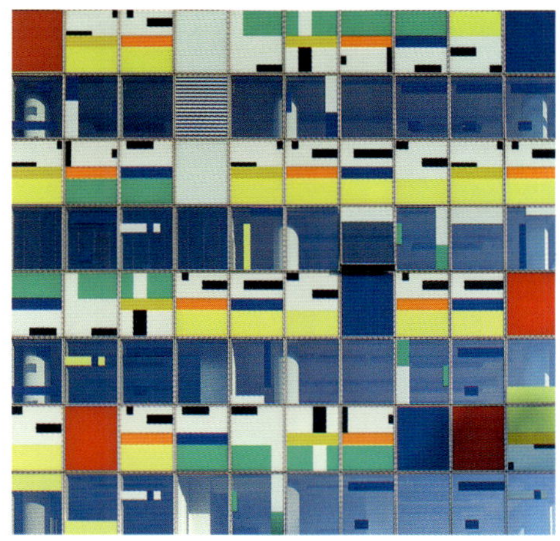
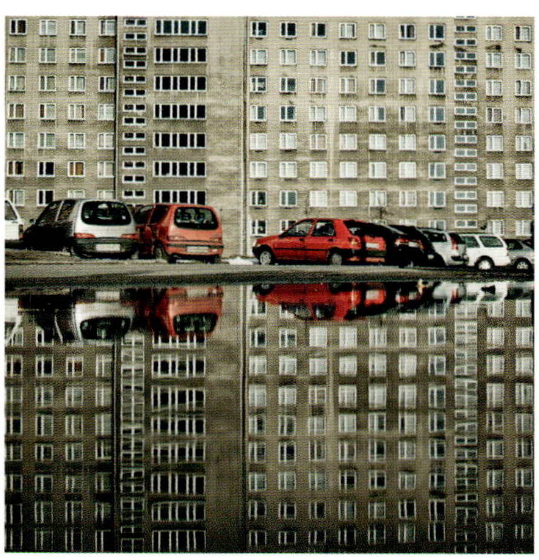
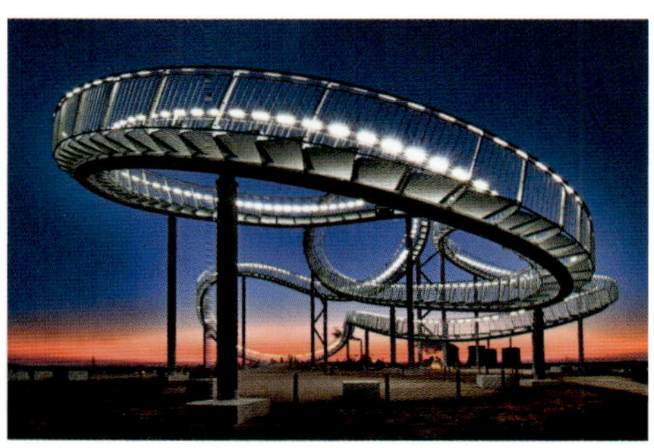
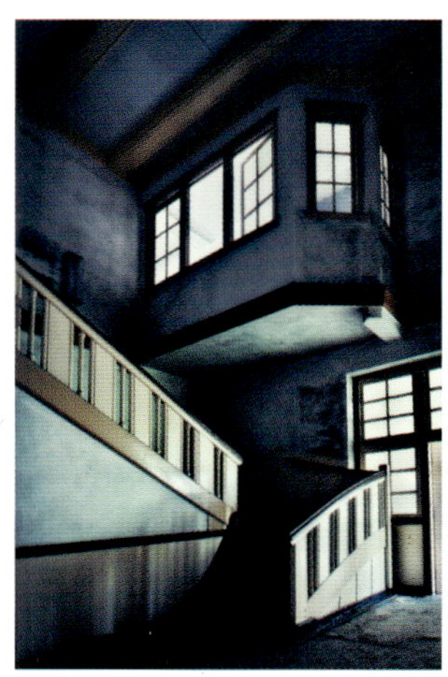

Top: **Flavio D'Aquino** Italy, **Igor Krieg** Germany, **István Forgács** Hungary.
Middle: **Jens Oliver Klaffs** Germany, **Aleksey Skripin** Russia, **Max van Son** Netherlands.
Bottom: **Paweł Karasiński** Poland, **Peter Mysticdidge Plorin** Germany, **Ralph Gräf** Germany.

ARTS & CULTURE

SHORTLIST
OPEN COMPETITION

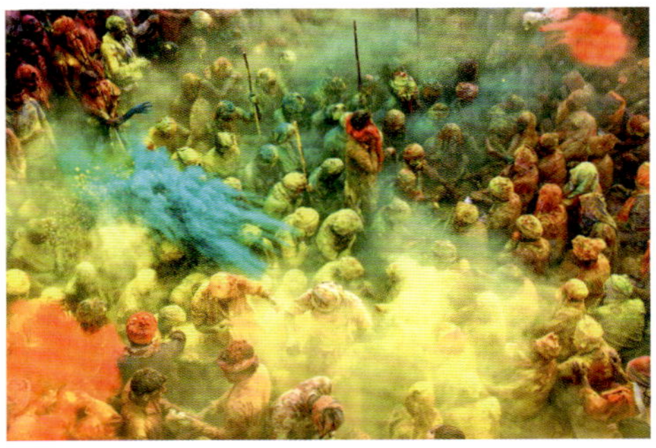
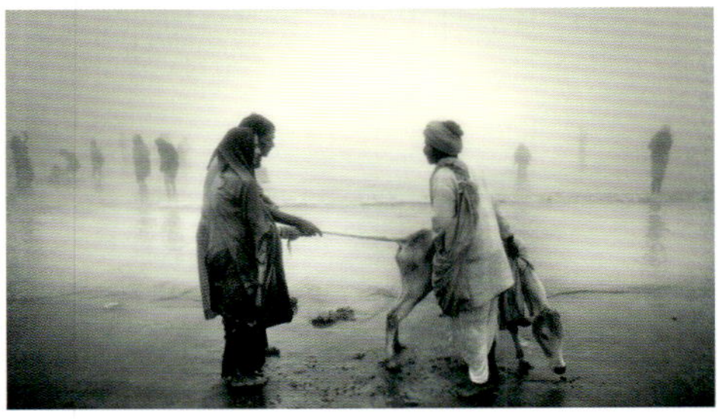
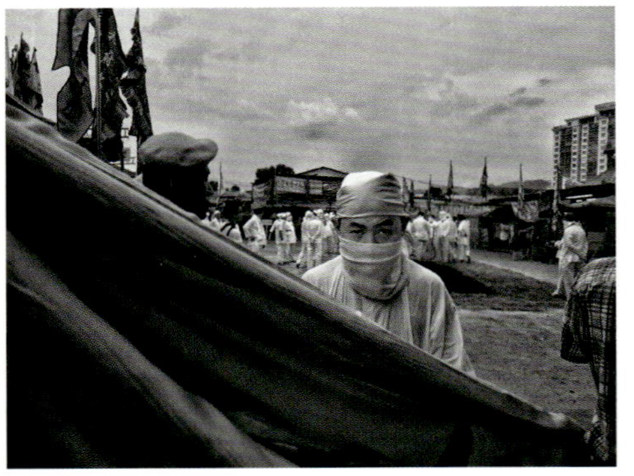
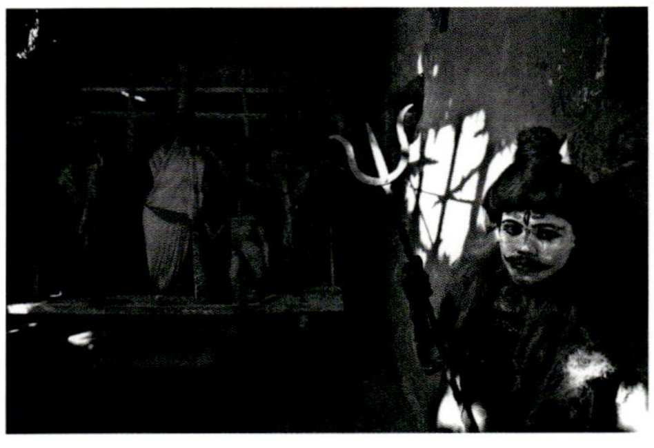
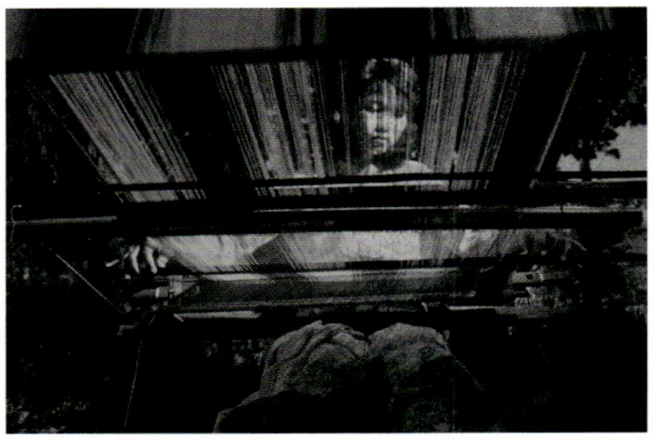
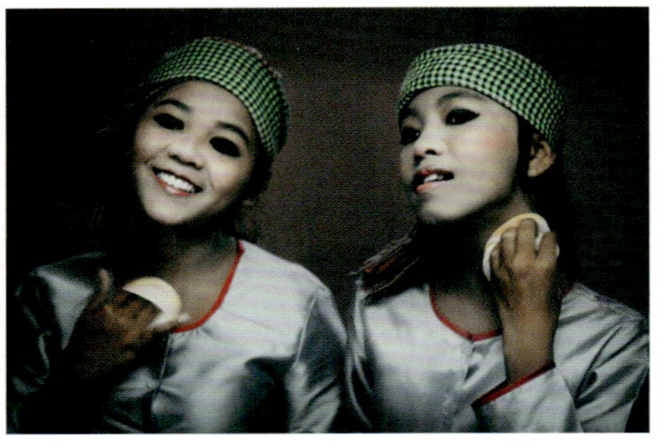
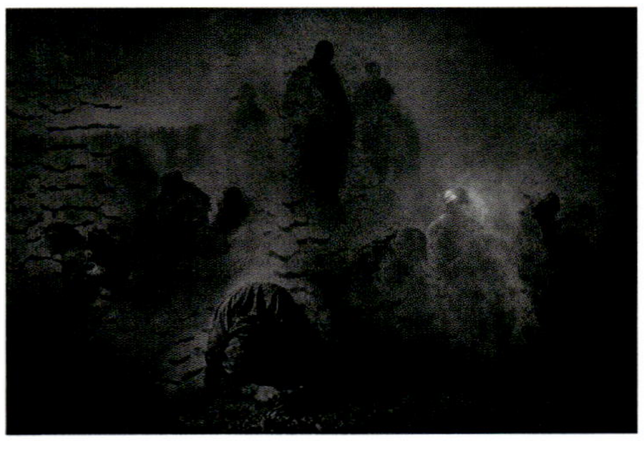
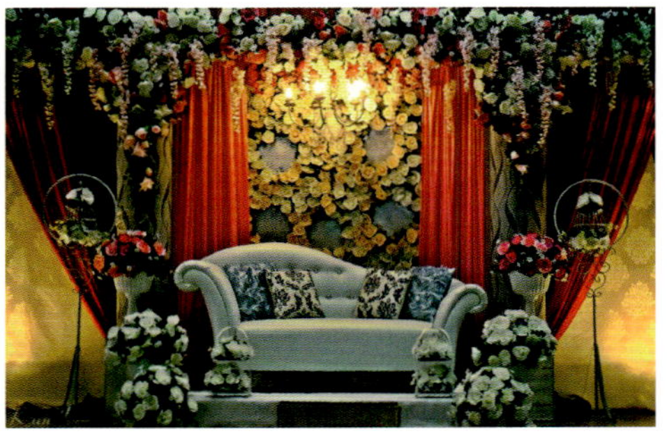
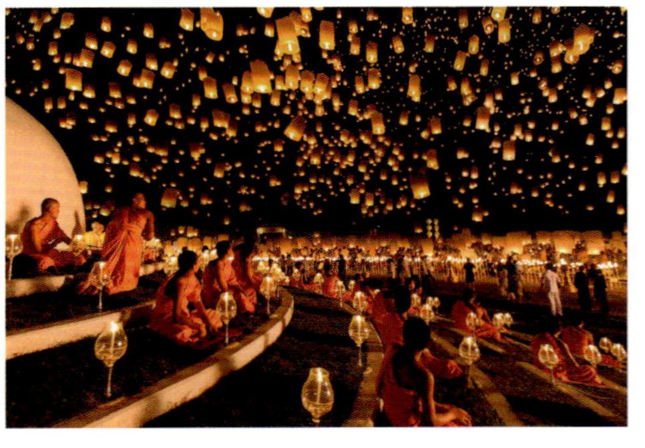

Top: **Anurag Kumar** India, **Arup Ghosh** India, **Chen Long Wen** Malaysia.
Middle: **Dibyendu Dey Choudhury** India, **Fahmy Husain** Indonesia, **Jessica Hetke** Germany.
Bottom: **Mohammad Reza Masoumi** Iran, **Mohdfaridzazhar Azhar** Malaysia, **Ng Chai Hock** Singapore.

ENHANCED

SHORTLIST
OPEN COMPETITION

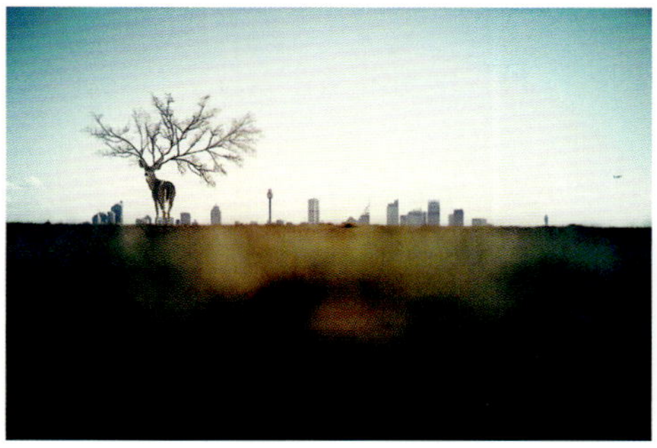
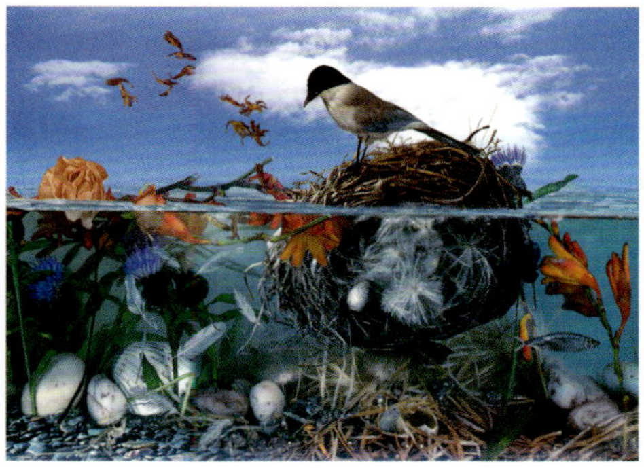
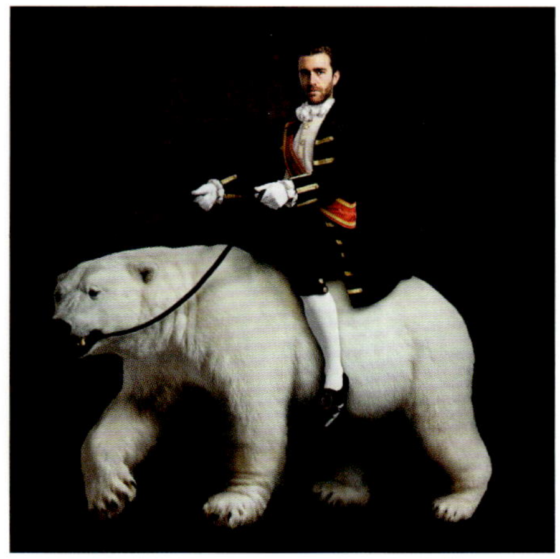
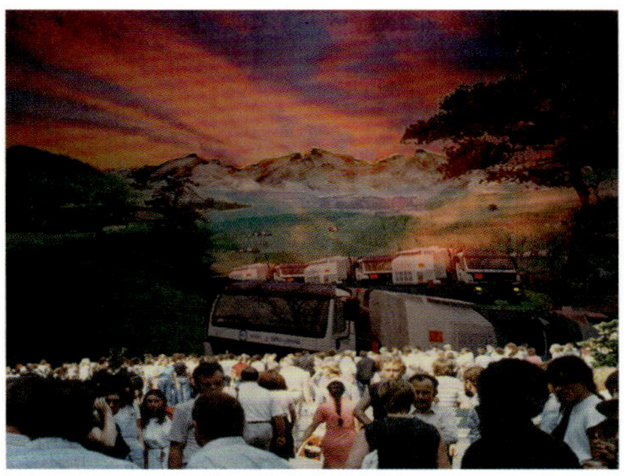
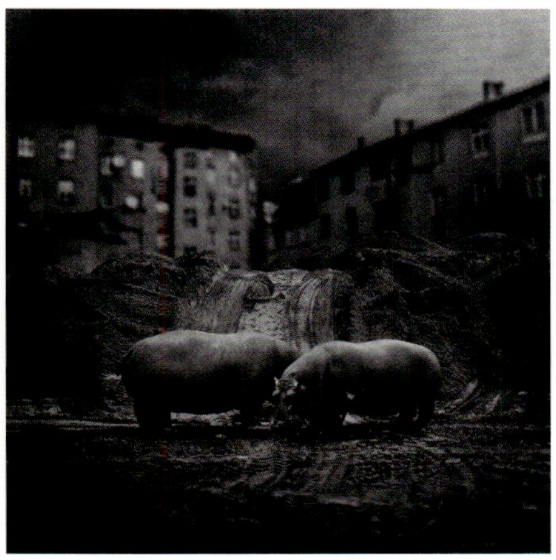
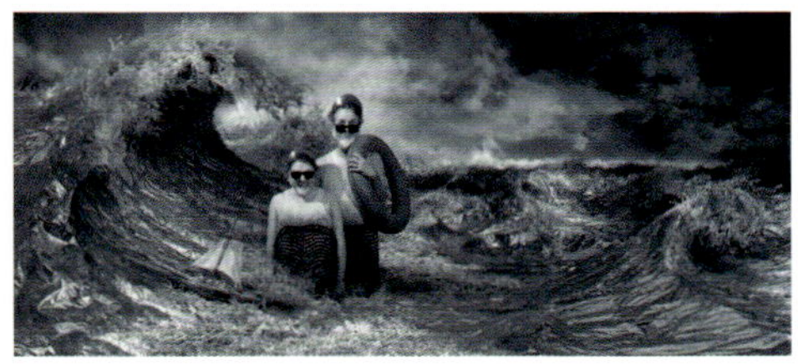
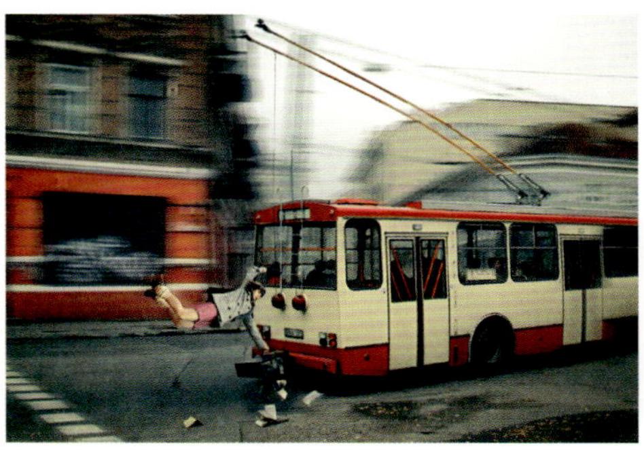
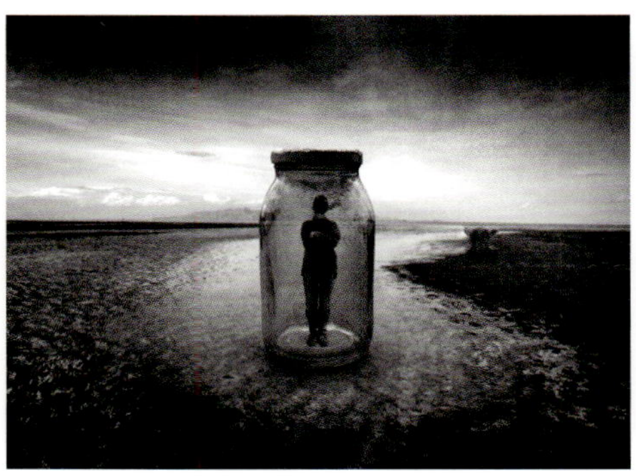
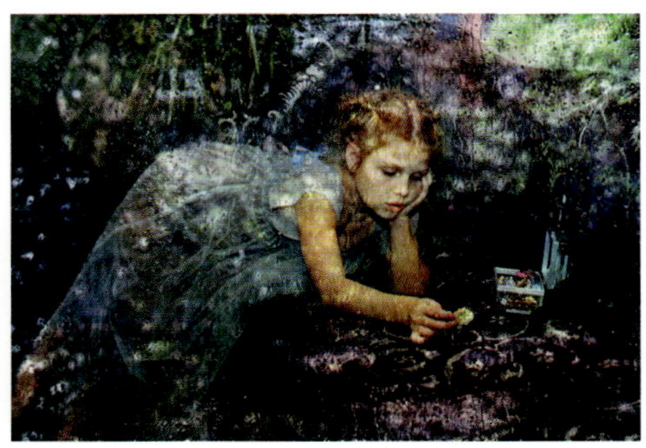

Top: **Chan Hoi Kim** Republic of Korea, **Christine Simpson** Ireland, **Danny Cohen** Australia.
Middle: **Gerhard Burger** Germany, **Michal Giedrojc** Poland, **Michel Lagarde** France.
Bottom: **Nina Piatrouskaya** Belarus, **Samad Ghorbanzadeh** Iran, **Viktoriya Panasenko** Ukraine.

LOW LIGHT

SHORTLIST
OPEN COMPETITION

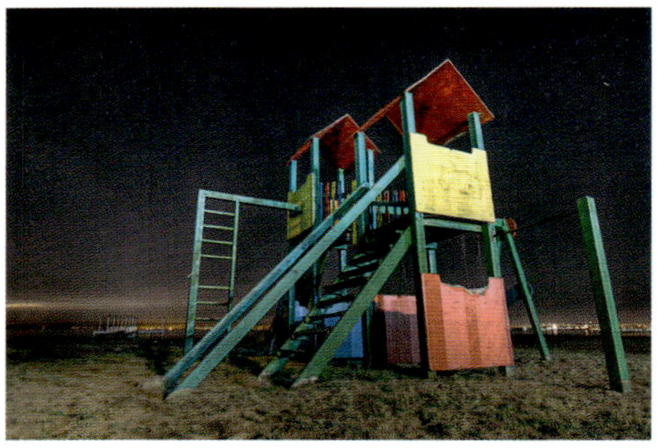

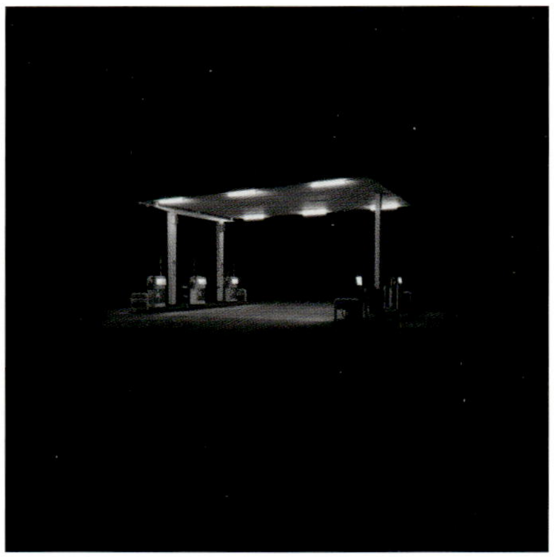

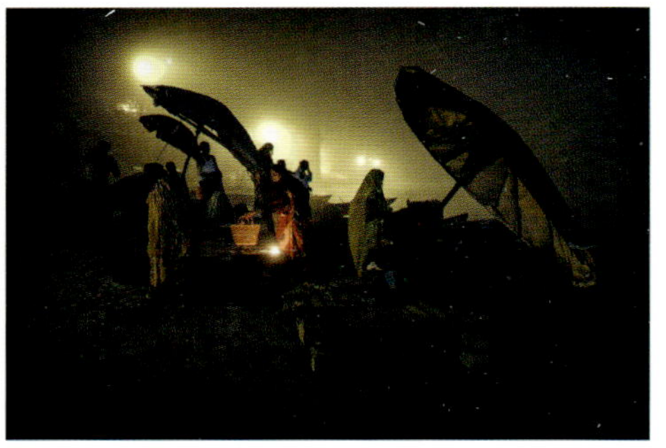

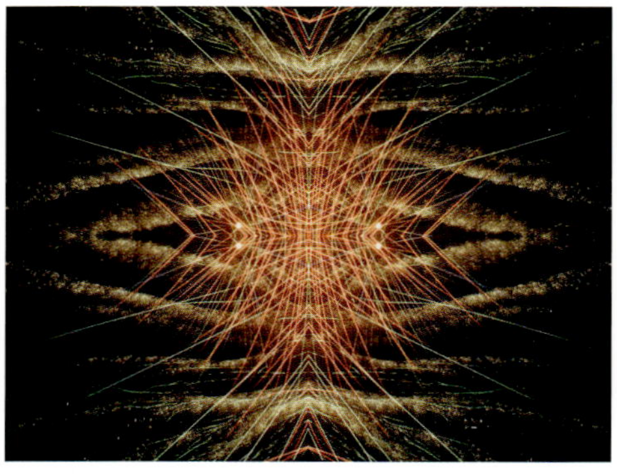

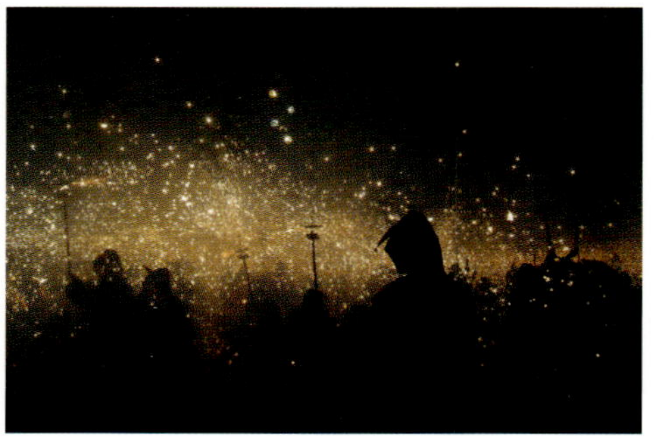

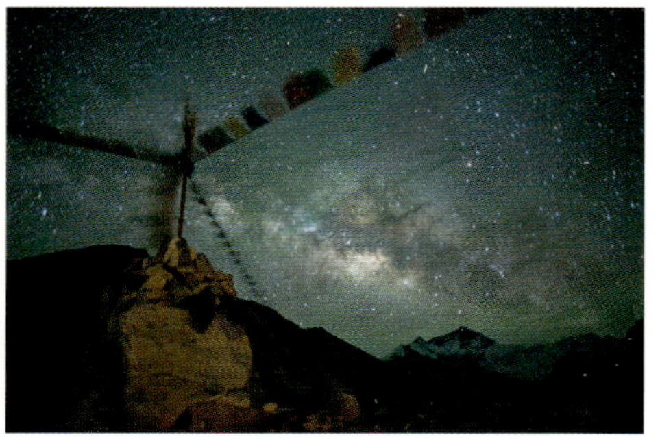

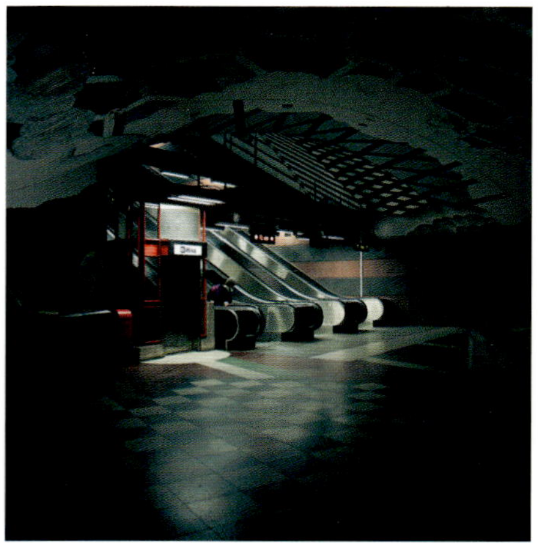

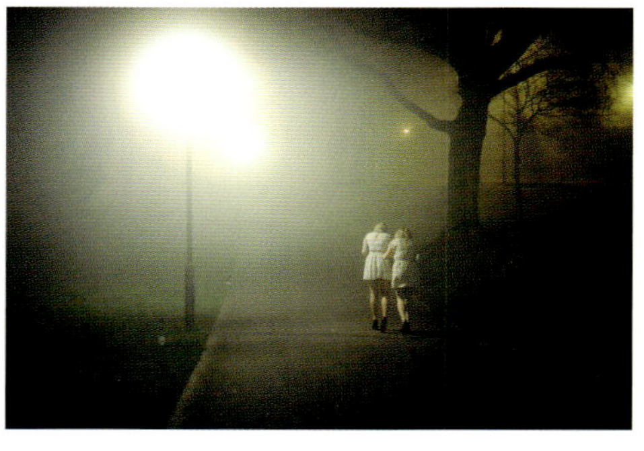

Top: **Cemil Seyis** Turkey, **Chris Round** Australia, **Harry Fisch** Spain.
Middle: **Manish Patel** United Kingdom, **Tatjana Bachmistova** Lithuania, **Tino Solomon** United Kingdom.
Bottom: **Torsten Muehlbacher** Austria, **Yi-Hsien Lee** Taiwan.

NATURE & WILDLIFE

SHORTLIST
OPEN COMPETITION

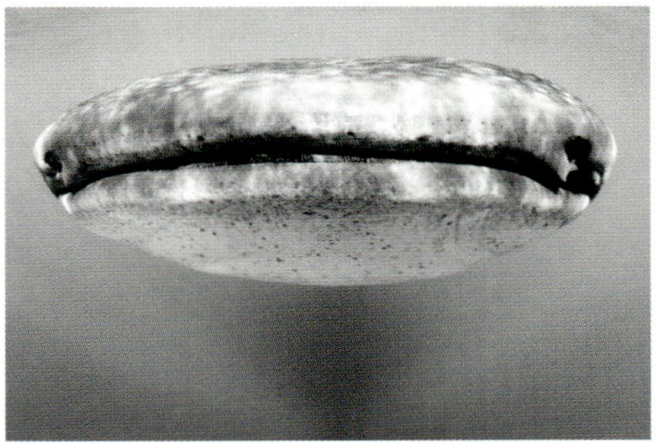
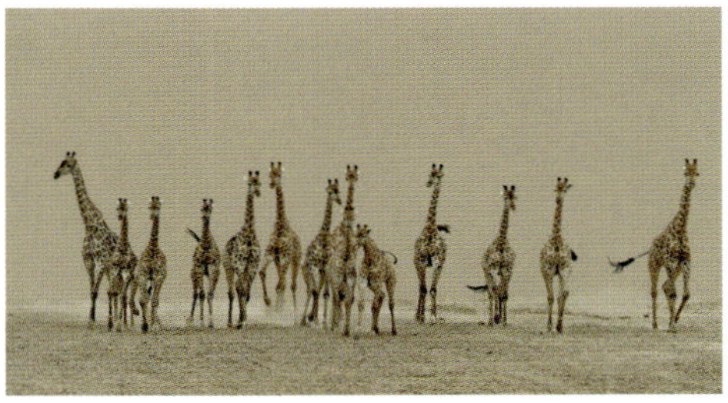
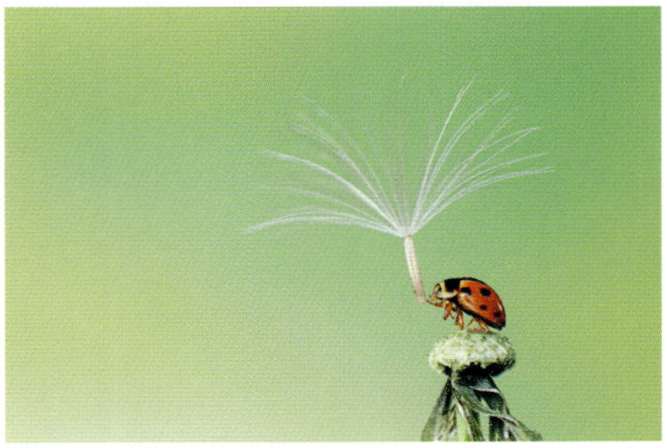
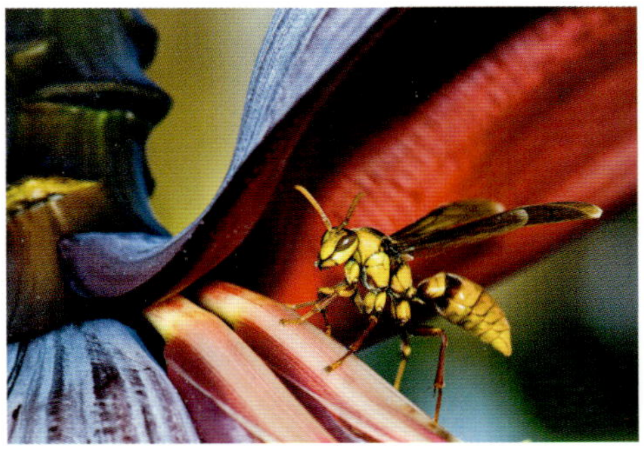
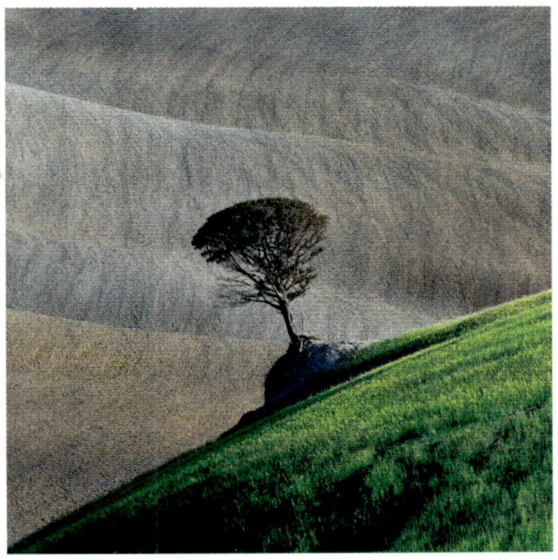
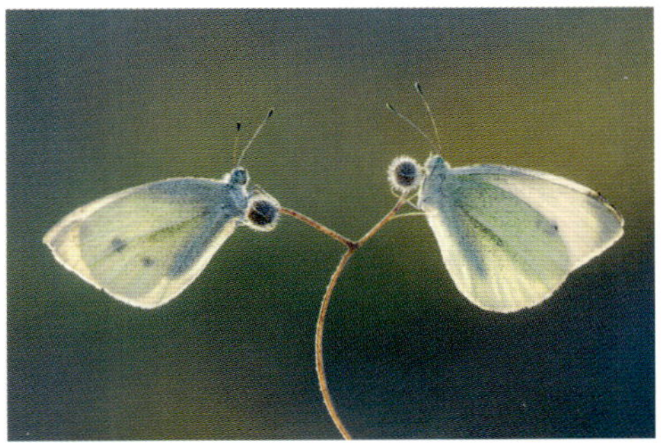
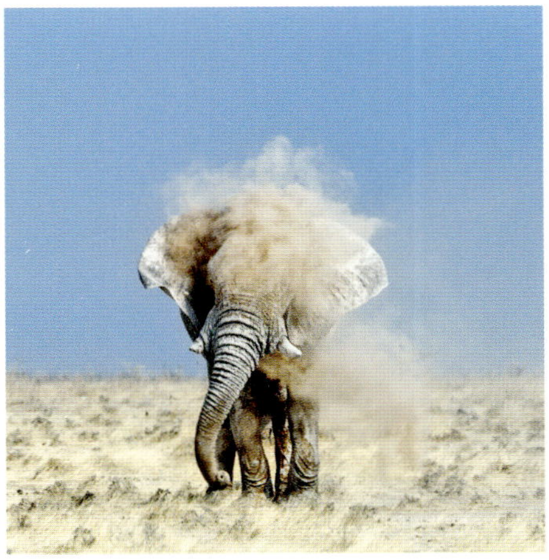
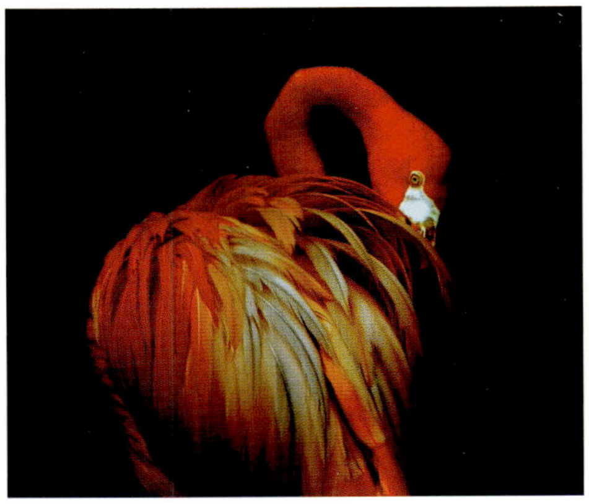
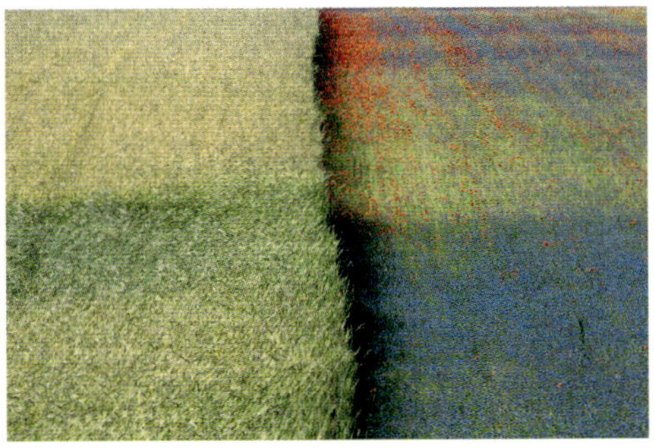

Top: **Christian Vizl** Mexico, **Frederick van Heerden** South Africa, **Nguyen Hoang Hiep** Vietnam.
Middle: **John Matzick** USA, **Marek Andrzejewski** Poland, **Petar Sabol** Croatia.
Bottom: **Peter Delaney** Ireland, **Ricardo Venerando** Brazil, **Roberto Bettacchi** Italy.

PANORAMIC

SHORTLIST
OPEN COMPETITION

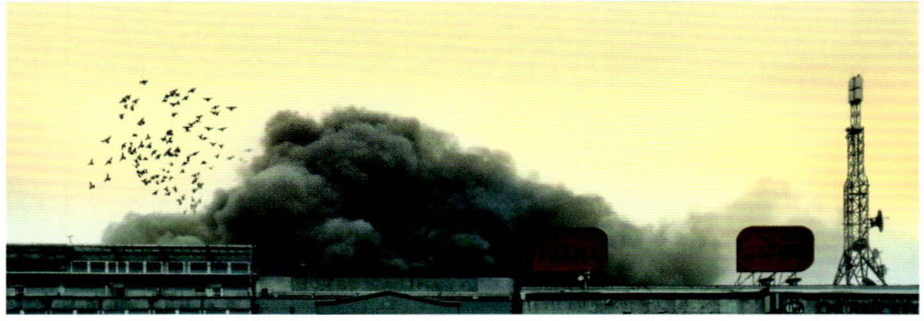

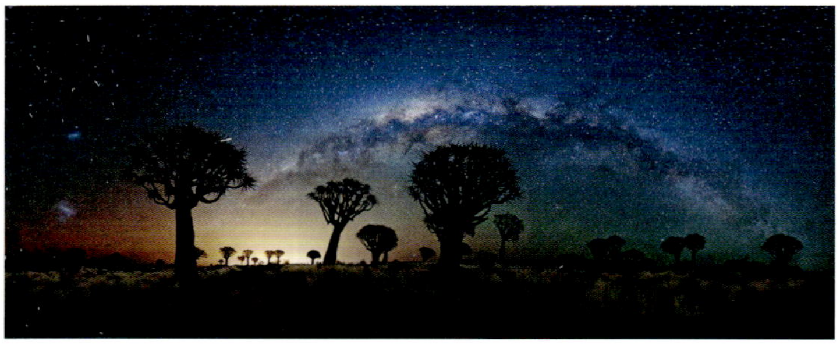

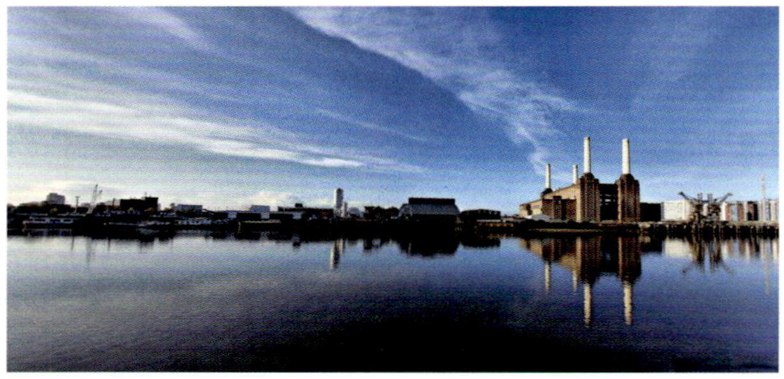

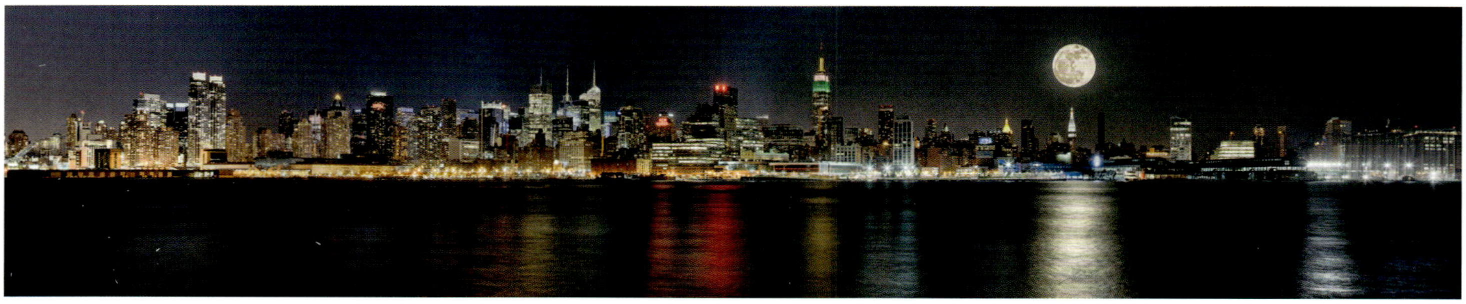

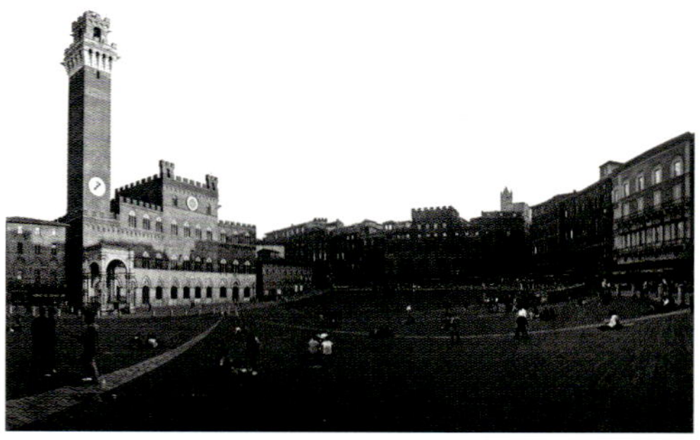

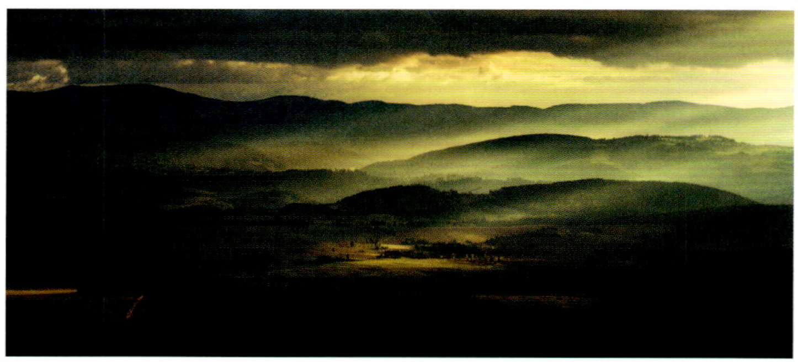

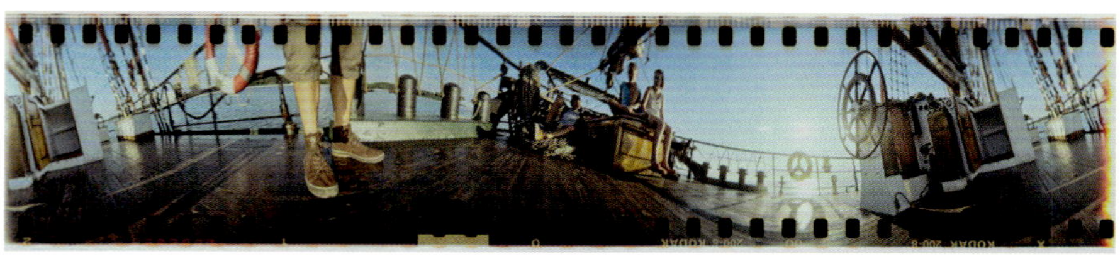

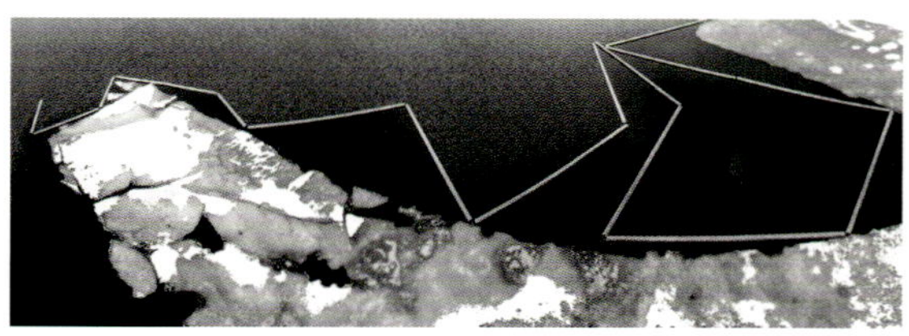

First row: **Anatoly Rudakov** Russia, **Christian Stangl** Austria. Second row: **Florian Breuer** South Africa, **Fabricio Pretti** Brazil.
Third row: **Jason Hipp** USA. Fourth row: **Luca Benini** Italy, **Pawel Uchorczak** Poland.
Fifth row: **Michael Schulze** Germany, **Konrad Lenz** Germany.

PEOPLE

SHORTLIST
OPEN COMPETITION

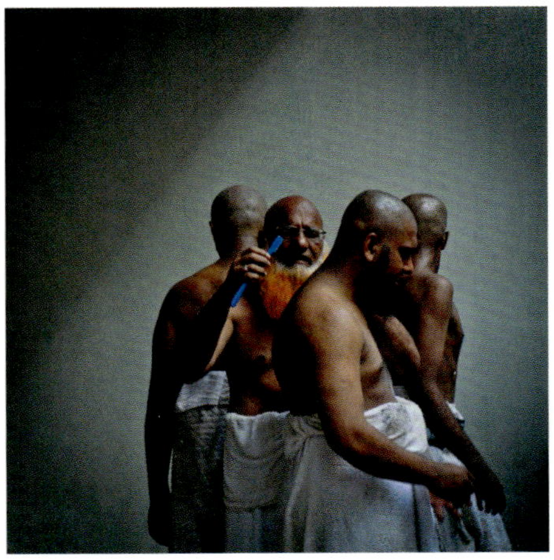
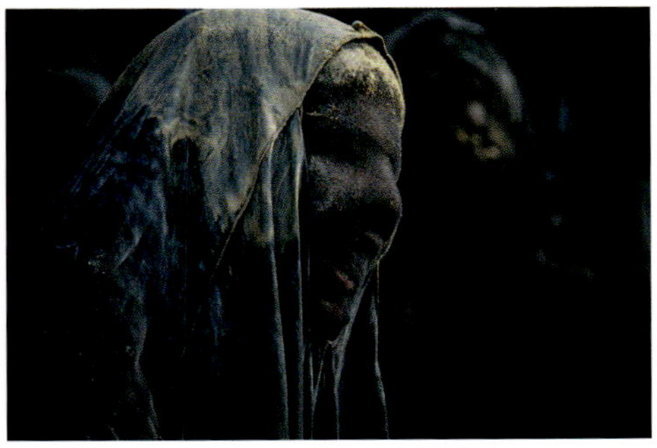
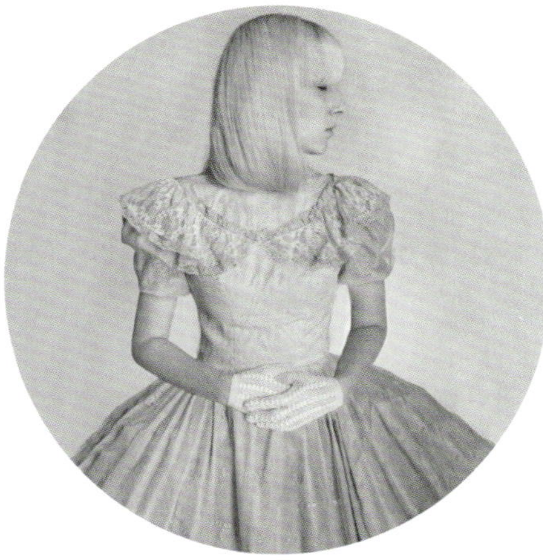
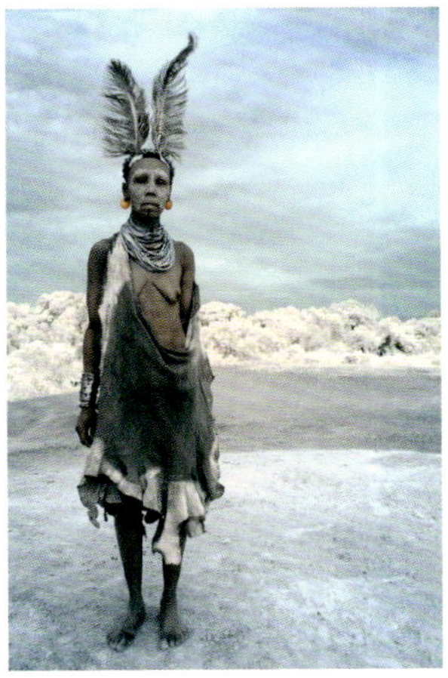
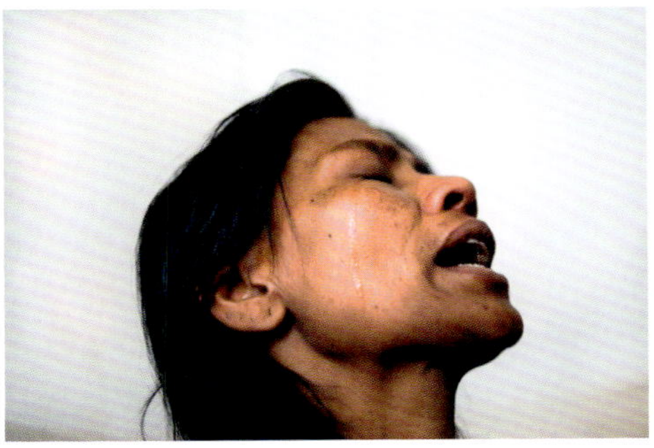
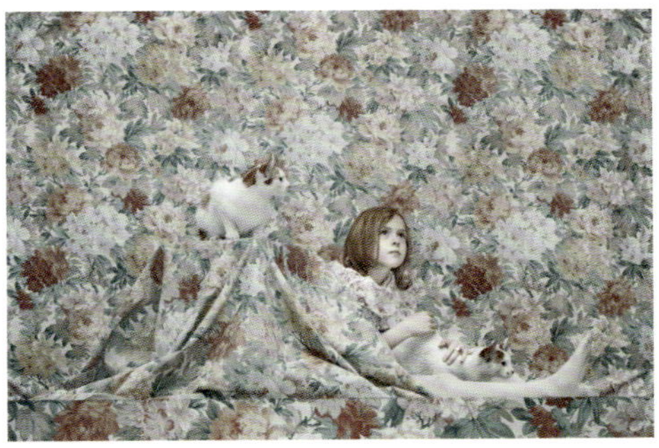
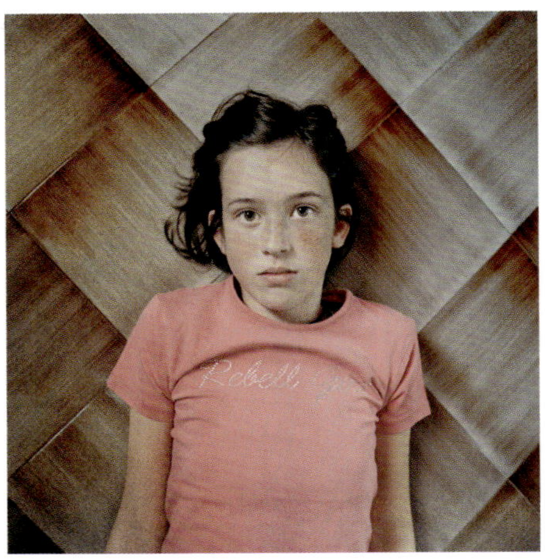

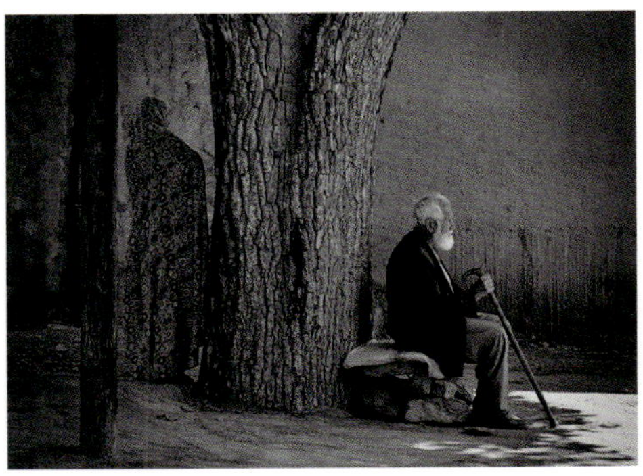
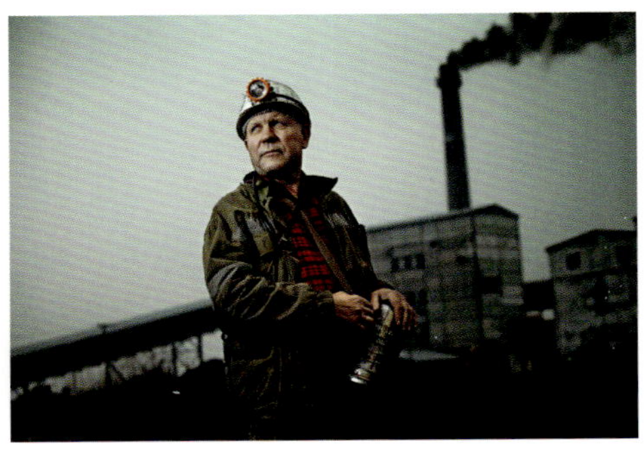

Top: **Ahmad Al Rikaby** United Kingdom, **Ali Asadi** Iran, **Karolina Grabowska** Poland.
Middle: **Louise Porter** USA, **Miguel Candela** Spain, **Natalia Wiernik** Poland.
Bottom: **Paolo Mezzera** Italy, **Reza Nezamdust** Iran, **Roman Shalenkin** Russia.

SMILE

SHORTLIST
OPEN COMPETITION

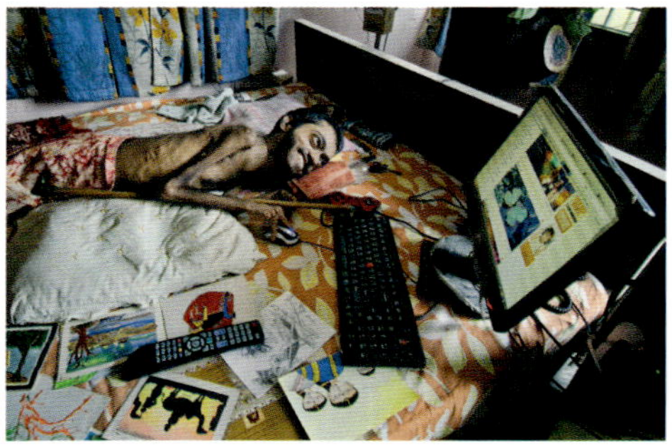

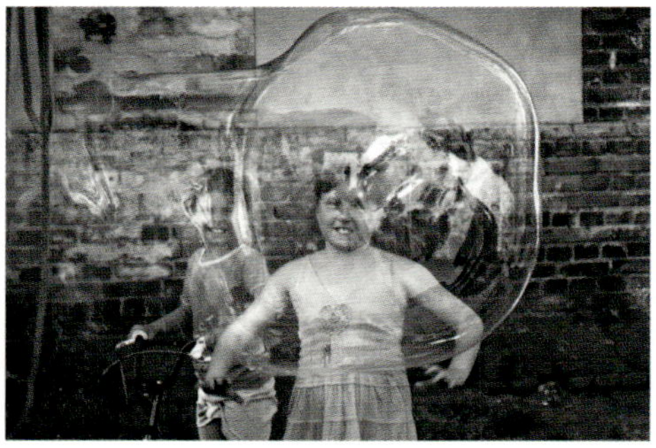

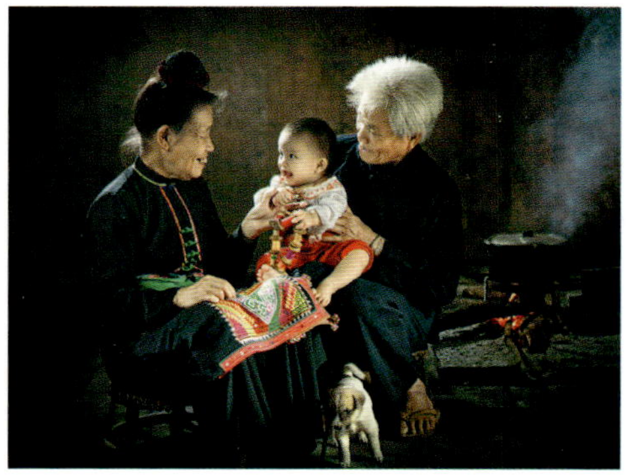

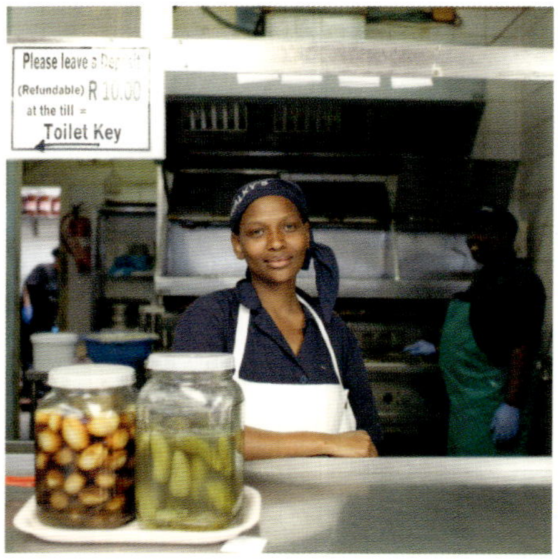

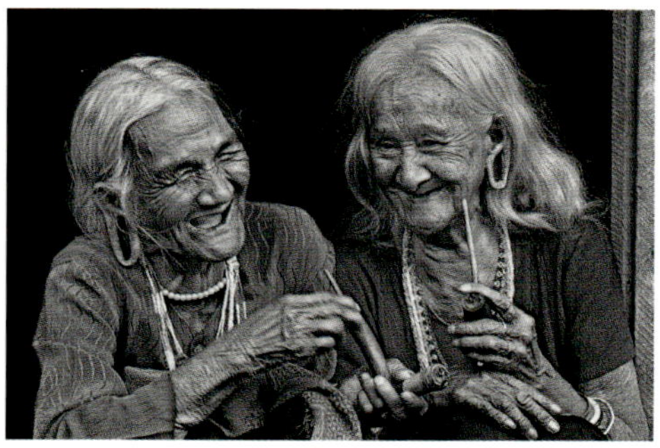

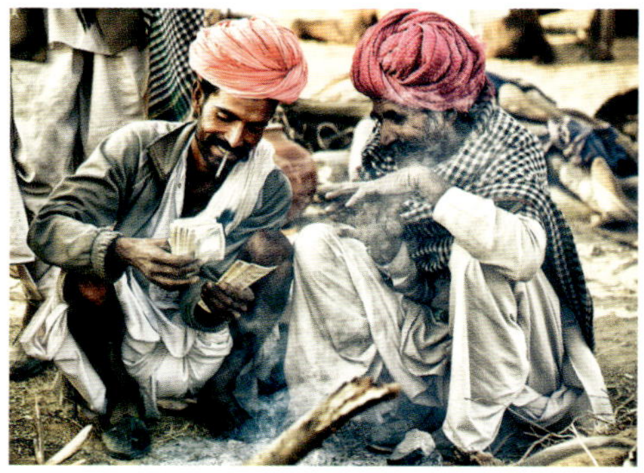

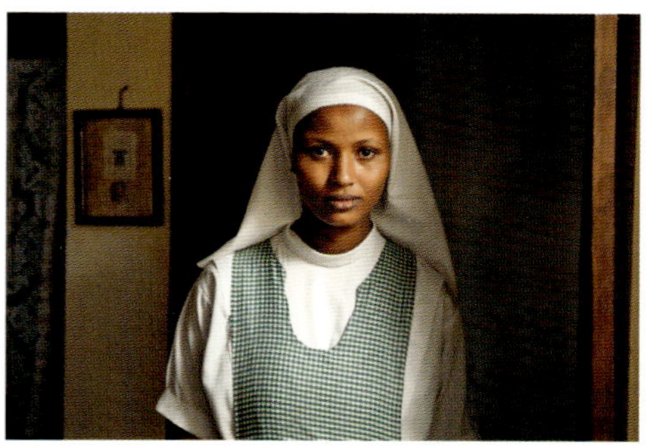

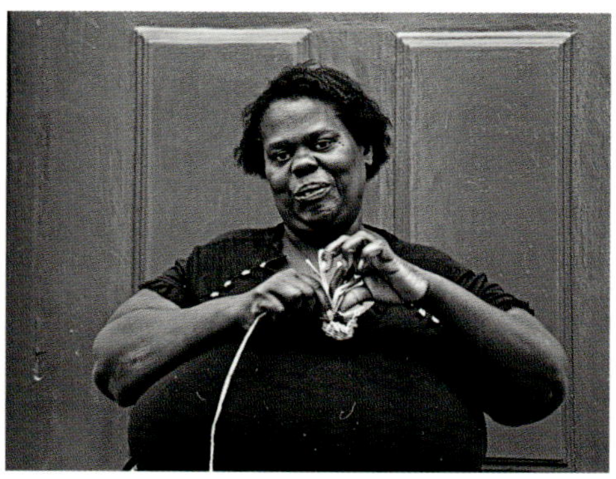

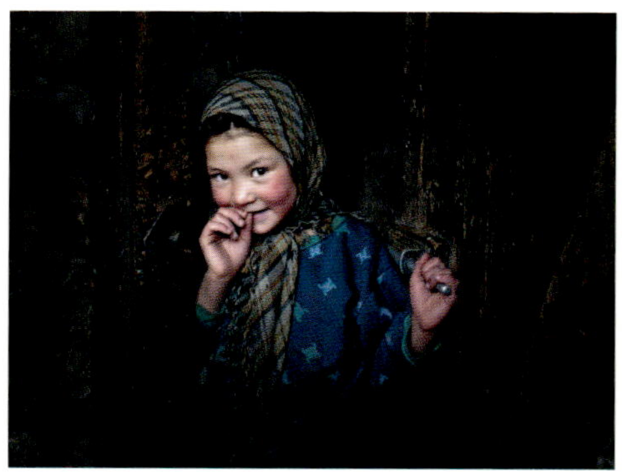

Top: **Abhijit Dey** India, **Boguslawa Trela** Poland, **Dinh Manh Tai** Vietnam.
Middle: **Eleri Griffiths** United Kingdom, **Huu Hung Truong** Vietnam, **Madhabendu Hensh** India.
Bottom: **Nick Riley** United Kingdom, **Paulo Mittelman** Brazil, **Sandipan Mukherjee** India.

SPLIT SECOND

SHORTLIST
OPEN COMPETITION

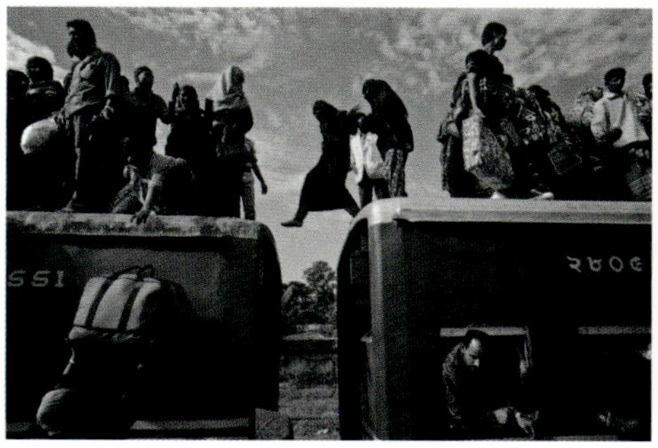
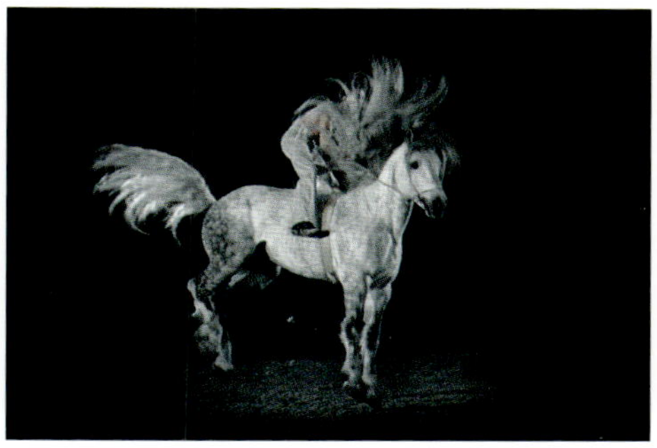
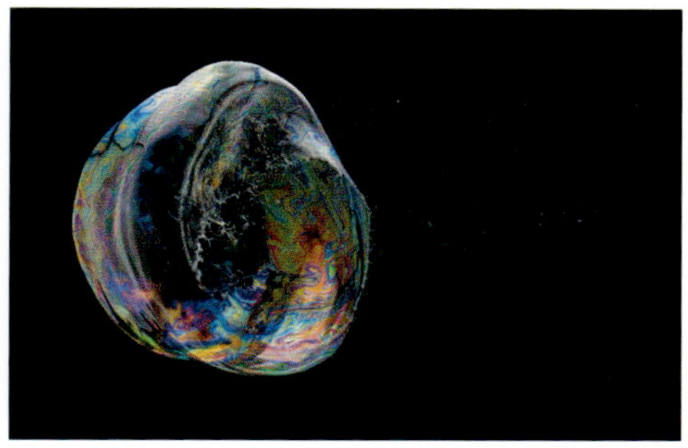
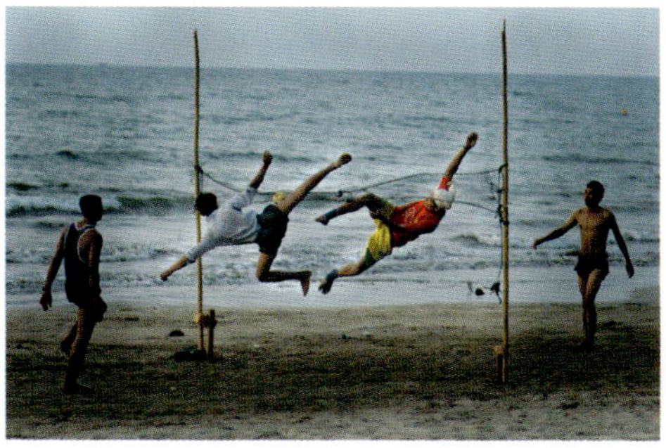
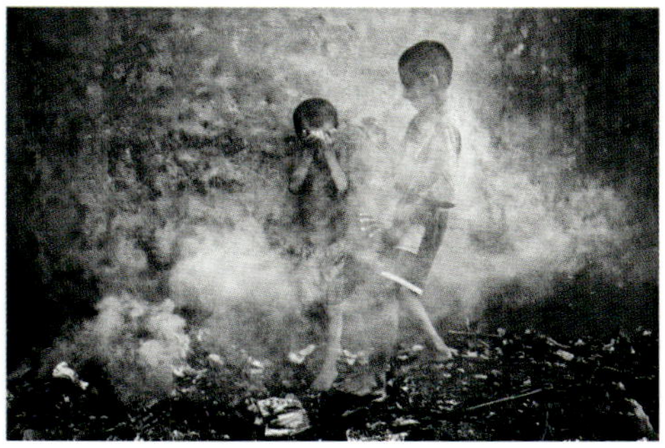
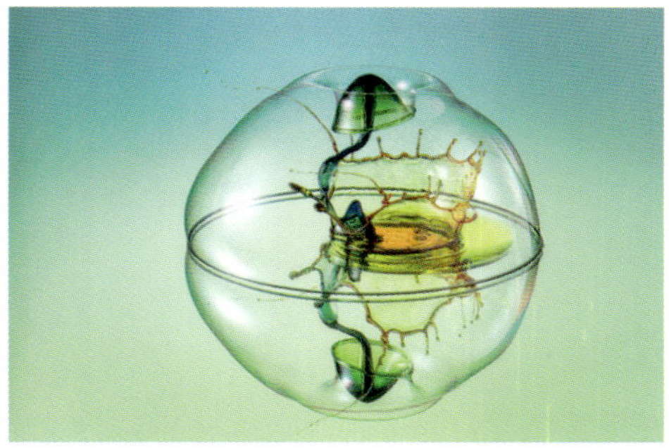
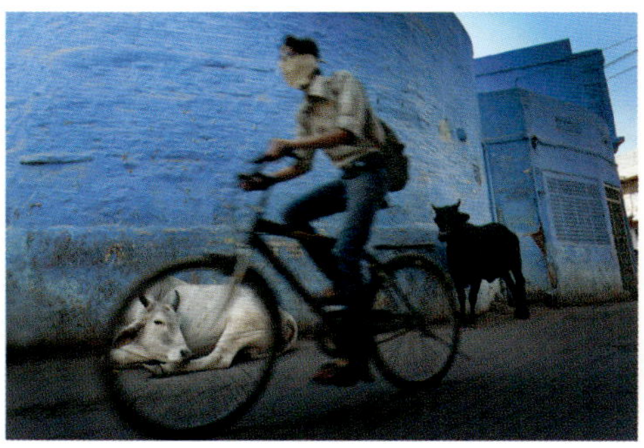
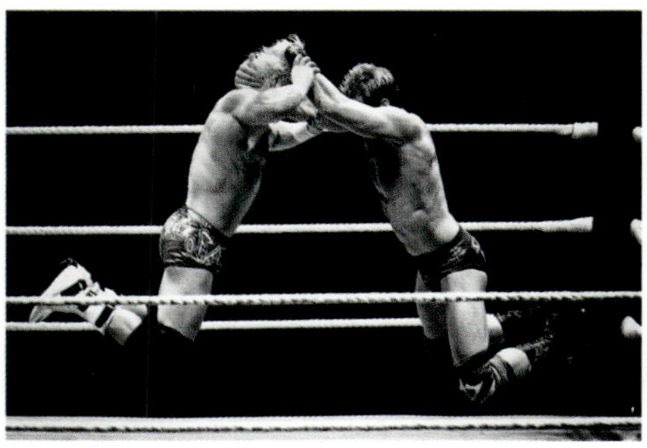
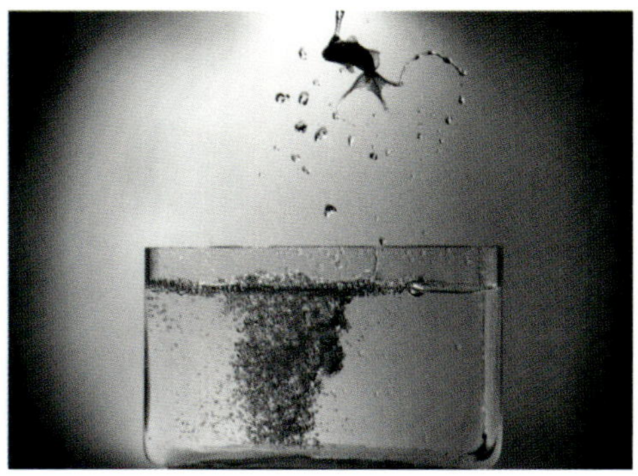

Top: **Ata Mohammad Adnan** Bangladesh, **Barbara Roppo** Italy, **Fabian Oefner** Switzerland.
Middle: **Gregory Bogaert** Belgium, **Kazi Riasat Alve** Bangladesh, **Markus Reugels** Germany.
Bottom: **Massimo Ferrero** Italy, **Nicola Genchi** Italy, **Tamás Nagy** Hungary.

TRAVEL

SHORTLIST
OPEN COMPETITION

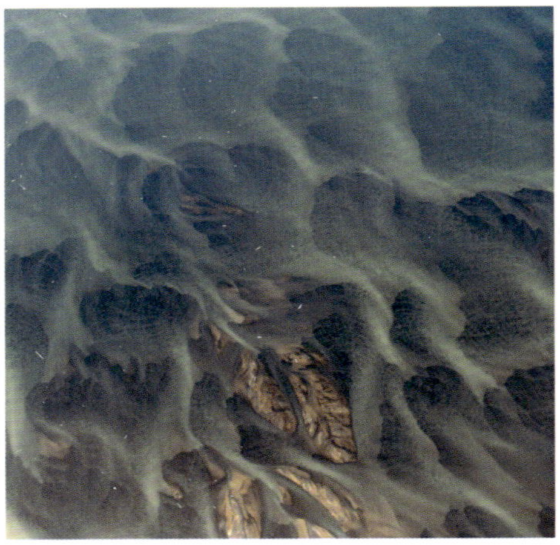
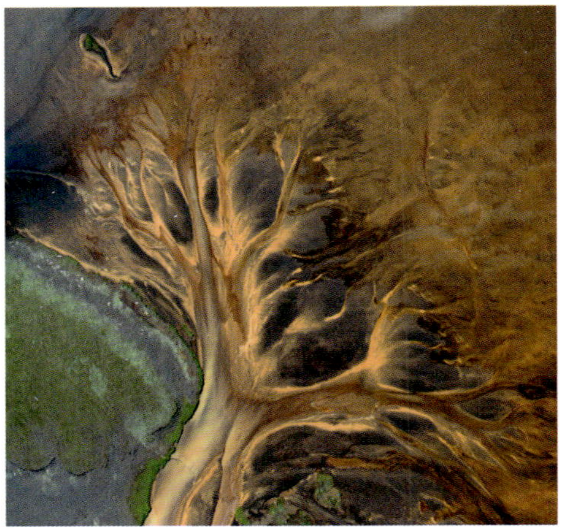
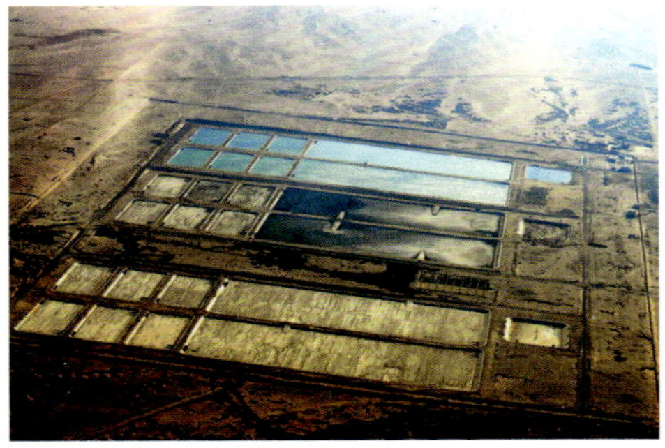
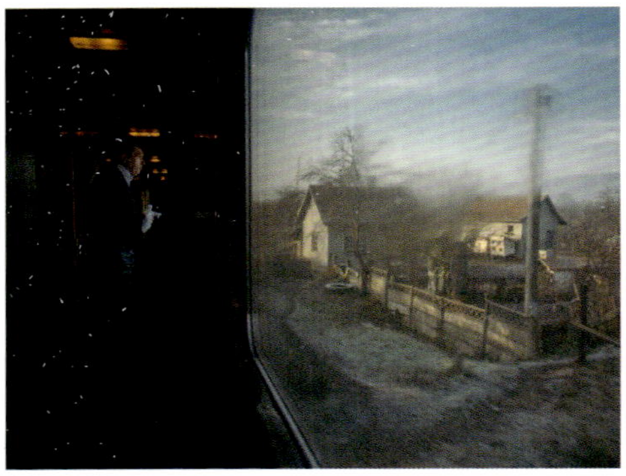
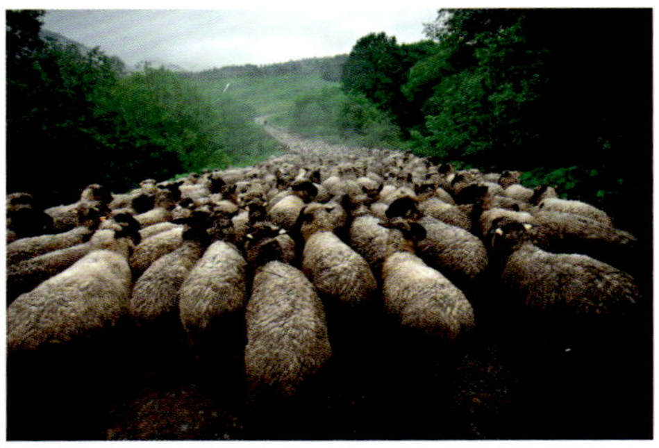
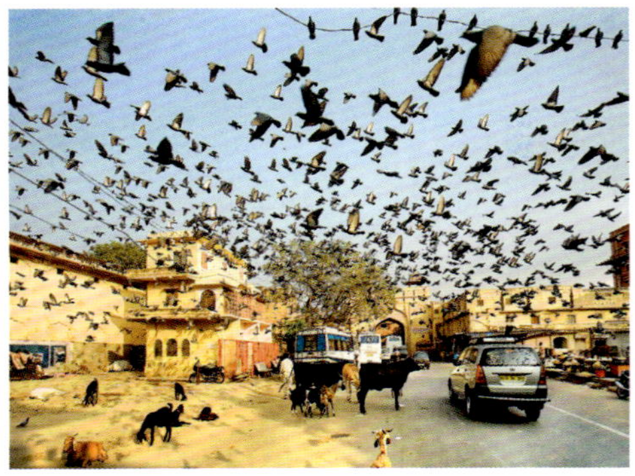
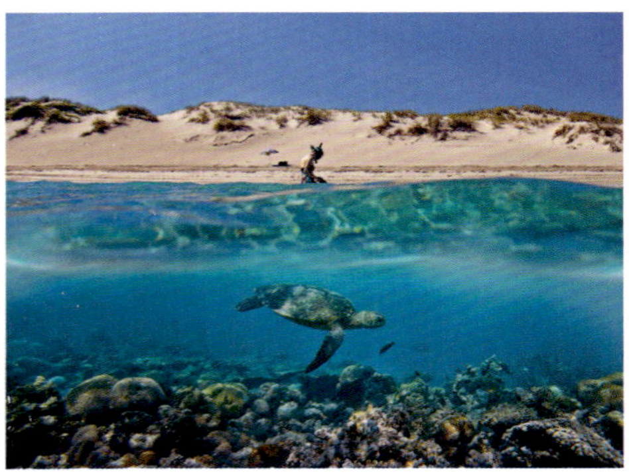
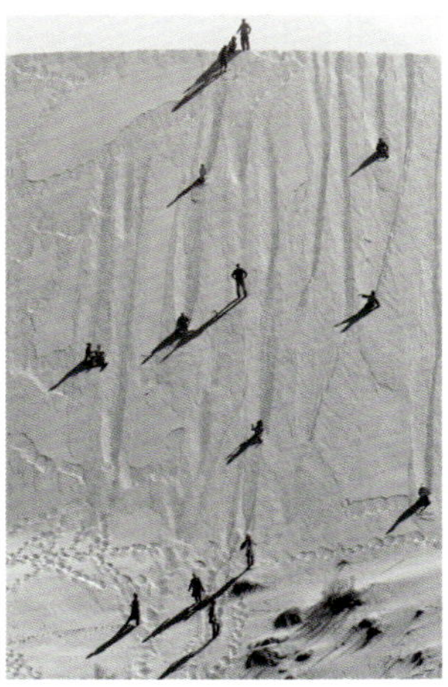

Top: **Andrey Ermolaev** Russia, **Andrey Ermolaev** Russia, **Olena Mozgova** Ukraine.
Middle: **Hajdu Tamas** Romania, **Maciej Grzegorzek** Poland, **Maciej Makowski** Poland.
Bottom: **Nathan Wills** Australia, **Peyman Bordbar** Iran.

A SPECIAL THANKS

To the **World Photographic Academy** members for their continued trust and support in our growing ventures.

2013 Honorary Judging Committee

Juana de Aizpuru
Chien-Chi Chang
Catherine Chermayeff (Presiding Chair of Jury)
Edmund Clark
Brandei Estes
Macduff Everton
Caroline Metcalfe
Tim Paton
Andrew Sanigar
Francesca Sears
Fiona Shields
Monica Suder

2013 Student Focus Judging Committee

Léonie Hampton
W.M. Hunt
Jonathan Worth

Open Competition

Damien Demolder (Presiding Chair of Jury)

William Eggleston Jr. for his kind assistance and support

Sony

Yoshiyuki Nogami
Katsuya Watanabe
Takashi Yasuda
Yann Salmon-Legagneur
Toby Shaw
David Edwards
Silke Schild
Emily Young
Naho Suginara

Candlestar

Michael Benson
Fariba Farshad
Matt Benson
Paul Cheetham
Tamsin Silvey

WPO Board Members

Sandy Angus and Damion Angus

Kraszna-Krausz Foundation

Spectrum Photographic

Somerset House

Alan Bates Design Ltd.
Isabel Solé López-Pinto